T0330791

Mexico, Central, and South America:
New Perspectives

Volume 4
Political Parties

Series Content

Volume 1
ECONOMICS

Volume 2
DEMOCRACY

Volume 3
SOCIAL MOVEMENTS

Volume 4
POLITICAL PARTIES

Volume 5
RACE AND ETHNICITY

Mexico, Central, and South America:
New Perspectives

Volume 4
Political Parties

Edited with introductions by

Jorge I. Domínguez
Harvard University

ROUTLEDGE
New York/London

Published in 2001 by

Routledge
29 West 35ᵗʰ Street
New York, NY 10001

Published in Great Britain by
Routledge
11 New Fetter Lane
London EC4P 4EE

Routledge is an Imprint of Taylor & Francis Books, Inc.
Copyright © 2001 by Routledge

Library of Congress Cataloging-in-Publication Data

Democracy in Latin America in the 1990s / edited with introductions by Jorge I. Domínguez.
    p. cm. -- (Mexico, Central and South America : the scholarly literature of the 1990s ;
    v. 2)
    Includes bibliographical references.
    ISBN 0-8153-3692-6 (set : alk. paper) -- ISBN 0-8153-3694-2 (v. 2 : alk. paper)
    1. Latin America--Politics and government--1980- 2. Democracy--Latin
America--History--20th century. I. Domínguez, Jorge I., 1945- II. Mexico, Central and
South America ; v. 2.

F1414.2 .D4317 2001
320.98--dc21
                                                              2001524240

ISBN 0-8153-3692-6 (set)
ISBN 0-8153-3693-4 (v.1)
ISBN 0-8153-3694-2 (v.2)
ISBN 0-8153-3695-0 (v.3)
ISBN 0-8153-3696-9 (v.4)
ISBN 0-8153-3697-7 (v.5)

Contents

vii Introduction

2 Electoral Strategy under Open-List Proportional Representation
Barry Ames

30 Shaping Mexico's Electoral Arena: The Construction of Partisan Cleavages in the 1988 and 1991 National Elections
Jorge Dominguez and James McCann

45 The Electoral Cycle and Institutional Sources of Divided Presidential Government
Matthew Soberg Shugart

63 Continuity and Change in the Chilean Party System: On the Transformational Effects of Electoral Reform
Peter Siavelis

87 Parties and Society in Mexico and Venezuela
Michael Coppedge

109 Presidents, Ruling Parties, and Party Rules: A Theory on the Politics of Economic Reform in Latin America
Javier Corrales

133 Presidential Power, Legislative Organization, and Party Behavior in Brazil
Argelina Cheibub Figueiredo and Fernando Limongi

153 Constituency Influence and Representation
Susan Stokes

171 Presidential Election Laws and Multipartism in Latin America
Mark Jones

189 Political Parties and Candidate Selection in Venezuela and Colombia
John D. Martz

210 Neoliberalism and the Transformation of Populism in Latin America: The Peruvian Case
Kenneth Roberts

245 The Populist Road to Market Reform: Policy and Electoral Coalitions in Mexico and Argentina
Edward Gibson

277 Acknowledgments

v

Introduction

Authoritarian regimes governed nearly all Latin American countries during the 1970s and still governed a majority of them during the first half of the 1980s. Elections had limited meaning; the citizens' political will was thwarted. Political parties were prohibited or greatly constrained in their work. In the 1990s, however, nearly all Latin American countries were under constitutional government. Imperfect as many of these regimes were, parties, elections, and voting behavior suddenly became central to settling crucial questions in politics: Who governs? Who gets what when? And, of course, the new political context made it much easier for scholars to analyze these matters using the normal tools of social science.

A topic of considerable intellectual and practical significance is the effect of rules on behavior and on the capacity of national institutions to function properly. The first three articles in this volume focus on these concerns.

A key issue for the normal functioning of democratic politics is the relationship between the institutions of constitutional democracy and the electoral cycle. All Latin American constitutions are presidential: presidents and parliaments are elected independently of each other. This can create a divided government when one party elects the president but the president's party lacks a legislative majority. This problem is not, of course, unique to Latin America; it is more marked in the United States and can appear in any system with similar constitutional rules. Matthew Shugart examines this problem comparatively. Because Latin American countries account disproportionately for the number of such presidential systems, his findings are especially pertinent to this region. Shugart shows that divided government is much less likely when legislative elections occur on the same day as presidential elections; concurrent elections foster unified government. The increased frequency of the constitutional requirement that presidents be elected by a majority of the voters has led to the spread of two-round presidential elections; this procedure makes divided government more likely because legislators are elected in the first round and the president is elected in the second round. In nonconcurrent elections, Shugart also finds, the president's party's share of parliamentary seats tends to increase in early-term elections but decline in later elections.

Mark Jones examines a closely related topic: What is the impact of presidential election laws on the likelihood that there will be many parties in a political system? He examines data from sixteen Latin American systems. He finds that those countries that use a plurality system ("first past the post") to elect their presidents are more likely to approximate a two-party system. Those countries that use a two-round majority framework have a larger number of parties competing in presidential elections; parties run "sincerely" in the first round and coalesce into two blocs, rather artificially, for the second round. Plurality systems for the president's election, moreover, reduce the number of parties in the legislature and in the wider political system. (Jones also confirms Shugart's finding that concurrent elections yield lower levels of multipartism than separately held presidential and legislative elections.) Finally, Jones found that the size of electoral districts only modestly increased the likelihood of multipartism. The presidential electoral formula and the timing of elections, therefore, have an impressive effect on the number of parties in a country.

The rules that have the most direct impact on parties are, of course, electoral rules about how to count votes. Peter Siavelis explores the effect of adopting a binomial (two-member) district legislative electoral formula in Chile with the return of democratic politics in 1989. According to the law, for elections to the Chamber of Deputies every party or electoral alliance could present two candidates in each of the sixty electoral districts; for elections to the Senate, the binomial system was used in nineteen districts. Voters may choose a single candidate from a series of two-candidate open lists. The individual gathering the highest number of votes wins the first seat in each district, but for the same electoral list to win both seats, it must double the vote of its nearest competitor. The effect of the binomial system was to subsidize the second-largest party or electoral coalition. Did this new electoral law transform the Chilean party system, long marked by competition among many parties? Siavelis argues that it did not. Neither the degree of party-system fractionalization nor the competitive dynamic of the party system was substantially changed, but the binomial formula increased the incentives for forming and maintaining coalitions.

Voters and politicians are the key actors in elections. The strategies of each help to shape the outcome and thus to determine the identity of a country's rulers. Three articles in this volume explore this issue.

Domínguez and McCann study Mexican elections for president in 1988 and for Congress in 1991, the founding elections of Mexico's democratization. They discover that voters were remarkably discerning. Mexican voters asked themselves, above all, whether they continued to support the long-ruling party, the Institutional Revolutionary Party (PRI). Thus the most statistically significant and consistent explanations for voting behavior in these two elections were past patterns of partisan choice, assessments of the president's performance, perceptions about whether the PRI was getting stronger or weaker, and expectations about what would happen to the economy if a party other than the PRI were to win. Voter behavior was not well explained by attachments to social cleavages, attitudes on policy issues, or general assessments about the present circumstances and the prospects for the nation's economy or personal finances. Once voters were ready to oppose the ruling party, but only then, issues, prospective economic assessments, and social cleavages shaped their choice between opposition parties. Moreover, a key minority of opposition voters voted strategically; that is, they suppressed their ideological preferences in order to vote for whichever opposition party was most likely to defeat the PRI.

Barry Ames analyzes the strategic behavior of rational politicians in Brazil. He spells out important characteristics of the Brazilian electoral system. There is open-list proportional representation; candidates are elected from party lists proportionate to the party's share of the votes, but voters can rank candidates on the party list at will. Electoral districts are large, and many legislators are elected from each district. Candidate selection occurs at the subnational level; national party leaders have little control over this process. Immediate reelection is permissible. What, then, should a politician do? Ames shows that most candidates for deputy pay little attention to ideological appeals and, instead, seek secure electoral bailiwicks, searching for municipalities where their wheeling and dealing will facilitate their election. Deputies deliver "pork" to constituents in their bailiwick. These rules and candidate behavior tend to hinder voter control over deputies, increase incentives for pork seeking, and weaken party programs and discipline.

But do the voters control those whom they elect, as might be expected in a democracy? Susan Stokes shows a worrisome breakdown in the responsiveness of elected politicians to the opinion of their constituencies, especially around 1990, a time of dire economic circumstances in most Latin American countries. Several elected Latin American governments switched to unpopular policies early in their terms because they thought that citizens were ill informed about policy and that their preferences would change in due course. Nearly a third of the presidential candidates elected between 1982 and 1995 implemented policies in office that were radically different from those they had promised. Carlos Menem in Argentina, Alberto Fujimori in Peru, and Carlos Andrés Pérez in Venezuela, all elected in 1989–1990, carried out the most shocking reversals of promised policies. Stokes finds that voters held governments that switched to a higher standard than governments that were consistent, yet, on average, switchers were not subsequently punished at the polls if their economic policy switch worked well (Menem and Fujimori were reelected with ample support).

In one way or another, all the articles discussed so far highlight the importance of political parties for the normal functioning of democratic politics. Parties mediate between citizens and the state. They respond to the opportunities and constraints evident in the nation's constitution and in voter preferences. The next four articles illustrate why parties matter and how they operate.

By comparing Mexico and Venezuela, Michael Coppedge illustrates that partisan competition matters greatly for the quality of political life. Before the 1980s, the differences between party-society relations in Mexico and Venezuela were slight in some respects, he shows. Nonetheless, he also demonstrates that Venezuela's competitive party system reduced violent repression and encouraged local officials to treat their clients with greater respect than was customary in "soft" authoritarian Mexico. Party competition also made for healthier relations between the government and the opposition in Venezuela than in Mexico. The Venezuelan government was more sensitive to criticism from the opposition. In turn, this government behavior encouraged a more moderate style of opposition behavior. Highway blockades, plant seizures, and various forms of civil disobedience were more likely in Mexico. Competitive party politics also made the opposition in Venezuela more independent and less subject to hidden co-optation by the government.

John Martz, like Coppedge, illustrates important differences in the entire political system by comparing candidate selection in Venezuela and Colombia. Martz found that Venezuelan parties were more likely to test their appeal directly with party loyalists; the Colombian candidate-selection process is more typically in the hands of top elites. These findings correspond to broad differences many scholars have noted between these countries. In both countries, however, an objective of party leaders during the candidate-selection process is to retain control over the party. For the most part, moreover, intrapartisan disputes are personalist; ideological issues rarely divide candidates within a given party. But in both countries party leaders have yielded to party-member preferences time and again even when this resulted in the nomination of a candidate they had opposed. In this sense, candidate choice retained a notable democratic quality within two of the oldest constitutional democracies in the Americas. Parties matter, therefore, and help to shape the nature of the political system in important ways. But can parties also foster effective democratic governance?

Scott Mainwaring and Aníbal Pérez Liñán inquire about the extent of party discipline in the 1987–1988 Brazilian Constitutional Congress. They ask, Do parties behave as sufficiently unified entities to transform voter preferences into party programs? They show that the biggest Brazilian parties were comparatively undisciplined, although the leftist parties were an important exception. They demonstrate that legislators who switched parties during the Constitutional Congress were more likely than others to be undisciplined before switching and their discipline increased markedly after their move to the new parties. The authors argue, as does Ames, that open-list proportional representation and little national party leader power over candidate selection, among other factors, explain undisciplined legislative behavior and make it impossible for Brazilian presidents to rely consistently on national party leaders to deliver the votes of their co-partisans. Presidential systems, they also suggest, permit legislators to vote on individual bills without fearing that their refusal to support the government might provoke its fall, in contrast to parliamentary systems. Thus electoral laws and the separation of powers explain much about party indiscipline. The breakdown of internal party discipline impedes effective democratic governance.

Argelina Cheibub Figueiredo and Fernando Limongi argue, however, that the obstacles to effective democratic politics in Brazil may be exaggerated. They show that Brazilian presidents had considerable success in enacting their legislative agenda after 1988. Presidents could also rely on support from the political parties in the presidential coalition. A presidential defeat in a roll-call vote was rare. The authors emphasize the effect of the president's legislative power and the internal organization of legislative work to explain party discipline, and they de-emphasize the explanatory utility of the separation of powers and the characteristics of electoral laws. In fact, the difference between Mainwaring and Pérez Liñán, on the one hand, and Figueiredo and Limongi, on the other, is more apparent than real: all agree that party discipline increased after 1989 and that the median level of party discipline in the early 1990s was around 85 percent— about the same or a bit higher than in the U.S. Congress. Parties did help democratic governance, even in Brazil. Did parties also contribute to effective governance of the economy?

Three articles shed light on this question. Javier Corrales shows that enacting market-oriented reforms produces dislocation in relations between the executive and the ruling party. He goes on to argue that the fate of those relations, and of the economic reforms, hinges on the strategies that the executive adopts to address that dislocation. He explores outcomes in Argentina and Venezuela. Corrales suggests that party-yielding strategies— that is, the executive's abandonment of the reforms— are counterproductive. Yet party-neglecting strategies, though at first they permit some progress in reform implementation, are ultimately tension-ridden and unsustainable. In Venezuela the reforms were reversed; the president was impeached. More effective, therefore, is a party-accommodating strategy, which was pursued in Argentina during the Menem presidency. The executive expands its capacity to deepen the reforms, but it also agrees to forgo seeking to achieve the original levels of reform implementation. Party accommodation is the economic reform strategy most likely to succeed, but it always entails concessions.

Edward Gibson's article picks up where Corrales's ends. Assume that the executive and the ruling party have enacted far-reaching market-oriented reforms. How can they win the next election if some of their constituents believe that the adoption of those reforms was a betrayal of party principles and came at a high cost? Gibson studies Mexico's PRI and the Argentine Justicialista (Peronist) Party. He argues that each party included two types of constituencies— those that cared about policy making and those that made it possible to win elections. Governing parties must bring together a policy coalition and an electoral coalition. He shows that Latin America's most important labor-based parties, the PRI and the Peronists, maintained their electoral dominance in the early 1990s while pursuing free-market reforms that adversely affected key social constituencies. Each party, in effect, had two distinctive regionally based subcoalitions: a metropolitan coalition that supported its development strategy and a peripheral coalition that generated electoral majorities. Contrary to the long-standing scholarly emphasis on the role of social classes and social sectors in these two parties, Gibson's approach suggests that regional dynamics were key to the parties' long-term success.

Finally, Kenneth Roberts examines economic reform in a no-party political system by focusing on Peru in the 1990s under President Alberto Fujimori. Fujimori enacted far-reaching market-oriented reforms in a neoliberal mold. Unlike the leaders who implemented the strategies highlighted by Corrales and Gibson, which relied on political parties to facilitate economic reform, Fujimori emphasized a personalist and paternalist pattern of political leadership. He dramatically weakened opposition political parties and eschewed founding and sustaining a political party as his partner in power. Instead, he nurtured a heterogeneous multi-class political coalition, with extensive support among poor Peruvians, through a top-down process of political mobilization guided by an eclectic set of ideas. He employed clientelist pork-barrel policies and tactics to build support. In these ways, he was a classic populist. Unlike populists of the past who emphasized state intervention in and regulation of the economy, Fujimori used populism to sustain his neoliberal economic program.

The near-complete destruction of political parties in Fujimori's Peru permitted the construction of a rather authoritarian political system under a thin veneer of constitutionalist governance and plebiscitary approval. The neglect of political parties in the process of enacting market-oriented economic reforms in Venezuela led to two military coup attempts, President Pérez's impeachment, and the marked weakening of democratic politics during the 1990s. Parties are highly regarded in virtually no political system today. Yet they remain essential pillars for the construction and maintenance of constitutional democracy and the preservation of public liberties. They are also the most effective instruments to explain, justify, and implement far-reaching economic reforms with the consent of the governed.

Mexico, Central, and South America:

New Perspectives

Volume 4
Political Parties

Electoral Strategy under Open-List Proportional Representation*

Barry Ames, *Washington University*

Theory: This paper develops a theory of candidate strategy from social-choice principles and from the workings of open-list proportional representation. The theory is used to explain the campaign behavior and the spatial patterns of vote distribution for candidates to the Brazilian Chamber of Deputies.
Hypotheses: Campaign strategy is evaluated with models that predict where deputies will offer budget amendments to benefit target municipalities whose votes they seek in subsequent elections. The choice of target municipalities is a function of the cost of erecting barriers to entry, the dominance of the deputy in the municipality, the spatial concentration of the deputy's statewide vote, the vulnerability of the municipality to invasion by outsiders, the weakness of the deputy in the last election, and the deputy's prior political career.
Methods: Logistic regression of amendments to the Brazilian national budget in 1989 and 1990 and OLS regression of municipal-level electoral results for the Brazilian Chamber of Deputies in the 1990 elections.
Results: Deputies seek secure bailiwicks, search for vulnerable municipalities, and strive to overcome their own electoral weakness by delivering pork. Candidates' tactics vary, partly because political backgrounds differ and partly because the differing demographic and economic contexts of Brazilian states reward some tactics and penalize others. Candidate behavior hinders voter control over deputies, increases incentives for pork seeking, and weakens party programs and discipline.

Latin America in the mid-1990s is a region of optimism. Fledgling democracies survive; economies stabilize and grow. But Brazil remains an enigma. While prices rise 30% per month and the distribution of income deteriorates, the legislature stalls attempts at stabilization until the executive provides low-level jobs for party faithful. Unprecedented corruption leads the Congress to remove the first popularly elected president in 30 years; within a year a new corruption scandal shakes the Congress itself.

Increasingly, observers blame Brazil's political institutions. Consider the party system and the legislature. Even by Latin American

·*The data utilized in this article will be deposited at the ICPSR by the end of 1995. Scholars interested in the data before that date may contact the author. This research has been supported by the National Science Foundation, Washington University, St. Louis, and IRIS—Institutional Reform and the Informal Sector, at the University of Maryland, College Park.

American Journal of Political Science, Vol. 39, No. 2, May 1995, Pp. 406–33
© 1995 by the Board of Regents of the University of Wisconsin System

2

standards, Brazil's party system is weak (Mainwaring and Scully 1992). Few parties have genuine roots in society. Party vote-shares are volatile over time and between presidential and legislative elections. In the Congress, party leaders exert little control over their delegations. Many if not most deputies spend the bulk of their time arranging jobs and pork-barrel projects for their benefactors and constituents. Though electorally successful parties span a wide ideological range, some of the largest "center" parties are really just shells for deputies with no policy interests at all. Few parties organize around national-level questions; the Congress, as a result, seldom grapples with serious social and economic issues.

Brazil's presidents benefit little from the weakness of the Congress. With only minimal chances to obtain stable legislative support, executives face independent governors, an electoral calendar imposing elections in three of every five years, municipalities depending for their very survival on federal largesse, and a substantial core of deputies who value their own incomes first, reelection second, and public policy a distant third. Presidents govern by forming coalitions based upon cabinet appointments. Because these appointments must satisfy both party and regional demands, cabinets tend to be very inclusive (Abranches 1988). The pork-barrel programs required to maintain them are costly, and policy innovation is extremely difficult.

At the core of Brazil's institutional crisis lies the electoral system. A unique set of rules, usually referred to as "open-list proportional representation," governs legislative elections. Scholars have explored Brazil's version of open-list proportional representation, but the absence of appropriate data has limited research both in scope and depth.[1] (See De Souza and Lamounier 1992; Fleischer 1973, 1976, 1977; Kinzo 1987; Lima Junior 1991; and Mainwaring 1993.)

In sum, the consolidation of democracy in Brazil may well depend on our understanding of the relationship between institutional structures, especially the electoral system, and the problems of the legislature and the executive. This paper examines elections for the Chamber of Deputies. I focus on the consequences of Brazil's version of open-list proportional representation for individual campaign strategies and for the types of deputies winning legislative seats, and I explore the ways in which campaign strategies operate in states with differing social and economic characteristics. The exposition begins with a sketch of the electoral system and a taxonomy of spatial vote patterns. I then offer a

---

[1]No multi-state studies have been undertaken, probably due to a scarcity of municipal-level voting data, an absence of digitized municipal maps, and unfamiliarity with spatial statistical techniques.

theory explaining the strategies adopted by individual Chamber candidates. The theory is based on notions of strategy developed in the social-choice literature and adapted to Brazil's political and social context. A test of the theory requires a measure of deputies' *intentions*. I utilize budgetary amendments: deputies submit amendments to benefit localities where they seek to reward allies and recruit new supporters. Thus the empirical analysis begins with a model predicting the chance that a given deputy will offer a budgetary amendment benefitting a particular municipality. I then test the efficacy of candidate strategies by modeling individual deputies' vote totals in the 1990 legislative election. In the conclusion I stress three broad consequences of deputies' strategic behavior: the loosening of the principal-agent tie between voters and deputies, the magnifying of incentives for pork-seeking, and the weakening of party programs and discipline.

1. The Brazilian Electoral System

In elections for the national Chamber of Deputies, each Brazilian state is a single, at-large, multimember district. The number of seats per state ranges from eight to 70. Lightly populated states are overrepresented; heavily populated states, principally São Paulo, are underrepresented. Electoral laws allow unlimited reelection, and parties cannot refuse to renominate incumbents. Voters cast single ballots either for the party label—in which case their vote merely adds to the party's total—or for individual candidates. Most opt for individuals. Candidate names appear nowhere on the ballot; rather, the voter must write in the candidate's name or code. The D'Hondt method determines how many seats each party earns; the individual ordering of votes then establishes which candidates receive those seats.[2]

Other nations, including Finland and pre-1973 Chile, have adopted open-list proportional representation, but Brazil's version differs in two ways: in Brazil state parties, not national parties, select legislative candidates, and the voting district (the state) is an important political arena in its own right. In some states, powerful governors control nominations and dominate campaigns; in others local leaders deliver blocs of votes to deal-making candidates; in still others neither governors nor local bosses have much influence over individual votes.[3]

[2] Until 1994, parties faced no minimum threshold for attaining seats in the legislature. In 1993, Congress approved a 3% threshold, but a loophole will minimize the law's effects.
[3] The strongest state machines are probably those of Maranhão and Bahia, both in the Northeast. While governor, Orestes Quércia dominated the PMDB in São Paulo, and he maintained much of that power during the administration of his hand-picked successor. Powerful local leaders are found mostly in less industrial areas.

4

Brazilian campaign regulations are both restrictive and permissive. Candidates may not, for example, buy advertisements on radio or television. Most candidates advertise in newspapers, but print ads have little impact (Straubhaar 1993). Candidates erect billboards and paint signs on walls, but they generally do so in conjunction with other campaign efforts, such as participation in rallies or delivery of public works to local leaders. Permissive spending laws allow candidates for the federal legislature to finance the campaigns of state assembly candidates. Because state assembly districts are also whole states, elected at large, politicians engage in *dobradinhas,* or double-ups, in which federal legislative candidates pay for the campaign literature of assembly candidates whose bases of support lie far away. The assembly candidates reciprocate by instructing supporters to vote for their benefactor for the national legislature. Such deals add little, of course, to linkages between representatives and their constituents.

A Taxonomy of Spatial Patterns

Legally, candidates seek votes everywhere in their states, but in reality most limit their campaigns geographically. The spatial patterns that result have two dimensions at the state level, each based on *municipal* performance. Suppose, for every candidate in each municipality, we calculate V_{ix}, candidate i's share of all the votes cast in municipality x. We define each candidate's *municipal dominance* as the candidate's share of the total votes cast for members of all parties. These shares represent the candidates' dominance at the municipal level.[4] Now suppose we use V_{ix} to calculate D_i, the average dominance for each candidate across all the state's municipalities, weighted by the percentage of the candidate's total vote each municipality contributes. Candidates with higher weighted averages tend to dominate their key municipalities; those with lower weighted averages share their key municipalities with other candidates. Thus "dominance-sharedness" is the first dimension of spatial support.

The second dimension also begins with V_{ix}, candidate i's share of the total vote cast in each municipality, but this dimension assesses the *spatial* distribution of those municipalities where the candidate does well. These municipalities can be concentrated, as close or contiguous neighbors, or they can be scattered. Combining the two dimensions yields four spatial patterns:

[4]Note that municipal dominance has nothing to do with actually winning seats; whole states, not municipalities, are electoral districts. I have also experimented with conceptualizing dominance solely in terms of votes for candidates of the candidates' own party.

5

Figure 1. A Concentrated-Dominant Vote Distribution: Municipal Vote Share of Laire Rosado Maia, PMDB-RN

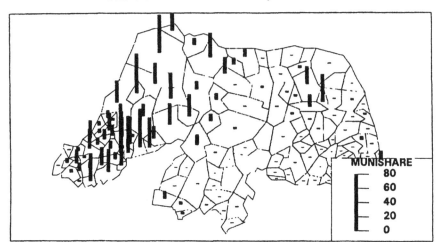

Concentrated-dominated municipalities. This is the classic Brazilian *"reduto"* (literally, "electoral fortress"), where a deputy dominates a group of contiguous municipalities. Candidates' families may have traditions of power in the region; they might climb the ladder of politics from local jobs; they may strike deals with local bosses. Figure 1, mapping the 1990 vote of Deputy Laire Rosado Maia, illustrates extreme concentration.[5] Rosado Maia received nearly all his votes in the Elephant's Trunk, the western section of Rio Grande do Norte. Maias have long controlled the West—one county even carries the family name. Note that where Rosado Maia received votes, he averaged at least 50% of all votes cast. So not only does Rosado Maia receive all his votes in this region, other candidates rarely dare to compete in his impermeable *reduto*.

Concentrated-shared municipalities. In large metropolitan areas such as greater São Paulo, a particular cohort of voters may be sufficient to elect many candidates. Working-class candidates, for example, often get three-fourths of their total statewide vote from one municipality, the city of São Paulo. But they might never receive more than 5% of the votes cast in the city or in any other county, because they share these municipalities with many other candidates.

[5]The Appendix discusses the construction of the map as well as other data problems.

Figure 2. A Scattered-Dominant Vote Distribution: Municipal Vote
Share of João Alves, PFL-Bahia

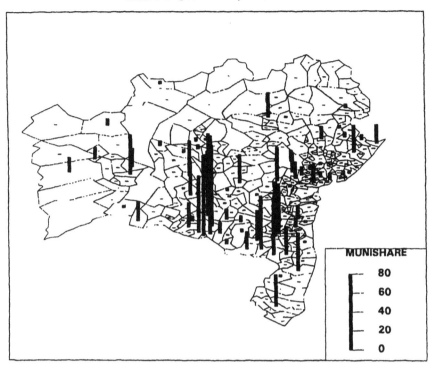

Scattered-shared municipalities. Some candidates appeal to voter
cohorts providing support that is numerically weak in any single municipality. Two common examples are Japanese-Brazilians and *evangélicos,*
Protestants who typically vote for evangelical candidates. These cohorts
are cohesive and loyal, but they are not very large, so candidates relying
on such voters construct coalitions composed of small slices of many
municipalities.[6]

Scattered-dominated municipalities. This pattern fits candidates
who once held such state-level bureaucratic posts as secretary of education, a job with substantial pork-barrel potential. The pattern is also
typical of candidates who make deals with local leaders. Figure 2 pre-

[6] For graphic illustrations of the scattered-shared and concentrated-shared patterns,
see my "Electoral Rules, Constituency Pressures, and Pork Barrel: Bases of Voting in
the Brazilian Legislature" (1995).

sents the 1990 vote of João Alves, an old-time Bahian politician. Alves' voting strength was scattered over the state, but he received many votes in those locations. He garnered 70–80% of the vote in such dispersed municipalities by making deals wherever he found willing local bosses. He delivered pork; the bosses paid off in votes. Alves chaired the congressional Budget Committee. In 1993 congressional investigators accused him of receiving tens of millions of dollars in kickbacks from construction companies. João Alves came to the Congress in 1966 with no money; by the early 1990s he had millions of dollars in real estate and a $6 million airplane.[7]

2. A Theory of Candidate Strategy under Open-List Proportional Representation

Optimal campaign strategies differ sharply between proportional and majoritarian electoral systems. Because small slices of the electorate may ensure victory in proportional elections, office-seekers pursue not the median voter but discrete voter cohorts (Cox 1990). How candidates define these cohorts depends, of course, on the size of potential targets and on the total votes required for election. Strategies also depend on the cost of campaigning as candidates move away from core supporters, the existence of local leaders seeking patronage, the spatial concentration of candidates' earlier political careers, and the simultaneity of elections for other levels of government.

How Candidates Calculate the Costs and Benefits of Appeals to Voters

Candidates know roughly how many votes guarantee a seat in their state's congressional delegation. This minimum depends on expected turnout and on the number of votes taken by the most popular candidates in their party.[8] Given a vote target, candidates imagine a variety of ways to construct winning coalitions. Their strategic calculations center on the costs and benefits of appeals to any potential group. This section examines some principles affecting candidate calculations under Brazil's electoral rules. These principles operate nationwide, i.e., with-

---

[7]Alves commanded a group of deputies known, due to their stature, as the Seven Dwarfs. The Chamber's internal investigating committee accused almost all of extorting and accepting kickbacks, but the full Chamber exonerated some. Nearly all have the same vote distribution: scattered pockets of very intense support.

[8]The votes of leading candidates may far outweigh laggards, but since the number of candidates elected is in direct proportion to the party's cumulative share of all votes cast, popular candidates make possible the election of those with far fewer votes.

out reference to subnational contexts. Subsequently, I consider aspects of Brazilian politics that vary across states.

Voters as members of politicized groups. A rational candidate seeks to expend the least resources for the most support. The ideal target is a self-conscious member of a large group carrying a politicized identification or grievance. Japanese-Brazilians, for example, always understand their ethnicity, and evangelical Protestants know they are not Catholics. Evangelicals, however, are more likely than Japanese-Brazilians to see themselves as victims; hence the evangelical vote is more unified. In both cases, outsiders see the cleavage less intensely, so candidates can win evangelicals without losing all the Catholics.

At the other extreme, in terms of the permanence and politicization of identifications, lie occupational groups. For industrial workers, class-consciousness depends on the nature of the production process, wages, and labor organization. Workers in small factories, especially in the informal sector, tend to be younger, less-skilled, more-recent arrivals in the city, and more deferential toward owners. Such workers support candidates offering particularistic benefits over candidates promising social reform.[9]

Community identification, especially in small communities, falls closer to the automatic side. Local politicians try to strengthen community identification, because their own influence depends on delivering voters to candidates. The centrality of government jobs facilitates voter mobilization in small communities, and the restriction of civil-service protection to low-level positions politicizes public-sector posts. Because elections for local executive posts and for legislatures are staggered, local officials know they will be on the job both before and after legislative elections, so they are encouraged to make deals with legislative candidates.

The difficulty of securing benefits for the group. Deputies seek support for their campaign promises in the legislature. They opt for geographically separable goods, for pork-barrel programs, when the decisional system is fragmented and the demand for public goods is strong, relatively stable and district-specific (Lowi 1964; Salisbury and Heinz 1970). Brazil is characterized by powerful states acting in their own interests, selection of congressional candidates at the state level, municipalities independently electing local governments, weak national party

---

[9]Paulo Maluf, a conservative populist politician, could not carry the state of São Paulo in the 1989 presidential election, but he won the mayoral contest of São Paulo city in 1992 precisely with the votes of such workers.

9

leaderships, and separation of powers between the president and the federal legislature. In addition, enormous regional inequalities leave some municipalities so poor that government employment and subsidies are crucial sources of income. Thus Brazilian politics favors the provision of local, geographically separable benefits.

The costs and benefits of barriers to entry. Deputies seek to insulate voter cohorts from the incursions of competitors because they know that barriers to entry, by eliminating competition, reduce the cost of campaigns. The difficulty of erecting barriers depends on the nature of the group to be shielded. Wage hikes, for example, require broad legislative coalitions, so it is difficult for anyone to claim exclusive credit. Barriers against ethnic outsiders, by contrast, are essentially automatic, but they are more costly to erect against insiders such as other ethnics.

Is it hard to erect barriers around particular localities? A simple "you're not from around here" shields a small, highly integrated community. Violence, in the form of disruption of campaign rallies or physical threats, is routine in rural areas. More diverse communities develop factional competition, with each side relying on strongly partisan supporters. In complex urban areas no single faction or leader controls a significant portion of the electorate, and the police are not beholden to individual politicians. Many candidates seek votes, and barriers to outsiders from any party are hard to maintain.

Suppose a broker controls access to a group of voters. This control stems from some combination of coercion and prior delivery of employment or services. Deputies seeking brokers' votes offer cash or a slice of the benefit secured, such as a road-building contract. If the broker successfully erects rigid barriers against the entry of other brokers, candidates will pay more for the broker's votes than the sum of the prices they would pay for each vote individually. If, by contrast, the broker cannot protect his turf, candidates pay a lower total price for these votes than their individual prices. Whatever the price and form of payment, brokers' fees require candidates to secure *separable* resources.

The Cost of Communicating with Potential Voters

Brazilian campaigning is a direct, grassroots activity.[10] Candidates visit small communities, holding meetings and rallies. Is it rational to

---

[10]Media access remains central to campaigning even though candidates cannot buy radio or TV time. Because radio and newspapers in Brazil are generally partisan, media connections provide an effective barrier to competition as well as a means of communicating with voters. In recent years many broadcasters, popular as a result of call-in shows, have become candidates.

campaign where one's message reaches few voters? Indeed it is. First, the more concentrated the target group, the lower the cost of constructing a winning coalition. Second, electoral coalitions that cover small areas are likely to be locational, i.e., based purely on community identification. While in theory locational and nonlocational criteria might match perfectly (all southerners are black, all northerners are white), few such cases exist in Brazil. Thus the physical distance between a candidate and the last voter, the voter whose support assures victory, is nearly always smallest for locational coalitions.[11]

The supply of politicians. Candidates' career trajectories constrain their campaign strategies and vote patterns. Local candidates, i.e., former mayors or city council members, should always be plentiful.[12] Except for those whose careers are rooted in large metropolitan areas, local candidates naturally develop *concentrated* distributions, because their name recognition decreases with the distance from their local job. What happens when candidates appear with backgrounds in state bureaucracy, or with no political history? Not a simple question, because at any given election the mix of careers among candidates depends on two sets of factors. One set (which may be called *endogenous*) depends on the context of the election itself, in the sense that new candidacies depend on the initial distribution of *incumbent* candidates. For example, where transportation costs are high, where statewide name recognition is low, where concentrations of workers or ethnics are weak, and where voters prefer candidates with municipal political experience, only local types will offer themselves. But the career mixes of candidates also depend on a second set of factors, *exogenous* in the sense that new candidacies respond to the opportunities and rewards of legislative activity. People with different backgrounds become candidates because they seek personal rewards from legislative activity.

My argument is simple: in campaigning, what you did affects what you do. For many local candidates, a run for the federal legislature is the first statewide political activity. Because locals begin with a single name-recognition peak, a *concentrated* campaign is the obvious choice. But suppose the candidate headed a government department that man-

[11]The exceptions include winning electoral coalitions based on class voting in the cities of Rio de Janeiro or São Paulo.

[12]Mayors must pursue another office, since they cannot seek immediate reelection. Federal deputy, however, is not necessarily a step up: in 1992 about one-fifth of all federal deputies went the other way, running for mayor. Local office holders are abundant as candidates except in frontier states, which develop so fast that local politics tends to be extremely weak. Frontier municipalities depend on state and federal largesse, and politicians often "parachute" in to pick up votes.

aged roads or schools. Surely bureaucrats considering a political career would locate projects to their political advantage, and such candidates would become well known in the communities benefitting from their largesse. Thus the voting support of such candidates should be *scattered* rather than concentrated. Whether they will dominate or share municipalities depends on the target municipality and on the program they directed. In rural communities, domination can result, either because a single program affects many people intensely or because the program may be designed to buy the support of local influentials rather than individual voters.[13] Urban communities absorb multiple programs— often directed by competing politicians—and voters are less easily controlled. Finally, suppose the candidate's career is in business. Business people may begin with some central recognition peak around the location of their business, but such peaks are seldom as large as those of local politicians. Their advantage is money: T-shirts, pressure cookers (bottom half before the election, top half after), and political jobs for voters. Money buys the political bosses who control voters, and money greases the *dobradinhas* between state assembly and federal Chamber candidates. For business types, then, scattered support results: the strategic business candidate buys support wherever available.

At this point let us distinguish between challengers and incumbents. Suppose a local politician challenges the incumbent in a concentrated-dominant bailiwick. Superficially, the challenge resembles a contest over an occupied seat in the U.S. House of Representatives, but it is actually more difficult. Local bailiwicks are usually sparsely populated. If the challenger picks up only 51% of the incumbent's vote, the confrontation leads to mutual defeat. Since pork matters more than national policy, neither local bosses nor individual voters want to replace a deputy who has delivered. Local vs. local contests, therefore, are so difficult they rarely occur.[14] Unless the incumbent neglects the district or angers the local boss, local challengers should await a retirement.

[13] A road, for example, may be intended to enrich a particular contractor or big farmer.

[14] In the 1990 election, the governor of São Paulo, Orestes Quércia, supported a challenge to a deputy who had previously been a member of Quércia's PMDB but had defected to the PSDB. Quércia's well-financed challenger won, but so did his target. For a broader test, consider the 1990 election in Paraná. Of the state's 30 congressional seats, non-incumbents won 24. Of these 24, 12 won with concentrated, local bailiwicks. Of the 12, 6 constructed bailiwicks where none had previously existed. Four essentially assumed the districts of incumbents who did not run. Only two took over the bailiwicks of incumbents who did compete. In one case the challenger constructed a much bigger bailiwick; in the other the challenger benefitted from the state's swing to the right, defeating two incumbents who had shared the same area.

What should we expect from local incumbents themselves? Given the infrequency of direct challenges within their bailiwicks, locals mainly fear a drop in the aggregate party vote. Were it to decline sufficiently, the same postelection rank might no longer guarantee a seat. Thus local incumbents have to fish for new voters either in the bailiwicks of party colleagues or in the bailiwicks of incumbents from other parties. Party identification in Brazil is weak, so deputies easily attract supporters of other parties. Since proportional representation rewards higher party totals with additional seats, party leaders discourage poaching in the bailiwicks of party allies. In sum, Brazilian candidates should forage for votes in *unfriendly* territory. And since shared municipalities are more vulnerable than dominated municipalities, domination as well as concentration should decrease for local candidates.

Changes in spatial concentration also occur among nonlocal candidates. The core constituencies of candidates relying on scattered distributions—evangelicals, broadcasters and state bureaucrats—are relatively stable in size, so such candidates need new followers. Since some of the pork these deputies deliver to their core supporters benefits others in the same municipalities, and since deputies save resources by remaining near their core support, their spatial concentration should increase.

Businessmen initially buy votes with payoffs to local bosses, but once in the legislature they are likely to seek more popular backing to fill in between areas of strength. Concentration among successful business candidates *rises*. Greater concentration, however, may not produce greater electoral success. The electoral support of business candidates is more fickle than the support enjoyed by local politicians. Better offers sway bosses loyal to the highest bidder. Thus businessmen face contradictory incentives. While opportunities are clearly better for candidates unconstrained by local careers, businessmen can lose support as quickly as they gain it. Business will supply many new candidates, but business incumbents will be more vulnerable to electoral defeat than candidates with other career trajectories.

3. Analysis

The broad outlines of the argument should stand or fall on empirical grounds.[15] Analysis begins with a model of campaign strategy that uses

---

[15]Given the considerable continuity between the last legislative elections of the dictatorship and those of the New Republic, there are no campaigns without incumbents. In addition, the availability of results for only four elections leaves open the stability of the system.

13

budgetary amendments as indicators of candidate intent. The following
section incorporates budgetary amendments in a model of actual electoral outcomes.

Campaign Strategy in the 1990 Election

Deputies submit budgetary amendments to retain old followers and
attract new ones. Congress did not regain the constitutional right to
modify the national budget until 1988, but deputies learned quickly.
Between 1989 and 1992, the annual number of budgetary amendments
climbed from 8,000 to 72,000, with over 90% targetting specific municipalities. The model assesses, for each municipality, the probability that
a deputy running for reelection will submit a budgetary amendment.[16]
Specifically, the probability that a deputy running for reelection in 1990
offered an amendment in 1989 or 1990 targeting municipality X is a
function of six factors: (1) the distance of X from the center of the
deputy's 1986 vote; (2) the dominance and concentration of the deputy's
1986 vote; (3) the vulnerability of municipality X to candidate invasion;
(4) the socioeconomic and demographic similarity of X to the deputy's
core constituency; (5) the deputy's electoral insecurity; and (6) the deputy's career trajectory.

Distance from 1986 vote center. The 1986 "vote center" of each
incumbent deputy is measured in two ways.[17] *Municipal center, C_m,* is
based on municipal domination, the percentage of each municipality's
total vote received by deputy *i*. *Personal center, C_p,* is based on personal share, the percentage of deputy *i*'s statewide total received in
each municipality. I then calculate the distance from C_m and C_p to every
municipality in the state. As municipalities become more distant, name
recognition declines and the cost of campaigning increases; distant municipalities are less likely to be targets for deputy *i*. At the same time,
deputies with personal vote centers in municipalities where they do not
also dominate (typically big cities) are likely to make amendments fur-

---

[16]Budgetary amendments are obviously not the only tactic deputies utilize. They
visit large numbers of municipalities, holding rallies and offering support to candidates
for other offices. Budget amendments are thus a proxy for a range of campaign activities.
For this reason, my analysis focuses on amendments *offered* rather than amendments
actually *approved* by the budget committee. The budget committee's actions represent a
legislative decision process, a process I treat in a work in progress.

[17]The center is the centroid of a plane surface in which a municipality's votes are
assumed to be cast at its center. Note that C_m and C_p are not necessarily at the actual
physical center of any particular municipality. The *socioeconomic* centers in the social-
match section, however, are indeed individual municipalities.

14

ther from their personal centers, because they share the central municipality with so many other candidates that credit claiming is hopeless.[18]

Dominance and concentration. Earlier, I defined dominance and concentration as characteristics of individual deputies measured at the level of the state as whole. Dominance, however, is also meaningful at the municipal level. A deputy could dominate minor municipalities, for example, but share large municipalities with others. Only municipal-level dominance should affect amending.[19] The higher the level of dominance in a given municipality, the more the deputy can claim credit for pork-barrel efforts, and, therefore, the more budgetary amendments he or she will offer. When dominance reaches very high levels, the deputy has a "safe seat" (as in the old one-party American South); hence amendments should decline.

Candidates with concentrated 1986 voting support should make more amendments, because they are vulnerable to the incursions of candidates with bureaucratic or business backgrounds. Concentrated candidates move out from their original bases in roughly concentric circles. They must be less selective than candidates with scattered votes, because they choose targets not just on the criterion of vulnerability but also on the criterion of nearness to their own core. As a result, concentrated candidates "over-amend."

Municipal vulnerablility. In municipalities dominated by strong incumbents seeking reelection, challengers have little incentive to invade. But conditions change; municipalities become permeable. A dominant deputy retires, leaving an electoral void. An influx of migrants signals an electorate free from control by old leaders and old loyalties. Invasion is encouraged by municipal fragmentation, either in the sense that many candidates from a single party share votes or in the sense that candidates from many parties enjoy electoral success.[20]

Social match. If incumbents identify certain occupational or ethnic groups as key supporters, they should target new municipalities where

---

[18] For a treatment of the effect of voter distance from candidates' home media markets, see Bowler et al. 1992.

[19] If *state-level* dominance has any effect at the level of the individual municipality, it must be true that deputies whose support comes mostly from municipalities they dominate are likely to make more amendments even in municipalities they only share. That is, dominant deputies' pork-barrel habit makes them behave irrationally.

[20] *Inter*party fragmentation is defined as 1 minus the sum of the square of each party's share of the total vote. *Intra*party fragmentation is defined equivalently at the level of the individual candidate, i.e., 1 minus the sum of the squares of each candidate's share of the party total.

similar groups reside. Deputies relying on working-class votes would seek industrial municipalities. Deputies appealing to civil servants should carry that appeal to localities where government is large. Thus deputies pursue new targets similar in socioeconomic composition to old bailiwicks. I begin by defining, on the basis of personal vote-share and municipal dominance, each deputy's core municipality.[21] Then I calculate the difference between each municipality and the core municipality on three socioeconomic indicators: size of electorate, per capita income, and percentage of work force employed by government. The first two indicators reflect the possibility of class-based vote seeking, while the third represents a well-organized interest. Given the general weakness in Brazil of appeals to social class, government employees are the most likely target. For each indicator, municipalities more like the deputy's core municipality should receive more amendments.[22]

Electoral insecurity. We know that individual votes largely determine deputies' electoral fortunes. Those whose 1986 rank was low, who barely escaped elimination, will work harder in the next election. Their overall number of amendments will increase.

Career trajectory. Because politicians with local backgrounds are more likely to maintain close ties with constituents than are politicians with bureaucratic or business backgrounds, local candidates should amend more. Locals should also concentrate their campaigns, including their budgetary amendments, closer to home. Bureaucratic and business candidates scatter campaign activities, buying support where they implanted projects and where they identify vulnerable municipalities. Candidates from families with long traditions in politics ought to be more pork-oriented, making more amendments.[23]

Pooling and estimation. Estimation began with observations at the level of individual deputies; that is, all deputies who served in 1986 and ran for reelection in 1990. I then pooled the deputies by state, and in

[21] If a deputy had a single municipality with a personal share clearly above any other, I selected that municipality as the core. If the deputy's personal shares in two municipalities were within a few percentage points, I chose the municipality with a higher municipal share as the core.

[22] The socioeconomic indicators come from the 1980 census, except for the size of the voting population, which is drawn from the 1989 electoral rolls.

[23] Deputies have political family if a relative of the same or older generation was or had been a mayor, state or federal deputy, federal senator, governor, or president. For biographical data see Câmara dos Deputados (1981, 1983, 1991); Brasil (1989), and Isto é (1991). Interviews with journalists supplemented the official sources.

two cases—six small northeastern states and three southern states—I pooled deputies in groups of states. This multi-state pooling, which increased the number of observations substantially, combines states that are similar in size, socioeconomic conditions, and political traditions.[24] Given that the number of amendments in each municipality cannot be less than zero, and given that most deputies make few amendments in any particular municipality, ordinary least-squares estimation is inappropriate. I experimented-with an event-count Poisson model, but the Poisson results revealed some statistical irregularities, so I collapsed the amendment data into a dichotomous variable and implemented a logistic regression.[25] Table 1 presents simplified results for six states or state groups: Bahia, the six small northeastern states, Minas Gerais, Rio de Janeiro, São Paulo, and the three southern states. Full results, including coefficients and standard errors, are available on request.

Interpretation. In each state or state group, the model achieved a high level of statistical significance, so the empirical results support the overall theory well.[26] In terms of the theory's specific elements, let us consider first the arguments confirmed in all or nearly all the six settings, followed by hypotheses failing to receive consistent support.

Everywhere municipal dominance strongly stimulated amendment making. The higher the percentage of a municipality's votes a deputy won in 1986, the more likely that deputy was to pursue more support in the same place in 1990. The negative slope on the squared term means that deputies at some point regard a municipality as "locked up," thus meriting no additional effort. Diminishing returns, in other words, set in, but the actual inflection points were beyond nearly all the cases.

The theory argued that vulnerable municipalities, those with high proportions of migrants or with high levels of party fragmentation, would be campaign targets. Only in the states of Rio de Janeiro and São Paulo (where the sign was correct) did municipalities with many mi-

[24]The six northeastern states included Alagoas, Paraíba, Pernambuco, Piauí, Rio Grande do Norte, and Sergipe. The three southern states included Paraná, Santa Catarina, and Rio Grande do Sul.

[25]In certain states or state groups, the diagnostics for both Poisson and negative-binomial models showed overdispersion; for others the Poisson worked well. Since the real issue is whether a candidate targeted municipality x, not how many amendments were made in x, the logistic form is perfectly suitable. Substantively, the results are a bit closer to the model's predictions with the original Poisson, but both forms are very close.

[26]Because this is an exploratory study—and to minimize references to insignificant coefficients with phrases such as "signs in the right direction"—I have adopted a .10 level of significance. However, over 80% of the significant coefficients also reach the .05 level.

17

Table 1. Will Deputy Submit Budgetary Amendment for Municipality?

Municipal and Individual Characteristics	Prediction	Logit Estimation					
		Bahia	Northeast	Minas Gerais	Rio de Janeiro	São Paulo	South
Distance from municipal center	−		−		+	+	+
Municipal distance squared	+	+	+	−			−
Distance from personal center	+		+	+	−	−	−
Personal distance squared	−		−		+		+
Municipal dominance	+	+	+	+	+	+	+
Municipal dominance squared	−	−	−	−	−	−	−
Concentration	+	+	+				
Percent of vote to retired deputies	+	+	+	+			+
Percent migrants	+	+	+	−	+		+
Match to core: Income distribution	?		+				
Match to core: Government employees	−	−	−	−	−	−	
Match to core: Population	?	+		+	+		+
Interparty fragmentation	+	+	+	−			
Intraparty fragmentation	+		+	+	+	+	−
Rank in party list in 1986	+	+	+	+	+	+	+
Local career	+	−	−	+	+		+
Local Career × Municipal distance	−	+	+	−	−	+	−
Local Career × Personal distance	−	−			+	+	+
Political family	+		−	+	+		−
N =		6666	3841	9106	1536	7410	6841

"+" means a positive coefficient, significant at the .10 level.
"−" means a negative coefficient, significant at the .10 level.
All likelihood ratios are significant at the .0001 level.

grants fail to attract deputies. Rio's deviance and the weakness of São Paulo probably stem from the high proportion of migrants in the cities of Rio and São Paulo themselves. Since so many deputies receive votes there, even a high proportion of migrants cannot make these cities appealing as amending targets, though they do attract other campaign tactics.

High levels of party fragmentation, both interparty and intraparty, increase everywhere the chances that candidates will target a given municipality. In Minas Gerais and São Paulo, only intraparty fragmentation increased candidates' amending activity. In these two states the Party of the Brazilian Democratic Movement, the PMDB, had attained a high level of dominance in 1986. In 1990 the PMDB would inevitably slip, so survival meant chasing the voters of party compatriots.

Deputies who finished low on their parties' postelection lists in 1986 certainly had reason to feel vulnerable. In every state except Rio, low ranking deputies (low ranks receive more positive scores) made significantly more amendments than their high-ranking colleagues. In Rio the relationship was positive but well below statistical significance. Most likely, the weakness of the vulnerability-amending relationship in Rio stems from the demographic importance of the capital combined with its unattractiveness as an amendment target.

At first glance, the distance hypotheses seem only weakly supported. Closer inspection, however, reveals that amending behavior reflects the distance of municipalities from deputies' core support in most cases. Minas Gerais and the six northeastern states support the original argument ("amend less with distance from municipal center").[27] In Rio, São Paulo, and the three southern states, deputies decreased their campaigning as a function of each municipality's distance from the core of their personal support rather than the core of their municipal domination.[28] Why the variation? In Minas and the northeast the average level of municipal domination is much higher than elsewhere; *mineiro* and *nordestino* deputies get substantial shares of their personal totals in places where they dominate. These localities remain crucial for them and they stay close to home. In Rio, São Paulo, and the South, the average level of domination (the deputy's percentage of the municipality's total votes) is less than half the level attained by *mineiro* and *nordestino* deputies. With low levels of domination, credit claiming is

---

[27] The absence of the predicted sign on the quadratic term simply means that amending behavior showed no diminishing returns.

[28] In both Rio and the South, the negative coefficient on the distance-from-personal-center variable dominates the coefficient of the distance-from-municipal-center variable.

19

more difficult, so the center of municipal domination is not the campaign reference point. Instead, deputies focus their campaigns where they receive the largest share of their personal totals.

Only in Bahia are budgetary amendments unrelated to the distance of municipalities from candidates' core support. Why is Bahia exceptional? Consider the political context. Bahia's governor, Antônio Carlos Magalhães (popularly known as ACM), is so powerful he can command candidates to campaign in particular municipalities. ACM's machine was built on his ties to the old military regime, ties that brought Bahia considerable federal largesse. ACM and his allies in the state bureaucracy reaped the political profits, and deputies with state-level bureaucratic backgrounds continue to dominate Bahia's congressional delegation. Only one of every eight *baiano* deputies has a local past—second lowest of any state—and purely local deputies are weak. Nonlocal Bahian deputies tend to have dominant-scattered vote distributions, so their amendments are necessarily dispersed. In a sense, the concept of a vote center means little to such deputies; they deal with local bosses wherever one is available.

What about the variables measuring the social match of each municipality to deputies' core constituencies? If deputies appeal to constituencies resembling those where they have done well, amendments ought to decrease as social distance increases. Government employees are a central constituency for many deputies, and such deputies do appear to seek similar municipalities: three states or state groups had significant results in the expected direction; only São Paulo had the wrong sign.[29]

The other social-match variables demonstrate that ideological appeals are indeed rare in Brazil. Similarities in income distribution and population produced insubstantial and inconsistent results.[30] In addition, if deputies seek targets on ideological bases, social matching ought to be strongest in the most developed regions of the country. Rio, São Paulo and the South, however, produced results no more consistent than the Northeast, Bahia, and Minas Gerais. The negative result is important: i.e., most deputies see the social and ideological characteristics of municipalities as minor factors in their decision to use pork-barrel politics as a campaign tool.

Consider now the hypotheses failing to receive consistent support. The original theory predicted, albeit hesitantly, that candidates with

[29] São Paulo's deviance probably results from the extreme unattractiveness of the highly competitive core city, where most bureaucrats live.
[30] The failure of candidates to seek municipalities of similar size may have another cause: small communities yield few votes, while big cities are too competitive.

backgrounds in local politics would amend more than those with business or bureaucratic careers. Only in Rio and São Paulo did the hypothesis receive support, and in Bahia and in the South local candidates made *fewer* amendments. These differences are not simply functions of the domination of candidates with local origins, because the South and Minas have the highest percentage of locals, while Bahia and Rio have the fewest. Local candidates' tactics depend on historical contexts. Bahia, for example, has few local candidates, and those who venture from their bailiwicks risk incurring the wrath of ACM. Rio has even fewer locals than Bahia, but for demographic rather than historical reasons. Rio has only 65 municipalities to serve as springboards for its 46 deputies (1.41 municipalities per deputy) while Bahia has 8.6 municipalities per deputy. Locals in Rio lack opportunities, but since they confront no coercive machine, they are free to compete with statewide candidates by over amending. São Paulo has a substantial number of locals, but between 1987 and 1990 many defected from the dominant PMDB. These defectors had to contend with Orestes Quércia's powerful PMDB machine, which sent candidates into the bailiwicks of the defectors. But the machine lacked the power to keep its opponents bottled up in their bailiwicks, so expansion was their optimal strategy.

Politics in the South and in the Northeast, by contrast, reflect distinct historical contexts. In the South, party labels are meaningful, no governor enjoys the hegemony of an ACM, spatial concentration is intense, and local candidates dominate. Candidates *lacking* a local base struggle to find support, so local politicians wisely stay in their bailiwicks, making fewer amendments. The Northeast and Minas Gerais support intermediate levels of local candidates; locals neither struggle, as they do in Bahia and Rio, nor dominate, as in the South.

Originally, I expected that local politicians would simply amend less as they moved farther from their bases. Instead, the results provide an instructive comparison to our distance measures, i.e., the variables measuring changes in amending behavior of all deputies, regardless of political career. In Bahia, the South and Minas Gerais, local deputies increase their amending activity as they move away from the municipalities where they are most dominant, but they decrease activity as they move away from the municipalities where they get most of their votes. Capital cities in these cases have little importance in total state electorates; few personal centers are found in cities where the presence of many deputies discourages credit claiming. For most deputies, therefore, it makes sense to stay close to the places contributing the bulk of their votes. In the Northeast and Rio, however, capital cities have much more weight in total state electorates, and more candidates have per-

sonal centers in exactly these capitals. But since these capitals are home
to many deputies, they discourage credit claiming, and local candidates
are forced to flee in pursuit of new voters.

Retirements (assessed by the percentage of the 1986 vote received
by candidates not competing in 1990) stimulated more amendments only
in Bahia. In the South amendments actually declined where retirements
freed more voters. This is a surprise, because in my interviews Southern
deputies mentioned municipalities made vulnerable through retirements.
Perhaps the timing was off: when deputies offered these amendments
in 1988 and 1989 (for the 1989 and 1990 budgets), they might not have
known who planned to retire.

The original argument suggested that candidates with spatially concentrated support would over amend to compensate for their geographically restricted vote bases. Only in Bahia and the Northeast did the
hypothesis prove correct. Perhaps the argument fails because concentration is often related to domination; i.e., what really matters is local
dominance rather than the spatial contiguity of votes. As a result, the
domination variable (which supported the prediction in every case) simply overwhelms concentration. The case of Bahia once again reflects
the power of Bahia's political machine. The machine discourages candidates from leaving their bases, so they overamend to increase local
dominance.

Finally, why do deputies from political families fail to distinguish
themselves? Political learning, I suspect, is very rapid. Whether members of political families or not, deputies quickly learn campaign tactics.
Interestingly, members of Northeastern political families made significantly *fewer* amendments than *nordestinos* without family ties. Such
ties are much more important in the Northeast than anywhere else;
about 30% of all deputies in these states have political relatives, compared to less than 10% in the South. Political family in the Northeast
often means old-style deal making, not populism; traditional *nordestino*
politicians do less for their constituents—especially in terms of social
assistance—and more for local bosses.

Recapitulation. The municipal-level campaign strategies of Brazilian deputies respond strongly to local dominance, to the vulnerability
to invasion of potential targets, to their own electoral weakness, and to
their previous careers. But the absence of campaign efforts in communities sociologically similar to deputies' core constituencies (exemplified
by the weakness of the social-match variables) confirms the impression
that few deputies seek votes along ideological lines. The absence of

party programs and the weakness of party discipline renders such appeals, except for the Workers' Party, unproductive.

Does Strategic Behavior Pay off Electorally?

Do the tactics of our vote-seeking deputies succeed? Table 2 estimates an "outcomes" model. It resembles the "strategy" model, but with important additions. The outcomes model incorporates 1986 vote as a predicter of 1990 vote. It also assesses the effects of overall (state-level) dominance—in addition to municipal-level dominance—to discover whether certain kinds of deputies were more successful. Each deputy's amendments, along with the amendments made by other deputies, are now explanatory variables. Finally, the model includes (to explore partisan realignment) variables measuring the gain of candidates from allied parties.[31]

The outcomes model works well, explaining more than 50% of the variance in candidates' 1990 vote everywhere except São Paulo.[32] Vote received in 1986 was the most powerful predicter. This result would be expected in most polities, but here it contradicts Brazil's conventional wisdom, which holds that deputies' unpopularity makes incumbency a disadvantage. Campaigning matters. In Bahia, the Northeast, Minas Gerais and the South, amendments increased votes.[33] Amendments made a difference in Rio de Janeiro and São Paulo as well, but only for more dominant deputies, i.e., amendments in these states became more important as municipal dominance increased. Municipalities in Rio and São Paulo are mostly competitive, with few dominant deputies. Where deputies share votes with many others (as in the capitals) amendments are futile, but as dominance increases they make more sense.

[31] In the construction of this indicator, PFL and PDS votes measure right-wing gain; PMDB vote measures left-wing gain. The latter is an imperfect measure, but in many municipalities the PMDB was the only opposition to the right. Each deputy was coded, on the basis of party affiliation, in terms of right or center-left orientation. Similar results are obtained by using 1978 and 1982 MDB-PMDB vote totals as a purer substitute for the 1986 PMDB vote.

[32] The poor performance of the model in São Paulo (although it easily attains overall statistical significance), may result from the state's high level of ideological politics, a function of the strength of leftist parties like the PT. The PT encourages voters to choose the party label instead of individual candidates.

[33] The model incorporates logged amendments to reduce the effect of each "additional" amendment. In the South, the negative coefficient on the term representing the interaction between amendments and dominance means that amendments are counterproductive above a certain level of dominance. About 5% of Southern deputies fall above this inflection point. Such deputies may be engaged in a hopeless struggle to maintain their bases in a region where dominance is increasingly rare.

23

Table 2. What Determines Electoral Success?

Municipal, Individual, and Electoral Characteristics	OLS Estimation of Results of 1990 Election					
	Bahia	Northeast	Minas Gerais	Rio de Janeiro	São Paulo	South
Vote in 1986	+	+	+	+	+	+
Amendments by deputy (logged)	+	+	+			+
Amendments* municipal dominance	+	+	+	+	+	–
Amendment by other deputies	–	–	–		–	–
Distance from municipal center						
Distance from personal center						
State-level dominance in 1986	+	+	+	+	+	+
Municipal dominance in 1986	–	–	–	+		–
Municipal dominance squared			+			–
Concentration in 1986			+			
Interparty fragmentation in 1986			+			
Intraparty fragmentation in 1986			–			
Match to core: Income distribution		+				
Match to core: Government employees		–				
Match to core: Population						
Rank in party list in 1986	–	+	+		+	
Local career				+		
Allied parties gain from 1986	+	+	+	+	+	+
PFL-PDS candidate	+	+	+		+	+
PMDB or left candidate		+	+			
Political family		+	+			
Political family* municipal dominance		–	–			
R^2 =	53%	57%	53%	53%	20%	56%
N =	8040	6629	13740	1536	16530	8803

"+" means a positive coefficient, significant at the .05 level.
"–" means a negative coefficient, significant at the .05 level.
All F tests for the entire model are significant at the .05 level.

24

Amendments by other deputies should lower a deputy's vote, because these amendments mean that opponents have also targetted the same municipality. Except in Rio and São Paulo—where other deputies' amendments had no impact—this is just what happened. The hypothesis failed in Rio and São Paulo for the same reasons we have seen above.[34]

Dominant deputies gained more votes than those with shared distributions, but concentration helped only in Minas Gerais.[35] In an election with more than 50% turnover of incumbents, and with substantial losses on the part of the center and center-left parties, this result has great importance. *Dominance protects deputies from partisan swings.* Most incumbents who lost seats in 1990 shared constituencies. Single-member municipalities, whether contiguous or scattered, are safer. In an environment of weak parties and pork-barrel politics, deal making with local *políticos*—the classic dominant-scattered pattern—makes sense.

The strategy model demonstrated that deputies rarely seek campaign targets socioeconomically similar to their core municipalities. Not surprisingly, they are equally unlikely to gain or lose votes on this basis. Although in big cities deputies make ideological or group appeals, they do not seek or receive support in *distant* campaign targets with such appeals. Given the high cost of poaching on the turf of fellow party members, candidates increase support by appealing to new groups in their base areas, not by pursuing similar but geographically distant groups. Consequently, although changes in the overall ideological composition of legislatures may result from electoral realignments, such realignments are not the product of individual campaign appeals.

Partisan shifts play an important role in the fortunes of individual deputies. In every state, overall gains by parties close on the political spectrum helped candidates. Since this election represented a defeat for the PMDB after its overwhelming success in 1986, right-wing candidates ("PFL-PDS candidate") gained, while PMDB and left candidates got a boost only in the Northeast and in Minas Gerais.

Finally, the career paths of deputies, at least as measured by previous occuptions or by membership in political families, had no consistent

---

[34] We know from the *strategy* model that deputies make fewer amendments as the distance from their vote centers increases. The *outcomes* model shows that their 1990 vote was generally unrelated to the distance from the core. Remember, however, that the model includes the 1986 vote, so the coefficient should only be significant if there is an additional, unexpected concentration of votes. This occurs in two cases, Minas and São Paulo, where deputies with more *concentrated* vote patterns did better in 1990 than in 1986. I cannot currently explain this result.

[35] The dominance variable masks any possible effects contributed by the two fragmentation measures. Obviously fragmentation is lower when deputies dominate municipalities.

effect on electoral outcomes. In the Northeast and Minas Gerais—areas where substantial percentages of deputies come from political families— these deputies had more success. But in Bahia, where political families are most common, such deputies received no help. In addition, local candidates did no better in any states. The election of 1990 represented an influx of big money into congressional campaigning. If this trend continues, local candidates, as these results demonstrate, are in serious trouble.

Recapitulation. The strategies of congressional deputies matter. Deputies profit by making their own amendments; they suffer when other deputies target the same municipalities. Deputies with dominant vote distributions are more successful at resisting partisan swings than those with shared distributions.[36] But most deputies gain little from concentrating their vote distributions or from making group or ideological appeals, and career patterns have no broad effect on electoral fortunes.

4. Conclusion

Most discussions of Brazilian politics stress its traditional, clientelistic roots. The theory developed here, by contrast, is grounded in the strategic behavior of rational politicians. Faced with an electoral system whose chief attributes include open-list proportional representation, large multimember districts, candidate selection at the level of politically active subnational units, and the possibility of immediate reelection, most deputies pay little attention to ideological appeals. Instead, they seek secure bailiwicks, search for vulnerable municipalities, and strive to overcome their own electoral weakness through "wheeling and dealing." Strategic candidates do not behave identically, because their own political backgrounds vary and because the differing demographic and economic contexts of Brazilian states reward some tactics and penalize others.

What is the significance of these results? Consider the principal-agent relationship between voters and deputies. Brazil's electoral system hinders voter control. It forces candidates to seek single-issue niches, to spend lavishly, and to make deals with candidates for other offices, candidates with whom they have nothing in common. The system cannot be faulted as undemocratic; indeed, by favoring no particular cleavage it allows all grievances to be articulated. But citizens learn little about the importance of national-level issues, and rational voters back candidates based on pork potential.

---

[36] Deputies can also switch parties to profit from partisan surges.

Brazil's electoral system motivates deputies to seek pork. When we combine these incentives with the state-centered quality of Brazilian politics, the results suggest that pork seeking may not have reached an equilibrium. Deputies in Brazil's South and in more industrialized states face more competition from candidates of other parties, but they also have more concentrated vote distributions. Higher levels of education and wealth increase voter interest and involvement in politics, but that interest magnifies incentives for deputies to focus on pork. At the same time, demands for local benefits may contribute to the elevated turnover rates and low seniority levels of southern congressional delegations, factors which shift the ideological center of the Congress to the right.

In the legislative process, Brazil's system produces parties without programs, parties sheltering an enormous range of interests and preferences. Open-list proportional representation is not a sufficient condition for weak parties; pre-1973 Chile combined open-list PR with fiercely ideological parties. But open-list PR in Brazil works differently, because state interests control nominations, because parties cannot control the behavior of their deputies, and because high district magnitudes increase both inter- and intra-party fragmentation.

This analysis has only scratched the surface of the theoretical argument.[37] What are the implications of spatial voting distributions for subsequent legislative behavior? De facto, Brazilian deputies represent a wide variety of constituencies, from dominated single-member districts to scattered special-interest cohorts, to scattered deals, to intensive working-class districts. Do some districts insulate deputies from presidential demands? Is corruption a natural outgrowth of certain constituencies? Are some deputies more oriented toward national legislation? Congress' acceptance or rejection of deputies' budgetary amendments also merits exploration. Why are some deputies more successful than others? Are there rules guaranteeing everyone a piece of the action? Can senior deputies buy the votes of needy junior members? The Brazilian case, a system allowing the formation of various constituencies within a single institutional framework, is a perfect laboratory for the study of electoral influences on legislative behavior.

Manuscript submitted 16 March 1994.
Final manuscript received 27 July 1994.

---

[37] These findings also have implications for other political contexts with similar rules, e.g., U.S. primary elections (both legislative and presidential) and at-large city council contests. With the spread of geographic information systems, it has become much easier to explore these settings.

APPENDIX
Data Sources and Problems

The map and Moran's I. I constructed the computerized maps with state road maps, a digitizing table, and Autocad. The data base also includes, in addition to electoral results, indicators from the 1980 census, all budgetary amendments offered for the 1989–91 budgets, and the results of the 1989 presidential election. The nearest-neighbor matrices used to calculate Moran's I derived from the map coordinates. Paul Sampson of the University of Washington provided the program creating these matrices. For an introduction to spatial analysis, see (Cliff et al. 1975).

The politically motivated tendency for municipalities to subdivide can seriously hinder mapping. Since the census data are based on 1980 borders, municipalities created after that date must be aggregated into old ones. In some cases the number of new units was so great that aggregation distorted political events. In other cases old states were compromised by the creation of whole new states. As a result, the analysis excludes Goiás, Tocantins, Mato Grosso, Mato Grosso do Sul, Acre, Amapá, Rondônia and Roraima. Although malapportionment gives these states considerable political force, most have very small populations.

Budgetary amendments. Each year the Joint Commission on the Budget publishes the amendments of deputies and senators (Brasil. Congresso Nacional, 1988–1990). Members submit these amendments on small cards, roughly 2″ by 6″, and the published volumes reproduce these cards, many of them hand written. Each card contains the name and state of the deputy or senator, the program modified, the municipality benefitted, the amount of money, and the program debited to finance the amendment. I coded all amendments in 1990 and 1991 but only a sample of the 72,672 amendments made in 1992. This paper does not utilize the 1992 group, because members of the new 1991–94 Chamber offered them. The analysis also excludes amendments (roughly 1%) benefitting no particular municipality. Thanks to Orlando de Assis and Carmen Pérez for help in obtaining the 1991 amendments.

The electoral results. For 1978 and 1982, the electoral results come from PRODASEN, the Senate's data processing arm. Thanks to Jalles and William for help. For 1986, the Tribunal Superior Eleitoral provided some data, but eight states never sent election results to Brasília. I copied results at the regional tribunals in these states. For 1990 the Tribunal Superior, with the assistance of Roberto Siqueira, Sérgio, Flávio Antônio, Conceição and Nelson, supplied data on diskette for fifteen states. Manuel Caetano in Porto Alegre helped with the *gaúcho* results.

REFERENCES

Abranches, Sérgio Henrique Hudson de. 1988. "Presidencialismo de Coalizão: O Dilema Institucional Brasileiro." *Dados* 31 (1):5-34.

Ames, Barry. 1995. "Electoral Rules, Constituency Pressures, and Pork Barrel: Bases of Voting in the Brazilian Congress," *Journal of Politics* 57.

Bowler, Shaun, Todd Donovan, and Joe Snipp. 1992. "Local Sources of Information and Voter Choice in State Elections: Micro-level Foundations of the 'Friends and Neighbors' Effect. *American Politics Quarterly* 21:473-489.

Brasil. 1989. *Assembléia Nacional Constituinte-1987.* Brasília: Câmara dos Deputados.

Brasil (Congresso Nacional). 1988-1990. *Projeto de Lei: Estima a Receita e Fixa a Despesa da União para o Exercício Financeiro de 1989-1991. Emendas.*

Câmara dos Deputados. 1981. *Deputados Brasileiros: 46th legislatura, 1979-1983.* Brasília: Câmara dos Deputados.

Câmara dos Deputados. 1983. *Deputados Brasileiros: 47th legislatura, 1983-1987.* Brasília: Câmara dos Deputados.

Câmara dos Deputados. 1991. *Deputados Brasileiros: 49th legislatura, 1991-1995.* Brasília: Câmara dos Deputados.

Cliff, Andrew, Peter Haggett, J. Keith Ord, Keith A. Bassett, and Richard Davies. 1975. *Elements of Spatial Structure: A Quantitative Approach.* Cambridge: Cambridge University Press.

Cox, Gary W. 1990. "Multicandidate Spatial Competition." In *Advances in the Spatial Theory of Voting,* ed. James M. Enelow and Melving J. Hinich. Cambridge: Cambridge University Press.

De Souza, Amaury and Bolívar Lamounier, ed. 1992. *As Elites Brasileiras e a Modernização do Setor Público: Um Debate.* São Paulo: Editôra Sumaré.

Fleischer, David. 1973. "O Trampolím Político: Mudanças nos Padroes de Recrutamento Político em Minas Gerais." *Revista de Administração Pública* 7:99-116.

———. 1976. "Concentração e Dispersão Eleitoral: Um Estudo da Distribuição Geográfica do Voto em Minas Gerais (1966-1974)." *Revista Brasileira de Estudos Políticos* 43:333-60.

———. 1977. "A Bancada Federal Mineira." *Revista Brasileira de Estudos Políticos* 45:7-58.

Isto é. 1991. *Perfil Parlamentar Brasileiro.* São Paulo: Editôra Tres.

Kinzo, Maria D'Alva Gil. 1987. "A Bancada Federal Paulista de 1986: Concentração ou Dispersão do Voto?" Presented at the meeting of the Associação Nacional de Pos-Graduação e Pesquisa em Ciências Sociais, Águas de São Pedro.

Lima Junior, Olavo Brasil, ed. 1991. *Sistema Eleitoral Brasileiro: Teoria e Práctica.* Rio de Janeiro: IUPERJ.

Lowi, Theodore. 1964. "American Business, Public Policy, Case-Studies, and Political Science." *World Politics,* July.

Mainwaring, Scott. 1993. "Brazilian Party Underdevelopment in Comparative Perspective." *Political Science Quarterly* 107:677-708.

Mainwaring, Scott and Timothy R. Scully, 1992. "Party Systems in Latin America." Presented at the 1992 LASA meeting, Los Angeles.

Salisbury, Robert and John Heinz. 1970. "A Theory of Policy Analysis and Some Preliminary Applications." In *Policy Analysis in Political Science,* ed. Ira Skaransky. Chicago: Markham.

Straubhaar, Joseph, Organ Olsen, and Maria Cavaliari Nunes. 1993. "The Brazilian Case: Influencing the Voter." In *Television, Politics, and the Transition to Democracy in Latin America,* ed. Thomas Skidmore. Washington, DC: The Woodrow Wilson Center Press.

American Political Science Review						Vol. 89, No. 1		March 199

SHAPING MEXICO'S ELECTORAL ARENA: THE CONSTRUCTION OF PARTISAN CLEAVAGES IN THE 1988 AND 1991 NATIONAL ELECTIONS

JORGE I. DOMÍNGUEZ *Harvard University*
JAMES A. McCANN *Purdue University*

*I*n the 1988 and 1991 national elections, Mexican voters asked themselves above all whether they continued to support the long-ruling official party. Voter behavior was not well explained by attachments to social cleavages, attitudes on policy issues, or general assessments about the present circumstances and the prospects for the nation's economy or personal finances. In both elections, moreover, the parties of the Left failed to mobilize voters that had chosen to abstain in past elections. Once voters were ready to oppose the ruling party, however, differences by issue, prospective economic assessments, and social cleavages shaped their choice between the opposition parties.

How do citizens who have long been governed by the same party in an authoritarian regime vote when there seems to be a chance that they could turn the incumbents out of office? In such elections, do citizens focus mainly on the future of the ruling party and its incumbents? Are these elections ideologically competitive, with party choice shaped by attitudes on policy issues and social cleavages? How do such citizens respond to the entry of a new party to challenge the rulers, and how strong is such a new party likely to remain from one election to the next? How stable and distinctive are blocs of voters once the electoral arena becomes more competitive? We seek to address these questions by focusing on the 1988 and 1991 national elections in Mexico.

In the July 1988 presidential elections, Mexico's electorate split into three large voting blocs (Table 1, see the note). The long-ruling Institutional Revolutionary Party (PRI) claimed just over half the votes for its presidential candidate, Carlos Salinas de Gortari. (In 1982, the PRI and small allied parties had claimed 71% of the votes cast for its presidential candidate, Miguel de la Madrid; in the 1960s and 1970s, the PRI and its allied parties always claimed over 80% of the votes cast in presidential elections.) The long-established opposition party, the National Action party (PAN), came in third, well behind a new political force, a coalition of several parties on the political Left led by Cuauhtémoc Cárdenas. Cárdenas himself, and many of his close associates in the new coalition, had once belonged to the PRI. In the August 1991 national congressional elections, the PRI's recorded votes soared and the PAN held steady, but the Cárdenas coalition splintered. The party that remained formally associated with Cárdenas, the Democratic Revolutionary party (PRD), received just over 8% of the recorded votes. Seven minor parties, the largest of which were former Cárdenas allies, each garnered from .6% to 4.4% of the recorded votes cast, for a total recorded vote of 12.7% for the minor parties.

We hope to show that the voting intentions o Mexican citizens as reported to our pollsters are bes explained in terms of voter judgments about th prospects for the ruling party and the voter's pas party preferences. These explanations are strongly significant statistically and hold for both nationa elections. Voters ask themselves, above all, whethe they continue to support the ruling party—the *part* *of the state* as Mexican scholars sometimes call it Contrary to the views of many commentators on thes Mexican elections (especially on the 1988 election), w also find that voter behavior is not well explained by (1) attachments to social cleavages, (2) attitudes or policy issues, or (3) general assessments about the present circumstances and the prospects for the nation's economy or personal finances.

We shall also argue that the organizational weaknesses among the parties of the Left help to explain important aspects of the outcomes in both elections. In 1988, the Cardenista coalition failed to mobilize voters who had chosen to abstain in past elections; in 1991, the Cardenista coalition splintered even though the pool of potential Cardenista voters remained large. That is, from 1988 to 1991 opinion alignments remained more stable than party alignments. Further, we suggest that the explanations for voting behavior in 1991 differ from those that obtained in 1988. In 1988, opposition voters were motivated by a range of political, social, and economic concerns; by 1991, opposition voters were motivated almost exclusively by their political judgments and by their place of residence: instead of national parties, the opposition parties had shrunk into regional parties. Finally, we shall propose and explain a two-step "model" of Mexican voting behavior. Mexicans decide first on their judgment about the ruling party; lurking beneath that judgment, especially in 1988, differences by issue, prospective economic assessments, and social cleavages shape voter choices between opposition parties and, therefore, the electoral arena.

Partisan Preferences in Mexico, 1988 and 1991

	Percent of Vote
1988 Presidential Election	
Institutional Revolutionary party (PRI)	55
National Action party (PAN)	20
Cardenistas	22
Minor parties	2
1991 Legislative Elections	
Institutional Revolutionary party (PRI)	68
National Action party (PAN)	15
Democratic Revolutionary party (PRD)	7
Minor parties	9

Source: Gallup interviews conducted in May 1988 and July 1991. *Note:* Respondents without a clear partisan preference have been dropped from this list. N = 1,914 (65% of the total sample) in 1988 and 2,029 (66%) in 1991. In 1988, the official tally gave 50% of the vote to the PRI, 17% to the PAN, 32% to the Cardenistas, and 1% to all other minor parties combined. In 1991, 61% of the vote went to the PRI, the PAN gained 18%, the PRD received 8% and the other minor parties polled 13%.

ASSESSING ARGUMENTS

The Institutional Revolutionary party (PRI) has long been a bureaucratic organization bearing its contradictions in its own name. The party claims legitimacy from both the Mexican revolution and its near opposite, institutional rule (Bailey 1988; Basáñez 1982). We shall now spell out the reasoning for our choice of independent and dependent variables.[1]

The Ruling Party

When citizens long governed by the same party in an authoritarian regime face a fairly open election, the fate of the ruling party becomes the central question for many voters; even those who oppose the ruling party do not necessarily oppose all of its policies, nor does their vote embody the social cleavages often evident in competitive politics (Huntington 1991, 74–92). We assess the importance of ruling-party factors through questions that ask respondents about their partisan loyalties and about the nation's prospects if a different party were to govern. If Mexico's voters were not focused mainly on the fate of the ruling party, then attitudes toward specific issues, general expectations about present and future economic circumstances, and ties to social groups would have a more salient role, while views about the ruling party's future would matter much less. To distinguish between these hypotheses, we take into account the Mexican context.

First, in Mexico, questions pertaining to, say, freer trade or foreign investment do not a priori tap support or opposition for the ruling party because the leaders of one major opposition party, the PAN, have officially favored such general policies. Responses to these questions thus measure attitudes on specific issues, not necessarily attitudes toward the ruling party. If attitudes toward issues were to explain Mexican voting behavior, we would conclude that the hypothesis about the preeminence of ruling-party factors in explaining voter choice does not hold.

Second, questions about prospective economic circumstances help to explain voter choice in many European countries where the same party has not governed alone for generations (Lewis-Beck 1988). We distinguish between responses to questions about the prospective economic situation posed in general terms from questions about the country's prospective situation that are specifically related to what would happen if a party other than the PRI were to gain power. If general questions about economic expectations explain Mexican voting behavior, we would conclude that the hypothesis about the preeminence of ruling-party factors in explaining voter choice does not hold.

Third, as the party of the state until 1988 by means fair and foul (at times including coercion and fraud), the PRI claimed election victories virtually without fail (Gómez Tagle 1989, 240–242). The PRI has never accepted defeat in a presidential election. It had never accepted defeat for a Senate seat until 1988, or for a governorship until 1989. The PRI had been integral to the authoritarian regime. Asked about a future without the PRI in power, Mexicans understand that they are not being asked about the fate of a "mere party." We asked voters whether the country's economic conditions or social peace would be hurt or helped if a party other than the PRI were to gain power; we also asked about general expectations concerning PRI strength. If these questions were to prove insignificant—or less important than questions about demographic factors, issues, or general economic expectations—in explaining voter choice, we would conclude that the hypothesis about the preeminence of ruling-party factors in explaining voter choice does not hold.

The Organization of the Ruling Party

Before the 1988 elections, PRI organization typically rested on collective affiliation, not individual membership. Various organizations belonged to the three "sectors" (one each for workers and peasants and a third more heterogeneous one for middle-class organizations) that have constituted the PRI since its major reorganization in 1938. Party leaders used this internal party organization to channel support and to manage conflicts. Paradoxically, this practice left the PRI without members: it sought the support of organizations but not directly of the nation's citizens (Garrido 1987).

The impact of this PRI internal structure on voting behavior was open to competing hypotheses. Did the PRI have a strong hold on individuals affiliated with the party in this indirect manner or did the indirect affiliation weaken individual loyalties to the party, rendering once PRI voters vulnerable to the appeals of a new opposition party, many of whose leaders had once belonged to the PRI? The PRI had long drawn strength from its peasant and labor unions whose members might be expected to vote PRI. Alternatively, the indirect nature of PRI "membership," the weakness of an internal party life, and some labor and peasant leaders' reputation for bossing their members might mean that lower-class voters had no special attachment to the PRI. As early as the 1960s and 1970s, there had been work-center revolts against traditional PRI-affiliated labor unions (Middlebrook 1989). This disconnection between the PRI and its presumed affiliates might cancel the effects of demographic factors. Under this alternative, voting would be unrelated to union membership, social class, religion, region, and other demographic factors.

The Presidency and the Issues

Mexico's political system has been highly centralized; the presidency has been "at its epicenter" (Bailey 1988, 30). The president has always come from the PRI since the party's foundation. We would be shocked if presidential performance were not to explain much about voting behavior in Mexico.

In the 1980s, Mexico's economy was in deep trouble. From 1981 to 1989, Mexico's gross domestic product (GDP) in constant prices per capita fell by over 9%; GDP per capita change was negative in five of those years. Consumer price inflation had been below 30% per year in the late 1970s and early 1980s; it was well above 60% per year every year from 1982 through 1987, when annual inflation peaked at 159%; the inflation rate in 1988 was 52%. In 1988, the minimum salary in real terms in Mexico city was 46% below its 1980 level. In 1988, the average salary in Mexican manufacturing was 28% below its 1980 level (United Nations, Economic Commission for Latin America and the Caribbean 1989).

From 1989 through 1991, gross domestic product per capita grew every year (on average, 1.7%). In each of those three years, inflation was below 30% per year, with an overall downward trend. The average salary in Mexican manufacturing recovered slightly, but in 1991 it was still 23% below its 1980 level. The minimum salary in real terms in Mexico city continued to drop; in 1991, it was 57% below its 1980 level (United Nations 1991).

The de la Madrid administration made two key economic policy decisions: it continued to service the foreign debt and to negotiate its rescheduling with its creditors, and it shifted away from the long-standing policies of industrialization by means of import substitution and heavy state involvement in the economy toward a market-oriented strategy and export promotion, reducing the state's impact on the economy. The Salinas administration accelerated these trends. It reached a comprehensive international debt settlement with its creditors, privatized many state enterprises, and removed many barriers to (and sought to promote) direct foreign investment. It greatly liberalized international trade and created a North American free-trade area with the United States and Canada. Many PAN leaders who had advocated similar policies supported the government's born-again eco-

nomic liberalism, but these policies helped to galvanize the Cardenista opposition.

In 1988, therefore, many voters had reason to worry about the country's and their own finances. In 1991, most Mexicans had yet to gain much from the economic recovery that was under way, even if some could have bright hopes for the nation's and their own economic future.

In terms of economic policy orientations, the speeches of politicians in 1988 and 1991 suggested some convergence between the PRI and the PAN in support for freer markets but also indicated that voters who disagreed with those policies could vote for Cárdenas. In 1988, for example, Cárdenas argued: "I think that this administration has been letting foreigners take over our fundamental decisions. It has acted not in the interest of the country but of foreigners who are against Mexico"; again: "Possibly, the present administration and the program of Carlos Salinas are rational in some way, but it is a rationality which goes against the majority. It is a rationality that has made many Mexicans poor, that leaves important economic decisions to foreigners, that closes the channels of democratic expression. A rationality conducive to repression and dictatorship" (WGBH Educational Foundation 1988). Although some policy differences were more muted by 1991, Cárdenas remained a clear alternative to the Salinas economic policies. Issue-oriented voting was certainly rational and conceivable in both 1988 and 1991. Indeed, commentators during both campaigns frequently portrayed the electoral choice in stark ideological terms.

The Opposition, Cleavages, and Parties

Did the shaping of Mexico's electoral arena in 1988 and 1991 conform to broader patterns of the construction of partisan cleavages? As Lipset and Rokkan (1967) argued in their classic work, in the genesis of party systems there are often territorial and religious bases for opposition because of a clash between the central nation-building political coalition and territorially or religiously defined oppositions. In Mexico, the PRI markedly centralized power in the capital city and, at moments in its history, has sponsored anticlerical policies.

The PAN might embody these territorial and religious cleavages. Although the PAN had had a long, if generally unsuccessful, electoral trajectory opposing the PRI, it has been a real political party, with its own members, activists, programs, and goals. Especially in some northern states such as Chihuahua, there was a genuine vibrancy to its internal life (Chand 1991). It may have won the 1986 gubernatorial elections in Chihuahua (though the official results gave the governorship to the PRI), and it won the Chihuahua governorship at last in the 1992 elections. In the PAN's history, fidelity to Roman Catholicism had played a significant role (Almond and Verba 1965, 93; Loaeza 1989, sec. 3). The PAN has also seemed stronger among middle-class voters. Thus we expected individual voter loyalty to the PAN in election after election, plus region, church attendance, and social class to help to explain voting for the PAN (Butler, Pick, and Jones 1991).

The Cardenista coalition was new in 1988. Formed around the person of Cuauhtémoc Cárdenas, a former PRI governor of the state of Michoacán and son of former President Lázaro Cárdenas, Cardenistas lashed out at the PRI's lack of internal democracy—at such practices as having the incumbent president de facto "appoint" his own successor or having most PRI candidates for governor and Congress be chosen by a few leaders or by the president himself. We expected Cardenistas to oppose the PRI, the official candidate, import liberalization, the sale of state enterprises, and continued servicing of the foreign debt. Consistent with the Lipset-Rokkan argument, the Cardenista coalition had some features of a socialist party in part because, in 1988, it included various parties that bore the name socialist and because, in both 1988 and 1991, it included the old Mexican Communist party. The Cardenista party's newness led us to ask how they got their votes. Did they mobilize the previously unmobilized? Did they take voters, as well as leaders, from the PRI? Had PAN voters in the past been "closet leftists" who had voted for the PAN mainly because there was then no viable left-wing alternative?

By the 1991 congressional elections, the Cardenista coalition had splintered into many of its initial components. Did this fragmentation reflect policy differences in the electorate or differences attributable to demographic factors? Did the collapse of the broad Cardenista coalition reflect factional infighting? If the latter, the voters for Cárdenas' own PRD in 1991 should resemble the voters for the minor parties in their concerns about the ruling party, the presidency, and the issues and in their demographic characteristics.

THE DATA

This study is based largely on two nationwide public opinion polls, both conducted by the U.S. Gallup Organization (Princeton, New Jersey) in collaboration with its Mexican affiliate, Gallup México (known as MOP S.A.). Sampling, questionnaire design, and overall direction were U.S. Gallup's responsibility; MOP's personnel, long experienced in polling Mexicans, did the field work.[3] The first poll was conducted from 12 May until 1 June 1988, carrying out a total of 2,960 personal interviews.[4] The second poll was conducted from 15 through 28 July 1991, carrying out a total of 3,053 personal interviews.

In both instances, each interview lasted on average about 40 minutes; the interviewees were all 18 years old (Mexico's voting age) or older. Mexico was divided into four regions (North, South, Mexico City Federal District, and Central Mexico minus the Federal District). The distribution of interviews was proportionate to each region's population. Cities, towns, and villages (with at least 1,000 residents) designated

as polling locations were chosen randomly within each region; there were 78 such locations in 1988 and 270 in 1991. Within each polling location, blocks, households and respondents in the household were selected at random, with about equal numbers of men and women. The margin of error attributable to sampling error is ±3% in 1988 and ±2% in 1991.

The 1988 poll ended five weeks before the presidential election. During those weeks, the support for Cárdenas grew dramatically (see Table 1 and its note). Many observers believe that the vote for Cárdenas was in fact higher. (The final result of the "real" election is neither known nor knowable, the ballots having been destroyed.) This discrepancy does not mean that the poll was in error. The poll probably reflected accurately the state of opinion in the second half of May, but the state of opinion changed (Basáñez 1992). In any highly charged campaign environment with a new party in the making, this is to be expected.

The 1991 poll ended three weeks before the congressional elections. In the official results, the PRI was credited with less support than the Gallup poll had found (see Table 1 and its note). The results for the PAN, the PRD, and the minor parties are fairly close between the Gallup poll and the recorded votes. As we shall see, there was a surge for the minor parties in the days just before the election.

In the case of both polls, there is a likely overestimate of the support for the PRI beyond the formal comparison between the polls and the respective official results. In both cases, some who told Gallup's pollsters that they would vote for the PRI did not, in fact, do so. It is impossible to use the poll to discern who changed their minds or who may have lied. The effect of these difficulties on our analysis is that our measure of support for parties other than the PRI is quite conservative. It identifies those who did not fear to tell the pollsters about their preferences. In the case of Cardenistas in 1988, these were the coalition's founders.

The design of each poll took into account the expectation that some voters would be reluctant to express their true preferences. Thus, in 1988, the question with regard to presidential candidate preference was phrased as follows: "Now, just for the sake of this study, let us imagine that today is election day and you are going to vote for the next President of the Republic. What you indicate will be completely confidential and will only be used for this poll. On this sheet (a sheet is handed out) please mark the political party for which you intend to vote for President of the Republic and deposit it in this box." Then a box is presented to attempt to convey the sense of confidentiality. In the 1991 poll, the same procedure was used to foster belief in, and to ensure, confidentiality (voters being asked to choose a party). In both years, the simulated secret ballot procedure was repeated for several questions deemed to be potentially controversial. We have only used questions asked via "secret ballot" to measure the dependent variable,[5] and we are fortunate that so many questions in these surveys were asked in this fashion.

DESCRIBING THE ELECTORATE

Our description of Mexico's electorate is summarized on Tables 2–4. The Appendix presents the questions in the sequence to which reference is made in these tables; the same sequence is repeated in Table 5. There was a very substantial increase in support for the PRI from 1988 to 1991; this increase is found in each and every category (see Tables 1 through 4). We have no doubt that President Salinas impressively turned around his party's fortunes during those three years.

Demographic factors delineate clusters of voters, although most relationships between demographic factors and party preferences are not very strong. The PRI drew more support from women, heavily rural southern Mexico, older voters, union members, the less well educated, and church-goers. The PRI did consistently less well in the Federal District. These findings hold for both elections. The PRI come through as a "traditionalist" party. The only deme graphic change in the PRI's basis of support fro 1988 to 1991 was its recapture of strong middle-clas support after having yielded more than half of th middle-class voters to the opposition in 1988. Even i 1988 the PRI got nearly half of the youngest voters while in 1991 it got a majority of those voters and wa strongest overall among voters aged between 26 an 29 years. At a time of economic duress, the PRI ability to corral these voters was impressive.

The PAN drew stable support in the North an more variable support in Mexico City. It had mor support among the youngest voters, the somewha better educated, and those who did not belong t unions. Gender and religion did not explain much o the support for the PAN. The consistent lack o relationship between church attendance and PAN support is surprising. In 1988 the PAN did less we with working-class voters, but in 1991 it improved it performance with these voters while it lost voter

TABLE 2

Demographic and Social Determinants of Partisan Choice (%)

DEMOGRAPHIC AND SOCIAL CHARACTERISTICS	1988				1991				
	PRI	PAN	CARD.	N	PRI	PAN	PRD	MINOR	N
Gender									
Male	53	20	25	973	63	16	10	11	975
Female	58	21	20	941	74	15	5	7	1,054
Region									
North	59	24	15	479	71	21	5	3	477
Central	56	17	24	474	72	15	6	7	532
South	67	12	20	446	78	6	4	11	421
Federal District	42	25	29	515	56	18	13	14	599
Age									
18–25	49	21	26	510	59	20	9	12	534
26–29	50	23	24	231	75	14	6	5	210
30–39	56	20	23	518	66	14	14	6	608
40–49	60	20	19	330	71	12	7	10	363
50+	64	17	17	325	74	14	6	6	334
Union Member?									
Yes	64	14	22	442	74	13	7	5	460
No	53	22	23	1,472	67	16	8	10	1,509
Class									
Professional	58	21	18	324	71	14	9	6	294
Middle	46	21	29	298	70	14	6	10	272
Working	59	15	24	325	62	17	10	11	386
Education									
Primary	63	17	18	677	73	11	7	9	792
Secondary	56	18	25	415	67	19	6	8	442
Preparatory	47	24	27	400	62	17	9	12	380
University	51	23	23	415	66	18	8	8	374
Church Attendance									
Weekly	59	21	18	953	70	16	6	8	925
Occasionally	54	19	25	793	69	14	8	9	966
Never	45	22	33	163	52	15	18	15	126

Source: Gallup interviews conducted in May 1988 and July 1991.

TABLE 3

Partisan Choice by Economic Perceptions and Policy Preferences (%)

ECONOMIC PERCEPTIONS AND POLICY PREFERENCES	1988				1991				
	PRI	PAN	CARD.	N	PRI	PAN	PRD	MINOR	N
Economic performance									
Current									
Good	66	16	16	462	73	13	6	8	1,071
Bad	52	22	24	1,404	63	18	10	10	907
Future									
Improve	68	12	19	465	73	15	5	7	937
Worsen	45	27	28	674	67	16	10	8	572
Personal financial situation									
Current									
Good	59	20	20	1,109	71	14	7	8	1,366
Bad	50	21	26	757	64	17	10	10	630
Future									
Improve	58	18	22	877	69	15	7	9	1,457
Worsen	52	24	23	461	67	14	9	11	239
Foreign investment									
Positive	57	21	21	1,065	72	16	5	7	1,292
Negative	50	20	27	583	61	15	13	12	452
Both	50	19	26	114	56	19	12	14	146
Imports									
Made easier	56	22	21	950	71	16	6	7	1,158
Limited	53	19	25	847	62	17	10	12	632
Continue paying foreign debt?									
Yes	58	20	20	1,335	—	—	—	—	—
No	47	21	29	477					
Retain state industries?									
Yes	56	16	25	854	—	—	—	—	—
No	52	25	21	859					
Environmental Protection									
Most important	—	—	—	—	68	15	8	9	1,218
Moderate importance					70	17	6	8	583
Not important					66	14	8	13	192

Source: Gallup interviews conducted in May 1988 and July 1991.

from the middle and professional classes. Except for this social class switch and the greater concentration of support for the PAN in the North in 1991, its demographic profile was stable between the two elections.

In 1988, the Cardenista coalition drew support from men (the gender gap widened from 1988 to 1991), younger voters, the middle class, the better-educated, and those who never went to church. (The latter were nearly twice as likely to vote Cardenista as those who went to church every week.) Its support was strongest in Mexico City and weakest in the North. Union membership did not matter. In 1991, the PRD had become a regional party, strong in Mexico City. It had lost support among the middle class. (In 1988, its middle-class support had exceeded its working-class support.) Support for the PRD was more evident among men, in the working class, and among those who did not go to church. Age, education, and union membership did not explain much.

In 1991, support for the minor parties resembled support for the PRD. The minor parties, too, drew disproportionate support from men, from the working class, and (strongly) from those who did not go to

church. Age and education did not explain much in a systematic way. As with the PRD, the minor parties were stronger in Mexico City. Unlike the PRD, the minor parties were also strong in southern Mexico and among union members.

Turning to views on general economic assessments and issues (Table 3), support for the PRI was not surprisingly higher among those who thought that Mexican economic performance had been good and would get better and that their personal finances were good and would also get better. Support for the opposition was stronger among the dissenters. These differences were notable in 1988 but narrowed markedly by 1991.

From 1988 to 1991, the PRI found more supporters among backers of foreign investment and freer trade. In 1988, support for the PRI was higher among those who favored servicing the foreign debt and somewhat so among those in favor of retaining state enterprises. In 1991, support for the PRI seemed unrelated to views on environmental protection.

Support for the PAN was unrelated to economic issues in both years. PAN supporters were found in comparable proportions among those who supported

TABLE 4

Partisan Choice by Political Interest, Prior Voting Behavior, and Perceptions of the PRI (%)

POLITICAL INTEREST, PARTISAN HISTORY, AND PARTY PERCEPTIONS	1988				1991				
	PRI	PAN	CARD.	N	PRI	PAN	PRD	MINOR	N
Interest in politics									
Much/some	56	20	22	809	69	16	9	7	693
Little/none	55	20	23	1,092	68	15	7	10	1,325
Prior Pres. Voting									
PRI	76	9	13	962	93	3	2	3	969
PAN	12	60	28	270	16	72	6	7	198
Cardenista					22	6	38	34	152
Not mobilized	51	20	28	240	67	17	7	9	377
PRI stronger or weaker in 10 yrs.									
Stronger	73	12	14	619	79	11	5	6	946
Same	64	17	18	470	69	15	7	10	494
Weaker	34	30	34	669	42	29	15	14	432
If another party wins									
National economy									
Better	31	30	36	749	47	27	14	12	565
Same	64	18	16	525	71	12	7	10	664
Worsen	82	9	8	396	87	7	3	4	542
Increase in Social Unrest									
Yes	61	18	20	1,068	75	13	6	7	1,151
No	45	25	28	683	57	20	10	13	698
Presidential Approval Rating									
Very high	79	10	11	364	81	11	4	4	971
Favorable	62	17	19	721	60	17	8	14	757
Mediocre	38	30	30	473	40	26	21	13	192
Poor	26	33	37	206	59	16	14	10	49

Source: Gallup interviews conducted in May 1988 and July 1991.

and opposed foreign investment, who supported or opposed trade liberalization, and who would or would not service the foreign debt. PAN supporters in 1991 were comparably split over their views on environmental protection. In 1988, PAN supporters did favor privatizing state enterprises. In both years, PAN supporters thought that the economy's performance was bad and its prospects not good, but the differences narrowed by 1991. PAN supporters were more closely divided (though, on balance, pessimistic) in both years on their views about their personal finances; these differences also narrowed by 1991.

Support for the Cardenistas in 1988 was also only weakly related to specific issues. By modest margins, support for the Cardenista coalition was higher among those who held negative views on foreign investment, freer trade, servicing the foreign debt, and privatizing state enterprises. In 1991, however, the smaller pool of PRD supporters was much more likely to be found among opponents of foreign investment and freer trade—an attitude profile that once again matches that of the minor parties. In 1991, PRD supporters had indistinct views with regard to environmental protection but the supporters of minor parties were more likely to be found among those who thought that this was not an important issue. In both years, Cardenistas believed that the economy's performance, their own financial circumstances, and their respective prospects were poor.

Policy attitudes differed on the whole along predictable lines, but in 1988 the differences between all the parties were not large. In 1991, differences over specific issues had arisen between the PRI on the one hand and the PRD and the minor parties on the other, while support for the PAN remained unrelated to specific issues.

Turning to political and institutional questions (Table 4), there is a strong association between presidential approval rating and party support. In both years, those who approve of the president's performance support the PRI; support for the opposition increases as presidential approval ratings drop. Nonetheless, in 1991, presidential approval was only moderately related to support for the minor parties.

Individual loyalty to party is strong. In 1988, the PRI retained three-quarters of its previous supporters, a figure that rose to nine-tenths in 1991. In 1988, the PAN had kept 60% of its previous supporters, a figure that reached nearly three-quarters in 1991. In 1988, the Cardenistas drew from the PRI but also substantially from the PAN and those not previously mobilized (e.g., eligible voters who chose not to vote in previous elections). Nevertheless, Cárdenas' relative success did not come about from a significant enlargement of the electoral space: the PRI still got 51% of those who had never been previously mobilized, while Cárdenas got only 28% of those voters. The Cardenista organization, moreover, had little staying power. In 1991, over a fifth of the 1988 Cardenistas returned to the PRI while nearly equal numbers split between the PRD and the minor parties (which explains their similar voter profiles).

In 1988 and 1991, PRI supporters were found especially among those who believed that the PRI would get stronger over time and that the economy would worsen and social unrest increase if some other party were to gain power. Fully 87% of the 1991 respondents who believed that the national economy would suffer under an opposition party voted for the PRI. Supporters of the opposition were much more likely to be found among those who held the opposite views. On this score, there was little difference among the opposition parties. These are among the strongest relationships we found.

We conclude, preliminarily, that attitudes toward the ruling party's future strongly shape voter choice. There was also stronger opposition in Mexico City. There was, however, a relatively weak connection between party choice and attitudes toward issues; general judgments about present and prospective economic performance were important in 1988 though they were not nearly as effective discriminators of voter choice as the question that connected the economy's future with the prospects that a party other than the PRI would gain power. Individual party loyalty was strong in the PAN, as expected, but even more so in the PRI. Attitudes toward presidential performance shaped party choice. The PAN was decidedly not a confessional party. Given the close parallel between the voter profiles for the PRD and the minor parties in 1991, the search for explanations about the Left's fragmentation should focus on factional struggles within the Left's parties and not in the electorate: the 1988 Cardenista voters did not go away in 1991, but they split their vote.

ANALYZING AND EXPLAINING PARTISAN CLEAVAGES

We turn now to explain the reasons for the vote for Mexico's opposition parties. Because we are interested in modeling discrete choices among a set of partisan alternatives, a multinomial logit specification for regression analysis is appropriate. Table 5 presents the results of this analysis, where the relative importance of demographic, economic expectation, issue attitude, and political and institutional factors can be judged.[6]

For both 1988 and 1991, we seek to explain the vote for the PAN. For 1988, we seek to explain the vote for the Cardenista coalition present on the ballot through four political parties: the Mexican Socialist party (PMS) included the old Communist party; the People's Socialist party (PPS), the Authentic Party of the Mexican Revolution (PARM), and the Frente Cardenista National Renovation party (PFCRN). The last, previously known as the Socialist Workers' party, had long been in coalition with the PRI but this time

bolted to the opposition. For 1991, Cárdenas founded a new party, the PRD, into which the PMS dissolved. In 1991, the PARM, the PPS, and the PFCRN competed on their own and are listed in the column for minor parties when, together, they got 8.4% of the vote. Also included among the minor parties in 1991 are the Mexican Ecologist party, the Workers' party, the Mexican Democratic party, and the Revolutionary Workers' party; in 1991, the vote for these four parties added up to 4.3%.

The Parties and the Presidency

The only variables that identify statistically significant relationships to explain voting for all opposition parties in both 1988 and 1991 are those that refer to the parties and the presidency. In both years and for all parties,

1. the greater the belief that the PRI would get stronger, the less the likelihood of voting for an opposition party;
2. the greater the belief that the economy would improve if a party other than the PRI would gain power, the greater the likelihood of voting for an opposition party;
3. the greater the approval for the incumbent president (Miguel de la Madrid or Carlos Salinas), the less the support for the opposition;
4. the more likely a voter was to have voted PRI in a prior presidential election, the less likely this voter was to support any opposition party in either 1988 or 1991; and
5. the more likely a voter was to have voted for an opposition party in a previous election, the more likely this voter was to support an opposition party in 1988 or 1991.

A core political cleavage existed across elections between the PRI and all opposition parties. The question of the ruling party's future was the central decision facing each voter.[7] First and foremost, the voter asked, Am I for or against the PRI and the president? Consistent with this argument, for the most part these Mexican elections were not about issues. There was no statistically significant relationship between attitudes on the issues on the one hand and voting for the PAN in either year or for the minor parties in 1991 on the other. There was a modest association between voting Cardenista in 1988 and favoring the state's retention of its enterprises and between voting Cardenista in 1991 and improving the quality of the environment. Also consistent with the argument that issues mattered little, political interest was the only political variable that was never statistically significant.

Voter views about the current state of the nation's economy had no direct impact on voter choice in either year. Voter views about their current personal finances had no direct impact on voter choice in 1988 nor on voting for the Cardenistas and the minor parties in 1991. In 1991, however, those who thought that their personal finances were not in good shape

TABLE 5

Predicting Support for Mexican Opposition Parties

INDEPENDENT VARIABLES	1988[a] PAN β	SE_β	CARD. β	SE_β	1991[b] PAN β	SE_β	PRD β	SE_β	MINOR β	SE_β
Female	−.16	(.20)	−.21	(.19)	−.22	(.20)	−.52	(.25)*	−.47	(.23)*
North	.38	(.26)	−.87	(.25)**	1.12	(.26)**	.48	(.35)	−.03	(.38)
South	−.29	(.28)	−.46	(.24)	−.13	(.30)	−.20	(.36)	.77	(.30)*
Federal District	.44	(.25)	.04	(.22)	.91	(.25)**	1.04	(.30)**	1.11	(.29)**
Age	−.12	(.09)	−.04	(.08)	−.12	(.09)	−.03	(.10)	−.04	(.10)
Union member	−.66	(.23)**	−.14	(.20)	−.02	(.23)	.08	(.27)	−.29	(.28)
Professional class	−.43	(.30)	−.68	(.28)**	−.55	(.32)	−.23	(.37)	−.48	(.37)
Working class	−.33	(.29)	.09	(.25)	.31	(.25)	.18	(.29)	−.12	(.28)
Education	.06	(.05)	.06	(.04)	.08	(.05)	−.04	(.06)	−.03	(.05)
Church attendance	−.01	(.06)	−.17	(.06)**	.02	(.06)	−.11	(.07)	−.06	(.07)
National economy										
Current	.09	(.12)	−.07	(.11)	−.13	(.15)	−.17	(.17)	−.13	(.16)
Future	−.36	(.12)**	−.08	(.11)	−.06	(.12)	−.19	(.15)	−.06	(.14)
Personal Finances										
Current	−.05	(.15)	−.15	(.13)	−.39	(.18)*	−.39	(.21)	−.31	(.20)
Future	−.18	(.09)*	−.11	(.08)	−.08	(.10)	.17	(.12)	−.04	(.11)
Foreign investment	.10	(.10)	.04	(.09)	.04	(.12)	−.15	(.14)	−.02	(.13)
Limit imports	−.09	(.09)	.03	(.08)	−.02	(.11)	−.05	(.13)	.12	(.12)
Pay foreign debts	.03	(.10)	−.14	(.09)	—		—		—	
State industries	−.12	(.09)	.18	(.09)*	—		—		—	
Environmentalism	—		—		.09	(.13)	.31	(.16)*	−.05	(.14)
Political interest	.01	(.09)	−.01	(.08)	−.02	(.10)	.11	(.11)	−.19	(.11)
Previous PRI supporter	−.93	(.25)**	−1.20	(.22)**	−2.04	(.29)**	−2.14	(.35)**	−2.23	(.31)**
Previous PAN supporter	2.54	(.33)**	1.12	(.33)**	2.66	(.32)**	.63	(.45)	.31	(.44)
Previous Cardenista					−.38	(.47)	1.62	(.36)**	1.28	(.34)**
Not previously mobilized	−.02	(.30)	−.14	(.27)	−.18	(.25)	−.59	(.32)	−.88	(.29)**
PRI getting stronger	−.52	(.11)**	−.52	(.10)**	−.52	(.11)**	−.53	(.14)**	−.61	(.13)**
Economy—other party	.97	(.13)**	1.20	(.12)**	.89	(.13)**	.71	(.16)**	.48	(.15)**
Unrest—other party	.30	(.18)	.30	(.16)*	.11	(.10)	.19	(.11)	.26	(.11)*
Presidential approval	−.16	(.04)**	−.15	(.04)**	−.12	(.06)*	−.23	(.06)**	−.14	(.06)*
Constant Term	.05	(.95)	.27	(.87)	−.20	(1.09)	.14	(1.33)	1.27	(1.23)

Source: Gallup interviews conducted in May 1988 and July 1991.
Note: Coefficients are multinomial logit estimates derived via maximum likelihood. Voting for the PRI served as the base category.
[a] N = 1,426, 70.1% correctly predicted.
[b] N = 1,766, 76.8% correctly predicted.
* p < .05.
** p < .01.

were more likely to vote for the PAN. On balance, these findings are inconsistent with a mode of analysis that emphasizes that citizens vote "retrospectively," that is, to reward or punish incumbent performance (Fiorina 1981).[8]

Voter views about the future of the nation's economy or about the future of their own finances had impact neither on the 1991 election nor, perhaps surprisingly, on voting Cardenista in 1988. In 1988, however, there was a strong negative association between expectations about the future of the nation's economy and voting for the PAN and a weaker negative association between expectations about the future of personal finances and voting for the PAN; that is, those who thought that the economy and their finances would get better were less likely to vote PAN. These results suggest that Mexico's 1988 presidential election had some similarities with many European elections in which voter behavior can be

forecast from expectations about the economic future. Nonetheless, this pattern did not recur in 1991. Even in 1988, expectations about the nation's economic future did not explain the Cardenista vote.

Let us compare the results on two variables: general expectations about the nation's economic future and expectations about the nation's economic future if a party other than the PRI were to gain power. The latter was a powerful and systematic predictor for all parties in both elections. The former was statistically significant only with regard to PAN voting in 1988. In 1988, the coefficient for the variable concerning the economy's future if a party other than the PRI were to gain power was more than twice that for the variable measuring general expectations about the economy's future.

We conclude, therefore, that Mexicans for the most part voted neither in terms of general retrospective or general prospective assessments about the economy or their finances nor on specific economic issues. Instead, they focused on a particular kind of prospective judgment—the connection between the future of the party of the state and the impact of its fate on the economy.[9]

Political Cleavages

This argument about the preeminence of ruling-party actors in Mexican elections must be tempered, however. There are some differences among the opposition parties. In 1988, these differences hinted at the development of distinct political cleavages. Consider the PAN. Union members were much less likely to support the PAN. Except for this feature, the most striking finding about the PAN in 1988 was its emergence as a national party; the PAN was not significantly stronger or weaker in any one of the nation's regions, nor was it more or less likely to draw support on the basis of church attendance. In contrast, Cardenistas were significantly less likely to attend church. As behooves a new party, Cardenistas were weaker in some regions (the North). Cardenistas were less likely to draw support from professionals. Cardenistas were more likely to believe that social peace would not be endangered if a party other than the PRI were to win, and they were also more likely to support retaining state enterprises. This was, perhaps, a socialist party in the making.

The 1991 election picture was rather different, however. The PAN's aspirations to become a national party had suffered a setback; the PAN again became mainly a regional party, strong in the North and in Mexico City. PAN voters were more likely to think that they were not financially well off, a view at odds with the party's stereotype. The PRD shrank regionally, to derive strength mainly in the Federal District. It was also less likely to retain support from women, and its supporters tended to give higher priority to environmental issues. The minor parties were less likely to have support from women; they were also regional parties, stronger in the South and (especially) in the Federal District. We do not minimize the importance of these regional cleavages but note that they were unrelated to other demographic or issue factors. The weakening of factors other than region accentuated the centrality of ruling-party questions in the 1991 election compared to that of 1988.

Organizational Factors

There was also an important organizational story. The PRI was, indeed, a party with members loyal to it in election after election. The statistical results are very strongly significant. So, too, was the PAN, which was significantly very likely to draw from its same pool of voters in successive elections. But the PAN voter believed in occasional political adultery; in 1988, the Cardenista coalition also drew support from voters who had previously supported the PAN.

Many past PAN voters were sophisticated strategic voters. Prior to 1988, many PAN voters were moti-

vated by their opposition to the ruling party but not by the PAN's views on particular issues. They voted for the PAN because that was the only way to oppose the PRI. Once a viable Cardenista option appeared in 1988, those who had voted for the PAN in 1982 flocked to Cárdenas. In a more ideologically competitive election focused no longer on the fate of one party but on the ideas of various parties, the issues, economic expectations, social ties, and candidates, this massive PAN-ista vote switching would be less likely to happen.

The Cardenista coalition's organizational skills were insufficiently developed, however. Although many Cardenista leaders had come from the PRI, voters who had voted PRI in previous presidential elections were significantly likely *not* to vote Cardenista. (PRI voters were more loyal to their party than comparable past PAN voters.) Moreover, the Cardenistas did a poor job at mobilizing voters who had been eligible to participate in the 1982 presidential election but had chosen not to do so: the coefficient linking these previously inactive citizens to the new partisan insurgency is clearly insignificant.

In 1991, the organizational story was also noteworthy. The PRI and the PAN each drew significantly from those who had voted for it in 1988. The 1988 Cardenista vote split between the PRD and the minor parties: both drew significantly from the 1988 Cardenista coalition. Neither was able to raid the PAN much, and they were again significantly unable to raid the PRI. The minor parties were also significantly unable to mobilize support among those who had been able to vote in 1988 but had chosen not to do so.

The organizational problems on Mexico's political Left explain its disarray. The voter profile was quite similar for the PRD and the minor parties; this voter profile made them different from the PRI and the PAN. The divisions within the Left, therefore, are not explained by different voter profiles for different left-wing parties. The Cardenista coalition got the PAN's strategic voters in 1988, but none of the coalition's splinters got significant numbers of votes from the PAN in 1991. The parties of the Left were equally unable in both elections to raid steady PRI supporters, despite the PRI origins of many Cardenista leaders and the long-lasting alliances between the PRI and several of the small parties. In each election, "new" parties (the Cardenistas in 1988 and the minor parties in 1991) could not mobilize previously uncommitted voters effectively. Instead, the parties of the Left in 1991 competed for each other's voters. This is a recipe for losing elections.

To underline the PRD's problems in 1991 but also to call attention to the fragile nature of the vote for the minor parties, we turn to Table 6. Based on a huge exit poll conducted by Gallup on election day in August 1991,[10] Table 6 presents information on the timing of the voting decision. It shows the PRI's impressive strength, deriving a majority of its votes from citizens who had made a standing decision to support the party even before the names of candidates were announced. Over a third of all voters for

TABLE 6

The Timing of Vote Decisions (%)

"WHEN DID YOU DECIDE TO CAST A VOTE FOR YOUR PREFERRED PARTY?"	PRI	PAN	PRD	MINOR
Yesterday or today	17	17	21	23
Within the last month	13	15	17	19
After candidates were announced	15	24	25	21
Relied on a standing decision	56	44	37	38
Number of cases	15,778	4,282	1,516	3,772

Source: Gallup exit polls conducted in August 1991.

all parties had made a standing decision to support the PRI even before candidates were announced. To overcome the PRI, the opposition needed the loyalty of its members and the organizational capacity to mobilize new voters. The PAN exhibited much loyalty from its voters, though more conditioned on the quality of its candidates. On the other hand, nearly 4 in 10 of the PRD voters decided quite late in the campaign. This was even more the case for the minor parties. Over a fifth of those who voted for the PRD or the minor parties made up their minds within the 24 hours prior to voting. The parties of the Left lacked strong loyalties; we have previously seen that they did not mobilize the previously unmobilized. This is a weak basis to build party strength and it helps to explain the Left's election defeats.

A TWO-STEP "MODEL" FOR MEXICAN VOTING BEHAVIOR

The results from Table 5 suggest that the Mexican voter approached the elections by focusing, above all, on the fate of the PRI and the presidency, which were

intimately interconnected. We believe, however, tha a more ideologically competitive election lurked jus behind this behavior. That is, once Mexicans got pas their judgment on the ruling party, demographic an issue factors played an important role in shapin; their voting decisions, and these factors divided th opposition parties between themselves. To clarif; these relationships, we report at Table 7 on th hypothetical probabilities of voting for the oppositio; parties. These probabilities are derived from ou regression analysis in Table 5. Our purpose is t show the interplay of perceptions of PRI strength an ideological predispositions.

At the top of Table 7, the expected voter choice: have been computed for two types of populations: Row 1 reports on those who believed that the PRI wa becoming weaker and that opposition parties coulc do a good job at getting the economy to grow maintaining social peace. Row 2 reports on those whc believed that the PRI was becoming stronger and tha the opposition parties could not do a good job ir getting the economy to grow and in maintaining social peace. In 1988, among those who thought that the PRI was becoming stronger and that the economy

TABLE 7

Expected Probabilities of Voting for an Opposition Party

VOTER PERCEPTIONS AND PREDISPOSITIONS	1988		1991		
	PAN	CARD.	PAN	PRD	MINOR
PRI becoming weaker	.31	.46	.26	.13	.16
PRI becoming stronger	.05	.05	.03	.02	.02
Voters with right-wing predispositions					
PRI becoming weaker	.47	.22	.19	.05	.12
PRI becoming stronger	.05	.02	.01	.01	.01
Voters with left-wing predispositions					
PRI becoming weaker	.08	.75	.27	.22	.14
PRI becoming stronger	.02	.09	.03	.03	.02

Source: Gallup interviews conducted in May 1988 and July 1991.
Note: These probabilities were derived from the estimated logit coefficients in Table 5 (N = 1,426 in 1988 and 1,766 in 1991). A voter's perception of the PRI's future viability is defined by three items: the expected strength of the PRI in the next 10 years, whether the national economy would prosper under an opposition party, and whether there would be increased social unrest if another party took control of the Mexican government. Left-wing or right-wing predispositions are indicated by four factors: socioeconomic status (professional versus working-class), religiosity (weekly vs. occasional church attendance), union membership, and national policy preferences. All other independent variables in Table 5 have been set to their mean values.

and social peace would suffer if a party other than the PRI were to gain power, the probability of voting PAN or Cardenista was only 5% each while the probability of voting PRI was 90%. Among those who thought that the PRI was becoming weaker and that the economy and social peace would not suffer if an opposition party were to gain power, the probability of voting PAN rose to 31%, the probability of voting Cardenista jumped to 46%, and the probability of voting PRI dropped to 23%; among these voters, Cárdenas would have been elected president. The same relationships are evident for 1991. In 1991, the PAN was still able to raise its share of vote from 3% to 26%; had they been united, the PRD and the minor parties together held 29%. In 1991, however, the PRI would win, getting 45% even among those who thought that it was becoming weaker and that the economy and social peace would not suffer if an opposition party were to gain power.

We modeled, then, two kinds of voters. One we call a left-wing voter. Such a person would come from the working class and belong to a union; attend church only occasionally; and oppose foreign investment, freer trade, continued payment of the foreign debt, and privatization of state enterprises. The other we call a right-wing voter. Such a person would come from the professional class and not belong to a union, attend church once a week, and favor the four policies opposed by the left-wing voter. (In 1991, the construction of the two hypothetical voters is the same, minus the items on the foreign debt and state enterprises, on which we have no data.)

Now consider Table 7, rows 3–6. Right-wing and left-wing voters who believed that the PRI was getting stronger and that the economy and social peace would be hurt if a party other than the PRI were to gain power were quite unlikely to vote for any opposition party in either election. They remained faithful to the PRI. What happens, however, if voters are ready to be governed by a party other than the PRI?

In 1988, among right-wing voters who believed that the PRI was getting weaker and that the economy and social peace would not suffer if an opposition party were to gain power, the probability of voting for the PAN rose to 47% while the probability of voting for Cárdenas dropped to 22%. Among left-wing voters who believed that the PRI was getting weaker and that the economy and social peace would not suffer if an opposition party were to gain power, the probability of voting for the PAN dropped to 8% while the probability of voting for Cárdenas rose to a whopping 75%. Among voters ready to live without the PRI, therefore, the PAN benefited substantially among right-wing voters and lost considerably among left-wing voters. Cárdenas benefited enormously among left-wing voters but lost more than half his vote among right-wing voters. Nonetheless, Cárdenas' support among right-wing voters was more than twice as high as the PAN's support among left-wing voters; this suggests strategic voting by

right-wing voters ready to support Cárdenas because he was more likely to beat Salinas.

In 1991, among voters not scared of the PRI's defeat, the PAN actually lost support among right-wing voters but held its own among left-wing voters. The minor parties also lost support among left-wing voters and lost a bit more among right-wing voters. The PRD gained substantially among left-wing voters and lost substantially among right-wing voters, but these swings are a pale version of the 1988 Cardenista performance: in 1988, among left-wing voters who thought that the PRI was getting weaker, the probability of voting for Cárdenas was 75%, whereas in 1991, the probability of such voters voting PRD had dropped to 22%. To put it differently, in 1991 only the PRD voters responded, albeit modestly, to issue and social cleavage motivations as had been more generally the case in 1988. (The voters for the minor parties, as we have seen, were late-deciders.) Some left-wing voters were the strategic voters in 1991 when, ready for the PRI's defeat, the probability that left-wingers would vote for the PAN was 27%, while the probability that right-wingers would vote for the combination PRD–minor parties was only 17%. This strategic voting behavior explains why the PAN performed better in 1991 among all voters than among right-wing voters: in 1991, for strategic left-wing voters, the PAN was the most likely to beat the PRI.

In both elections, among voters ready to replace the party in power, issues and demographic cleavages mattered. In 1988 especially, such voters were more likely to split between the opposition parties in ways that conform to the evolution of a political party and cleavage system. Even so, we are impressed by the strategic voting behavior of an important minority of Mexico's electorate. Some right-wing and left-wing voters made electoral judgments that sought to maximize the PRI's defeat—thereby reinserting traits that focused on the fate of the ruling party (especially in 1991) even after we attempted to dampen their impact.

CONCLUSION

After decades of single-party rule and well-founded suspicions about the conduct of their rulers and the fairness of their elections, in the late 1980s and early 1990s Mexican citizens approached elections by focusing on the fate of the party that had long governed them. First and foremost, they asked themselves, Am I for or against the party of the state and its leader? The most statistically significant and consistent explanations for voting behavior in two national elections were related to these concerns: What would happen to the economy if a party other than the PRI were to win? Was the PRI getting stronger or weaker? How might one judge the president's performance? What were past patterns of partisan choice? Supporters of the PRI strongly believed in the continued viability of the party's rule, and this belief shaped their voting behavior.

41

Most Mexican politicians and journalists—and many scholars—interpreted these Mexican elections (especially the 1988 election) as an ideological struggle with significant social class, regional, and religious dimensions. Our conclusions differ markedly. Consistent with an explanation of voter behavior focused on the ruling party's fate, attitudes on issues hardly mattered; nor did social cleavages matter in a consistent fashion from election to election.[11] In addition, general expectations about the economy's future were important only in shaping the vote with regard to the PAN in 1988, but they did not affect voting for the PAN in 1991 nor for the Left in either election. Prospective economic expectations became significant in the analysis mainly when the question explicitly connected the economy's future to the fate of the PRI.

A related implication is that no newly politicized bloc of voters had entered Mexico's "political space." In 1988 and 1991, the principal effect of the entry of Cardenismo was to reshuffle the voters among existing parties, not to mobilize the previously unmobilized. In 1991, the parties of the Left fought each other but failed to mobilize new voters. The 1991 vote for the minor parties was more spontaneous than focused. Contrary to the views of many observers of Mexico, especially in 1988, highly charged issue-oriented conflicts, or voting behavior based on general economic expectations (as opposed to economic expectations tied to the ruling party's fate), had not replaced the old basis for division, namely, whether to retain or reject the PRI. Mexican politics changed slowly because its voters had changed little in their views.

In reaching such conclusions, we have also shed light on three matters important to Mexicanists: (1) the PRI had indeed retained the loyalty of its members despite its peculiar internal structure, (2) the PAN was not a confessional party, and (3) a large pool of potential left-wing voters awaited the organizational reconstruction of Cardenismo given the nearly identical 1991 voter profiles of the parties that in 1988 belonged to the Cardenista coalition.

There was an ideologically competitive election lurking just beneath this focus on the fate of the ruling party. To find it, however, required a heuristic exercise to identify these voters and model their hypothetical behavior. We developed a two-step "model" to suggest the typical behavior of some Mexican voters. These voters decided, first, their view on the ruling party. Many voters stopped there. The voting behavior of those open to the possibility of being governed by another party, however, resembled (especially in 1988) what might be expected in an ideologically competitive election. Issues mattered. Social cleavages mattered. There were important differences between the PAN and the Cardenistas in 1988, while the PRD's distinctive traits as an issue-and-social-cleavage-oriented opposition party came through in 1991. There is evidence, moreover, of substantial strategic voting behavior among both

right-wing and left-wing voters depending on the specific context of each election.

For the PRI, these findings suggest the importance of partisanship and presidential performance as well as its need to cast doubt on any opposition party's ability to govern. For the parties of the Left, these findings point to the imperative need to rebuild a united coalition. For the PAN, these findings indicate that it should position itself as an alternative ruling party, taking advantage of its victories in some gubernatorial elections in the early 1990s; once Mexican voters believe that a party other than the PRI can govern, the PAN does well among right-wing voters and can draw on left-wing strategic voters.

For Mexico, the shaping of its political arena is under way. Mexicans differed on issues; the various parties could express various social cleavages. But the full flowering of these issue and social cleavages the political arena awaited further democratization. The preeminent concern over the fate of the ruling party in Mexican elections still prevented the full emergence of the representative and contestatory roles that parties perform in ordinary elections in other countries. Mexican democracy was still slouching to be born, and the issues that would one day enliven its politics remained hidden until that Bethlehem would be reached.

APPENDIX: THE VARIABLES

For the purpose of our analysis, we have focused on the independent variables measured by the following questions, which are listed in the sequence in which they appear in Tables 2–4, the same sequence being repeated in Table 5.

Demographic Questions (Tables 2 and 5)

Male/Female
From Mexico's North
From Mexico's Center (excluding Mexico City)
From Mexico's South
From the Federal District (i.e., Mexico City)
Age
Union Member: Yes/No
Class, as measured by the respondent's profession: "Please tell me which of these kinds of work best describes the work that you do." A card is then shown listing many different kinds of work. *Professional* includes lawyer; medical doctor; professor; engineer; nurse; public accountant; computer programmer; systems analyst; musician; government or state enterprise director; manager or official; and owner or manager of a factory, store, or other private firm. *Middle* includes white-collar positions such as secretary, postal worker, bank clerk, sales clerk, vendor, salesman, police officer, fire fighter, restaurant personnel, pharmacist, hairdresser, and the like. *Working* includes skilled-trades such as mechanic, plumber, electrician, and painters, as well as factory worker (at various levels of skill), cab driver, chauffeur, machine operator, lumberman, farmer or farm worker, and fisherman.
Education: "What was your last year in school?" We coded as *primary* those who have at most completed primary education; *secondary*, those who have begun secondary schooling or, at most, completed it; *preparatory*, those who have begun the upper end of university-oriented high school education or, at most, completed it; *university*, those who have some university education or who may have completed it.
Church attendance: "With what frequency do you attend church?"

More than once a week, once a week, two or three times per month, every month, from time to time, or never? *Weekly* refers to those who attend church at least once a week, *occasionally*, those who attend church at least "every once in a while" but no more than two or three times per month. *Never* means just that.

Issue Questions (Tables 3 and 5)

"How would you assess the current condition of the nation's economy? Would you say that the nation's economy is doing very well, well, badly, or very badly?" We have collapsed the four-point response into *good/bad. 1988 Version.* "Would you say that at the end of the forthcoming six-year presidential term Mexico's economic situation would be better than it is now, would be the same, or would be worse?" We have used the *better/worse* responses. *'91 Version* "Would you say that in three years Mexico's economic situation would be better than it is now, would be the same, or would be worse?" We have used only the *better/worse* responses.

"How would you assess your own personal economic situation? Would you say that your personal economic situation is very good, good, bad, or very bad?" We have collapsed the four-point response into *good/bad. 1988 Version.* "How do you expect that your own economic situation will be within a year—much better, a bit better, a bit worse, or much worse than it is now?" We have collapsed the four-point response into *better/worse* and ignored those respondents who volunteered "the same." *1991 Version.* "How do you expect that your own economic situation will be within three years—much better, a bit better, a bit worse, or much worse than it is now?" We have collapsed the four-point response into *better/worse* and ignored those respondents who volunteered the same."

"Considering all the consequences, good and bad, in your view is investment in Mexico by foreign companies positive or negative for the country? *1988 Version.* "With regard to imports of foreign products into Mexico, should the next government facilitate the import of those goods or should it limit their importation?" *1991 Version.* "With regard to imports of foreign products into Mexico, is your view is the policy of facilitating the import of those goods basically a good policy or is it basically a bad policy for the people of our country?"

Asked Only in 1988. "In your view, should the next government continue to pay the country's foreign debt or should it stop payment?"

Asked Only in 1988. "With regard to state enterprises, what do you think that the next government should do: keep most of them or sell most of them to private enterprises?"

Asked Only in 1991. "Thinking [of] all the areas in which the government has to invest its effort and money—such as education, road building, agricultural output, etc.—how much importance would be given to the protection and improvement of the environment? Would you say that improving the quality of air and water should be the government's most important priority, should be an important but not the most important priority, should have a moderate level of importance, or should have no importance at all?" For our analysis, the two middle answers have been combined as *moderate importance.*

Political Questions (Tables 4 and 5)

'88 Version. "Using a scale from 1 to 10, how would you rate President Miguel de la Madrid's job as president?" *1991 Version.* "Using a scale from 1 to 10, please rate on this paper, without showing it to me, the job performance of Carlos Salinas de Gortari as President of the Republic." (Then a "secret ballot box" was used.) In both years, respondents were told that 1 is least favorable and 10 is most favorable. For both years, we coded ratings of 9 or 10 as *very high*, 7 or 8 as *favorable*, 4–6 as *mediocre*, and 3 or below as *low*.

"Referring to the card I'm showing you, please tell me how much interest in politics would you say you have? None, little, some, much?"

In both 1988 and 1991, the same procedure was followed to ask about past voting behavior: "Did you vote in the previous presidential elections?" Those who said yes were then asked, "For which candidate did you vote?" Voters then were given the "secret ballot box" to answer this question. We recoded their answers into the party affiliations of the candidates. *Net previously mobilized* refers only to those respondents who were eligible to vote in the previous presidential election but chose not to do so.

"Ten years from now, do you expect that the PRI will be a stronger party than it is today, a weaker party than it is today, or about as strong as it is today?"

"If a party other than the PRI were to gain power, do you think that Mexico's economic conditions would improve, remain the same, or worsen?"

"If a party other than the PRI were to gain power, do you think that there would be problems for the country's social peace or that there would not be problems with social peace?"

Notes

1. We are very grateful to Jeffry Frieden, Jennifer Widner, and Ashutosh Varshney for many thoughtful and constructive comments.

2. This section draws in part from Dominguez and McCann 1992.

3. Most public opinion polls in Mexico are sponsored by a political party and are of dubious quality. Ours, on the other hand, were financed by independent media organizations; they are the best available to study Mexican political behavior. The 1988 poll was commissioned by ECO, Inc., a Los Angeles television station that is a subsidiary of Mexico's large private television network, TELEVISA. The second poll was financed directly by TELEVISA. One of us (Dominguez) worked as a consultant for both polls. We are grateful to Richard W. Burkholder, vice president, Gallup Organization, and Ian M. Reider, president, IMOP/Gallup México, for allowing us to use the data for this research.

4. Originally 3,000 interviews were planned. Gallup México discarded 40 of those interviews because they were unreliable.

5. Almost half of those who said through the "secret ballot" that they would vote for Cárdenas or for the PAN said something different when they were asked a similar question openly.

6. The functional form of our logit equations may be written as follows. If we code a preference for the PRI in 1988 as 1, PAN support as 2, and Cardenista as 3, the probability of an individual voting for each of the parties is

$$Prob(Vote\ PAN) = \exp(x\beta_1)/[1 + \exp(x\beta_1) + \exp(x\beta_2)]$$

$$Prob(Vote\ CARD) = \exp(x\beta_2)/[1 + \exp(x\beta_1) + \exp(x\beta_2)]$$

$$Prob(Vote\ PRI) = 1/[1 + \exp(x\beta_1) + \exp(x\beta_2)].$$

In these equations, exp refers to the exponential function, x stands for a vector of independent variables, and β_1 and β_2 correspond to the logit regression coefficients computed via maximum likelihood for the two equations in 1988. For 1991, the dependent variable has four categories rather than three, with the minor parties taking on a value of 4. The functional form in this case is a simple extension of these specifications. Included in each denominator are the coefficients from the additional equation for the minor parties category. For example,

$$Prob(Vote\ PAN\ 1991) =$$

$$\exp(x\beta_1)/[1 + \exp(x\beta_1) + \exp(x\beta_2) + \exp(x\beta_3)],$$

where the β_i values are taken from the coefficients listed on the far right-hand column of Table 5. By coding the dependent variable in this way, the probability of voting for the PRI serves as our base alternative.

7. The 1988 poll asked questions that permit the construction of an index of personality trait ratings for each of the presidential candidates. Inclusion of such an index would not change these substantive conclusions. To be sure, a favorable impression of the three presidential candidates in 1988 influenced voting choice quite significantly, but the independent variables reported in Table 5 remain significant (with the exception of the item on state enterprises). The effect of including an index of candidate ratings would reinforce the finding that explicitly political factors explain voting choices.

8. It is possible, of course, that economic evaluations indirectly influenced vote choice through perceptions of the PRI's long-term viability and its future governing capabilities. To illustrate, consider the following multinomial logit coefficients (with standard errors in parentheses) based on the 1988 sample. The estimates in columns 1 and 2 are taken directly from Table 5, while those in columns 3 and 4 come from an equation that did not include the three predictors related to the PRI as an institution (*PRI getting stronger, Economy—other party*, and *unrest—other party*).

National Economy	Including "Institutional"		Excluding "Institutional"	
	PAN	Cardenista	PAN	Cardenista
Current	.09 (.12)	−.07 (.11)	−.11 (.14)	−.22 (.11)*
Future	−.36 (.12)**	−.08 (.11)	−.39 (.14)**	−.09 (.11)

*p < .05.
**p < .01.

When the three prospective judgments related to the PRI are left out of the equations, evaluations of Mexico's economic performance in 1988 are more closely connected to voting choice. This suggests that attitudes toward the economy have some bearing on presidential preferences but that such effects are largely mediated by the more powerful items that tap into the PRI's future viability and governing capabilities.

9. Of course, it is possible that judgments regarding the PRI's viability and capabilities were inferred or rationalized on the basis of the respondent's vote choice. Given all presently existing data sets, it remains impossible to model this potential dynamic thoroughly. Nevertheless, our findings from a series of regressions estimated via instrumental variables (available from the authors upon request) suggest that prospective evaluations of the PRI did, indeed, cause voters to support or oppose the party.

10. We use the exit poll only for Table 6. The exit poll relied on a multistage-area-probability sample, with each geographic entity having the same probability of falling in the sample according to its weight in the electoral registry. There were 350 sampling sites throughout the country; the statistical margin of error was ±1%.

11. That issues have little impact on the voting choice is not surprising from a comparative perspective; that demographic factors matter so little is more surprising, both in general and for Mexicanists. For comparative findings, see Harrop and Miller 1987, chaps. 6–7.

References

Almond, Gabriel, and Sidney Verba. 1965. *The Civic Cultur* Boston: Little, Brown.

Bailey, John J. 1988. *Governing Mexico: The Statecraft of Cris Management*. New York: St. Martin's.

Basáñez, Miguel. 1982. *La lucha por la hegemonía en Méxic* Mexico: Siglo XXI.

Basáñez, Miguel. 1992. "Encuestas de opinión en México." I *México: auge, crisis y ajuste*. Eds. Carlos Bazdresch, Nise Bucay, Soledad Loaeza, and Nora Lustig. Mexico: Fondo c Cultura Económica.

Butler, Edgar W., James B. Pick, and Glenda Jones. 199 "Political Change in the Mexico Borderlands." In *Sucesic Presidencial: The 1988 Mexican Presidential Election*. eds. Edg: W. Butler and Jorge A. Bustamante. Boulder: Westview.

Chand, Vikram. 1991. "Civil Society, Institutions, and D mocratization in Mexico: The Politics of the State of Chihu: hua in National Perspective." Ph.D. diss., Harvard Unive sity.

Domínguez, Jorge I., and James A. McCann. 1992. "Whith: the PRI? Explaining Voter Defection in the 1988 Mexica Presidential Elections." *Electoral Studies* 11:207–22.

Fiorina, Morris P. 1981. *Retrospective Voting in American Ele tions*. New Haven: Yale University Press.

Garrido, Luis Javier. 1987. "Un partido sin militantes." In *L vida política mexicana en la crisis*, ed. Soledad Loaeza an Rafael Segovia. Mexico: El Colegio de México.

Gómez Tagle, Silvia. 1989. "La dificultad de perder: el partid oficial en la coyuntura de 1988." *Revista mexicana de sociolog* 51:239–260.

Harrop, Martin, and William L. Miller. 1987. *Elections an Voters*. London: Macmillan.

Huntington, Samuel P. 1991. *The Third Wave: Democratizatio in the Late Twentieth Century*. Norman: University of Okla homa Press.

Lewis-Beck, Michael. 1988. *Economics and Elections*. Ann A: bor: University of Michigan Press.

Lipset, Seymour Martin, and Stein Rokkan. 1967. "Cleavag Structures, Party Systems, and Voter Alignments." In *Part Systems and Voter Alignments*, ed. Seymour Lipset and Stei Rokkan. New York: Free Press.

Loaeza, Soledad. 1989. *El llamado de las urnas*. Mexico: Cal Arena.

Middlebrook, Kevin J. 1989. "Union Democratization in th Mexican Automobile Industry: A Reappraisal." *Latin Amer ican Research Review* 24:69–93.

United Nations Economic Commission for Latin America and the Caribbean. 1989. *Balance preliminar de la economía de América Latina y el Caribe, 1989*. LC/G.1586.

United Nations. 1991. *Preliminary Overview of the Economy o Latin America and the Caribbean, 1991*. LC/G.1696.

WGBH Educational Foundation. 1988. "Mexico: End of ar Era, 1982–1988." Public Broadcasting System.

Jorge I. Domínguez is Professor of Government, The Center for International Affairs, Harvard University, Cambridge, MA 02138.

James A. McCann is Professor of Political Science, Purdue University, West Lafayette, IN 47907.

THE ELECTORAL CYCLE AND INSTITUTIONAL SOURCES OF DIVIDED PRESIDENTIAL GOVERNMENT

MATTHEW SOBERG SHUGART   *University of California, San Diego*

*P*residents often lack legislative majorities, but situations of opposition-party majorities ("divided government") are much less common outside the United States. The president's party's share of seats tends to increase in early-term elections but decline in later elections. Thus opposition majorities often result after midterm elections. Opposition majorities rarely occur in elections held concurrently with the presidential election but are more likely to do so if legislators enjoy electoral independence from their parties due to features of electoral laws.

ivided government has been a common occurrence in the United States. A substantial literature has developed,[1] mostly arguing that divided government leads to undesirable policies and interbranch stalemates (e.g., Cutler 1980; McCubbins 1991; Robinson 1985; Sundquist 1986), although at least one important work (Mayhew 1991) has challenged the negative assessment. Surprisingly, there seems to be no literature specifically devoted to divided government in other presidential systems. However, almost all of the more general literature on presidentialism (e.g., Linz 1990, 1994; Mainwaring 1993; Valenzuela 1994) argues that lack of presidential majorities imperils government stability.

In a two-party system like that of the United States, a president lacking a copartisan majority is the same as a president facing an opposition majority. However, in the multiparty systems typical of most other presidential systems, these phenomena must be kept conceptually distinct. I shall use the term *divided government* to refer only to those situations in which a legislative majority is held by a party or preelection coalition that is different from that of the president. Divided government of this sort can be seen as a form of coalition government (Sundquist 1988)—indeed, as a grand coalition leaving no room for a distinction between government and opposition. The result is often alleged to be a lack of accountability, as no party is uniquely responsible for policy and there is no "out" party to which voters can turn if they want a change.

A situation in which no party holds a majority in a presidential system likewise can be seen as a form of coalition government. However, unlike opposition-majority situations, no-majority situations do not necessarily mean the absence of an opposition that can serve as an alternative governing formula. That is, although the category of no-majority situation is a residual category (neither "unified" nor "divided"), it is useful to keep it distinct, as it includes phases in which the chief executive's party, albeit a minority in the legislature, may be a part of most legislative coalitions along with one or more other parties. Such situations in parliamentary regimes do not necessarily obviate accountability or majority rule (Powell 1989; Strom 1990), as opposition-majority situations (divided government) may.

As we shall see, no-majority situations are much more common than divided government in presidential systems outside the United States as common as unified government. Thus it may be surprising to see the literature on presidential systems outside the United States speaking of such themes as "dual democratic legitimacies" (Linz 1994), conjuring up images of an executive and congress at loggerheads because each responds to a different majority of voters. The problem of competing legitimacies would seem to be most acute under divided government, yet one never encounters the phrase *dual legitimacies* in studies of the United States. Indeed, these two literatures on presidentialism (studies of divided government in the United States and studies of other presidential systems, esp. in Latin America) rarely address one another. It is time to start putting these literatures together to seek a more comprehensive explanation of the phenomenon of nonunified government. Then we may be in a better position to explain why divided government in the United States apparently does not cause such bad performance as "mere" nonmajority government allegedly does elsewhere.

I shall not attempt to resolve the debate about why presidentialism survives in the United States but often fails elsewhere. Nor shall I attempt to discern whether divided government produces better or worse governance than unified party control, though my conclusions have implications for these questions. Rather, I shall seek to answer a prior question, Why do patterns of divided, unified, and no-majority government vary? Do basic institutional differences among presidential systems give us much leverage over this question?

Party system variables are obviously important, but a reliance on such factors alone would not tell us if there are features in the design of constitutional and electoral rules themselves that affect the probability that the president's party will hold a majority or face majority opposition. For instance, divided government is likely to be more common in two-party systems than in multiparty systems, but so is unified government, for the simple reason that of two parties must have a majority. While the occurrence of unified or divided government is thus mediated through the party system, there may be other structural variables that affect the pattern of presidential or opposition majorities by either (1) making it more likely that voters will vote for different parties for each of the two branches, or (2) reducing the number of parties.

One feature of institutional design that I find to be especially important is the timing of elections, or (as I shall call it here) the *electoral cycle*. In the data analysis that follows, I find that opposition majorities are uncommon when elections are concurrent, that is, when presidential and legislative elections are held on the same day. Expanding on earlier studies of the timing of elections (Jones 1994; Shugart and Carey 1992), I find that as elections are held later in a president's term, the share of seats won by the president's party tends to decline. Therefore, later-term elections often result in opposition majorities. This is a generalization of the well-known phenomenon of "midterm decline" in the United States (Erickson 1988; Hinckley 1967; Kernell 1977; Tufte 1975).

The second factor is the "localizing" or "nationalizing" effect of legislative electoral rules. Localizing rules are those in which candidates and incumbents can tailor their campaigns to suit local constituencies rather than rely mainly on voters' perceptions of the national party to which they belong. I argue that in such systems, as in the United States, there is a lesser sensitivity of legislative elections to the presidential electoral cycle. Thus occasionally divided government results even in concurrent elections. I show, too, that localizing electoral rules reduce the number of parties if elections are concurrent. Other things equal, a lower number of parties would mean a greater frequency of majorities for either the president's party or for the major opposition party. A third factor, the presidential veto—which may encourage voters to split their tickets if they desire more moderate policies than either of two major parties could deliver through unified government (Ingberman and Villani 1993)—does not appear to have a significant effect on the probability of an opposition majority.

Below I review some of the causes of divided government given in the U.S. literature and develop a theoretical justification for why the electoral cycle and electoral rules might matter for the observed variations in the tendency towards divided government. I present data on the incidence of presidential and opposition majorities and analyze the effects of the electoral cycle in more detail and explore how the incidence of divided government is mediated through the effects of institutional variables on the party system. Finally, I test for any effect of presidential vetoes on the probability of opposition majorities.

CAUSES OF DIVIDED GOVERNMENT

The Electoral Cycle and "Midterm Decline"

The electoral cycle refers to the relative timing of elections. In explaining divided government in the U.S. case it would have been sufficient, at one time,

to look to this. Before 1956, divided government wa almost exclusively a result of midterm elections. N concurrent election in the twentieth century and on two in the previous century (1876 and 1884) ha produced a majority in either chamber for a part other than that of the incoming president.[2] Over th whole period from 1868 to 1992, opposition majoritie have resulted from 21.9% of concurrent elections. O the other hand, the frequency of divided governmen resulting from midterm elections was more tha twice as high—48.4%. Clearly the electoral cycle i only part of the explanation for divided governmen in the United States, but it is a big factor.

The literature on the United States is necessaril restricted to the dichotomous classification of con gressional elections into *concurrent* and *nonconcurren* (usually called *on-year* and either *off-year* or *midterm*) Still, we can turn to the U.S. literature for guidance a to why the electoral cycle might matter. To the exten that the timing of an assembly election influences th degree of convergence or divergence of votes for th two branches, it is also likely to have an effect on th incidence of divided government. I shall not preten to review comprehensively the immense literature o the phenomenon of midterm decline in the Unitec States. However, we need to consider some of th main strands of theorizing on the topic.

The most obvious answer to the question why there are midterm losses is simple: over time, more voters become disillusioned and defect to the oppo sition (see Kernell 1977). However, there are many explanations that either compete with or embellish this one. Some scholars have stressed differences in the composition of the electorate in concurrent and midterm elections (Born 1990; Campbell 1960). Others have seen midterms as referenda on presidential popularity or economic performance (Kernell 1977, Tufte 1975) or as a means of moderating policy by strengthening the opposition (Alesina and Rosenthal 1989). Some see midterm losses driven mainly by larger-than-average gains in the preceding concurrent election (Hinckley 1967). Erickson (1988) considered these and other explanations and concluded that a simple notion of "presidential penalty" had the greatest explanatory power. The notion of presidential penalty is the easiest to test in a multicountry data set, as it simply posits that parties that hold the presidency do not fare well in national legislative elections that are held during the term of a copartisan president.

Explanations Based on Divergent Voter Expectations

Another class of explanations for divided government in the United States is based on voters' divergent expectations of legislators and presidents. It should be noted that this class of explanations is not in competition with those based on midterm decline. Indeed, explanations based on *midterm* decline obviously are not intended to explain divided government that results from *concurrent* elections. Explanations based on divergent expectations purport to explain why we sometimes have divided government, regardless of the electoral cycle.

Jacobson (1990) argues that voters simply want different things from their congressional and presidential candidates. Democrats win congressional elections because they offer programs that voters like, but Republicans more often win the presidency because they are judged to be better at ensuring prosperity and security. The problem with this argument is that it appears to rest on peculiarities of the U.S. parties, each of which is identified with specific policies that voters tend to want from one or the other branch of government.[3] Jacobson's argument does not tell us whether this difference in voters' policy expectations is a general feature of presidentialism or is specific to some aspect of the U.S. system. I shall argue that the electoral-rule variable (localizing vs. nationalizing) allows us to explain the phenomenon that Jacobson has identified and generates expectations about how widespread ticket-splitting motivated in this way should be in presidential systems.

Explanations Based on Balancing to Achieve Moderation

Another set of explanations suggests that divided government results from voters' balancing of one party with the other. Examples of this general approach include Fiorina 1992 (pp 67–73) and Zupan 1991, which provide similar arguments about how voters may respond if they desire to break a long period of dominance by one party. It is more difficult to change the majority of the legislature than it is to change the executive in a presidential system, because voters in any given district face a dilemma. If they vote for the out party but voters in a majority of all districts do not, they will deprive themselves of the distributive benefits of having a legislator of the majority party but will not have produced a change in who controls policy. So, instead, they vote for the out party's presidential or gubernatorial candidate, as a check on the actions of the legislature.

Other variants of the balancing argument posit that voters, in splitting tickets and thereby contributing to divided government, are acting as if they favored a more moderate policy outcome than government under the unified control of either party can deliver. Thus, in a time in which the two major parties have located themselves farther from the center of the policy space than most voters desire, ticket splitting and divided government become common (Fiorina 1988). Ingberman and Villani (1993) endogenize the divergent policy preferences of the two parties, hypothesizing that given the institutional structure of the American regime, a party's best way of maximizing its influence over the total policymaking apparatus is to locate away from the center of the policy space. In this way, voters seeking moderation will cast split votes.

Is the balancing hypothesis generalizable to presidential systems outside the United States? In principle, it is, but it will encounter a serious problem in many other presidential systems. As I shall show, situations in which no party holds a majority are common outside the United States, largely because of proportional representation. The balancing models assume that voters are balancing *two* divergent parties. Yet in a system with important minor parties, it is as likely that ticket-splitters are casting their congressional vote for a more extreme party on the same side of the political spectrum as their (more moderate)[4] presidential choice as it is that they are going to the other side of the spectrum to provide "moderation."[5] The argument in favor of moderation between two relatively extreme parties appears to work only in systems in which majorities for one or another party are regularly expected.

JUSTIFICATION AND OPERATIONALIZATION

The timing of elections is operationalized as the share (of unity) of the time between scheduled presidential elections that has elapsed at the time that a given assembly election takes place.

The Electoral Cycle

For concurrent elections, TIME = 0 and for true midterms, TIME = .5. In the data analysis that follows, concurrent elections are nonetheless treated separately from nonconcurrent elections. The following thought experiment will help clarify why concurrent and nonconcurrent elections must be kept analytically distinct.

Suppose that a legislative election would be held the day after the winner of the presidential election is known. In this case, it is possible that there is a reward, rather than a penalty, to the party having won the presidency. If so, then this hypothetical "honeymoon" election should produce the biggest surge in support. Some voters who supported the winner after having been torn between the two front-runners (assuming for the moment that there are just two candidates perceived as being likely winners) would be inclined to switch to the winner. The party of the loser would be left only with its hard-core support.[6] In a concurrent election, on the other hand, even voters who favor a presidential candidate who winds up losing would be expected to support the slate of legislative candidates associated with this candidate, holding constant for the moment possible incentives for ticket splitting. Thus there is a sharp discontinuity between elections at TIME = 0 and those for which TIME > 0. As a result, we can dichotomize elections as concurrent versus nonconcurrent and use the TIME variable to test for differences within the class of nonconcurrent elections. From the way that the "time" variable is operationalized, the assumption is that it is not so much real time as relative time that matters. We could use real time in months in the regressions presented and get results that are nearly identical. The notion of relative time is theoretically appealing for two reasons, however. First, the model to be tested suggests that the more a president has left of his term, the stronger the incentive is to line up behind the president. Conversely, the model suggests that the later it is in the term, the more jockeying for position for the next term may matter in shaping voters' decisions. For such an effect, it matters less how many months away that election is than whether the legislative election is held with three-fourths of the term left, half a term, or a third of a term. Second (and related to the first reason) the sample of actual presidential terms contains little variation. Most presidential terms are of four or five years. None are shorter than four or longer than seven (see the Appendix). For this reason, in this data set, time measured in actual months and time measured relative to presidential elections are very highly correlated (r = .96). However, there is no reason why terms could not be shorter or longer, thus making the two definitions of time measure very different things.[7]

Legislative Electoral Rules

The premise that there would be any responsiveness at all of assembly elections to the electoral cycle rests on the assumption that voters generally cast their votes on the same basis for the two branches. Under some electoral rules, however, that assumption may be less valid than in others. Let us first consider the logic that undergirds this assumption in the first place; then we shall see under what conditions it may not hold or may hold less strongly.

In endorsing a given presidential candidate, voters are choosing one party label over another, in the process either endorsing the program offered by their preferred candidate or, at least, rejecting that of another.[8] But electing a president is not enough. The president will need legislative support; voters know this, and so they vote for the legislative ticket affiliated with their preferred presidential candidate. If voters behaved in this way, we would always have identical vote totals for parties in presidential and congressional elections, when those elections are concurrent.[9] In nonconcurrent elections, the preferences for or against the president may have shifted over time in the manner already depicted; still, it is on the question of feelings toward the president that voters select their legislative ticket or candidate, according to the theory.

What institutional factors might encourage many voters to behave contrary to this stylized portrayal? One such feature is an electoral process that encourages *local-oriented* voting notwithstanding that what is being elected is a *national* legislative body. For example, where candidates for assembly seats rely on their own initiative rather than the prior endorsement of their parties in order to run for office, they have an

incentive to cultivate a "personal vote" based on service to their locality (Cain, Ferejohn, and Fiorina 1987; Carey and Shugart n.d.). The personal vote allows legislators to identify themselves in the voters minds independently of the national reputation of their party. Even if party organizations control nominations, party decentralization encouraged by some electoral rules may make it difficult for voters to express a vote based on national priorities even if they wish to. In either scenario, we may speak of *localizing electoral rules*, in that the rules create opportunities for legislators to cultivate ties to their local constituencies. Under localizing electoral rules, then, members' personal reputations as good servants for a geographical constituency provide them with voter support independent of or in addition to voters evaluations of the national party. Given such electoral independence, assembly elections are likely to be less responsive to the cycle of elections and partisan control of the presidency.

Features of electoral rules that may create localizing tendencies are those that inhibit party cohesion and the control of national leaders over locally elected rank-and-file. For example, open primaries on the U.S. model greatly decentralize party control and allow members to tailor their campaigns to their districts. Other countries' electoral laws also have provisions that prevent national party leaders from denying the use of the party name to candidates who use it to suit their own purposes rather than out of loyalty to a party platform, for example, Brazil (Mainwaring 1991); Colombia (Archer 1990, Cox and Shugart n.d.); and the Philippines (Pinckney 1971; Sours 1970). Before a reform was passed in 1958, the Chilean electoral law employed a complex set of procedures that made it difficult for voters to know which candidates (or even which parties, given a frequent tendency of parties to form poorly publicized coalitions) would benefit from their vote (Geddes 1990; Gil 1966; Valenzuela 1994). After 1958, however, the process of registering lists and allocating seats became more transparent (Cruz-Coke 1984); and, largely as a result, national policy came to be more important in campaigns than service to a geographic constituency (Valenzuela 1994). Finally, in Ecuador, a series of party and electoral law provisions encourage loose and uncohesive parties whose members have little connection to any common platform (Conaghan 1994). All of these systems (Brazil, pre-1958 Chile, Colombia, Ecuador, the Philippines, and the United States) are thus coded as having localizing electoral rules. All the other cases (Argentina, post-1958 Chile, Costa Rica, El Salvador, France, Portugal, and Venezuela) are coded as having *nationalizing electoral rules*.

RESULTS

This reasoning leads to two hypotheses: (1) the incidence of divided government will be greater in nonconcurrent than in concurrent elections; and (2)

TABLE 1			
Ratio of Presidential to Opposition Majorities in Sole or Lower Houses			
	ELECTORAL RULES		
ELECTORAL CYCLE	NATIONAL-IZING	LOCAL-IZING	TOTAL
Concurrent	10.0:1	2.3:1	3.1:1
Noncurrent	2.5:1	1.4:1	1.7:1
Total	4.0:1	1.8:1	2.2:1

the incidence of divided government resulting from concurrent elections will be greater if electoral rules are localizing than if they are nationalizing.

The Ratio of Presidential to Opposition Majorities

The simplest means to test these two hypotheses is to compute the ratios of presidential to opposition majorities for each of the combinations of our two variables, the electoral cycle, and the electoral rules. The results, derived from the data displayed in the Appendix, are summarized in Table 1. We see that presidential majorities occur 3.1 times as often as opposition majorities in concurrent elections, but only 1.7 times as often in nonconcurrent elections. This accords with the first hypothesis. Disaggregating the concurrent elections by nationalizing and localizing electoral rules, we find striking correspondence with the second hypothesis. Presidential majorities occur 10 times as often as opposition majorities in concurrent elections under nationalizing rules, but only 2.3 times as often in concurrent elections under localizing rules.[10] Thus my reasoning appears to be sound.

The Transition to Divided Government

A further check on the argument presented is to see if in systems of localizing electoral rules opposition majorities are more likely to result from a partisan change in the presidency than from a partisan change in the assembly majority. The reason for such an expectation is rooted in the electoral independence afforded by localizing rules. Even if a plurality of

voters has chosen to change the partisan composition of the executive branch, enough legislators may survive the adverse presidential outcome to preserve the preexisting majority in the legislature.

In fact, we have nine cases of opposition majorities in systems of localizing electoral rules and just five in systems of nationalizing rules. Table 2 shows that of the nine transitions to divided government under localizing rules, six resulted from a partisan change in the presidency. Four of those cases were in concurrent elections. Only three occurrences of opposition majorities, all from midterms, resulted from a change in the party controlling the assembly.[11] Under nationalizing electoral rules, on the other hand, only one occurrence of an opposition majority resulted from a partisan change in the presidency.[12] Four (all midterm or later) resulted from a partisan change in the assembly.

The findings reported in Table 2, although based on a relatively rare phenomenon, conform to the theoretical expectations. The theory led us to expect localizing electoral rules to grant electoral independence such that even when voters opt to change the partisan control of the presidency, sometimes the legislative majority does not change hands. Under nationalizing electoral rules, on the other hand, the fates of legislators are more closely bound to partisan tides in presidential elections. Also, as expected, change in the legislative majority leads to opposition majorities only in midterm or later-term elections, when voters punish the president's party. No opposition majority has ever resulted from a concurrent election in which voters elected to change the legislative majority but to retain the presidency in the hands of the incumbent party.

Fit to Theory

These findings are consistent with the expectation of the theory presented. Recall that I have suggested that concurrent elections would ordinarily be expected to result in limited ticket splitting. Although I provide no direct data on ticket splitting, the results are consistent with a theory that explains variation in presidential versus opposition majorities by reference to variations in the tendency of voters to vote differently for the two elected branches. When voters are

TABLE 2		
Transitions to Opposition Majorities under Different Institutional Configurations		
ELECTORAL RULES	PARTISAN CHANGE IN PRESIDENCY	PARTISAN CHANGE IN LEGISLATURE
Localizing	Colombia 1946, Colombia 1982, Philippines 1961,[a] Philippines 1965,[a] United States 1968,[a] United States 1980[a]	United States 1918, United States 1946, United States 1954
Nationalizing	Costa Rica 1966[a]	Chile 1973, El Salvador 1988, France 1986, France 1993

[a]Concurrent election.

selecting the executive and legislature at the same time, they would be expected to select legislative candidates of the same party as their preferred presidential candidate. Ticket splitting would be higher, however, if legislative elections were conducted to a large degree on the basis of local or personal concerns rather than on support or opposition to a given presidential candidate. The divide between localizing and nationalizing electoral rules in concurrent elections (Table 1) powerfully confirms this line of reasoning. So does the finding that the transition to divided government after concurrent elections is most common under localizing rules and when it is the presidency that changes hands.

THE ELECTORAL CYCLE IN DETAIL

I shall disaggregate the notion of electoral cycle. Instead of considering simply concurrent versus nonconcurrent, we shall look at the specific time at which each assembly election is held relative to a presidential election. Elections occur at nearly every point within a president's term, although few occur very late in a president's term,[13] so that we have plenty of observations.

Time and Support for Presidential Parties

Figure 1 shows a plot of TIME and change in percent seats.[14] The regression line reflects only the nonconcurrent elections.[15] We find that there is a striking downward trend in seats won by presidents' parties in elections over time. As expected, the coefficient on time is negative and significant. When considering only nonconcurrent elections, this one variable explains nearly 50% of the variance. When concurrent elections are added (as in model 1 in Table 3), the variance explained drops to around 33%, but this is still impressive for a specification that includes only the electoral cycle.

The main reason for the decline in R-squared when including the entire data set is that those systems in which all elections are concurrent add "noise." In such cases, the congressional election that provides us with our observation is being compared with the election held at the time when the outgoing president was elected. A related factor is that concurrent elections (even when the preceding election was a midterm) are by definition held when it remains uncertain who will be the president facing the Congress being elected. In a nonconcurrent election, on the other hand, that president is a known quantity. These considerations provide further justification for considering concurrent and nonconcurrent elections separately, rather than simply coding concurrent elections as TIME = 0.[16]

The relation found between TIME and change in percent votes or seats provides strong support for the "presidential penalty" explanation for midterm loss (Erickson 1988). However, note that there is also a presidential reward in the early part of a term. This

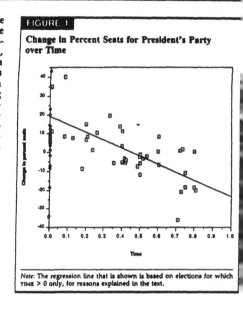

FIGURE 1

Change in Percent Seats for President's Party over Time

Note: The regression line that is shown is based on elections for which TIME > 0 only, for reasons explained in the text.

finding is consistent with the expectations for honeymoon elections I have articulated. This presidential reward could not have been found in the United States, although the general notion of a presidential honeymoon is widely understood. It takes comparative work such as this to find that the honeymoon is indeed translated into greater voter support of the president's party, given an opportunity afforded by the electoral cycle.

A particularly striking feature of the data plot in Figure 1 is the near intersection of this line with a point that would represent no change in percent seats at the midterm.[17] What this suggests is that in a system in which only midterm elections were used, presidential elections would have virtually no impact on the seat shares of the parties. This is support for the notion of surge and decline, where the decline at the midterm merely represents a reassertion of longer-term electoral patterns following a surge at a concurrent election (Born 1990).

Time and Divided Government

These regressions and data plot show that presidential parties' seats decline as elections are held later in the presidents' term. But what effect does this decline have on the tendency toward divided government? We can answer this question with probit analysis, using an equation specified as follows:

$$\text{OPPMAJ} = a + \beta_1 \text{TIME} + \beta_2 \text{NUMPAR} + \beta_3 \text{USA},$$

where OPPMAJ is a dummy variable equal to one if an opposition party controls a majority of seats, and zero

TABLE 3

Regression Results for Electoral-Cycle Variables and Change in Percent Seats

INDEPENDENT VARIABLE	MODEL 1 ELECTORAL CYCLE VARIABLES ONLY		MODEL 2 WITH ELECTORAL-RULE VARIABLES	
	EST. COEF.	S.E.	EST. COEF.	S.E.
Constant	19.10***	4.34	19.06***	3.49
TIME	−42.73***	8.60	−63.52***	15.20
TIME • LOCAL	—	—	12.13*	6.31
TIME • PRESVOTE	—	—	.32	.28
CONC	−12.32***	4.96	−29.58**	11.02
CONC • LOCAL	—	—	3.16	4.35
CONC • PRESVOTE	—	—	.32	.21
R^2	.33		.49	
No. of observations	64		60	

Note: The dependent variable is change in percent seats for president's party. TIME is the share of the president's term elapsed when the assembly election is held, LOCAL is a dummy set to 1 if electoral rules are localizing, PRESVOTE is the percent of vote received by the president, and CONC is a dummy set to 1 when the election is concurrent with the presidential election.
*$p \leq .10$.
**$p \leq .05$.
***$p \leq .01$.

therwise; TIME is the electoral cycle variable, as efined earlier; NUMPAR is the effective number of arties represented in the legislature; and USA is a ummy variable for the United States.

NUMPAR is entered as a control variable, simply ecause majorities of either type (presidential or pposition) are expected to be rarer, the larger the umber of parties. The dummy for the United States ¬ included to be sure that an increasing incidence of pposition majorities in elections as TIME increases ¬if found—is not simply a result of the many U.S. udterm elections that result in divided government. he results are that TIME is a statistically significant redictor ($p < .05$) of the frequency of opposition ajorities, even controlling for the effective number ¬ parties and including a dummy for the United tates.[18] Thus the probability of an opposition major- y increases the later an election is held in a presi- ent's term.

¬ringing in Electoral Rules and Other Variables

¬ model 2 in Table 3, I test for a difference in slope on ¬e TIME variable according to the electoral rules. The ¬eory presented suggests that the time and electoral ¬le variables are interactive. That is, if the electoral ¬dependence afforded by localizing electoral rules ¬lows members to shield themselves from evalua- ¬ns of the party controlling the president, then the ¬ope of the decline according to TIME should be less ¬eep in systems of localizing electoral rules than in ¬stems of nationalizing rules. We can test for this ¬fect by specifying a regression as follows:

$$\Delta SEATS = k + TIME (\beta_0 + \beta_1 LOCAL + \beta_2 PRESVOTE)$$

$$+ CONC (\mu_0 + \mu_1 LOCAL + \mu_2 PRESVOTE),$$

where $\Delta SEATS$ is the change in percent seats for the president's party since the last legislative election; TIME is the electoral cycle variable, as before; LOCAL is a dummy variable that equals one if legislative rules are localizing, and zero otherwise; PRESVOTE is the percent votes received by the president; and CONC is a dummy that equals one if the elections is concurrent, and zero otherwise.

By making the variables interactive, this specifica- tion lets us test for the hypothesis that the slope of the line for TIME is significantly different according to which type of legislative electoral rule is used. If this hypothesis holds, the coefficient on TIME will remain negative and significant and the coefficient on TIME • LOCAL will be positive and significant, indicating that the decline over time is less steep for localizing rules than for nationalizing rules. If concurrent elections also vary according to electoral rule type, then CONC should remain negative and significant, while CONC • LOCAL should be positive and significant.

Further, I expect that the standard errors on TIME • LOCAL and CONC • LOCAL will be larger relative to their estimated coefficients than will be the standard errors on TIME and CONC. The reason is that the sheltering from the cycle effect afforded by localizing rules is only facilitating and potential; members are still subject to varying degrees of reward or penalty according to TIME when their party holds the presi- dency. If they were not, then TIME would have no effect at all in systems with localizing rules; at the extreme, perhaps we should indeed expect no effect of TIME. Realistically, however, we should expect the effect of evaluations of the president only to be dampened—and possibly to varying degrees in dif- ferent elections and for different legislators. Again, the reason is simply that localizing rules provide the *opportunity* for members to shelter their fates from evaluations of the president. On the other hand, I have argued that under nationalizing rules, legislators' fates are inextricably bound to voters' evaluations of a president from the same party. Therefore, *the standard errors on* TIME *and* CONC *should be much smaller relative to their estimated coefficients than for the terms that are interacted with* LOCAL.

PRESVOTE, the percent of votes won by the president, is included and also interacted with the cycle variables because a president who has won a larger "mandate" may experience a greater late-term loss. This expectation is simply a generalization of the "regression to the mean" explanation for varying degrees of midterm losses seen in the United States (e.g., Hinckley 1967). The coefficient on TIME * PRESVOTE might be negative, so that a larger share of votes for the president portends greater-than-average penalty later in the term. The coefficient on CONC * PRESVOTE, however, should be positive, as a president elected with larger shares of the vote ought to have more "coattails" in a concurrent election.

The results of this regression are displayed in Table 3 as model 2.[19] The expectations on the electoral rule variables are largely confirmed. The coefficient on TIME indeed remains negative and highly significant ($p < .01$), and the coefficient on TIME * LOCAL is positive and significant ($p < .1$, almost $p < .05$). The standard error on TIME * LOCAL is indeed larger relative to its coefficient than the standard error on TIME.[20] CONC also remains negative and significant. The coefficient on CONC * LOCAL is of the expected sign but is statistically insignificant. In part, this is because (as was discussed in connection with model 1), there is already a lot more scatter on CONC than on TIME, because the reference point for ΔSEATS is often a full presidential term in the past.

The estimated coefficients on the two interactive terms involving the president's vote are utterly insignificant. Indeed, the coefficient on TIME * PRESVOTE is of the wrong sign as well. Model 2 thus suggests that the electoral cycle and electoral rule variables are more important in predicting the change in percent seats held by the president's party than is the share of votes won by the president.

The Electoral Cycle, Electoral Rules, and the Party System

So far, I have dealt with two tasks. First, we saw how the ratio of presidential to opposition majorities varied with different institutional configurations. Then we saw the effects of presidential reward in early-term elections and presidential penalty in elections held later in the term. Our task is now to expand our scope to include an important aspect of the relationship between party systems and majority situations—the phenomena of multipartisan and *no-majority* situations. Such situations are actually the second most common in presidential systems, according to the data presented in Table A-1, in the Appendix. No-

majority situations account for 29% of all observ tions, compared to 49.1% of cases in which tl president has a majority and 21.9% in which a opposition party or alliance has a majority.[21] I seek determine whether the occurrences of no-majorit situations are randomly distributed across the case or depend on institutional variables in any systemati way. We shall see that localizing elections appear t reduce the number of parties in concurrent elections However, the best predictors of increased number o parties (and therefore of no-majority situations) ar district magnitude and, especially, the combinatio of nonconcurrent elections with localizing rules.

Let us consider the effects of localizing electora rules and how such rules might operate differently o the number of parties in systems that use concurren elections versus systems that use (exclusively) nor concurrent elections. If the party label can be adapte to the needs of local candidates and incumbent leg islators (as it can under localizing rules), then there I reduced incentive to establish separate parties whe disagreements arise between local chapters and th national leadership. When elections are concurrent the focus of the campaign is likely to be on th nationwide race for the presidency. Thus candidate who can freely choose their party label or mold it t suit local concerns have the incentive to line u behind one or the other presidential candidate, rather than behind a party that will not attract mucl attention in the presidential race. At least as long a the election for president is conducted under plural ity or pluralitylike rules,[23] ordinarily this logic woul imply just two principal parties (Shugart and Care; 1992, chap. 10). Other things being equal, then, thirc parties should be less common under the combina tion of localizing electoral rules and concurrent elec tions with plurality (or pluralitylike) electoral rules fo the presidency. Thus the way in which this combina tion structures incentives of members of legislature: and candidates for the legislature should make major ities—whether presidential or opposition—likely. In nonconcurrent elections, on the other hand, the absence of the presidential contest to structure the party system implies that there may be no adverse cost to candidates' being associated with third parties (Shugart and Carey 1992). There may even be some benefit to *not* being identified with the president's party, given the decline observed in midterm or late-term elections (albeit a dampened one, as model 2 in Table 3 showed).[24]

To summarize, the combination of concurrent and localizing elections leads to an expectation of a two-party system and frequent majorities (for either the president or the opposition). The nonconcurrent-localizing combination would suggest a tendency toward multipartisan and no-majority situations. To see if these expectations hold, we can perform two statistical tests, one of which appears to support this reasoning and the other of which casts some doubt on it. As I shall discuss, there are reasons having to do with the sample of cases to accept the logic of my hypothesized effect of concurrent elections and localizing electoral rules. The two statistical tests are (1) a regression of various institutional variables on the effective number of parties and (2) a probit analysis of these same variables on the probability of legislative majorities.

The first test uses ordinary least squares regression analysis in an equation specified as follows:[25]

$$NUMPAR = a + \beta_1 CONC + \beta_2 LOCAL$$
$$+ \beta_3 NCLOCAL + \beta_4 MAG,$$

where NUMPAR is the effective number of parties in the assembly; CONC is a dummy variable equal to one if the election is concurrent, and zero otherwise; LOCAL is a dummy variable equal to one for localizing electoral rules, and zero otherwise; NCLOCAL is a dummy variable set to one for localizing electoral rules *combined with* nonconcurrent elections, and zero otherwise; and MAG is the magnitude (number of seats per district) of the electoral system.[26]

If my explanations are valid, then CONC and LOCAL should have negative and significant coefficients, because concurrent elections should encourage voters to support the larger parties that have a chance at the presidency and because localizing electoral rules should allow parties to be affiliated with a major-party presidential candidate and simultaneously loose enough to let members respond to local concerns. NCLOCAL should be positive and significant. Of course, MAG should be positive and significant.

Table 4 shows the results. CONC and LOCAL are both of the expected sign, though the coefficient on LOCAL ($p < .1$) is less significant than the coefficient on CONC ($p < .05$). Surprisingly, district magnitude is not significant. The results suggest that when elections are concurrent, the effective number of parties is reduced from 3.2 on average (the constant term) to around 2.4. When electoral rules are localizing, it is reduced by a further .72 effective party (the coefficient on LOCAL). Thus, when both CONC and LOCAL are set to one, the average effective number of parties is predicted to be about 1.6, which is a value that obtains when there are just two major parties with one holding a substantial majority. The insignificance of magnitude in this equation is surprising, given that magnitude has been called the "decisive factor" in determining the number of parties (Taagepera and Shugart 1989). However, most studies of the effects of electoral systems have dealt overwhelmingly with parliamentary systems. The finding here confirms that presidential systems should be analyzed in their own right and not as though they were just like parliamentary systems, other than their manner of executive selection. The reductive effect of concurrent elections on the number of parties (at least when a pluralitylike rule is used to elect the president) is such that even large-magnitude presidential systems have low number of parties. To cite a couple of specific examples, both Costa Rica and Venezuela have fairly high effective magnitudes (8 and 27, respectively), yet both have fairly low numbers of legislative parties (well under three in most elections), in part because

TABLE 4

Effective Number of Parties in the Legislature and Probability of Legislative Majority

INDEPENDENT VARIABLE	EFFECTIVE NUMBER OF PARTIES		PROBABILITY OF LEGISLATIVE MAJORITY	
	EST. COEF. (OLS)	S.E.	EST. COEF. (PROBIT)	S.E.
Constant	3.18***	.29	.86**	.33
CONC[a]	−.82**	.36	−.23	.43
LOCAL[b]	−.72*	.40	.67	.52
NCLOCAL[c]	1.64***	.49	−1.45**	.61
MAG[d]	.03	.02	−.06**	.03
R^2	.38		—	
% correctly predicted	—		77.5	
No. of observations	71		71	

[a]Concurrent election.
[b]Localizing electoral rules.
[c]Nonconcurrent election with localizing electoral rules.
[d]Effective magnitude.
*$p \leq .10$.
**$p \leq .05$.
***$p \leq .01$.

of concurrent elections and two-candidate competition for the presidency in most contests.

Thus we can say that concurrent elections reduce the number of parties and that the combination of concurrent elections and localizing electoral rules tends to reduce the number of parties to two. This is consistent with the expectation that this configuration would give legislative candidates the advantages of being aligned with a major presidential contender, but also the electoral independence to tailor their message and behavior to suit the needs of local constituents. Next we test whether the CONC + LOCAL combination also produces a greater probability of majorities.

Table 4 also shows the results of a probit equation with the same independent variables. The dependent variable is MAJ, a dummy variable that equals one if any party has a majority of seats. The coefficients on CONC and LOCAL are of the expected signs but (especially CONC) far short of being significant. Magnitude is significant in this equation ($p < .05$).

What accounts for the contradictory result? Although presidential majorities are common with concurrent elections, no-majority situations are so common as well that there is no statistically significant effect of concurrent elections alone on the probability of majorities. That is, the number of parties may be reduced by concurrent elections but not enough that majorities become significantly more probable for either the president or the opposition. Although this equation suggests that magnitude is a stronger factor in predicting majorities, there are reasons based both on the sample of cases and findings already demonstrated not to reject the hypothesis that localizing rules in concurrent elections are also a significant factor. First, in the data sample, two countries that contribute a number of observations, the Philippines and the United States, both use low magnitude (M = 1) in addition to localizing electoral rules.[27] Because these cases (plus Colombia, where localizing electoral rules are combined with relatively high magnitude and near-concurrent elections) are the only ones that consistently have majorities for one party regardless of the value of TIME, the probit analysis on a dichotomous dependent variable naturally picks up magnitude as the more important factor. However, the regression that has a continuous dependent variable (effective number of parties) has already shown us that CONC and LOCAL are more significant predictors of a reduced number of parties than is magnitude. Moreover, model 2 in Table 3 showed us that in general, localizing electoral rules dampen the degree of responsiveness of the electoral cycle to the partisan control of the presidency. These findings provide some reason to suspect that if we had a sample in which there were more cases of localized electoral rules and concurrent elections with magnitude greater than one, we might find a greater probability of a majority, just as we find a reduced number of parties. As it is, however, the two models presented in Table 4 alone do not sort out fully the effects of the different variables.

A further justification for not abandoning the reasoning that localizing electoral rules are an important variable in their own right in contributing to majorities (including opposition majorities) can be seen by reference to Table 2. In this table we saw that six of seven transitions to divided government resulting from a partisan change in the presidency—but only three of seven transitions resulting from a partisan change in the legislative majority—occurred under localizing electoral rules. The table also showed that five of the seven transitions occurring from a partisan change in the presidency resulted from concurrent elections, while all the transitions resulting from a partisan change in the legislature occurred in midterm elections.

If the electoral system's magnitude were a more important cause of majorities, we should not expect such patterns. Low magnitude contributes to majorities not only by reducing the number of parties but also by producing "manufactured" majorities—those in which a party did not have a majority of votes but won a majority of seats (Lijphart 1994; Rae 1967). If low magnitude were a more important predictor of opposition majorities than are localizing electoral rules, then we should expect some concurrent elections to produce divided government from a change in the partisan composition of the legislature (i.e., there should be some cases of concurrent elections in the right side of Table 2). Particularly in close elections, a low-magnitude electoral system would from time to time give the legislative majority to a party different from that which won the presidency—possibly even different from that which won the most

legislative votes. Instead, we find that oppositi majorities that result from concurrent elections occ under localizing electoral rules and from a partis change in the presidency. This was the pattern th was predicted on the basis of a theory that postulate that voters in systems of localizing electoral rul would sometimes vote to change the presidency b would find that their local representatives had serve them well enough that they would split tickets.

Moreover, another result in Table 2 supports m contention that concurrent elections and localizir rules are more important than magnitude for bot reducing the number of parties and predicting d vided government. If, as I have argued, voters ar more interested in and capable of punishing th president's party in midterm elections under nation alizing rules than under localizing rules, then magn tude should matter relatively less under nationalizin rules. That is, while a very high magnitude woul make it unlikely that a single party would claim majority, voters' focus under nationalizing rules o the performance of the governing party would pro duce opposition majorities after midterm elections i medium-magnitude as well as low-magnitude sys tems. Under localizing rules, on the other hand, th greater insulation of legislators should mean tha only in low-magnitude systems (with their greate tendency to magnify small changes in votes percent ages into relatively larger changes in seats percent ages) would we see changes in partisan control of th legislature at midterm. Indeed, very low magnitude do not appear to be required to turn the partisar control of the legislature against the president i midterm elections if the electoral rules are national izing. Of the four cases of a transition to divide government resulting from a partisan change in th legislature under nationalizing rules, only one (France 1993) occurred under single-member dis tricts. On the other hand, all three cases of transitior to divided government resulting from change in th party controlling the legislature under localizing rule occurred with single-member districts—and all in th United States.

This discussion of effects of electoral cycle and nationalizing or localizing electoral rules has sug gested ways in which the incidence of divided gov ernment may be affected by the impact of these variables on the party system. Although we have too few cases of opposition majorities to draw firm con clusions, I have presented an argument about why divided government would be more likely to result from (1) concurrent elections in which localizing electoral rules are used and (2) midterm or later elections, especially those in which nationalizing rules are used.

Testing the Balancing Hypothesis

As noted previously, Ingberman and Villani (1993) have a model in which divided government results from parties' taking divergent policy stances and voters' preferring moderation. Given the president's veto, both parties must compromise to enact policy under divided government. I shall test this hypothesis on the present data set. I have identified the conditions under which a two-party system is most likely in presidential systems—concurrent elections (with plurality presidential elections) and localizing electoral rules. Two-partism is crucial to Ingberman and Villani's argument, as well as to any other that posits balancing as an explanation of divided government, because it assumes that one party or the other will win a majority of legislative seats. The veto is also crucial, as a president who lacks a veto cannot "moderate" the policy output of the legislature. Many presidents do not wield a veto; many who do confront multiparty systems.

A probit equation is specified:

$$\text{OPPMAJ} = a + \beta_1 \text{VETO} + \beta_2 \text{NUMPAR},$$

where OPPMAJ is the dummy for whether or not there is an opposition majority, VETO is a dummy equal to one if there is a presidential veto requiring at least a two-thirds vote to override, and NUMPAR is the effective number of assembly parties. If balancing is a valid explanation, VETO should have a positive and significant effect. That is, opposition majorities are certain to be more common in two-party systems than in multiparty systems, simply because either kind of majority is more common. But if balancing as a result of the veto is a predictor of divided government, then VETO should be a significant predictor of the probability of OPPMAJ beyond that given by NUMPAR.

However, VETO is not significant, holding NUMPAR constant, whether or not a dummy variable is included for the United States. In both specifications, TIME and NUMPAR remain significant even when the effects of a presidential veto are considered.[28] Thus I find no support in a data set on comparative presidential systems for the balancing hypothesis that has been developed with respect to the specific conditions of the United States.

DISCUSSION

The results of this article allow us to place the study of divided government in the United States into a broader comparative perspective than has generally been attempted. The evidence from 12 countries suggests that the electoral cycle is of great importance in determining whether presidents enjoy legislative support in the form of a copartisan majority or face an opposition majority, as well as in the growth or decrease in that support over time. Legislative elections that are concurrent with presidential elections[29] are more likely than those that are nonconcurrent to produce unified government. Nonconcurrent elections, other than those held early in the president's term, are more likely to produce divided government. This is a generalization of the on-year/off-year pattern in the United States that was especially pronounced before 1956.

Other major results include the following. Elections held early after a presidential election are likely to produce a surge in support for the new president's party, with a simple linear model fitting the data and predicting a decline over time in elections held later in the term. Electoral rules that facilitate legislators' cultivation of ties to local constituencies[30] reduce the degree of decline in support for presidential parties over the course of an electoral cycle. Such independence of legislators from party also may make for a greater likelihood of divided government even in concurrent elections, as voters who opt for one party for the presidency may find that a candidate of another party has served local interests well. Thus, while presidential majorities are more common in concurrent elections, the electoral rules variable is also a significant predictor of the number of parties in concurrent elections. The reduction in the number of parties that is associated with localizing electoral rules in concurrent elections may account in part for the incidence of divided government in United States and Philippine concurrent elections.

One question that arises is, if the tendency toward opposition majorities is inherent in the institutional design of the United States (and some other countries), why has divided government in concurrent elections been almost entirely a recent phenomenon in the United States? There are two responses. First, a more sophisticated measure of the degree of electoral independence than the dichotomy used here might capture differences over time in the United States. States adopted primaries at different times and have changed the degree of "openness" of primaries over time. At least through the nineteenth century and into the early twentieth, the degree of party control (at least at the state level) was no doubt greater than it has been in the post–World War II era, when members have increasingly been able to cultivate a "personal vote" at the level of their own districts (Cain, Ferejohn, and Fiorina 1987). Second, nothing in the theory articulated here implies that localizing electoral rules guarantee the divergent voter expectations that may produce divided government. Such electoral rules do, I agree, make the articulation of such divergent preferences easier than do other institutional formats. And I further claim that nationalizing rules practically guarantee that legislative elections reflect voters' evaluations of the president. The data analysis supports this idea strongly.

There is a need for much more systematic research on the consequences of divided government. As noted in the introduction, there is some dispute about its supposedly negative effects in the United States. In the comparative presidentialism literature, on the other hand, there is no dispute at all about the "perils" (Linz 1990) of a lack of presidential majorities, let alone opposition majorities. As far as the United States is concerned, Mayhew's (1991) excellent study calls into serious question the claims made in the literature (both American and comparative) about the perniciousness of divided government. He cites electoral incentives of members of Congress as one plausible reason for the lack of a serious divergence between unified and divided government in patterns of either congressional investigation or the passing of major legislation. The present analysis provides support for Mayhew's explanation, as in systems with localizing electoral rules, members of the legislature are much less tied to the collective fates of their parties than in other systems. Thus members are more self-reliant in building their careers on legislative or constituent-service-oriented reputations. The resulting less-cohesive parties imply that executive-legislative relations would be less sensitive to which party controls the branches under localizing electoral rules. In systems with nationalizing electoral rules, on the other hand, divided government may be much more difficult to cope with, as parties may have a stronger collective incentive to accentuate their differences.

To return to themes about divided government versus no-majority situations, we can draw some tentative conclusions about the effects of different patterns of nonunified government on the performance of presidential government. If parties are less cohesive (as I have argued they are likely to be under the combination of concurrent elections and localizing rules), then divided government may not in fact be a form of grand coalition. Rather, less cohesive parties imply that much policy would be made by one cross-party coalition opposing another cross-party coalition. In such a situation (which appears to fit the experience of the United States, and probably the Philippines and Colombia as well), party lines may not be the best predictors of policy stance; but it may not be accurate to charge that nobody is responsible for policy because everyone is responsible, as criticism of American divided government in the popular media often suggests. It is, however, undoubtedly valid to say that determining this responsibility is a much tougher task for voters, because it is necessary to look beyond the party label into the record of individual politicians.[31]

On the other hand, if parties are cohesive and nationally focused (as I expect them to be under nationalizing electoral rules), divided government may mean de facto grand coalitions or even crises of "dual legitimacies." That is, under such party systems, cross-party alliances would be much harder to craft and governance might indeed be made more difficult unless there were other constitutional rules to mitigate such stalemates, such as the French provision that control over the government is ceded to the legislative majority when it is different from the party of the presidency (Pierce 1990; Shugart and Carey 1992; Suleiman 1994).[32]

Opposition majorities are not unique to the United States, but they also are not the norm in other systems that elect their chief executives directly. They are the product of specific institutional configurations about which there is considerable variation cross-nationally.

APPENDIX

Case Selection. Table A-1 shows the countries and time periods included in this study, along with the lengths of presidential and assembly terms and information on electoral rules and cycles. The table also indicates the number of assembly elections from which observations were taken and gives the percent of these observations that produced each of the three possible majority situations (presidential, opposition, or no majority). Cases were selected as follows. First, a country had to have a popularly elected president. Where elections are indirect, a country was included only if the electors who make the final selection must vote only once and therefore are unable to broker the outcome. If the legislative assembly sometimes make the final selection from among candidates who first ran in a direct popular vote, the country was included. Thus Argentina, Chile, and the United States are all included because no candidate who won a plurality of the popular vote has been denied the presidency in the time of the study, but Finland is excluded.

Second, voters had to be free to cast their presidential and legislative votes for different parties. Thus Bolivia, the Dominican Republic, Honduras, and Uruguay are excluded, as voters in most or all of the elections in these countries have been required to vote a straight ticket.

Third, the president must exercise real political powers. Such powers could be legislative (veto or decree) or nonlegislative (e.g., appointing cabinet ministers, dissolving parliament); but where the secondary literature indicates that presidents do not exercise such powers as they are formally granted, the case was excluded (Duverger 1980; Nogueira 1986; Shugart and Carey 1992). Thus the data set does not include Austria, Iceland, or Ireland.

No fewer than three elections are used for each country. Where a country changed its institutional configuration between elections, it is given multiple entries in Table A-1. The table shows the variety of term lengths used in the countries studied. It also indicates whether a country's constitution permits elections for either branch to be called ahead of schedule. For instance, in Chile, France, and Portugal, there is no vice-president, so if a president dies or otherwise vacates the office, a new election is held for a new full term. In France and Portugal, presidents may dissolve parliament, thereby ordering early elections. The values of the variable TIME indicate the share of the scheduled presidential term that had elapsed at the time an election was held. That is, even if a president does not complete the term for which he was elected, an election held while that president is in office can be assumed to reflect the portion of the planned term that had elapsed. All that is required to accept this assumption is for presidents not to announce in advance of legislative elections that they plan to retire early.

56

TABLE A-1

Summary of Data

Country	Years in Data Set	Presidential Term		Assembly Term		Electoral Rules[a]	Effective Magnitude	Electoral Cycle	% of Observations with Majority for ...			
		Years	Early Elections?	Years	Early Elections?				N	Pres.	Opp.	Neither
Argentina	1983–89	6	no	4[b]	no	National	6.2	Mixed	5	40.0	.0	60.0
								Concurrent	2	50.0	.0	50.0
								Nonconcurrent	3	33.3	.0	66.7
Brazil												
I	1945–50	5	no	5	no	Local	12.5	Concurrent	2	50.0	.0	50.0
II	1954–62	5	no	4	no	Local	12.5	Nonconcurrent	3	.0	.0	100.0
III	1990	5	no	4	no	Local	19.3	Nonconcurrent	1	.0	.0	100.0
Chile												
I	1937–57	6	yes	4	no	Local	4.0	Nonconcurrent	6	.0	.0	100.0
II	1958–73	6	yes	4	no	National	4.0	Nonconcurrent	4	25.0	25.0	50.0
Colombia												
I	1945–49	4	no	2	no	Local	8.7	Nonconcurrent	3	33.3	66.7	.0
II	1974–91	4	no	4	no[c]	Local	7.7[d]	Nonconcurrent[e]	6	83.3	16.7	.0
Costa Rica	1953–90	4[d]	no	4[f]	no	National	8.1	Concurrent	10	60.0	10.0	30.0
Ecuador	1979–90	4[e]	no	2[g]	no	Local	2.8	Mixed	5	.0	.0	100.0
								Concurrent	3	.0	.0	100.0
								Nonconcurrent	2	.0	.0	100.0
El Salvador	1985–91	5	no	3	no	National	4.9	Nonconcurrent	3	33.3	33.3	33.3
France	1967–93	7	yes	5	yes	National	1[h]	Nonconcurrent	8	50.0	25.0	25.0
Philippines	1953–69	4	no	4	no	Local	1	Concurrent	5	60.0	40.0	.0
Portugal	1979–87	6	yes	4	yes	National	12.0	Nonconcurrent	5	60.0	.0	40.0
United States	1912–90	4	no	2	no	Local	1	Mixed	41	61.0	36.6	2.4
								Concurrent	21	66.7	28.6	4.8
								Nonconcurrent	20	55.0	45.0	.0
Venezuela	1958–88	5	no	5	no	National	27	Concurrent	7	42.9	.0	57.1

[a]Localizing or nationalizing, as explained in text.
[b]Staggered terms, with one-half renewed every two years.
[c]One early election called to replace congress according to new constitution of 1991.
[d]4.9 in 1991.
[e]Concurrent in 1974.
[f]Five-year term after election of 1953.
[g]Four-year term for deputies elected from nationwide district, five years for all deputies and president elected in 1979.
[h]5 in 1986.

ectoral Rule Variables. Electoral rules were coded on dichotomous variable according to whether they ere nationalizing or localizing in their effects on gislative campaigns. If legislative aspirants may not n for office except as candidates of a legally regis-red party and if voters cast votes for party lists, as Costa Rica and Venezuela, rules are nationalizing. on the other hand, party names are either absent om the ballot or may be adopted by candidates on e basis of their own entrepreneurial activities— aying a deposit or collecting signatures of voters— en electoral rules are localizing because such can-dates have more freedom to tailor their campaigns local concerns. For example, in the United States, ndidates receive the right to run under the label of party by winning a primary contest. Nor do parties Colombia (Archer 1990) and the Philippines (Pinck-ey 1971; Sours 1970) control the use of their labels. In Brazil, local party organizations can admit a ndidate onto the party list without the approval of e state-level party, let alone the national party

organization. Moreover, once elected, a legislator cannot be denied the use of the party label in the future (Mainwaring 1991). The change in electoral rules in Chile after 1958, from localizing to national-izing, was discussed in the main text.

Effective magnitudes are determined using the method discussed in Taagepera and Shugart (1989, 126–35, 266–69), which takes into account varying magnitudes of individual districts in some countries, as well as thresholds. For electoral systems in which all seats are allocated in districts, effective magnitude (M_{eff}) is calculated as

$$M_{eff} = E/S, \qquad (1)$$

where E is the number of electoral districts and S is the number of seats in the legislature. For electoral systems with thresholds, we use the formula

$$M_{eff} = 50\%/T, \qquad (2)$$

where T is the percent of votes required for a party to win a seat. The Venezuelan electoral system is highly complex, and we suggest and justify using the geometric average of the values of effective magnitude that result from equations 1 and 2 (ibid., 269). We provide values for several countries included here (ibid., 136–37). For most others, our methods are applied to the descriptions in Nohlen 1993. Effective magnitude in this data set ranges from 1 to 27. The mean magnitude in the entire data set is around 7; the median is around 4.

Votes and Seats Data. Data on votes and seats won by presidential parties are from Mackie and Rose 1992 and Nohlen 1993. For the Philippines, data are from the *Report of the Commission of Elections to the President of the Philippines and the Congress.* A party was considered to be aligned with the president only if sources indicated that the party had endorsed the president at the time of the presidential election (the first round, in the case of a two-round electoral system). In most cases, only a single party was so listed. If several party organizations listed themselves on the ballot as a single alliance (as in Chile in 1973 and France in 1986), the alliance was counted as a "party."

Dealing with U.S. Observations. The one country from which there are especially numerous observations is the United States. Accordingly, for the regressions (but not for Tables 1 and 2), to avoid having this one case swamp the results, the number of observations was reduced to nine. Five consecutive elections were chosen from 1924 to 1932 and four more from 1980 to 1986. The results on the TIME variable from these elections were checked against those from the entire set of U.S. elections (1912–88) to ensure that the elections chosen were not atypical. They were not. For example, in all U.S. observations, the president's party, on average, gained 2.8% votes in the on-year election and lost 3.8% at the midterm. In the smaller sample, the figures were an on-year surge of 3.9% and an off-year decline of 2.5%. Given standard deviations of greater than 2, the difference is not significant.

Upper and Lower Houses. All data are from lower houses. We might expect the pattern of divided versus unified government to be different in upper and lower houses, perhaps because the two houses are elected on a different basis or because staggered elections are used in the upper houses. In fact, the overall rates of divided government are almost identical in upper and lower houses. For example, presidents held majorities in 36.8% of lower-house observations and in 39.1% of upper-house observations. Opposition majorities occurred at rates of 15.8% and 13.0%, respectively. This similarity results partly from the rarity, except for the United States, of presidential systems in which the electoral system or districting arrangements for the upper house differ much from those of the lower house. By using only

lower houses, we avoid multiplying the number observations for some countries, but not for othe that happen to be unicameral. There are 23 election in unicameral systems in the data set, plus eigh elections from France, which for present purpose may be considered effectively unicameral, given th weakness of its Senate (Lijphart 1984). That makes total of 31 effectively unicameral observations. Ther are 38 lower-house elections in the data set from countries with what Lijphart (ibid.) calls symmetri bicameralism (leaving the numerous U.S. observa tions for now). Adding upper houses would have added an additional 46 elections, but all from countries already covered. (Upper-house elections for at least some seats, occur more frequently in many countries than do lower-house elections.)

Veto Variable. A president is coded as having a vet only if a vote of at least two-thirds of the legislators is required to override it. In systems in which som types of legislation have different override require ments than others, the coding depended on what th veto override procedure is on the more important legislation, such as budgets. For example, the Cost Rican and Ecuadorian presidents have vetoes with a least two-thirds required to override on all legislation *except the budget.* Thus Costa Rica and Ecuador are scored as having no presidential veto. In Colombi before 1991, the situation was reversed, with th stronger veto being on most types of expenditure.

Legislators' Party Switching. Among the Philippine legislatures in the period of study, it was common fo members to be elected under the label of one party but subsequently switch to another party (Sour 1970). The same is currently true in Brazil (Mainwar ing 1991) and Ecuador (Conaghan 1994). In all cases, the label that a candidate bore in the election (i.e., the one revealed to voters) is the one that is counted Changing party affiliation once elected is not of concern here. Thus my data show episodes of divided government in the Philippines, even though presidents of the previously "out" party were generally able to entice sufficient defectors from the erstwhile majority party to cross party lines and form a congressional majority.

Notes

The author is grateful to John Carey and Gary Cox for several long discussions that helped clarify points and to Mark Jones, Scott Morgenstern, Steve Swindle, Rein Taagepera, and Michael Thies for their comments. Morgenstern also served as a research assistant, funded by the Ford Foundation. Octavio Amorim-Neto provided research assistance, funded by National Science Foundation Grant No. SES-9208753.

1. This vast literature cannot be reviewed thoroughly here. General studies of divided government include Cox and Kernell 1991; Fiorina 1992; and Jacobson 1990.

2. One twentieth-century concurrent election, that of 1916, had left neither party with a majority of seats.

3. Fiorina (1992) makes a similar point about another form

of comparative study of divided government—that focused on the states.

4. For the sake of illustration, I am assuming that there are only two parties with a realistic chance of winning the presidency and that they are competing for the median voter (Downs 1957). In the stylized proportional representation congressional election, however, there are more parties, some of which cater to more extreme policy positions.

5. To illustrate this argument, suppose the United States had several minor parties that stood to win congressional seats in addition to the Democratic and Republican parties. In such a case, some voters who currently vote straight tickets would become ticket-splitters (e.g., some who voted Democratic for president might vote for a Rainbow Coalition legislative slate).

6. This intuition is recognized by some who advocate reform of the United States system. Robinson suggests that congressional elections be held one month after presidential elections (when TDME = .021) in order to increase the probability of presidential majorities (1985, 117–19).

7. Indeed, until recently, some U.S. governors served for only two-year terms. The Chilean constitution of 1980 called for eight-year terms. If the effects of time are to be generalized, term length could make a large difference at the extremes. Might the choice of relative or absolute time depend on whether one posits that the electoral cycle effect stems from voter or elite calculations? An explanation based on voters may imply absolute time, as voters update their perceptions of the president's party based on new information upon which to base retrospective voting. An explanation based on elites may imply relative time, as elites look ahead to the remaining time in the term and thereby shape election outcomes. Because of the high correlation between absolute and relative time in the data, it is impossible to sort out these intriguing possibilities. However, this reasoning may help drive future modeling of the effects of timing of elections.

8. I add rejecting that of another to take account of the notion that voters may seldom vote with the idea of conferring a "mandate." Rather, they may vote retrospectively (Downs 1957; Fiorina 1981). For a very useful review of these perspectives, see Powell 1989.

9. Such a theory would leave no room for ticket splitting. However, increasing district magnitude (M) in the assembly election would predict greater ticket splitting, even if all voters were motivated by national policy priorities. Some voters would vote for a minor party for Congress but vote strategically between the two viable contenders for the presidency, for which M = 1. For detailed models with data, see Shugart 1988 and Shugart and Carey 1992.

10. To be sure that the results were not being swamped by the large number of observations from the United States, I checked the ratios with those observations excluded. The spread between the ratios of presidential to opposition majorities actually widens—4.7:1 for concurrent elections and 2.3:1 for nonconcurrent. The ratio in concurrent elections under localizing rules barely changes (2.0:1). The one result that is affected substantially is the ratio for nonconcurrent elections under localizing rules, which is identical to that seen for the concurrent elections (2.0:1). This is because the two-party system in the United States results in many more cases of presidents retaining their majorities even after (typically) losing seats at midterms than do the more typical multiparty systems elsewhere.

11. Is the United States in 1930 an additional occurrence? In that election the voters returned a majority of Republicans in the House of Representatives (while the Republicans continued to control the presidency), but by the time Congress convened, deaths and Democratic by-election victories gave the Democratic party a majority. As this study concerns itself with election day outcomes, it is reasonable to classify this case as one in which unified government was maintained by voters, albeit precariously.

12. The one case with opposition majority resulting from a change in the presidency in a system of nationalizing electoral

rules was a close call: in Costa Rica in 1966, the party with the legislative majority lost the presidency 50.5% to 49.5%.

13. Colombia is the one country that regularly uses very-late-term elections, held about two months before the next presidential election. These elections have been excluded from the regressions on cycle effects because they are less likely to be influenced by evaluations of the incumbent than they are to serve as part of the campaign for the successor. Indeed, Jones (1994) has classified the Colombian cycle as neither concurrent nor nonconcurrent, because while the elections are technically nonconcurrent, the terms of office are concurrent.

14. I have used seats rather than votes because what we are ultimately concerned with here is seats. The results are similar if we use votes (not shown for reasons of space) but less pronounced, owing to the tendency of nearly all electoral systems to give some bonus in seats to the party with the most votes (Rae 1967).

15. I have already justified the separate treatment of concurrent and nonconcurrent elections.

16. What about coding concurrent elections as TIME = 1, based on the outgoing president? I tried such a specification, and the results were unsatisfactory. Concurrent elections are therefore different in kind, not just in degree, from nonconcurrent elections.

17. The actual figures for TDME = .5 are −2.3% for seats. The corresponding figure for votes is −1.3%.

18. The coefficients (and standard errors) are (1) a constant of −.16 (.66), (2) 1.22 (.56) on TIME, (3) −.44 (.22) on NUMPAR, and (4) .80 (.52) on the U.S. dummy. If we exclude the USA dummy, NUMPAR becomes more significant and TIME remains significant. Thus it is the impact of the effective number of legislative parties, not that of TIME, that is weakened by the U.S. observations.

19. Other specifications were run with dummy variables for several countries for which there were many more observations than for others or that appeared to be possible outliers. None of these country dummies was significant and none had a more than negligible effect on the coefficients of the other variables. I also attempted to test for effects of economic growth, expecting that the sensitivity of seat shares to the electoral cycle might be affected by economic performance. However, data are available for most of these countries and time periods (if they are available at all) only on an annual basis, while what is needed is performance over the interval between elections. I tried several specifications and none produced a significant coefficient on the economic variable.

20. The t-score on TIME is −4.18. On TIME * LOCAL, it is 1.92.

21. With the United States excluded, the percentage of no-majority situations is much higher, 43.8%, but mainly because of the far less frequent occurrence of opposition majorities outside the United States (only 13.7%). Presidential majorities are only slightly less common outside the United States than in the United States—42.5%.

22. If the president is elected by plurality, that usually means just two major parties. If the president is elected by a majority-runoff system, the number of major parties may be higher. See Shugart and Taagepera (1994). Of the concurrent elections systems analyzed here, only Ecuador uses the majority-runoff system.

23. Pluralitylike rules include the U.S. electoral college, given that the electors themselves are chosen by plurality rule (on a statewide basis in most states), and the Costa Rican provision that a runoff is held only in the event that no candidate obtains 40% of the vote.

24. Such a conclusion would be supported also by the example of Colombia, where elections are technically nonconcurrent (except for 1974) but are generally held at the point at which over 90% of the time between presidential elections has elapsed. Therefore, they are nearly always concurrent, being held during the campaign for the next president. Their pattern resembles that of concurrent elections and localizing electoral

rules—an almost "pure" two-party system with occasional divided government.

25. Observations from Ecuador are excluded in these two statistical tests, as this is the only case for which concurrent elections and majority-runoff presidential elections are used in combination. As noted, the logic of the argument being tested applies to plurality rule for the presidency.

26. What is actually entered here is "effective" magnitude, which takes into account the effects of interdistrict variations in magnitude and of thresholds. See the Appendix.

27. Indeed, single-member districts are themselves localizing in the sense that they give each member a defined geographical constituency that he or she uniquely represents. However, the degree to which members can tailor their messages to their own districts varies according to how nationalizing other features of electoral and party rules are. Thus single-member districts in systems where the vote turns more on national concerns (e.g., in the United Kingdom and Canada), rather than on district characteristics (as in the United States) have a lower personal vote (Cain, Ferejohn, and Fiorina 1987) and also a greater number of parties (Epstein 1967; Shugart and Carey 1992, 226–29).

28. The coefficients (and standard errors) are as follows. With no dummy for the United States, the constant is .05 (.92), the coefficient on TDME is 1.14 (.55), and that on NUMPAR is −.52 (.25). With the U.S. dummy, the results are −.40 (.88), 1.20TDME (.56), −.39NUMPAR (.23), and .87USA (.52).

29. For reasons noted, these arguments about concurrent elections apply only when the president is elected by plurality or a similar electoral formula, not when majority runoff is used.

30. I have tried to avoid implying that the causal effects run in only one direction, from institutions to party organization to voter behavior. For instance, where, for whatever reasons, parties emerge as decentralized organizations, rules are likely to be adopted that weaken the nationalizing potential of elections. For present purposes, however, I am concerned with the proximate effect on voters' perceptions of whether or not their presidential and legislative votes have the same meaning with regard to national policy. Once chosen, rules affect behavior; such a statement by no means obviates the importance of analysis of the interests that lie behind the choice of rules.

31. In this vein, Palmer (1993) notes that unlike elections in Westminster parliamentary systems (and by extension in presidential systems that use nationalizing elections), which give voters policy options at election time, elections in what he terms the "congressional" U.S. system do little more than establish the identities of the players, who then "transact" with one another to produce policy.

32. The French constitution also provides for no presidential veto, thus obviating the need for coalitionlike government when the president faces an opposition majority. However, if (unlike France, but as in the United States and in Latin American presidentialism) the president retained control over the cabinet even in an opposition-majority situation and had no veto, it does not follow that governance would be smooth. Such a president remains chief executive, yet is practically assured of being marginalized in the legislative process, a situation that may have pernicious effects of its own, even tempting the president to use extraconstitutional measures to try to influence policy. For a fuller discussion of these issues and data on how often presidents have insufficient legislative support to be able to sustain vetoes, see Shugart and Mainwaring (n.d.)

References

Alesina, Alberto, and Howard Rosenthal. 1989. "Partisan Cycles in Congressional Elections and the Macroeconomy." *American Political Science Review* 83:373–98.

Archer, Ron. 1990. "Paralysis of Reform: Political Stability and

Social Conflict in Colombia." Ph.D. diss., University of California, Berkeley.

Born, Richard. 1990. "Surge and Decline, Negative Voting, and Midterm Loss Phenomenon: A Simultaneous Analysis." *American Journal of Political Science* 34:615–45.

Cain, Bruce, John Ferejohn, and Morris Fiorina. 1987. *The Personal Vote: Constituency Service and Electoral Independence.* Cambridge: Harvard University Press.

Campbell, Angus. 1960. "Surge and Decline: A Study of Electoral Change." *Public Opinion Quarterly* 24:397–418.

Carey, John M., and Matthew S. Shugart. N.d. "Incentives To Cultivate a Personal Vote: A Rank Ordering of Electoral Formulas." *Electoral Studies* 13:4. Forthcoming.

Conaghan, Catherine M. 1994. "Loose Parties, 'Floating' Politicians, and Institutional Stress: Presidentialism in Ecuador, 1979–1988." In *The Failure of Presidentialism Democracy*, ed. Juan J. Linz and Arturo Valenzuela. Baltimore: Johns Hopkins University Press.

Cox, Gary W., and Samuel Kernell, eds. 1991. *The Politics of Divided Government.* Boulder: Westview.

Cox, Gary W., and Matthew S. Shugart. N.d. "In the Absence of Vote Pooling: Nomination and Allocation Errors in Colombia." *Electoral Studies.* Forthcoming.

Cruz-Coke, Ricardo. 1984. *Historia electoral de Chile, 1925–1973.* Santiago, Chile: Editorial Jurídica de Chile.

Cutler, Lloyd N. 1980. "To Form a Government." *Foreign Affairs* 59:126–43.

Downs, Anthony. 1957. *An Economic Theory of Democracy.* New York: Harper & Row.

Duverger, Maurice. 1980. "A New Political System Model: Semi-presidential Government." *European Journal of Political Research* 8:165–87.

Epstein, Leon. 1967. *Political Parties in Western Democracies.* New Brunswick, NJ: Transaction Books.

Erickson, Robert S. 1988. "The Puzzle of Midterm Loss." *Journal of Politics* 50:1011–29.

Fiorina, Morris P. 1981. *Retrospective Voting in American National Elections.* New Haven: Yale University Press.

Fiorina, Morris P. 1988. "The Reagan Years: Turning to the Right or Groping Toward the Middle?" In *The Resurgence of Conservatism in Anglo-American Democracies*, ed. Barry Cooper, Allan Kornberg, and William Mishler. Durham, NC: Duke University Press.

Fiorina, Morris. 1992. *Divided Government.* New York: Macmillan.

Geddes, Barbara. 1990. "Democratic Institutions as a Bargain among Self-Interested Politicians." Presented at the annual meeting of the American Political Science Association, San Francisco.

Gil, Federico. 1966. *The Political System of Chile.* Boston: Houghton Mifflin.

Hinckley, Barbara. 1967. "Interpreting House Midterm Elections: Toward a Measurement of the In-Party's 'Expected' Loss of Seats." *American Political Science Review* 61:694–700.

Ingberman, Daniel, and John Villani. 1993. "An Institutional Theory of Divided Government and Party Polarization." *American Journal of Political Science* 37:429–71.

Jacobson, Gary C. 1990. *The Electoral Origins of Divided Government: Competition in U.S. House Elections, 1946–1988.* Boulder: Westview.

Jones, Mark P. 1994. *Electoral Laws and the Survival of Presidential Democracies.* Ph.D. diss., University of Michigan.

Kernell, Samuel. 1977. "Presidential Popularity and Negative Voting: An Alternative Explanation of the Midterm Congressional Decline of the President's Party." *American Political Science Review* 71:44–66.

Lijphart, Arend. 1984. *Democracies: Patterns of Majoritarian and Consensus Government in Twenty-One Countries.* New Haven: Yale University Press.

Lijphart, Arend. 1994. *Electoral Systems and Party Systems in Twenty-Seven Democracies, 1945–1990.* Oxford: Oxford University Press.

Linz, Juan J. 1990. "The Perils of Presidentialism." *Journal of Democracy* 1:51–69.

Linz, Juan J. 1994. "Democracy, Presidential or Parliamentary: Does It Make a Difference?" In *The Failure of Presidential Democracy*, ed. Juan J. Linz and Arturo Valenzuela. Baltimore: Johns Hopkins University Press.

McCubbins, Mathew D. 1991. "Party Politics, Divided Government, and Budget Deficits." In *Parallel Politics*, ed. Samuel Kernell. Washington: Brookings Institution.

Mackie, Thomas T., and Richard Rose. 1992. *The International Almanac of Electoral History*. Washington: Congressional Quarterly Press.

Mainwaring, Scott. 1991. "Politicians, Parties, and Electoral Systems: Brazil in Comparative Perspective." *Comparative Politics*, October, pp. 21–43.

Mainwaring, Scott. 1993. "Presidentialism, Multipartism, and Democracy: The Difficult Combination." *Comparative Political Studies* 26:198–228.

Mayhew, David R. 1991. *Divided We Govern: Party Control, Lawmaking, and Investigations, 1946-1990*. New Haven: Yale University Press.

Nogueira Alcala, Humberto. 1986. *El régimen semipresidencial: Una nueva forma de gobierno democrática?* Santiago, Chile: Editorial Andante.

Nohlen, Dieter, ed. 1993. *Enciclopedia electoral Latinoamericana y del Caribe*. San Jose, Costa Rica: Instituto Interamericano de Derechos Humanos.

Palmer, Matthew S. R. 1993. *Constitutional Design and Law: The Political Economy of Cabinet and Congressional Government*. J.S.D. diss., Yale University.

Philippines, Republic of. Commission of Elections. Various years. *Report of the Commission of Elections on Elections to the President of the Philippines and the Congress*. Manila: Bureau of Printing.

Pierce, Roy. 1990. "The Executive Divided against Itself: France 1986-1988." Paper presented at the annual meeting of the American Political Science Association, San Francisco.

Pinckney, Thomas M. 1971. *Third Parties in the Philippines*. Ph.D. diss., University of Tennessee.

Powell, G. Bingham, Jr. 1989. "Constitutional Design and Citizen Electoral Control." *Journal of Theoretical Politics* 1:107–30.

Rae, Douglas W. 1967. *The Political Consequences of Electoral Laws*. New Haven: Yale University Press.

Robinson, Donald L., ed. 1985. *Reforming American Government: The Bicentennial Papers of the Committee on the Constitutional System*. Boulder: Westview.

Shugart, Matthew S. 1988. *Duverger's Rule, District Magnitude, and Presidentialism*. Ph.D. diss., University of California, Irvine.

Shugart, Matthew S., and John M. Carey. 1992. *Presidents and Assemblies: Constitutional Design and Electoral Dynamics*. New York: Cambridge University Press.

Shugart, Matthew S., and Scott Mainwaring. N.d. "Conclusion: Varieties of Presidentialism." In *Presidential Democracy in Latin America*, ed. Scott Mainwaring and Matthew S. Shugart. Forthcoming.

Shugart, Matthew S., and Rein Taagepera. 1994. "Plurality Versus Majority Election of Presidents: A Proposal for a Double Complement Rule." *Comparative Political Studies* 27:323–48.

Sours, Martin H. 1970. "Philippine Political Parties: A Background Analysis in Political Development." *Philippine Journal of Public Administration* 14:384–96.

Strøm, Kaare. 1990. *Minority Government and Majority Rule*. New York: Cambridge University Press.

Suleiman, Ezra N. 1994. "Presidentialism and Political Stability in France." In *The Failure of Presidential Democracy*, ed. Juan J. Linz and Arturo Valenzuela. Baltimore: Johns Hopkins University Press.

Sundquist, James L. 1986. *Constitutional Reform and Effective Government*. Washington: Brookings Institution.

Sundquist, James L. 1988. "Needed: A Political Theory for the New Era of Coalition Government in the United States." *Political Science Quarterly* 103:613–35.

Taagepera, Rein, and Matthew S. Shugart. 1989. *Seats and Votes: The Effects and Determinants of Electoral Systems*. New Haven: Yale University Press.

Tufte, Edward R. 1975. "Determinants of the Outcomes of Midterm Congressional Elections." *American Political Science Review* 69:812–26.

Valenzuela, Arturo. 1994. "Party Politics and the Crisis of Presidentialism in Chile: A Proposal for a Parliamentary Form of Government." In *The Failure of Presidential Democracy*, ed. Juan J. Linz and Arturo Valenzuela. Baltimore: Johns Hopkins University Press.

Zupan, Mark A. 1991. "An Economic Explanation for the Existence and Nature of Political Ticket Splitting." *Journal of Law and Economics* 34:343–69.

Matthew Soberg Shugart is Associate Professor of Political Science, University of California at San Diego, La Jolla, CA 92093-0519.

The party system consequences of Chile's "binomial" (two-member-district) legislative electoral formula have been the subject of much debate. For some analysts, the binomial system limits party system fractionalization and encourages centripetal competition, enhancing the prospects for democratic stability. Others emphasize elements of continuity within the country's historic multiparty system and contend that the electoral formula may prove destabilizing. This article, arguing that limited electoral reform has limited party system consequences, provides comparative empirical measures showing that neither the degree of party system fractionalization nor the competitive dynamic of the party system has been substantially transformed. However, the binomial formula does increase the incentives for coalition formation and maintenance. The article concludes that the ultimate consequences of electoral reform depend on whether these new incentives for coalition formation can overcome the elements of continuity within the party system in the long term.

CONTINUITY AND CHANGE IN THE CHILEAN PARTY SYSTEM
On the Transformational Effects of Electoral Reform

PETER SIAVELIS
Wake Forest University

During the 1980s and 1990s, many of the world's democracies have experienced an erosion of public confidence in democratic institutions and electoral processes. Notably, these crises have occurred not only in new and fragile democracies where they have come to be expected but also in democracies with impressive records of longevity. In countries as diverse as

AUTHOR'S NOTE: *I acknowledge the support of a Fulbright-Hays fellowship that financed the fieldwork in Chile on which this study is based. Research for this article was undertaken while I was a visiting professor at the Institute of Political Science at the Catholic University of Chile. I am grateful to Gary Cox, Mark Jones, Arend Lijphart, Burt Monroe, Matthew Shugart, David Samuels, Arturo Valenzuela, Helga Welsh, and two anonymous reviewers from CPS for their useful comments and suggestions.*

COMPARATIVE POLITICAL STUDIES, Vol. 30 No. 6, December 1997 651-674
© 1997 Sage Publications, Inc.

651

Brazil, Israel, and Italy, proportional representation (PR) electoral systems have been identified as one of the main culprits contributing to a severe crisis of representation. Political leaders and the public have responded with calls for electoral reform, often underscoring the need to adopt systems of plurality election or to fundamentally reform PR systems, given the underlying assumption that such changes will lead to party system transformation and increased political effectiveness.

The question of how distinct electoral formulae affect party systems has occupied a central place in the study of electoral laws. Perhaps the most debated questions in the field of electoral theory are whether majority/plurality electoral formulae or small magnitude electoral systems have the capacity to exercise a reductive effect on the number of political parties and whether such systems encourage centripetal drives within the party system (Cox, 1984, 1990; Lijphart, 1990a; Lijphart & Grofman, 1984; Sartori, 1986; Shugart, 1985).

Advocates of plurality electoral systems often underscore the superiority of this type of formula based on the supposition that it leads to the formation of two-party systems or at the very least to centripetal competition in multiparty systems. This logic has also been extended to suggest that small magnitude PR systems exert similar effects on the party system (Sartori, 1968). Given the integrative dynamic these types of formulae are said to produce, proponents argue that they rationalize electoral choice, provide greater identification between the legislator and the elector, and produce more consistent parliamentary majorities— all of which contribute to more effective public policy and enhanced democratic stability (Duverger, 1954; Hermens, 1941; Lardeyret, 1991; Quade, 1991).[1]

However, an issue that has often gotten lost in this academic and political discussion of "stability" and "governability" is whether the reform of PR systems in multiparty contexts will actually lead to party system integration and centripetal competition. How relevant are established theoretical connections between electoral and party systems when dealing with a change in electoral laws in countries where there is already a developed, well-entrenched party system? Despite a great deal of theoretical discussion, little empirical evidence has been offered measuring the actual effects of such a change in the context of consolidated multipartism.

---

1. A strong counterargument can and has been made. Sartori (1976, p. 139) underscores the important role that PR systems can play in ensuring the loyalty of all party sectors to the institutions of democracy by providing an opportunity for participation within them, whereas Lijphart (1991) points to the importance of the role of PR systems in providing mechanisms for negotiation and consensus in divided societies.

This lack of empirical treatment is understandable for two reasons. First, in consolidated democracies there are relatively few cases in which this type of comprehensive change in electoral systems has taken place on the national level. Because electoral systems serve the interests of governing parties, there is little incentive for elites to change the system that brought them to power. Second, in polities where fundamental electoral system change has been undertaken on the national level, it is often carried out in a situation of democratic crisis or reformulation, where the effects of such a change are difficult to gauge because of the attendant problems that often exist.

Given the increased tendency to attempt to rectify performance problems in diverse democracies through electoral reform, it is important to analyze the consequences of changing electoral formulae in polities characterized by well-institutionalized parties. How do the theoretical assertions outlined above apply in this context? Can the actions and decisions of party actors exert forces that are stronger than those produced by the electoral system? What strategies do party organizations adopt to counteract the potential transformational effects of electoral system change? How does other electoral legislation affect the party system impact of electoral reform?

THE CHILEAN DEBATE

Chile serves as an excellent case study to explore some of the questions elaborated above. The case offers a rare test of the electoral/party system relationship, because the electoral formula in use since the return of procedural democracy in 1989 did not emerge as a result of negotiations and choice by political parties themselves but rather was imposed by an outgoing military regime. During the democratic transition process, military reformers and their civilian allies used their considerable leverage to impose a series of constitutional and electoral changes aimed at party system transformation in an effort to remedy what they perceived as the unhealthy nature of polarized and ideological party competition in the country. The most important of these reforms was the adoption of an electoral formula with two-member districts, or a *binominal* system, designed to temper the negative consequences of the often fractious and ideological party system.[2]

---

2. I employ the term *binominal*, a similar cognate in English. Two-member districts are not common, although they do exist at the state level in the United States. The mechanical effects of this electoral formula are discussed by Taagepera (1984) and by Cox (1984).

65

Echoing civilian and military reformers, some scholars argue that the new electoral system encourages centripetal competition and will limit party system fragmentation (Guzmán, 1993; Rabkin, 1996). Other proponents of the binomial electoral system have underscored that, whereas the new system has not reduced the number of parties, it has changed the competitive dynamic of the party system (Gutiérrez, 1989; Guzmán, 1993). They point to the pattern of competition between the center-left Concertación coalition and the center-right Unión por el Progreso electoral alliance (which has existed since the return of democracy) as evidence of a fundamental change in the traditional pattern of party competition.³ Although the binomial reform has not succeeded in creating a two-party system, they contend that it has created a bipolar pattern of party competition that represents a departure from the historical pattern of three-bloc competition between ideological pillars of the right, center, and left. These scholars argue that when coupled with the ideological transformation of Chilean society, this pattern of competition may eventually lead to a two-party system or, at the very least, to the routinization of the extant pattern of bipolar competition.

Others argue that although there has not been a significant reduction in the number of political parties, numerical criteria are less important than they have been in the past. For these scholars, much of the literature on the effects of the binomial system misses the point by focusing on parties rather than electoral lists as the units of analysis. What really matters is the number of lists vying for electoral support in the long term. They point out that in Chile the binomial system has encouraged a pattern of competition between two major party lists, making for what amounts in practice to competition between two parties (Baldez & Carey, 1996, p. 12).

Contrary to these arguments, proponents of a PR option for Chile argue that the binomial system fails to discourage party fragmentation, does not encourage centripetal competition, and actually promotes divisiveness, posing a threat to democratic governability (Siavelis, 1993; Valenzuela & Siavelis, 1991). These scholars assume that parties rather than lists are the fundamental units of analysis for understanding the composition of the Chilean party system. They argue that the elements of continuity that characterize party competition are more important than advocates of the binomial system suggest, and that the electoral formula is both inappropriate and potentially destabilizing given this reality.

This article evaluates the tenability of the arguments discussed above by analyzing empirical evidence from the Chilean case. It asks a number of

3. The Unión por el Progreso coalition was called Democracia y Progreso during the 1989 elections.

questions: First, has the electoral system reduced the number of relevant political parties in Chile? Second, has the electoral system succeeded in transforming the competitive dynamic of the party system? In other words, is the competitive dynamic bipolar, tripolar, or something else? Is the direction of competition centripetal or centrifugal? Finally, even if the number of parties has not been reduced, what is the significance of the emergence of a more coherent form of coalition politics in Chile? Are pacts, rather than parties, a more significant unit of analysis for evaluating the effects of the binomial system?

This article argues that Chilean parties have adopted strategies to overcome any of the reductive tendencies that the electoral system might produce. Party leaders have engaged in frenzied negotiations before each election to construct electoral lists that allow the participation of a number of significant political parties very close to those that characterized the preauthoritarian era. Just as before the military regime, the most recent parliamentary elections in 1989 and 1993 demonstrated that there are four or five parties with significant levels of support and several minor parties that also gained legislative representation.

A number of indications also make it clear that the three-way competitive dynamic that has traditionally characterized the Chilean party system continues to persist both at the electoral and elite levels, despite an emerging pattern of bipolar competition. In addition, rather than encouraging centripetal competition, as scholars have suggested, the binomial system may do exactly the opposite.

Finally, there are increased incentives to form electoral pacts under the binomial system, and participation in a pact is more important for electoral success than it was in the preauthoritarian era, particularly for smaller parties. However, it is a mistake simply to treat the current coalitions that exist as if they were parties. Although pacts have been of undeniable importance in the immediate postauthoritarian period, their significance has been exaggerated by the pattern of bipolarity produced by the democratic transition.

In essence, this article argues that the Chilean binomial system has not had the party system transformational effects that some authors have suggested nor is it likely to in the future. Rather, in the Chilean case, limited electoral reform has had, and will have, limited party system consequences. One might expect the binomial system to have had more of an effect on the party system if a more restrictive or *stronger* electoral system (in Sartori's, 1968, terms) had been adopted. For example, if joint party lists had been banned, if a single-member district system had been adopted, or if a similar two-member electoral system had been employed for local and national elections, perhaps the electoral system would have had more party system consequences.

This does not suggest that the binomial system has had no effect. Given that only two seats are available in each district in a country characterized by four to five significant parties, the system does provide increased incentives for the formation of electoral pacts. Thus, the binomial system has made coalition formation both more likely and more important for electoral success than it was during the preauthoritarian era. Once the somewhat unique contextual features of the transition to democracy fade in importance, perhaps the most significant question for the future is whether the forces of continuity within the party system in terms of the number of parties and the underlying ideological divisions will prove stronger than the incentives for the formation of electoral pacts.

THE TRANSITION TO DEMOCRACY
AND ELECTORAL ENGINEERING

Despite the systemic political crises of the late 1960s and early 1970s, for most of its history Chile was a relatively stable multiparty democracy with well-institutionalized parties and a PR electoral system. Following an almost 17-year interregnum of military rule beginning in 1973, and a pacted democratic transition characterized by negotiation between civilian political elites and the incumbent military regime, the party system reemerged with many of the salient features that characterized it in the preauthoritarian period (Scully & Valenzuela, 1993; Siavelis, 1993; Valenzuela & Siavelis, 1991).[4] However, civilian authorities inherited a fundamentally different institutional and legal landscape.

Military reformers contended that the intensely competitive and often polarized nature of the Chilean party system and the political deadlock it produced were among the principal precipitating conditions of the military intervention of 1973. Military authorities made it clear that they sought to design an electoral formula that would help lead to centripetal competition, party system integration, and eventually, the establishment of a two-party system or limited multipartism.

The most obvious choice would seem to have been the adoption of the Anglo-American, single-member-district system. However, military authorities, relying on the counsel of civilian constitutional advisors Jaime Guzmán

---

4. This does not suggest the absence of important changes in the party system. A process of ideological reorientation has occurred within the parties of the right and the left. I refer to similarities in terms of the number of major parties and the nature of the most significant cleavages within Chilean society. For a discussion of the continuity of the Chilean party system in the post-Pinochet era, see Scully and Valenzuela (1993).

and Sergio Fernández, rejected a pure plurality formula because of the likely short-term political implications it would have had. Judging from the results of the 1988 plebiscite on the continued rule of General Augusto Pinochet, reformers anticipated that the political right could only rely on approximately 40% of the national vote. If the forces of the democratic opposition succeeded in forming a broad-based coalition, they could easily win almost all of the seats in congress with a single-member system. This would result in the near exclusion of parties of the right from congress, the majority of which were supporters of the preceding military regime.

The designers decided on the adoption of an electoral system with district magnitudes (M) of two (M = 2). By instituting such a system, they believed they could achieve both the long-term goal of party system transformation and at the same time guarantee representation and legislative veto power for the political right. Military reformers and their civilian allies developed a system that, in theory, ingeniously balances these two goals.

According to the law, for the elections to the Chamber of Deputies, every party or electoral alliance can present two candidates in each of the 60 electoral districts. For elections to the Senate, the binomial system is also employed in 19 senatorial districts. Electors may choose a single candidate from a series of two-candidate open lists. The individual garnering the highest number of votes wins the first seat in each district. However, given the operational characteristics of the D'Hondt PR system in two-member districts, for an electoral list to win both seats, it must double the vote of its nearest competitor. Therefore, certain thresholds exist for parties to obtain seats. In each district, to obtain one seat, a party or coalition must have at least 33.4% of the votes of the two largest parties or coalitions, and to win both seats it must win 66.7% of said vote. The military and parties of the right doubted that the electoral list of the democratic opposition would be able to muster 66.7% of the vote across districts nationally. Therefore, the binomial system would enable the right to win one of the two seats in each district (or 50% of the seats) with only 40% of the vote.

The binomial system did, indeed, favor the parties of right in the 1989 and 1993 elections, although not to the extent predicted by military reformers.[5] For both elections, the parties of the center left were quite successful in forming a broad-based coalition rather than falling victim to squabbling and division as the parties of the right and the military had hoped. The complete unity of purpose of the center left Concertación coalition prevented the right from winning a majority in the Chamber of Deputies in both elections. The

5 Valenzuela and Siavelis (1991, pp 39-48) provide proportionality indices measuring the extent to which the parties of right were favored in the 1989 elections.

center-right Unión por el Progreso alliance also failed to achieve an elective majority in the Senate. However, the existence of nine "institutional" Senators appointed by the outgoing military regime has given the right de facto veto power in the upper house during the two postauthoritarian governments of Christian Democratic Presidents Patricio Aylwin and Eduardo Frei.

THE NUMBER OF PARTIES

Although the designers of the electoral system were moderately successful in their effort to provide overrepresentation of the right in legislative elections, did they achieve their second goal of party system transformation? The effect of electoral formulae on the number of political parties was addressed in its most classic form by Duverger (1954), in one of what have become known generally as "Duverger's laws." Duverger's thesis that the "simple majority, single ballot system favors the two-party system" has been debated in the literature for decades, as has his contention that this relationship approaches the status of a "true sociological law" (p. 217).

Sartori (1986) correctly underscores the tendency of scholars to dismiss Duverger's (1954) laws instead of "giving them another and better try." In an attempt to do so, Sartori updates Duverger's thesis in the form of a tendency statement contending that, "Plurality formulas facilitate (are facilitating conditions of) a two-party format and, conversely, obstruct (are an obstructive condition of) multipartyism" (p. 64). Most scholars of electoral theory would accept this kind of theoretical relationship between plurality systems and their effects on the party system.[6]

However, the debate on the relationship between electoral laws and their party system effects is complicated by the question of variations within what are commonly considered the two major "types" of electoral formulae: majority/plurality and PR. The distinction between the two is often a false one, given that many variables affect the proportionality of PR systems, including district magnitude, minimum thresholds, and the counting system. In this sense, plurality and proportional systems are really the two end points on a continuum of electoral systems.

Indeed, because the Chilean system is characterized by district magnitudes of two, one could argue correctly that it is not a pure plurality system but

6. In his study of 22 democratic regimes, Lijphart (1984, p. 158) found that in every case but two there was a correlation between plurality formulae and two-party systems or a corresponding relationship between PR and multipartism. Riker (1986) discusses in detail some of the exceptions to this general rule.

rather a proportional system characterized by magnitudes of two. Nonetheless, district magnitude has come to be recognized as one of the most important variables affecting the functional dynamic of electoral systems (Lijphart, 1990b). As Lijphart and Grofman (1984) have convincingly demonstrated, the effects of low-magnitude proportional formulae on party systems are often more similar to those exerted by majority/plurality systems.[7] In this regard, the most important variables that distinguish electoral systems from one another are the proportionality between seats and votes that a given system produces and whether large and small parties are penalized or helped by it. Given the strong effect of low district magnitude on these two variables, in theoretical terms one would expect that a system with M = 2 should have a similar, but slightly less forceful, reductive effect on the number of political parties in comparison to a single-member system. Thus, the functional dynamic of the Chilean electoral system is certainly much closer to that of a plurality system t
han a proportional one

MEASURES OF RELEVANT PARTIES

Given that there have only been two legislative elections since the return of democracy to Chile, it is difficult to draw definitive conclusions concerning the number of parties that will remain relevant in the future. Nonetheless, one can arrive at a preliminary comparative measure of the number of parties that exist in Chile today and compare it to the historical average.

In determining relevance, it is not sufficient to simply count the number of parties with representation in parliament. Given the permissiveness of the preauthoritarian Chilean PR system, many of the parties with small parliamentary contingents in the past were neither very relevant nor did they have a significant level of national support. Also, given the exclusionary characteristics of the binomial system, it is possible for parties to have relevance and receive a significant share of the national vote without winning much representation in congress. Simply counting the number of parties in congress does not reveal much, but how relevant is a party if it does not even have one representative in congress?

Table 1 reflects these considerations. First, the table presents data on the number of parties that elected at least one deputy in each election between

7. Lijphart and Grofman (1984) underscore the importance of whether a particular electoral system satisfies the principle of proportionality on which PR systems are based. Lijphart (1990b) has more recently and forcefully restated the importance of district magnitude and particularly its relation to the degree of proportionality electoral systems are able to achieve.

Table 1

Measures of Electoral Parties in Chilean Chamber of Deputies Elections, 1925-1993. Based on Percentage of National Vote Received

Year	Number of Parties With Representatives in Chamber	Number of Parties that are of "Simple Relevance"[a]	Percentage of Vote Received by Parties With "Simple Relevance"[a]	Laakso and Taagepera Index (N_v) "Effective Parties"	Molinar Index (NP_v) "Number of Parties"
1925	4	4	95.9	4.17	3.34
1932	17	6	72.5	9.31	7.44
1937	11	4	71.9	6.93	5.75
1941	12	5	85.5	6.50	5.55
1945	12	6	84.6	6.66	5.19
1949	14	5	74.1	7.08	5.72
1953	18	7	68.7	11.89	9.63
1957	13	7	79.0	8.62	6.19
1961	7	7	99.5	6.44	5.40
1965	7	6	93.4	4.07	1.92
1969	5	5	94.9	4.92	3.58
1973	8	4	84.2	5.19	3.91
Mean	10.67	5.5	83.68	6.82	5.30
Median	11.50	5.5			
1989	10	4	75.40	7.83	4.69
1993	7	5	82.48	6.29	4.38

Source. 1925 to 1969: Nohlen (1993), 1973: Valenzuela (1978), 1989: Nohlen (1993), 1993 Participa (1993). All indices were computed by the author.
a. Those parties with at least one representative in the Chamber of Deputies and that polled at least 5% nationally.

also summarizes the number of parties that elected a minimum of one member to the lower house and also received at least 5% of the national vote, or what I call a measure of *simple relevance*. Despite the existence of more sophisticated criteria for determining party relevance, it is important not to ignore this elementary measure. Although not definitive, it provides valuable information about the basic characteristics of the party system.

In addition, two widely accepted measures of party relevance are also presented: Laakso and Taagepera's (1979) "effective number of parties" (*N*) and Molinar's (1991) "number of parties" (*NP*). Both can be computed either on the basis of the percentage of votes received or the percentage of parliamentary seats held by each party. Those presented here are based on the percentage of national vote. The Laakso and Taagepera index is a measure of the effective number of parties, based on Rae's (1971, pp. 47-64) "index of party fractionalization" (*F*), but it provides the added benefit of a more tangible depiction of fractionalization that closely approximates the actual number of parties.[8] The Molinar index (NP) is also a measure of the number of parties, but it seeks to provide a more realistic depiction of the actual importance of parties by controlling for the tendency of other indices to give too much numerical weight to large parties and to be excessively sensitive to small ones.[9] Table 1 presents all of this data for Chilean Chamber of Deputies elections between 1925 and 1973, the mean indices from all elections during this period, as well as the indices for the 1989 and 1993 elections.

It is clear from Table 1 that the binomial system has not resulted in a notable decrease in the number of political parties. Although Chile's preauthoritarian PR system permitted the representation of a greater number of small parties in the Chamber of Deputies, the binomial system has not succeeded in substantially reducing the number of *relevant* political parties. In the 1989 and 1993 elections, the number of parties that were successful in garnering more than 5% of the vote and gaining representation in the chamber is about the same as in the preauthoritarian period, as is the percentage of the total vote received by these parties. Indeed, it is interesting that for the 1993 elections, the number of parties that fit the criteria of "simple relevance" actually increased from the 1989 election.

More important, the more sophisticated measures of party relevance also demonstrate remarkable continuity. The Laakso and Taagepera (1979) index demonstrates a number of "effective parties" very close to the historical average. Although the Molinar (1991) measure of the NP shows slightly less fractionalization than the historical average, it is not a significant difference.

8. Rae's (1971) index measures the probability that any two randomly selected voters will have chosen a different party for each election: (F_e), where T_i = any party's decimal share of the vote.

$$F_e = 1 - \{ \Sigma T_i^2 \}.$$

The Laakso and Taagepera (1979) index of the effective number of parties is really a variation of Rae's index. N = number of relevant parties, where P_i = share of votes garnered by the ith party

$$N = 1/(\Sigma p_i^2).$$

9. To control for difficulties with other indices, Molinar (1991) argues for counting the winning party as one, regardless of its size (because it is surely relevant), and then determining the effect of minority parties. Molinar's index (NP) is as follows:

$$NP = 1 + N \frac{(\Sigma P_i^2) - P_1^2}{\Sigma P_i 2}, \text{ where } N = 1/\Sigma P_i^2$$

and P_1^2 is the proportion of votes of the winning party, squared.

average. Although the Molinar (1991) measure of the NP shows slightly less fractionalization than the historical average, it is not a significant difference. What is more, Table 1 demonstrates a downward trend in the fractionalization of the party system and in the number of relevant parties from an historic high in 1953, despite the fact that a PR electoral system was used throughout the 1953 to 1973 period. The mean indices for fractionalization and the number of relevant parties, then, really are above the historical norm for the past 20 years of Chilean democracy. If the mean indices for the period between 1961 and 1973 are considered, the current indices of the NP and N are actually higher. Despite the adoption of an electoral system characterized by small district magnitudes, all of the measures of party fractionalization and the number of relevant parties demonstrate a strikingly consistent pattern to when the PR electoral system was in force.

EXPLAINING PARTY SYSTEM CONTINUITY: MORE THAN JUST MAGNITUDE

What explains this continuity, and why has there not been a significant reduction in the number of relevant parties as some scholars have argued has been or should be the case? For those students of Chilean electoral politics who argue that the binomial system will lead to the formation of a two-party system, part of the answer lies in having overlooked theoretical and empirical work on the effect of district magnitude. Expecting that $M = 2$ should translate into the formation of a two-party system is as fallacious as the presumption that $M = 1$ will create a one-party system. Taagepera and Shugart (1989, p. 144) have suggested an empirical equation for the effective number of electoral parties (N_v) based on district magnitude, which for the binomial system produces an $N_v = 2.9$. Taagepera and Shugart (1993) also propose a theoretical measure for the effective number of parliamentary parties (N_s)

10. Miranda (1982) analyzes this process of "defractionalization" in the Chilean party system during the 1960s.

11. This conclusion departs from some other work analyzing the effect of electoral system change. Shugart's (1992) study of electoral reform in PR systems concludes that although there are no immediate effects following electoral system transformation, parties adjust "after just a few elections" (p. 207). It also departs from Sartori's (1968, p. 61) conclusion that a "strong" party system subject to the effects of a "strong" electoral system will exert reductive pressures within the party system.

12. Taagepera and Shugart's (1989) equation for the number of effective electoral parties is $N_v = 1.25(2 + \log M)$. Taagepera and Shugart's (1993) theoretical model for the number of parliamentary parties is $N_s = 85(MS)^{1/16}$ where M = magnitude and S = assembly size.

From another perspective, the indices that result from the Taagepera and Shugart (1989, 1993) models would seem to provide support for those who avoid the narrow presumption that a two-party system will emerge and make a more general argument for decreased party system fractionalization. However, predictive models based only on magnitude and assembly size are incomplete. In the Chilean case, there are additional variables that hamper the potential reductive capacity of the electoral system, suggesting that the actual number of relevant parties will remain higher than these two models predict and can help to explain why the data in Table 1 suggest the existence of such an elevated number of relevant political parties.

First, to ensure their continued existence, small parties have adapted to the electoral system and retained the ability to achieve congressional representation by negotiating with large parties for positions on electoral lists. Given the importance of the 33.4% and 66.7% electoral thresholds referred to earlier, larger parties may feel a need to include in their coalition a smaller, ideologically nearby party to attract extra support. Because small parties can hold forth the promise of attracting additional votes, large parties are willing to share in the allocation of a small number of electoral slates in exchange for extra anticipated votes that can help electoral alliances cross one of the crucial thresholds. Smaller parties also are aware that the only way to win legislative seats is to negotiate to join a larger coalition. By forcing a process of negotiation among all party sectors to form joint lists for legislative representation, the binomial system, contrary to its designers intentions, has actually contributed to the continued existence of small parties.

Second, although the binomial formula is employed on the national level for the election to the Chamber of Deputies and the Senate, a PR system is used for the election of local authorities. This helps to guarantee the continued existence of and differentiation among smaller parties given their ability to achieve representation on the local level with relatively smaller percentages of the votes than they need to win representation on the national level. Even if the national electoral system were capable of producing something of a reductive effect, the local electoral system has the capacity to keep the multiparty system alive, because smaller parties retain the ability to effectively compete in at least one electoral arena. The existence of two levels of elections, each of which is based on a different principle of representation, reinforces the continued existence of small parties. It also serves to increase the leverage of smaller parties in the national negotiation process if they can demonstrate significant electoral appeal on the local level.

THE BINOMIAL ELECTORAL LAW AND THE COMPETITIVE DYNAMIC OF THE CHILEAN PARTY SYSTEM

Party systems cannot be adequately described by simply counting the number of parties or coalitions. The nature, direction, and pattern of competition must also be taken into consideration.

Some analysts of Chilean electoral politics have argued that, although the binomial system has not reduced the effective number of parties, it has changed the competitive dynamic of the party system (Guzmán, 1993; Rabkin, 1996). They contend that the dynamic of three-way competition between the center, right, and left—often referred to as a pattern of *tres tercios* (three thirds)—has been fundamentally transformed. Although the binomial system has not succeeded in creating a two-party system, they contend, it has created a bipolar and centripetal pattern of party competition that may eventually lead to the formation of a two-party system. How valid is this contention?

These analysts are correct in noting that for the last two congressional and presidential elections something of a bipolar pattern of competition has existed between an alliance of the center left (the Concertación) set off against another of the center right (Unión por el Progreso). Since the return of democracy, in both presidential elections each electoral coalition was successful in choosing a single presidential candidate, for what essentially amounted to a two-candidate race. In addition, each of the coalitions presented joint electoral lists following negotiations between its various component parties, making for a pattern of competition between two major coalitions for both presidential and legislative elections. Although these phenomena suggest the appearance of an incipient bipolar dynamic, they do not necessarily signal a fundamental transformation in the dynamic of party competition from the preauthoritarian period.

The simple existence of two major presidential candidates and two legislative lists does not necessarily signal the advent of a long-term pattern of bipolar competition. Historically, the three-bloc configuration of party competition in Chile has elicited certain types of coalition behavior that are generalizable for most of the preauthoritarian period. Since 1932, with only two exceptions (Jorge Alessandri in 1958 and Salvador Allende in 1970), every elected president has been a center-party candidate relying on either the support of the left or the right. A center candidate was elected with the support of the left on three occasions (1938, 1942, and 1946), once with the support of the right (1964) and twice with the support of both the right and the left (1932 and 1952). It is possible that the current dynamic is simply a recurrence of a similar historical phenomenon. That is to say, rather than a bipolar pattern of competition, what really occurred in 1989 and in 1993 was the election of centrist candidates with the support of the moderate left.

In terms of legislative elections, coalition formation has also been a historic necessity. Only once, in 1965, did a party (the Christian Democrats-PDC) garner a majority in a national congressional election. Given this pattern of competition and despite the existence of three major ideological blocs, legislators often coalesced into two groups—one supporting the government and one acting as an opposition. So, just as in the case of presidential elections, the current coalescence of legislative membership into two major groups does not necessarily signal a pattern of bipolar competition.

Indeed, although the Christian Democrats are certainly the dominant party in contemporary Chile, no party is capable of garnering a majority in legislative elections. It is important to bear in mind that the landslide victories for the party's presidential candidates (55.2% for Patricio Aylwin in 1989 and 58.01% for Eduardo Frei in 1993) have led analysts to overstate support for the party (Ministerio del Interior, 1993). In the congressional elections, the Christian Democrats received only 26.0% and 27.1% of the vote, respectively, in elections for the Chamber of Deputies in 1989 and 1993 (Ministerio del Interior, 1993). Thus, coalition formation and the politics of pacts in all probability will be an enduring feature of the Chilean political landscape.

Second, as Table 2 shows, if returns from the two postauthoritarian congressional elections held in 1989 and 1993 are disaggregated into forces representing the right, center, and left, the support for each of the historic blocs displays remarkable continuity with the preauthoritarian period.[13]

Third, some analysts point to the diminishing ideological distance between Chilean parties as a sign that the competitive dynamic of the system has been transformed (Gutiérrez, 1989; Guzmán, 1993; Larraín, 1984). Although it is undeniable that the ideological spectrum of the Chilean party system has substantially narrowed, this is due more to the effects of the ideological reorientation of individual parties and the influence of world events than to the drives exerted by the electoral system.[14] Although political parties may be closer ideologically, this does not necessarily mean that the

13. The proscription of the Communist Party between 1938 and 1958 produced a significant under-reporting of the left's real magnitude of support during this period. A truer measure of the support for parties of the left would probably bring the historic average of support closer to the current level. Table 2 presents how parties were categorized as right, center, or left. In the 1989 elections, several candidates ran as independents because of laws prohibiting certain parties or registration problems. In all cases, I was able to identify the "real" partisan orientations of candidates.

14. Cuevas Farren (1993) analyzes the ideological reorientation of Chilean political parties across the political spectrum.

Table 2

Percentage of Total Vote Received by Parties of the Right, Center, and Left in Chilean House of Deputy Elections 1937-1993

Party	1937	1941	1945	1949	1953	1957	1961	1965	1969	1973	Mean (1937-1973)	1989	1993
Right[a]	42.0	31.2	43.7	42.0	25.3	33.0	30.4	12.5	20.0	21.3	30.1	34.1	29.8
Center[b]	28.1	32.1	27.9	46.7	43.0	44.3	43.7	55.6	42.8	32.8	39.7	33.1	31.6
Left[c]	15.4	33.9	23.1	9.4	14.2	10.7	22.1	22.7	28.1	34.9	21.5	24.3	30.9
Other	14.5	2.8	5.3	1.9	17.5	12.0	3.8	9.2	9.1	11.0	8.7	8.5	7.7

For 1937 to 1973:

a. Right: Conservative, Liberal, National after 1965.

b. Center: Radical, Falangist, Christian Democrats, Agrarian, Laborist.

c. Left: Socialist, Communist.

Source: Valenzuela (1978, p. 6).

For 1989 to 1993:

a. Right: National Renovation, Independent Democratic Union, National, Independents on Congressional Lists of the Right (for 1989 this also includes the Union of the Center-Center).

b. Center: Radical, Christian Democrats, Social Democrats, Center Alliance Party.

c. Left: Party for Democracy, Socialist Party, Almeyda Socialist Party, National Democratic Party, Christian Left, Humanists, Greens, Independents of Congressional Lists of the Left.

Source: 1989 elections, Programa de Asesoría Legislativa. (1992, pp. 54-57). 1993 , nondefinitive data, *La Epoca*, December, 13, 1993, p. B1.

number of relevant parties and ideological groupings has necessarily been reduced or that the dynamic of competition between them will change. What is more, despite a so-far conciliatory pattern of interaction between the parties of the center and the left, profound differences between the parties of the Concertación remain in terms of platforms, political interests, and party subcultures. The traditional class and religious cleavages that differentiated parties in the past have been displaced by divisions over controversial issues such as crime, poverty, divorce, and abortion. Interparty friction on these issues may overshadow the conflicts of the transition that put the parties of the Concertación on the same side of the democracy/authoritarianism cleavage, resulting in a resurgence of competition between the parties of the center and the left.

Purely political issues may also divide the Concertación coalition, making for a more traditional pattern of competition between the center and left. In the interest of coalition unity, the parties of the left have agreed to support Christian Democratic presidential candidates in both postauthoritarian elections. The parties of the left refrained from presenting presidential candidates of their own, despite the fact that Socialist leader Ricardo Lagos has been a tenable and popular potential candidate. If the centrist Christian Democrats insist that one of their candidates be the Concertación standard-bearer in the next presidential election, the left may decide it has more to gain by leaving the Concertación and presenting a presidential candidate of its own.

Finally, in terms of the direction of competition that the binomial system encourages, some analysts have applied theoretical generalizations that are not relevant to the Chilean case to argue that the electoral system will produce centripetal competition (Guzmán, 1993, Rabkin, 1996). Although the binomial system is not a single-member-district system, the centripetal tendencies suggested by Downs's (1957) median voter hypothesis are simply said to apply to party competition in Chile. On this basis, these analysts have argued that the binomial system exerts a centralizing effect on party competition, without considering that M = 2 produces a distinct competitive pattern from the M = 1 Downs assumed in elaborating his hypothesis. More careful analysis has shown that the binomial system actually may encourage centrifugal competition, given that it creates two electoral equilibria rather than the single one suggested by Downs's theory (Magar, Rosenblum, & Samuels, 1996).

THE BINOMIAL SYSTEM, ELECTORAL PACTS, AND THE DYNAMIC OF COALITION FORMATIONS

The preceding section provides strong evidence that there are important elements of continuity within the Chilean party system in terms of the number of significant political parties, underlying ideological divisions, and the pattern of coalition formation and competition. Nonetheless, one could argue that this entire discussion misses the fundamental point that electoral coalitions have displaced parties as the most important units of analysis for characterizing the Chilean party system. For example, one might ask how the Concertación differs from parties composed of discrete factions such as the Japanese Liberal Democratic Party. Indeed, in much of the literature on postauthoritarian Chilean politics, analysts have categorized the effective number of parties in Chile at or about two, based on the existence of two strong electoral coalitions (Baldez & Carey, 1996, p. 12; Shugart & Carey, 1992, p. 220).[15]

The increasing treatment of Chile as a two-party system in the literature is troubling and overlooks several important realities— not the least of which is the failure to recognize Chile as a case of multiparty presidentialism, with all the problematic consequences that this configuration has the potential to produce (Mainwaring, 1993; Mainwaring & Shugart, 1997; Siavelis, 1997). At the same time, although it is undeniable that the binomial system has made the politics of coalition formation and electoral pacts more important, individual parties and individual party organizations do not cease to be significant units of analysis for understanding the party system. Despite coalition formation and the strength of alliances in the posttransition period, parties in Chile have distinct platforms, historical identities, and constituencies. It may also be premature to conclude that current coalitional configurations are somehow permanent, given the relatively recent return of party politics to the country.

Individual Chilean parties have roots that run very deep and predate the advent of authoritarian rule. Even the so-called new Chilean political parties such as the Unión Demócrata Independiente (UDI), Renovación Nacional (RN), and the Partido por la Democracia (PPD) have important historical antecedents, particularly with regard to party elites and core constituencies. Individual parties in both coalitions maintain separate organizations, independent party offices, and distinct leadership and decision-making structures. The interparty conflicts that have already erupted in both coalitions suggest

15. Shugart and Carey (1992) list the effective number of parties as 2.6 (p. 220). Baldez and Carey (1996) contend that the system "now performs effectively as a two-party system" (p. 12).

that these marriages of necessity may break down, making way for new and different marriages.

What is more, Chilean voters continue to vote for individual party candidates rather than lists. Election returns demonstrate that individuals do not vote only on the basis of electoral pacts. The often large differentials between candidates on the same lists with different party credentials are more than a function of the personalities of candidates.[16] In popular debate, Chileans still ask, "Is candidate X UDI or Renovación?" and they know and care about the difference. In addition, although many voters will enthusiastically cast ballots for Christian Democratic candidates, they find it difficult—given historical baggage and differing platforms on divorce, abortion, and social issues—to vote for PPD or Socialist (PS) candidates, even though they share the same electoral lists with the Christian Democrats.

But most important, one must bear in mind that it was the democratic transition that produced the pacts that exist in Chile today. Although few expect a renewed military incursion into politics, it is entirely too soon to make definitive statements about the nature of the party system given the temporal proximity of transition politics. In the period leading up to the 1988 plebiscite, parties had a strong incentive to band together to achieve one goal: an end to the authoritarian regime. The reality of a yes/no plebiscite allowed the parties of the center left to subordinate their programmatic differences to agree on the fundamental goal of regime change. The plebiscite also clearly drew the lines of battle and provided a strong incentive for the parties of the center right to coalesce. These alliances were maintained for the first two presidential and legislative elections following the defeat of the authoritarian regime. The context of the democratic transition provided strong incentives to maintain coalitions, making it premature to categorize current pacts in Chile as simply parties made up of distinct factions.

Since the return of democracy, there has been no fundamental crisis to challenge the unity of either coalition. The Concertación has not yet faced the challenge of maintaining an electoral alliance with more than one presidential candidate. Given the favorable economic and political circumstances that characterized the democratic transition, parties of the left have had no real incentive to distance themselves from the Christian Democrats or to present separate congressional lists. A significant crisis that undermines the core support of the Christian Democrats could produce strong incentives for the left to present its own presidential nominee and a separate slate of legislative candidates.

16. There are often very large differentials in the number of votes received by candidates on each list. For the 1989 elections, there was an average difference of 11.4% between candidates. For a discussion, see Valenzuela and Siavelis (1991, p. 52).

Finally, the current coalitional configuration and the potential combination of future coalitional configurations are much more complex than analysts of Chilean politics have suggested. Perhaps the overriding concern with the democratic/authoritarian dichotomy in recent years has led theorists to think in "bipolar" terms without realizing the very likely potential for a more fluid pattern of coalition formation in the future. As partisan differences become more pronounced with the fading of the urgency that characterized the immediate postauthoritarian period, a pattern of shifting alliance formation revolving around coalitions of the center and either the right or left may reemerge. The ideological distance between the Christian Democrats and the major moderate party of the right—Renovación Nacional—is not so wide as to preclude the formation of a center-right coalition in the near future.

The incentives for pact formation produced by the binomial system are undeniably strong. However, in certain situations the elements of underlying continuity within the party system can overcome these incentives. Analysts of Chilean politics often forget that coalition formation was also important in the past and that there were incentives to form alliances even with a PR electoral system. However, despite this reality at key junctures (and particularly in situations of governmental crisis), parties decided it was in their interest to go it alone or to change coalition partners. Alliance formation is likely to become much more fluid than the very limited experience with postauthoritarian politics suggests. In short, although pacts and alliances are important, parties do still very much matter.

CONCLUSIONS

This article has argued that the party system transformational effects of the binomial system predicted by many scholars and Chilean policy makers have not materialized nor are they likely to in the near future. Evidence presented here suggests that there has been neither a decrease in party system fragmentation nor has the dynamic of preauthoritarian political competition been substantially transformed. What is more, although electoral pacts are certainly important, individual parties have not ceased to be relevant.

Parties have not fused to improve their chances of victory in congressional elections. Because of an unwillingness of individual parties to abandon their separate constituencies and historical identities, the mechanical reductive effects predicted by military authorities, and by some electoral theorists, have been overcome by the parties themselves. The development of an elaborate system of pacts and negotiations between parties has resulted in joint congressional lists and allowed access to congress for small- and medium-sized parties. The ability of coalitions to provide electoral spoils for smaller parties to gain wider support has provided for a level of party system fragmentation very similar to that which existed in the preauthoritarian period.

Analysts are correct in noting that the binomial system provides increased incentives for the formation and maintenance of electoral coalitions. However, it is questionable whether these incentives are strong enough to fundamentally transform the dynamic of party competition in the country or to lead to centripetal drives within the party system.

In Chile, limited electoral reform has had, and will continue to have, limited effects on the party system depending on the dynamic interaction of the incentives and drives operating within the party system, a few of which have been described here. Given the elements of continuity within the party system, the continued ability of parties to form joint lists, and the existence of a PR electoral system for municipal elections, it is doubtful that the binomial system will discourage party system fragmentation or necessarily lead to a pattern of centripetal competition as many scholars have suggested. The question for the long term, as the shadow of the authoritarian regime fades, is whether the incentives for the maintenance of coalitions are stronger than those produced by the elements of continuity within the party system.

In more general terms, this case study suggests that there is no uni-causal or direct relationship between electoral system change and party system transformation within well-institutionalized party systems. The ability of electoral formulae to exert transformational effects on party systems, both in terms of numbers and the dynamic of competition, depends on many variables of which district magnitude is only one. Others include the strength, number, and cultural importance of political parties; the continued salience of ideological cleavages that brought them into existence; and the nature of electoral systems at the local and municipal level. Although these results certainly do not represent a test case of the transformational potential of small-magnitude formulae to decrease party fragmentation or encourage centripetal competition, they do demonstrate that theorists and policy makers should exercise a great deal of caution in their assumptions concerning any mechanical or automatic effects of electoral reform.

Given these realities, the utility of electoral reform as a palliative for the crises of democracy in many parts of the world is probably limited. In situations in which party proliferation is viewed as an obstacle to cooperation and effective policy making, it is clear that a simple change in electoral formulae will not necessarily elicit the transformational effects imputed to plurality or small magnitude systems. Although these types of electoral systems may encourage party system integration in the formative stages of party system evolution, within the context of a well-entrenched party system, electoral reform can have unanticipated consequences.

REFERENCES

Baldez, L, & Carey, J. (1996, May). *The Chilean budget process* Unpublished manuscript presented at the World Bank Conference on policy making in Latin America, University of California, San Diego.

Cox, G. (1984). Electoral equilibrium in double member districts. *Public Choice, 44*, 443-451

Cox, G. (1990). Centripetal and centrifugal incentives in electoral systems. *American Journal of Political Science, 34*, 903-935.

Cuevas Farren, G. (Ed.). (1993). *Renovación ideológica en Chile: Los partidos y su nueva visión estratégica* [Ideological renewal in Chile: Political parties and their new strategic vision] Santiago: Universidad de Chile, Instituto de Ciencia Política.

Downs, A. (1957). *An economic theory of democracy.* New York: Harper Collins.

Duverger, M. (1954). *Political parties.* New York: John Wiley.

Gutiérrez, H. (1989). Chile 1989: ¿Elecciones fundacionales? [Chile 1989: Founding elections?]. *Documento de trabajo, serie estudios públicos No. 3.* Santiago, Chile: FLACSO.

Guzmán, E. (1993). Reflexiones sobre el sistema binominal [Reflections on the binominal system]. *Estudios Públicos, 51*, 303-325.

Hermens, F. A. (1941). *Democracy or anarchy? A study of proportional representation.* South Bend, IN: Notre Dame University Press.

Laakso, M., & Taagepera, R. (1979). Effective number of parties. A measure with application to Western Europe. *Comparative Political Studies, 12*, 3-27.

Lardeyret, G. (1991). The problem with P.R. *Journal of Democracy, 2*(3), 30-48.

Larraín, H. (1984). Democracia, partidos políticos y transición: El caso chileno [Democracy, political parties and democratic transition: The Chilean case]. *Estudios Públicos, 15*, 88-115.

Lijphart, A. (1984). *Democracies.* New Haven, CT: Yale University Press.

Lijphart, A. (1990a). Double checking the evidence. *Journal of Democracy, 2*(3), 42-48

Lijphart, A. (1990b). The political consequences of electoral laws, 1945-1985. *American Political Science Review, 84*, 482-496.

Lijphart, A. (1991). Constitutional choices for new democracies. *Journal of Democracy, 2*(1), 72-84.

Lijphart, A., & Grofman, B. (1984). Introduction. In A. Lijphart & B. Grofman (Eds.), *Choosing an electoral system.* New York: Praeger.

Magar, E., Rosenblum, M., & Samuels, D. (1996) *Can the center hold?* Unpublished manuscript.

Mainwaring, S. (1993). Presidentialism, multipartism and democracy: The difficult combination. *Comparative Political Studies, 26*, 198-227.

Mainwaring, S., & Shugart, M. (1997). Conclusion: Presidentialism and the party system. In S. Mainwaring & M. Shugart (Eds.), *Presidentialism and democracy in Latin America.* Cambridge, UK: Cambridge University Press.

Ministerio del Interior de Chile. (1993). Informativo elecciones 1993 [Election bulletin, 1993]. *Computo, 4.* Santiago, Chile: Author.

Miranda, M. T. (1982). El sistema electoral y el multipartidismo en Chile: 1949-1969 [Electoral system and multipartism in Chile: 1949-1969]. *Revista de Ciencia Política, 4*(1), 59-69.

Molinar, J. (1991). Counting the number of parties: An alternative index. *American Political Science Review, 85,* 1383-1391.

Nohlen, D. (1993). *Enciclopedia electoral latinoamericano y del caribe* [Electoral encyclopedia of Latin America and the Caribbean]. San José, Costa Rica: Instituto Interamericano de Derechos Humanos.

Participa. (1993). *Resultados de las elecciones de diputados* [Results of the House of Deputies elections]. Santiago, Chile: Author.

Programa de Asesoría Legislativa. (1992). *Análisis de actualidad No. 43* [Current analysis No. 43]. Santiago, Chile: Author.

Quade, Q. (1991). P.R. and democratic statecraft. *Journal of Democracy, 2*(3), 36-41.

Rabkin, R. (1996). Redemocratization, electoral engineering, and party strategies in Chile, 1989-1995. *Comparative Political Studies, 29,* 335-356.

Rae, D. (1971). The political consequences of electoral laws. New Haven, CT: Yale University Press.

Riker, W. (1986). Duverger's law revisited. In B. Grofman & A. Lijphart (Eds.), *Electoral laws and their political consequences* (pp. 19-42). New York: Agathon Press.

Sartori, G. (1968). Political development and political engineering. In J. D. Montgomery & A. O. Hirschman (Eds.), *Policy* (Vol. 17, pp. 261-298). Cambridge, UK: Cambridge University Press.

Sartori, G. (1976). *Parties and party systems: A framework for analysis.* Cambridge, UK: Cambridge University Press.

Sartori, G. (1986). The influence of electoral systems: Faulty laws of faulty methods? In B. Grofman & A. Lijphart (Eds.), *Electoral laws and their political consequences* (pp. 43-68). New York: Agathon Press.

Scully, T., & Valenzuela, J. S. (1993). De la democracia a la democracia: Continuidad y variaciones en las preferencias del electorado y en el sistema de partidos en Chile [From democracy to democracy: Continuity and change in electoral preferences and the Chilean party system]. *Estudios Públicos, 51,* 195-228.

Shugart, M. (1985). The two effects of district magnitude: Venezuela as a crucial experiment. *European Journal of Political Research, 13,* 353-364.

Shugart, M. (1992). Electoral reform in systems of proportional representation. *European Journal of Political Research, 21,* 207-224.

Shugart, M., & Carey, J. (1992). *Presidents and assemblies: Constitutional design and electoral dynamics.* New York: Cambridge University Press.

Siavelis, P. (1993). Nuevos argumentos y viejos supuestos: Simulaciones de sistemas electorales alternativos para las elecciones parlamentarias chilenas [New arguments and old assumptions: Simulations of electoral system alternatives for Chilean parliamentary elections]. *Estudios Públicos, 51,* 229-267.

Siavelis, P. (1997). Executive-legislative relations in post-Pinochet Chile. In S. Mainwaring & M. Shugart (Eds.), *Presidentialism and democracy in Latin America.* Cambridge, UK: Cambridge University Press.

Taagepera, R. (1984). The effect of district magnitude and properties of two seat districts. In A. Lijphart & B. Grofman (Eds.), *Choosing an electoral system* (pp. 91-102). New York: Praeger.

Taagepera, R., & Shugart, M. (1989). *Seats and votes.* New Haven, CT: Yale University Press.

Taagepera, R., & Shugart, M. (1993). Predicting the number of parties: A quantitative model of Duverger's mechanical effect. *American Political Science Review, 87,* 455-464.

Valenzuela, A. (1978). *The breakdown of democratic regimes: Chile.* Baltimore: Johns Hopkins University Press.

Valenzuela, A., & Siavelis, P. (1991). Ley electoral y estabilidad democrática: Un ejercicio de simulación para el caso de Chile [Electoral law and democratic stability: A simulation for the Chilean case]. *Estudios Públicos, 43,* 27-88.

Peter Siavelis (Ph.D., Georgetown University, 1996) is an assistant professor of political science at Wake Forest University in Winston-Salem, North Carolina. His recent publications include "Executive-Legislative Relations in Post-Pinochet Chile" in Presidentialism and Democracy in Latin America (edited by S. Mainwaring and M. Shugart, Cambridge University Press, 1997) and, with Arturo Valenzuela, "Electoral Engineering and Democratic Stability: The Legacy of Authoritarian Rule in Chile" in Institutional Design in New Democracies (edited by A. Lijphart and C. Waisman, Westview Press, 1996). He has been a visiting professor and visiting scholar at the Institute of Political Science at the Catholic University of Chile, Santiago.

Parties and Society in Mexico and Venezuela

Why Competition Matters

Michael Coppedge

Mexico and Venezuela are not usually considered similar political systems. Since most observers classify Venezuela as a democracy and Mexico as an authoritarian regime, it is commonly assumed that political life in these two countries is fundamentally and thoroughly dissimilar. The distinction between democracy and authoritarianism, however, masks striking similarities in the political institutions and practices of the two countries, in particular, the ways in which political parties have penetrated and gained control over other actors in civil society. This article highlights these similarities, not to tar Venezuela's good reputation nor to whitewash Mexico's political shortcomings, but to concentrate attention more narrowly on the essential remaining difference—the competitiveness of the party system. This comparison of Mexico and Venezuela, while odd, reveals some of the differences that democracy can make in developing countries.

This article argues that these differences can be discerned at the grass-roots level. In labor unions, when the party system is competitive, there is less violent repression of workers. Also, whether workers vote, and how they vote, depends less on the unions' or parties' mobilization efforts than on the workers' own abilities and interests. In rural and urban communities, party competition makes local bosses (*caciques*) less abusive, intimidating, and violent toward their clients, and therefore more respectful of citizens' property, persons, and opinions. In national politics as well, a competitive party system encourages governmental responsiveness, moderate opposition, and peaceful evolution of the political system.

While this article is by no means the first examination of the consequences of party competition, it is one of only a handful of empirical studies that compare competitive and noncompetitive systems to draw conclusions about the impact of party competition below the macro level of regime change, stability, and national public policy.[1] Most of what we know about the impact of party competition is based on comparisons of democratic countries. Since all of these countries possess, by definition, competitive party systems, the conclusions drawn from such comparisons reveal the impact of a relatively small difference in levels of competition, that is, two-party versus multiparty systems.[2] This article looks at the more fundamental difference between a competitive party system (Venezuela) and an uncompetitive system (Mexico). Studies that compare democratic and nondemocratic systems have tended to focus on either the conditions for stable democracy or the consequences of democracy for elite decision making on national public policy.[3] This article, in contrast, focuses on the immediate, personal, day-to-day consequences for ordinary citizens. Democratic theorists have long asserted that democracy matters even at the grass roots, and almost all of the recent writing on democratization assumes that the

253

theorists are correct.[4] This study provides evidence to support their assertions and assumptions.

The dominant position enjoyed by the Mexican Institutional Revolutionary Party (PRI) before the near-victory of Cuauhtémoc Cárdenas in 1988 is well-known. Not only was it a dominant party in every sense of the word, it was a highly penetrative party as well, one that effectively controlled most organizations in Mexican society by formal incorporation through its labor, peasant, and popular "sectors" (wings) or by informal means such as cooptation and intimidation.

Venezuela's parties were very much like the PRI in their relations with other groups in civil society, with the crucial difference that they operated in a competitive system. Two large parties, *Acción Democrática* (AD) and the Social Christian Party COPEI, shared 80–90 percent of the vote after 1973 and alternated in the presidency four times since 1958. While neither of these parties was dominant, both were structured like the PRI: they were built on labor, peasant, and middle class wings subject to tight party discipline, and they actively coopted and infiltrated other organizations in society in order to extend their control, relying on state resources (when available) to achieve their ends.

The conclusions of this particular comparison would not necessarily hold for all varieties of democracy or authoritarianism. However, a comparison of Mexico and Venezuela is appropriate in isolating the most basic consequences of democracy or its absence in certain types of political systems: relatively well-institutionalized regimes based on strong party control of society. The competitiveness of the party systems in Mexico and Venezuela differs just enough to make one system authoritarian and the other democratic.

Since fundamental changes have been taking place in both countries in the last decade, the generalizations made in these pages about the political environment at the grass roots refer to periods in each country's history during which political institutions were changing less drastically and less rapidly. For Mexico, these are the years of "stabilizing development," roughly 1946 to 1970; for Venezuela, they are the years between the founding of the democratic regime in 1958 and the onset of the debt crisis in the mid 1980s. Some of the generalizations would be valid beyond those dates, but delimiting the periods in this narrow fashion simplifies the argument and avoids confusion. However, this analysis is also relevant for politics at the national level, and in some respects the generalizations about the earlier periods help explain differences in the two countries' subsequent evolution. The concluding section contains a brief case study of contemporary reform efforts that illustrates the continuing relevance of party competition.

Parties and Organized Labor

From 1946 through the 1970s, most trade unions in Mexico cooperated with the PRI through one institutional arrangement or another, most commonly through formal affiliation with the *Confederación de Trabajadores Mexicanos* (CTM), which was the official labor "sector," or wing, of the PRI. In 1978, 63.9 percent of the unions in the largest peak labor organization, the *Congreso del Trabajo*, were affiliated with the CTM.[5] In practice, members of affiliated unions were automatically members of the PRI as well.

While some important unions stayed outside the CTM and engaged in short-lived

254

militance that caused problems for the government, during most of their history these unions were as cooperative as any union in the CTM. Among them were the FSTSE (white collar federal employees incorporated separately in the PRI's CNOP, or "popular," sector), the STFRM (railway workers), SUTERM (electrical workers), SNTIMSS (social security workers), and the STMMSRM (miners and metallurgical workers). The railway workers, for example, were led in the 1940s and 1950s by the original *charro*, whose nickname has become the slang for a corrupt and coopted labor leader. The smaller confederations that now belong to the *Congreso del Trabajo* — CROM, CROC, and CGT — were coopted much like these unions.[6] The CROC, in fact, was created in 1952 as a loyal counterbalance to the CTM during a period of labor disturbances. There were independent confederations, notably the *Unidad Obrera Independiente* (UOI) and the Christian-Democratic *Frente Auténtico de Trabajo* (FAT), but they were small in comparison to the official and semiofficial organizations.

The relationship between the PRI and PRI-affiliated unions was asymmetrical, but there was give as well as take. For example, all of the affiliates of the *Congreso del Trabajo* were heavily dependent on government subsidies for their operating expenses, since they were not able to collect dues from an estimated ninety percent of their membership.[7] The government also indirectly subsidized some unions and federations by awarding them contracts from state enterprises, which the unions subcontracted to private firms in exchange for a percentage of the award, reportedly up to 35 percent.[8] Other benefits went directly to individual labor leaders. Loyal labor leaders were recruited by the PRI as candidates for congress, and once elected, they had few legislative responsibilities but enjoyed extra income, greater prestige, and access to additional money-making opportunities.[9] Similar benefits came with appointments to positions in the PRI itself and in executive agencies and government boards. Needless to say, leaders who accepted these benefits were expected to cooperate with the PRI. Davis summarizes the result, saying that the CTM "tends, ultimately, to close ranks in support of PRI economic policies even when workers' interests seem to be sacrificed by the party. The rules of the Mexican political game are generally respected. These norms preclude open criticism of the president, limit mobilization, and call for the closing of ranks around presidential policy decisions."[10] Leaders who refused to cooperate found that they were vulnerable to charges of corruption or subversive activity and were easily removed from their positions.

Union leaders who were coopted in turn coopted the rank and file in their unions. Again, the relationship was asymmetrical, but not without benefits for the members. Unionized workers, estimated to comprise about 15 percent of the national work force and 25 percent of the urban work force, were a labor elite in Mexico that received much better wages, access to subsidized credit and housing, health care, basic consumer goods, technical training, and participation in profit-sharing plans.[11] Real wages for unionized workers remained fairly constant from the 1950s until the mid 1970s, and many union leaders enjoyed genuine support for years after the prolabor Cárdenas government (1934–1940).[12]

All of these benefits, however, were manipulated to maximize the leadership's control. The *cláusula de exclusión* of the Federal Labor Law established a closed shop, which in effect gave union officials control over hiring and firing decisions, and they abused this control to sell jobs (for as much as $2,000) to workers who would not make trouble and to get rid of workers who challenged their leadership.[13] In some plants, workers had to be in

255

good standing with the union leadership even to receive benefits to which they were entitled by law. And union politics were far from democratic, especially in the CTM and unions not considered strategically important: assemblies to hear grievances and elect new leaders were sometimes postponed, votes were manipulated, and voters intimidated.[14]

These tactics worked very effectively to keep opposition to PRI dominance under control. While some unions, even some CTM-affiliated unions, were militant in their wage demands, ties with political organizations outside the "revolutionary family" of the PRI were likely to bring down repression. Unions and federations outside the PRI structure were discouraged by the government's authority to withdraw their legal registration and to declare their strikes illegal (and therefore subject to violent repression), as well as by the disadvantage of not having access to all the subsidies, concessions, and benefits used to coopt the other organizations.

Despite these obstacles, the history of the Mexican labor movement has been punctuated by bouts of militant strike activity, and strikes by railway workers, electrical workers, petroleum workers, and teachers have received considerable scholarly attention.[15] Furthermore, some unions have stood out as being relatively democratic, and efforts to achieve union democracy have intensified in recent years. The work of Ian Roxborough and Kevin Middlebrook has provided a healthy corrective to the earlier notion that all Mexican unions were completely docile and violently repressed by the state.[16] These studies must be kept in perspective, however. The unions studied by Roxborough and Middlebrook are large unions in one of the most modern and strategic sectors of the economy—the automobile industry—and are therefore not typical of the small unions in nonstrategic, labor-intensive industries that make up the majority of the unions. Also, it must be remembered that the most militant unions were eventually repressed, and that some of the most important unions, such as the STPRM in the petroleum industry, were dominated by archetypical *charros*. Finally, even the more militant unions that defected to confederations free of the CTM, such as the UOI and the FAT in the 1970s and 1980s, were careful to avoid explicitly political activity and chose to concentrate their efforts on plant-level wage and benefit demands.[17]

As in Mexico, most of the Venezuelan labor movement was effectively subordinated to the general policy aims of a single party—*Acción Democrática*.[18] The Venezuelan labor movement in general was highly politicized, since most unions were founded by party organizers starting in the late 1930s. Unlike Mexico, however, Venezuela had a competitive system: union leadership was chosen in union elections using party slates. This was the practice at all levels, including elections within the *Confederación de Trabajadores de Venezuela* (CTV), which was the peak association for over 80 percent of Venezuela's organized workers.[19] AD had the largest representation in the CTV ever since its second national congress in 1944.[20] Except during a brief period following a division of AD in 1967, 50 to 70 percent of the members of the national congresses and executive committee of the CTV were affiliated with AD from 1959 to the present.[21]

Party loyalty was very strong among AD labor leaders, as it was among the labor leaders of all the other parties. It is useful, however, to distinguish between the loyalty of labor leaders to their respective party labor wings and the loyalty of the labor wings to the national party leadership as a whole. The loyalty of AD's representatives on the executive committee of the CTV to their party's labor bureau (*buró sindical*) was absolute and unvarying, just as

256

one would expect the representatives of the CTM to behave in the *Congreso del Trabajo* in Mexico. During research conducted during 1985, I asked sixteen of the seventeen AD members of the CTV executive committee the following question: "Does the Executive Committee of the CTV sometimes make decisions about legislative bills, political demonstrations, strikes, or other important matters before they have been discussed by the labor bureaus of one or more of the political parties, or only afterwards?" Eighty-one percent (thirteen) said that the parties must discuss the matters first, and the three who claimed otherwise, when asked to support their claim, were unable to come up with a counterexample.

This fact, combined with AD's majority, means that AD's labor bureau enjoyed at least veto power over the CTV's actions. When asked whether "the Executive Committee of the CTV sometimes makes decisions that the Labor Bureau of AD opposes," all but one AD representative (94 percent) replied that it does not. In light of the overlap in the membership of the two bodies, the situation could hardly be otherwise: three-quarters of the *Adecos* in the CTV leadership were also members of the labor bureau.

The relationship between the AD labor bureau and the party as a whole was more complicated, but it was strikingly similar to the relationship between the CTM and the PRI. Both are best described as loose alliances that benefited both the labor wing and the party while reserving ultimate authority for the party.[22]

Top AD labor leaders, like other AD leaders, knew that AD was not a labor party, and the great majority of them did not wish that it were. They believed that the interests of the Venezuelan working class were best served by having a close relationship with a powerful political party.[23] There is ample reason to believe that they were right. For example, labor conflicts were referred automatically to tripartite commissions on which labor and government representatives loyal to AD could always outvote management.[24] And many of the benefits enjoyed by organized workers were not the product of collective bargaining but were decreed by Venezuelan presidents.[25] In this environment, labor leaders were wise to maintain close ties to the government, and one way to accomplish this goal was to be a powerful base of support for the governing party.

Labor got access because the politicians placed a high value on labor support. No group was more useful than the labor unions in getting out the vote in general, as well as internal, elections. The human resources of the labor unions and federations of the state were at the disposal of the state labor secretary (frequently because he was a leader of the state labor federation), and this power allowed him to act as a powerbroker in state politics. Labor leaders even became general secretaries at the state level.[26]

The cooperation of the unions was also valuable to a government faced with a political or economic crisis. Betancourt's government gained legitimacy in the eyes of conservatives and the military in part because he and the AD labor leaders were able to convince the unions to avoid strikes in the crucial first years of democracy and even to accept wage cuts in the face of an economic crisis.[27] Conversely, the CTV's cooperation was also useful to AD in the opposition, as a way of embarrassing COPEI governments with spectacular increases in strike activity. Figure 1 leaves no doubt that the ties between the president's party and organized labor were the principal regulator of labor militancy in Venezuela: the two peaks in man-hours lost to strikes both occurred during COPEI governments, while AD was leading the opposition.[28]

257

91

Figure 1 Man-Hours Lost to Strikes (millions)

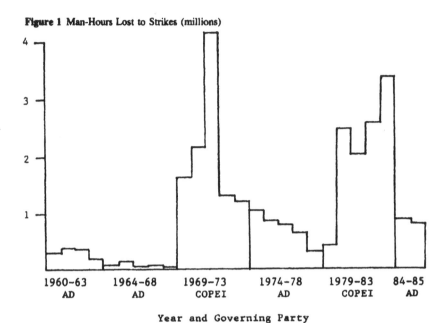

Year and Governing Party

SOURCE: Graph drawn from statistics in Carlos Eduardo Febres, "El movimiento sindical: Actor social o gestor institucional?" in Moisés Naím and Ramón Piñango, eds., El caso Venezuela: una ilusión de armonía (Caracas: Ediciones IESA, 1984), pp. 306-307 (1960-1980) and the Year Book of Labour Statistics 1987 (Geneva: International Labour Office, 1987), table 9A (1981-1985).

Ultimately, however, the labor bureau's right to act autonomously was limited, and the limitations were placed there by the national labor leaders themselves. They were unwilling to challenge party or government policy in ways that would bring their loyalty to the party into question. They tried to defend the interests of their class by exerting pressure privately through proper channels, asking, arguing, and persuading. In extreme instances they also took their case to the media. But they stopped short of threatening or condoning strikes, demonstrations, or other forms of force.[29] Such actions would have been considered embarrassing and damaging to the party or government and could have endangered the chief benefits the labor wing received from its alliance with the party—the trust and good will of the politicians. One might expect that AD labor leaders were ashamed of their position, but in reality they defended it as "politically responsible."[30]

The party loyalty of union leaders was reinforced by many of the same practices that were common in Mexico. All of the labor confederations in Venezuela were heavily subsidized by the national government; labor leaders were rewarded with seats on official boards, party

258

leadership positions, and seats in congress by AD and other parties; many labor leaders (from all parties) benefited handsomely from large government subsidies and lax government regulation of union enterprises such as the *Banco de los Trabajadores de Venezuela* (BTV);[31] and unionists who embarrassed an AD government, such as those who supported the "wrong" presidential precandidate within AD in 1967–68, were expelled from the party, voted out of union posts, harassed, and intimidated.[32]

Many union leaders in Venezuela controlled their members in much the same way as Mexican *charros*. The genuine benefits of unionization were as important in Venezuela as they were in Mexico, as organized labor had privileged access to higher wages, social security and health care, food and transportation subsidies, and other benefits, compared to the nonunionized work force.[33] But control was also maintained through more coercive means. Venezuela had no closed shop, but union leaders found other ways to keep challengers to their leadership in line:[34] entitlements were distributed preferentially along party lines, and some unions were notorious for the lack of turnover in their leadership, which perpetuated itself in power by postponing assemblies or manipulating union elections.[35]

The high degree of party penetration of unions created a similar style of unionism in Mexico and Venezuela. In both countries, union leaders preferred to concentrate on wages and the resolution of plant-level grievances rather than on political unionism designed to transform the system.[36] Furthermore, strike rates were rather low by international standards. In Venezuela, never as many as three percent of the unions went on strike in any given year between 1970 and 1985.[37] Despite all the attention paid to the more militant unions in Mexico, strike activity there was lower than in most of the rest of Latin America. In one of the few systematic attempts to compare the autonomy of labor movements in Latin America, Mexico and Venezuela were both rated "medium-low" (along with Colombia, Uruguay before 1985, and Chile under the last decade of the Pinochet regime).[38]

Nevertheless, the fact of party competition in Venezuela created a less violent and more open environment for workers than was possible in dominant-party Mexico. In Venezuela, the labor bureau of AD had to at least appear to defend working class interests actively because it was competing with other parties for the allegiance of workers within the unions, federations, and the CTV. Competition required a greater respect for workers' property, persons, and opinions than was necessary in the PRI-dominated unions of Mexico. In his excellent comparative study of the political socialization of workers in Mexico and Venezuela, Charles Davis reported that "such extralegal repression as the use of thugs to disrupt opposition activities, arbitrary firings, or disappearances and assassinations are far more common in Mexico than in Venezuela."[39]

While this observation was based on impressionistic evidence, Davis reached firmer conclusions on the basis of a survey of nearly one thousand workers in the two countries. One conclusion was that Venezuelan workers were marginally more likely to vote independently of the "hegemonic" parties AD and COPEI and instead cast protest or leftist votes and that the competitive party system in Venezuela explained more of this cross-national difference in leftist/protest voting than any other variable.[40] Another conclusion was that, compared to Mexican workers, Venezuelan workers had greater "cognitive mobilization" and psychological involvement in politics, that is, their participation was motivated more by their own interests than by external inducements.

259

> Workers vote in Mexico primarily because of ties to the PRI, not because of resources or cognitive mobilization. . . . By contrast, evidence of more self-directed participation in elections is found among workers in the more competitive electoral system of Venezuela. . . . Loyalty to the PRI leads to perfunctory voting with minimal psychological involvement in politics or attention to government performance. By contrast, hegemonic partisans [*Adecos* and *Copeyanos*] in Venezuela are likely to be attentive to politics and to form their partisan loyalties consistent with their assessments of performance. Hence, hegemonic partisans in Venezuela have greater potential to become autonomous participants in the political process than do their counterparts in Mexico.[41]

Mexico versus Venezuela: State versus Societal Corporatism?

It has been suggested that this comparison of Mexico and Venezuela yields conclusions about the differences between state and societal corporatism.[42] On first consideration, this interpretation is appealing. Mexico has long been considered a classic example of state corporatism, and some authors have noted certain societal corporatist features in Venezuela.[43] In its use of party slates in union elections, social democratic party dominance in the peak labor confederation, and the prominent place of a labor wing within the social democratic party, Venezuela's institutional structure was virtually identical to that of two societal corporatist states, Germany and Austria.[44] Furthermore, representation of the CTV on the boards of ministries and state enterprises was made mandatory in 1966, and Venezuelan presidents created several tripartite commissions to consider questions of price increases, immigration, and worker dismissals.[45]

A more careful consideration of the question, however, suggests that the distinction between state and societal corporatism is neither the most appropriate analytic tool nor the best interpretive framework for a comparison of Mexico and Venezuela. In the first place, the boards and commissions that allegedly provided for corporatist representation in Venezuela were not as well institutionalized as those in the European cases. The peak tripartite commission on economic policy set up by President Pérez in the late 1970s was dismantled when his successor, Luis Herrera Campíns, came to power. President Lusinchi's *Comisión sobre Costos, Precios, y Salarios* (CONACOPRESA), set up in 1984, was, in Ellner's words, "gutted of the binding power with which its CTV architects had originally endowed it," boycotted by business representatives in 1985, and abandoned by the CTV itself in 1987.[46] Moreover, many of the lower-level commissions never became operational.[47]

Second, Venezuelan labor did not enjoy the same degree of autonomy that is found in the European instances of societal corporatism. As an ideal type, corporatism is "the formal recognition by the state of the social power of strategic interests, [which] entails the institutionalization of such interests as permanent public clients who may claim a legitimate share of power as a function of their economic role."[48] This ideal type implies complete autonomy for strategic interests such as labor which is never realized in practice even in the most liberal societal corporatist systems. Labor autonomy is usually compromised to some degree by the mediating role of parties. There has always been some ambiguity in the "new corporatist" literature on this question, stemming from the need to claim that labor has less

260

autonomy in state corporatism than in the societal variant, while insisting that its autonomy is also limited in societal corporatism.[49] Lehmbruch resolves this tension most satisfactorily by treating societal corporatism as an auxiliary channel of representation in which-parties delegate authority to labor to bargain directly with capital and the state on certain issues of high economic policy.[50]

The problem in applying the corporatist label to Venezuela is that its parties played such a dominant mediating role that they delegated little authority to the labor representatives, and consequently the auxiliary channels played a relatively unimportant role in the policymaking process. As one Venezuelan writer observed:

> Even when the labor and peasant representatives began to participate more regularly in the plural bodies [tripartite boards] after the late sixties, their presence continued to be markedly irrelevant. The unions have not been able to affect the formation and execution of government policies on their own, that is, without prior assimilation of their positions by the sponsoring party, especially AD. . . . In sum, the economic plural organs established by the government during the democratic period have been, fundamentally, arenas for carrying out negotiations between the respective party elite in the government and the representatives of the so-called private sector, in spite of the constitutional requirement of a broad representation of the corporate groups with interests in economic life.[51]

Because Venezuela's corporatist structures were poorly institutionalized and its labor sector enjoyed little autonomy vis-à-vis parties, conclusions about societal corporatism based on the Venezuelan case are not likely to hold for the standard European cases of societal corporatism. If any conclusion about corporatism is to be drawn from a comparison of Mexico and Venezuela, it is that Venezuela belonged in some intermediate position between societal and state corporatism and that, to the extent that labor enjoyed more autonomy in Venezuela than in Mexico, this extra autonomy should be credited to the competitiveness of the Venezuelan party system.

However, such a conclusion would miss the larger implications of the comparison, for the phenomenon whose characteristics are being analyzed here is not confined to the arena of corporatist bargaining. It is a phenomenon that is also present in the politics of rural communities and urban barrios, in corporatist countries of either stripe, and in countries that are hardly corporatist at all. This phenomenon—the degree of competition in the party system—is more narrowly defined than the multifaceted corporatist syndrome, but the simplicity of the phenomenon allows for much broader applicability and therefore supports conclusions that transcend the literature on corporatism. Mexico and Venezuela were chosen, not because they might be corporatist or support conclusions about corporatism, but because the similarities in the way their parties penetrated society, corporatist or not, largely satisfy the assumption of "other things being equal." Mexico and Venezuela are unusually good candidates for comparative analysis, since they are strikingly similar in many respects but not in the most basic one—the democratic or authoritarian nature of the regime.

Parties and Rural Communities

In the rural communities and small towns of Mexico and Venezuela, politics took on a different character. It was not party politics in the national sense, because the national issues

261

around which parties build their symbols, ideologies, programs, and rhetoric have little meaning at the local level. It was, instead, clientelism, built around personalities and connections and favors. Political brokers maintained asymmetric face-to-face relationships with clients in the communities, exchanging particularistic benefits for votes in elections and attendance at rallies. The exact nature of the tie between these brokers and political parties varied—sometimes the brokers were party officials themselves, sometimes they were party loyalists holding positions in government or sectoral organizations, and other times they were independent mediators between clients and parties—but the effect of the brokerage was the same: they obtained and enforced the support, cooperation, or acquiescence of anyone who mattered in the community.

The terms of the exchanges between these brokers and their clients varied considerably, depending on the resources at the broker's disposal. In Mexico, a *Confederación Nacional Campesina* (CNC) leader would win support by agitating for titles to land; an irrigation district chief would manipulate the distribution of water during the crucial weeks of the growing season; a *presidente municipal* would find a job for a supporter on the public payroll; a *juez conciliador* would have dissidents arrested or arrange for their release.[52]

Most of these brokers had counterparts in Venezuela. For example, while there was no official peasant confederation, the *Federación de Campesinos de Venezuela* (FCV) was not all that different from the CNC: its constituent peasant leagues were organized by party militants, it grew rapidly by brokering the distribution of land titles after the Agrarian Reform of 1961, it was heavily subsidized by the government, and an estimated 80 percent of its leagues were dominated by one party, *Acción Democrática*.[53] The peasant population was never organized collectively like the *ejidos*, and the FCV was never quite as important to AD as the CNC was to the PRI, but the FCV was always a most reliable ally of AD and AD governments. Outside the FCV, local party officers and government officials (all of whom were tied to party clienteles) actively used the resources at their disposal—jobs, food baskets, authority over the placement of public works, and access to higher officials—to negotiate support for their party or clientele.

The clienteles built by these brokers ultimately translated into support for a political party due to the brokers' own clientelistic relationships with higher party and government officials. In Mexico, the local bosses (*caciques*) may or may not have attained their positions with the help of the official party, but once in power they invariably allied with a PRI governor, deputy, or senator to insure good connections with the government.[54] In exchange, they mobilized their local clienteles to support the PRI in staged protests, demonstrations, and elections.[55] Eventually, many of these *caciques* became PRI deputies, senators, or governors themselves.[56]

In Venezuela, local brokers were much more likely to owe their positions to their party, which nominated them for a council position, appointed them to a judicial or administrative post, or commissioned them to organize the peasants in the community.[57] Their functions, however, were the same as in Mexico: they mobilized their clienteles to support a political party in rallies, demonstrations, and elections in exchange for favors from higher government and party officials, possibly including their own candidacy for a legislative seat, or even an appointment as governor.[58] The effect was similar because in both countries the line separating government and governing party became increasingly blurred as one descended from the national to the local level. Mexico was notorious for this, but even in

262

Venezuela local and state officials routinely used public vehicles to transport "supporters" to rallies, government printing presses to print party leaflets, and legislative funds to play host to visiting party leaders.[59]

Still, there was a tremendous difference between local brokers in Venezuela and the *caciques* in Mexico, and the difference was one of competition. Since 1958 no party has been so dominant in Venezuela that competition has been eliminated, even at the local level. Municipal elections are usually more lopsided than national elections in Venezuela, but even in the most lopsided year (1984), when AD won nearly two-thirds of the municipal council seats overall, there was no district (the smallest unit of representation) in the country in which some other party failed to win at least one seat. In the median district, the opposition won two seats out of seven.[60] In Mexico, the only officials elected at the local level were chosen under winner-take-all rules until 1977.[61]

This lack of complete dominance by AD had an important consequence: it meant that citizens in the rural communities had a choice among brokers whose clientelistic hierarchies remained separate all the way to the national level. If promises were not kept or rights were abused, there were brokers from other parties who had an interest in exposing the failure and offering redress.[62] Moreover, these alternative brokers had connections to powerful state and national party leaders who were constantly looking for incidents they could publicize in order to embarrass the governing party. If the local brokers for the governing party were exposed in this way, they would risk losing their chief advantage over the local opposition—their connections with the government—for the leaders of the governing party would very likely disown them. The prospect of political isolation created incentives for local officials to be respectful of and responsive toward their clients.

In Mexico, the *caciques* were truly dominant in their local communities. Almost all local authorities, whether police or judges or municipal presidents or peasant leaders, had been coopted or intimidated by the *cacique* and his faction. In some communities, a dissident faction might arise from time to time, but it was not likely to be nearly as effective as local opposition in Venezuela, for two reasons. First, the *cacique* himself would harass the faction ruthlessly.[63] If he could not coopt its leaders, the *cacique* would threaten, extort, or arrest and imprison his opponents (with the cooperation of the judge and police in his faction). Murder was also a possibility.[64]

Second, dissident factions were necessarily isolated factions. Most of them had no ties to any larger organization, and those that did had ties to parties or confederations that were at best regionally strong, and often either embattled themselves or only ambiguously in the opposition. There was no opposition party that was organized in every state and community, large enough to have a chance of actually winning a national election, and consequently important enough to provide significant protection for a small group fighting a *cacique* backed by the PRI. Eventually, most dissident factions were coopted or eliminated by the *cacique*.[65]

The lack of competition at the local level gave rise to, and then reinforced, other aspects of political life in Mexican rural communities. While it is hard to document, I believe that *caciques* were more intent on abusing their power for self-enrichment than Venezuelan party brokers were. This is not to say that all of the Venezuelans were beyond reproach; my impression is that many local leaders sought bribes and kickbacks and insider deals, and a few of them became quite wealthy. But there is a world of difference between this level of

263

abuse and the notorious greed of the *caciques*, men who enlarged their estates by tricking, intimidating, and murdering peasant farmers, who stole harvested crops, who made themselves partners in any profitable ventures in their region, and who gained monopolistic control over the local economy in order to extract the greatest possible profit from farmers living at lower-than-subsistence levels.[66] A *cacique* necessarily was, or became, not just the most powerful figure in the community, but also the wealthiest. Indeed, it is hard to escape the impression that this was the whole point of being a *cacique* in the first place.

Hand in hand with this depth of greed was brutality. *Caciques* were known to maintain networks of informants and enforcers with instructions to threaten and physically intimidate anyone who spoke out against the *cacique*. There are tales of dissidents who were buried up to their necks and then trampled on by horses, peasants behind on their debts who were kept in cages in the *cacique*'s patio, peasants who were forced off their land at gunpoint, and so on.[67] It is hard to imagine such things taking place in contemporary Venezuela. There was violence in Venezuela, too, but word of it tended to get out, and when it did, the opposition had a field day. In Mexico, the victims were often afraid to tell anyone. Explanations that point to cultural differences rooted in the Conquest and the preceding Aztec culture are not convincing, because no cruelty has been committed under PRI rule that was not equaled by the Gómez dictatorship in Venezuela. The crucial difference between then and now, and between Mexico and Venezuela, is a competitive party system. *Caciques* who have to compete use more carrots than sticks, while a broker who is the only game in town can operate with impunity.

Parties and the Urban Barrios

The *caciques* of Mexican rural communities had counterparts in the urban *caciques* of the Mexican *colonias proletarias*. Residents were incorporated into the PRI through the *Confederación Nacional de Organizaciones Populares* (CNOP, now renamed UNE) rather than the CNC; they sought land for squatter settlements rather than for agriculture; and their most frequent government contacts were with the Federal District government rather than the agrarian reform or agriculture ministries. But these were superficial differences.[68]

In most important respects, urban *caciques* played a broker role very similar to that of the rural *caciques*.[69] They established clientelistic relationships with the residents of their squatter communities by organizing, and then manipulating, the distribution of land, building materials, titles, and services; in exchange they expected participation in committee meetings and rallies and financial contributions for public services, bribery, and remuneration for work on behalf of the *colonia*. In turn, the urban *caciques* mobilized their clienteles for elections and progovernment rallies, persecuted or ostracized dissidents, and defended the government in exchange for personal rewards and access to government and party officials to press for satisfaction of the clientele's demands.[70] While the porousness of urban life prevented most urban *caciques* from becoming as wealthy or as brutal as their rural counterparts, many of them came to exercise absolute dominance over the affairs of their *colonia*, to the point of evicting uncooperative residents and requiring heavy and unexpected contributions to, for example, purchase a car for their personal use.[71]

One important difference between rural and urban *caciquismo*, however, lay in the greater degree of organization in city politics. In the rural areas, there were few politically relevant organizations besides the CNC, the *ejido*, the schools, the church, and government boards. In Mexico City there was a greater variety of organizations (for example, for sports, occupational groups, mothers, public service interest groups, the *colonias*) that could conceivably become politically relevant. Consequently, the PRI had to resort to a broader variety of strategies of cooptation and control, and the nature of *cacicazgo* varied depending on the type of organization being controlled.

Nevertheless, the same basic tactic was used again and again to accomplish the party's purposes: if an organization started to move into opposition, the PRI or the government would divide it, coopt one half, and repress the other.[72] In the *colonias*, for example, if a leader embarrassed the government, he might simply find that government officials were no longer responsive to his petitions for the community and at the same time find that one of his clients was becoming increasingly critical of him for not "delivering the goods." Soon, his movement would be split between his supporters and those who sided with the critical client, and eventually the former client would replace him as the new *cacique*. Naturally, the new leader was being encouraged in his boldness by the PRI all along, and after winning some benefits for the community to consolidate his position, he would turn out to be no more effective than his predecessor.[73]

Politics in the barrios of Venezuela was very similar to the Mexican situation just described. By 1958, Caracas was surrounded by a large migrant population living in squatter settlements, seeking titles to the land, and petitioning for roads and utilities. *Caciques* (the same term was used) arose to champion the concerns of each of the barrios; they perpetuated themselves in "office" by manipulating local junta elections with party backing and returned the favor by mobilizing their clienteles for party rallies and demonstrations and general elections.[74] While it is hard to be sure without rigorous comparative study, Venezuelan *caciques* seem to have been less abusive of their clienteles and less secure in their positions. Still, this is a difference of degree. Both Mexican and Venezuelan urban *caciques* brokered the exchange of land titles and community development assistance for mobilization of squatter communities in favor of a political party.

Even the tactics used to control organizations within the barrio were similar to those applied in Mexico. There were attempts to establish organizations that would be free of domination by the political parties. The parties, however, recognized that such autonomy posed a threat to their power and actively subverted such attempts.[75] Sometimes party loyalists were sent to infiltrate a new organization and eventually elect one of their own as its leader. More often, a party would coopt an independent leader with an offer of a position in the government or a seat on a commission, in a party body, or in the congress. Since there were so few channels for influence outside the parties, few leaders could resist these offers. Indeed, especially during campaign season, enterprising leaders would create "independent" organizations in order to invite cooptation, a practice well known to Mexicans.[76]

If cooptation failed, parties would create parallel organizations that tended to attract more support than the independents because, having a party connection to the government, they could achieve better results. This strategy, known as *paralelismo*, was used often to recruit support in the squatter settlements in the early 1960s.[77] This was also the parties' response to the neighborhood association movement beginning in the late 1970s.[78] In urban areas, many *asociaciones de vecinos* sprang up to petition city councils for better police protection,

265

road repairs, better sewer systems, and other improvements in public services. *Acción Democrática*'s response was to set up a municipal affairs department with a seat on its national executive committee, which actively encouraged AD's municipal councilmen to create AD-affiliated neighborhood associations to preempt the creation of independent ones.[79]

Nevertheless, Venezuela was unlike Mexico in having a multiparty system. In urban communities, this meant that barrio residents had someone to turn to besides the *cacique* if their demands were not met. As Talton Ray observed in the mid 1960s:

> . . . the most realistic means of exerting pressure is through the opposition parties. Those are the only organized groups available to the barrio man which represent a serious threat or challenge to the government because they are the only ones that compete with it for what it really needs in order to exist—votes.[80]

And party competition was especially intense in the Caracas metropolitan area in the 1960s because the largest party in the system was weak there. In 1963, AD received less than 13 percent of the vote in the Federal District. It took years of intense party competition to bring the urban AD vote up into its "normal" national range. In the meantime, Venezuelan parties and their representatives in government assiduously courted the barrios.

> In sharp contrast to the stereotyped image of the Latin American official who stands aloof from the activities of the lower-class citizens, government officials in Venezuelan cities . . . leave their doors open to petitioners and receive them warmly. . . . Officials frequently visit the barrios, attending inaugurations of improvement projects, sports events, and junta meetings. In some cities, mayors and even state governors take Saturday excursions through the poorer communities and talk with the people about their problems. This contact with the urban poor is very important to the officials: on the one hand, it keeps them abreast of the people's political tendencies; and, on the other, it gives them exposure to the families whom they must persuade to vote for them.[81]

Why Competition Matters

The differences between party-society relations in Mexico and Venezuela before the mid 1980s were so slight that they cause one to wonder how meaningful it is to distinguish between authoritarian and democratic regimes. In some ways, Mexico was about as democratic as a country could be and still be authoritarian: no other authoritarian regime can claim to have had as many elections over as long a period of time, or as well-organized a party that campaigned so hard. Most observers agree that, until recently, the PRI would have won elections (without a majority, of course) even without the fraud and coercion that have become customary.[82] And Venezuela, with its aggressively penetrative parties obsessed with controlling other organizations, was about as authoritarian as a country could be and still claim to be democratic. Criticisms that it was really a *partidocracia*, or partyarchy, are warranted.[83]

Yet, even though Venezuelan democracy was not up to first world standards, and even though it shared some surprising similarities with Mexico, the comparison of political life at

266

the grass roots has shown that Venezuela's competitive party system reduced violent repression and encouraged local officials to treat their clients with greater respect than was customary in Mexico. Critics on the extreme left used to argue that the benefits of democracy are overrated, especially in developing countries, because voting and civil liberties supposedly mean little to people who lack adequate shelter or enough to eat. Even writers who praise democracy as an ideal sometimes criticize actual "democracies" for falling so far short of those ideals that they bring few real benefits to ordinary citizens. Comparison of Venezuela and Mexico offers strong evidence that one essential component of democracy—party competition—does make a difference, even at the grass roots, even in a "democracy" that is far from perfect.

Comparison of Mexico and Venezuela also suggests that three of the benefits of party competition carry over into the arena of national politics. First, it makes for healthier relations between government and opposition. In a competitive party system, the government is more sensitive to the criticism of the opposition. This does not mean that the government is necessarily more responsive to the opposition after criticism; it does necessarily mean that the government anticipates possible criticisms and acts so as to rob them of force. It empowers the opposition through anticipated reaction. The latent power of the opposition is revealed in the meetings of the parliamentary fraction of AD, in which the leadership frequently justifies its decisions by saying that they were necessary "in order not to play into the hands of the opposition."[84]

The sensitivity of the government encourages a more moderate style of opposition behavior as well. In Venezuela, the opposition parties rarely went beyond verbal criticism and peaceful demonstrations, because this was all they had to do to get a reaction. The opposition's energies were all directed towards embarrassing or shaming the government. In Mexico, however, the government could ignore mere criticism as long as the PRI's dominance was secure. In order to provoke a reaction, the opposition had to take more drastic measures—highway blockades, plant seizures, and other forms of civil disobedience. The severity of the governments' responses corresponded to the severity of opposition actions. In Venezuela, the governing party would respond with rhetoric, denial, cooptation, infiltration, and *paralelismo*. The Mexican government's response would include all of the above tactics, plus violent repression, which is rarely used against political opponents in Venezuela.[85]

A clarification may be necessary at this point. Not all democracies with competitive party systems exhibit the same sensitivity of the government and moderation of the opposition that Venezuela did, but this does not mean that this conclusion is invalid. The polarization, praetorian struggle, extreme tactics, and even violence found in the "democratic" experience of Ecuador, Peru, Bolivia, Argentina, El Salvador, and other countries are not properly associated with democratic regimes, because their democracy was not consolidated. A comparison based on stable, institutionalized regimes, such as Mexico and Venezuela, yields the most reliable generalization.

A second benefit of competitive party politics pertains to the autonomy of the opposition. In Mexico it was not always clear which groups were in the opposition and which were supporting the government. There were "parastatal" political parties with independent origins and separate representation in the congress that always voted with the PRI on important questions;[86] labor unions outside the CTM that were nevertheless dominated by

267

classic *charros*; sports clubs founded independently for nonpolitical purposes that ended up turning out their membership for PRI rallies. It was in the interest of both the leaders of these organizations and the PRI to encourage this ambiguity, because the costs of both autonomy and subservience were high. In Venezuela, the lines between government and opposition were clearly drawn. Parties were either cooperating with the government (through a formal coalition or an explicit pact) or openly opposing it. Leaders of labor unions and other social organizations might deny any partisan affiliation of their organization, but not because party ties were murky but rather, because they were clear but pluralistic. This behavior reflects a fundamental difference between an authoritarian, dominant party system and a democratic, competitive system: in the former, real opposition is not legitimate in the eyes of the government, and explicit cooperation is viewed as a sell-out by the opposition. In the latter, opposition is recognized as legitimate, and honest cooperation with the government is respected, because collaboration does not require a surrender of autonomy.

The final and perhaps the most important benefit of party competition is that it affords a greater potential for peaceful evolution of the political system. In the long run, all political systems need to evolve in order to respond to changes in society. New groups arise, people expect different things from their leaders, and new issues become salient. If a regime does not adapt to these changes, leaders lose their ability to govern effectively and must rely less on institutional mechanisms of control and more on repression if they are to stay in power. This adaptation is difficult in a dominant party system because most of the actors who have the power to change the system have a personal stake in preserving it the way it is. In a competitive party system, the opposition parties have a stake in proposing popular political reforms that will return them to power. Therefore, other things being equal, a competitive system is better able to adapt than a dominant party system.

A comparison of political trends in Mexico and Venezuela in the 1980s will serve as a brief case study that supports these broad generalizations. By the mid 1980s the need for political reform in both countries was impossible to ignore. The system of stability built on cooptation and party penetration had been in place for decades, and a more urban, better educated, more middle class population was no longer willing to support this old political style.

In Mexico, it took a long time before the government responded to the population's new aspirations, and when it did, the response was inadequate. Demands for change began surfacing earlier than in Venezuela, with the student demonstrations of 1968, the autonomous peasant organizations of the 1970s, and the independent currents within the unions in the 1980s.[87] Mexican presidents periodically announced reform efforts to deal with some of the complaints about the regime—Echeverría's Integrated Rural Development designed to undermine the rural *caciques*, López Portillo's electoral reform of 1977, de la Madrid's Moral Renovation campaign against corruption—but all of these programs either were largely symbolic or were frustrated by opposition to them within the PRI. When the de la Madrid government committed obvious fraud to prevent Cuauhtémoc Cárdenas from winning the 1988 presidential election, democratization became a much more distant goal.[88]

The Salinas government elected in that year finally carried out significant reforms, including the first recognition of an opposition victory in a gubernatorial election, a reorganization of the PRI that has begun the shift from indirect corporate membership to direct individual membership, and the arrest or replacement of several corrupt *charro* leaders. Nevertheless, a new biased electoral law, continuing electoral fraud, and resistance to reform by state and local PRI cadres have made it clear that the PRI will not surrender power at the national level to another group anytime soon.[89]

In Venezuela, demands for "democratization of democracy" hardly began to be voiced before the government responded with serious reform, and its quick response can be traced directly to the incentives created by party competition. In 1984, to fulfill a minor campaign promise, President Lusinchi created a Presidential Commission for the Reform of the State (COPRE). The commission, composed of representatives of all of the major parties as well as highly respected business, church, and university leaders, produced a surprisingly sharp critique of Venezuelan democracy and proposed far-reaching reforms that would have the effect of weakening the political parties.[90]

The government could have ignored COPRE's recommendations, since no interest groups were actively calling for such reforms, and the governing party had many self-interested reasons to resist them. But during the election campaign of 1988, the presidential candidate of COPEI, Eduardo Fernández, sensed that he stood little chance of winning the election unless he found a powerful new issue. COPEI had done poorly in the 1983 elections, and according to the opinion polls of 1987–88 its position had hardly improved. Fernández therefore began advocating the implementation of COPRE's recommendations. The presidential candidate of AD, Carlos Andrés Pérez, understood that this issue could give COPEI an edge in the competition and decided to make the issue his own.

After that point, the two parties competed to present themselves as the champions of political reform, and as a result the first legislative actions were taken even before the election was held. A consensus on the need for reform took hold and has led to the adoption of further reforms during the Pérez government. Direct elections were held for state governors and mayors in 1989, and the electoral law was modified to make legislators more accountable to local constituencies.[91]

Some of these reforms may be partially frustrated by entrenched interests, and further reforms will certainly be needed if Venezuela is to attain the kind of democracy associated with the industrialized countries. Still, it is a developing democracy that has shown its ability to reform itself peacefully, while remaining politically stable. The Mexican regime has been at least as stable as Venezuela, but in several ways it is not as democratic. One telling proof of its authoritarian nature is the fact that it has not been able to reform itself without major turmoil and may not be able to reform itself peacefully at all.

The recent histories of political reform in Venezuela and Mexico support the superior adaptability of democracy only if *ceteris paribus* conditions hold. Obviously, other things are not always equal. In the wake of the 1989 riots and the 1992 coup attempts in Venezuela, Mexico seems to be the superior adaptor. Due to the superior leadership and skill of Carlos Salinas and his technocratic team, Mexico's more realistic prospects for free trade with the United States, and the opposition's wish to avoid a second bloody Mexican revolution, the limited reforms sanctioned by the Mexican government have been more efficacious than the sweeping reforms passed in Venezuela. However, the Venezuela regime's greater *willingness* to adapt is demonstrated by the fact that it adopted deeper reforms, earlier in the game, and in response to milder protest. At this writing, a thorough

269

constitutional reform is being debated. In the long run, Venezuelan democracy may yet demonstrate a superior ability to evolve peacefully.

NOTES

I am grateful to the Department of Education for a Fulbright Grant for Doctoral Dissertation Research Abroad, which financed research in Venezuela on which parts of this article are based, to Alejandra Grosse, who provided superb research assistance, and to two anonymous reviewers.

1. Questions similar to those in this study were also examined in Seymour Martin Lipset, *Political Man* (New York: Doubleday, 1960), and Sidney Verba, Norman Nie, and Jae-On Kim, *Participation and Political Equality: A Seven-Nation Comparison* (Cambridge: Cambridge University Press, 1978).

2. Prominent examples are Arend Lijphart, *Democracies: Patterns of Majoritarian and Consensus Government in Twenty-One Countries* (New Haven: Yale University Press, 1984); David Cameron, "The Expansion of the Public Economy," *American Political Science Review*, 72 (December 1978), 1243–1261; and G. Bingham Powell, *Contemporary Democracies: Participation, Stability, and Violence* (Cambridge, Mass.: Harvard University Press, 1982).

3. Larry Diamond, Juan J. Linz, and Seymour Martin Lipset, eds., *Democracy in Developing Countries*, 4 vols. (Boulder: Lynne Rienner, 1988), considers each country's democratic and nondemocratic experiences to explain the evolution of democracy, but not to justify it. On policy consequences, see Valerie Bunce, *Do New Leaders Make a Difference? Executive Succession and Public Policy under Capitalism and Socialism* (Princeton: Princeton University Press, 1981); and Karen L. Remmer, "The Politics of Economic Stabilization: IMF Standby Programs in Latin America, 1954–1984," *Comparative Politics*, 19 (October 1986), 1–24.

4. Robert Dahl, *Polyarchy: Participation and Opposition* (New Haven: Yale University Press, 1971), argues the assertion well in chapter 2. The most ambitious study of democratization is Guillermo O'Donnell, Philippe C. Schmitter, and Laurence Whitehead, eds., *Transitions from Authoritarian Rule* (Baltimore: The Johns Hopkins University Press, 1986); their most extensive discussion of the justification for democracy is contained in the final volume, *Tentative Conclusions about Uncertain Democracies*, written by O'Donnell and Schmitter. Myron Weiner, "Empirical Democratic Theory," in Myron Weiner and Ergun Özbudun, eds., *Competitive Elections in Developing Countries* (Washington: AEI, 1987), pp. 3–34, is concerned primarily with institutionalizing democracy rather than justifying it. See also Terry Lynn Karl, "Dilemmas of Democratization in Latin America," *Comparative Politics*, 23 (October 1990), 1–21, which distinguishes among types of democracy and speculates about their consequences.

5. Charles L. Davis, *Working Class Mobilization and Political Control: Venezuela and Mexico* (Lexington: University Press of Kentucky, 1989), p. 62. However, Dale Story, *The Mexican Ruling Party: Stability and Authority* (New York: Praeger Publishers, 1986), p. 86, reports that 70 to 90 percent of the unions were affiliated with the CTM.

6. Evelyn P. Stevens, *Protest and Response in Mexico* (Cambridge, Mass: The MIT Press, 1974), p. 171.

7. Story, pp. 87–88.

8. Ibid, p. 89.

9. Peter H. Smith, *Labyrinths of Power: Political Recruitment in Twentieth-Century Mexico* (Princeton: Princeton University Press, 1979), p. 224.

10. Davis, p. 65. As Wayne Cornelius, Judith Gentleman, and Peter H. Smith, "Overview: The Dynamics of Political Change in Mexico," in Wayne Cornelius, Judith Gentleman, and Peter H. Smith, eds., *Mexico's Alternative Political Futures* (La Jolla: Center for U.S.-Mexican Studies, University of California, San Diego, 1989), p. 22, have noted, the Mexican taboo against direct criticism of the president has been broken in the last decade. The mere fact that these violations are noteworthy, however, indicates the gap between the two systems: in Venezuela, disrespectful criticism of the president by opposition politicians, radio commentators, newspaper editorialists, and television satirists is taken for granted. What is newsworthy in Venezuela is any presidential attempt to stifle such criticism, such as Jaime Lusinchi's ban on coverage of his divorce. The gaps have narrowed in some respects but are still wide.

11. Davis, pp. 36–40.

12. Barry Carr, "The Mexican Economic Debacle and the Labor Movement: A New Era or More of the Same?," in Donald L. Wyman, ed., *Mexico's Economic Crisis: Challenges and Opportunities* (La Jolla: Center for U.S.-Mexican Studies, University of California, San Diego, 1983), pp. 91–116.

13. Story, p. 89, and Stevens, p. 106.

270

14. Raúl Trejo Delarbre, "El movimiento obrero: Situación y perspectivas," in Pablo González Casanova and Enrique Florescano, eds., *México, hoy* (Siglo Veintiuno Editores, 1979), pp. 121–151. One example of the strategy of postponing elections is described in María Lorena Cook, "Organizing Opposition in the Teachers' Movement in Oaxaca," in Joe Foweraker and Ann L. Craig, eds., *Popular Movements and Political Change in Mexico* (Boulder: Lynne Rienner, 1990), p. 209.

15. Stephens, *Protest and Response*, is the best survey of the turbulence in Mexico's labor history.

16. Ian Roxborough, *Unions and Politics in Mexico: The Case of the Automobile Industry* (Cambridge: Cambridge University Press, 1984); Kevin J. Middlebrook, "Union Democratization in the Mexican Automobile Industry: A Reappraisal," *Latin American Research Review*, 24 (1989), 69–93.

17. Davis, pp. 26–27.

18. For more information on party penetration of the labor movement in Venezuela, see Andreas Boeckh, "Organized Labor and Government under Conditions of Economic Scarcity: The Case of Venezuela" (Ph.D. diss., University of Florida, 1972); Stuart I. Fagen, "Unionism and Democracy," in John D. Martz and David J. Myers, eds., *Venezuela: The Democratic Experience* (New York: Praeger Publishers, 1977), pp. 174–194; Julio Godio, *El movimiento obrero venezolano, 1965–1980*, vol. 3 (Caracas: ILDIS, 1982); Margarita López Maya and Luis Gómez Calcaño, "Desarrollo y hegemonía en la sociedad venezolana: 1958 a 1985" (mimeo, Centro de Estudios del Desarrollo, Caracas, June 1985); and Carlos Eduardo Febres, "El movimiento sindical: Actor social o gestor institucional?," in Moisés Naím and Ramón Piñango, eds., *El caso Venezuela: Una ilusión de armonía* (Caracas: Ediciones IESA, 1984), pp. 288–309.

19. *Latin American Regional Report*, 85–05 (June 21, 1985). The figure is approximately correct for 1985. Thirteen to twenty percent of the organized work force is affiliated with the Christian Democratic CODESA or the leftist CUTV.

20. Boeckh, pp. 173–178.

21. Charles L. Davis and Kenneth M. Coleman, "Political Control of Organized Labor in a Semi-Consociational Democracy: The Case of Venezuela," in Edward C. Epstein, ed., *Labor Autonomy and the State in Latin America* (Boston: Unwin Hyman, 1989), p. 259.

22. Ellner describes the relationship between the political and labor leaders of AD in detail but exaggerates the labor bureau's autonomy and influence within the party during the 1960s. Steve Ellner, "Organized Labor's Political Influence and Party Ties in Venezuela: Acción Democrática and Its Labor Leadership," *Journal of Inter-American Studies and World Affairs*, 31 (Winter 1989), 91–129. The labor wing did not prevail over the political leaders of AD in the mid 1960s so much as side with a majority faction against Rómulo Betancourt, who had lost his preeminence within his own party during those years. Many of Ellner's examples of labor's independence involved minority factions within the labor bureau whose actions were overruled by the majority of its leadership or who were expelled. See Michael Coppedge, "Strong Parties and Lame Ducks: A Study of the Quality and Stability of Venezuelan Democracy" (Ph.D. diss., Yale University, 1988), ch. 1.

23. In a 1985 survey of AD leaders, 78 percent of the labor leaders and 63 percent of AD members of congress agreed that the labor leaders should push their demands even if they lacked party support. Coppedge, "Strong Parties and Lame Ducks," p. 41.

24. Jennifer L. McCoy, "Labor and the State in a Party-Mediated Democracy: Institutional Change in Venezuela," *Latin American Research Review*, 24 (1989), 35–67. According to a management source, the labor ministry sided with the unions over 80 percent of the time on appeals of "unjustified" dismissals. U.S. Embassy Annual Labor Report of 1977, cited in Cecilia Valente, *The Political, Economic, and Labor Climate in Venezuela* (Philadelphia: Industrial Research Unit, The Wharton School, University of Pennsylvania, 1979), p. 121.

25. McCoy, pp. 50–51.

26. Confidential interview with an AD labor leader, August 3, 1985.

27. Public employees' salaries were twice cut by ten percent in 1960 and 1961. The second reduction provoked criticism by labor leaders affiliated with leftist parties, but the AD (and COPEI) leaders of the CTV supported the cuts and expelled the PCV and MIR from the CTV. Robert J. Alexander, *The Venezuelan Democratic Revolution: A Profile of the Regime of Rómulo Betancourt* (New Brunswick: Rutgers University Press, 1964), pp. 155–156 and 241–242.

28. McCoy, "Labor and the State in a Party-Mediated Democracy," has argued that labor militancy increased after 1969 due to the CTV's increased financial independence and its new corporatist role. Simple inspection of Figure 1 shows that, if there was any such secular increase, it was dwarfed by the effects of party control.

29. Davis and Coleman, pp. 253–254.

30. Manuel Peñalver, "La crisis y las bases de la democracia social" (Caracas: FETRATEL, 1985); and Manuel Peñalver, "Los trabajadores y la política" (Caracas: UTRAVE, 1985).

271

31. McCoy, "Labor and the State in a Party-Mediated Democracy."

32. Ellner, pp. 91–99.

33. Davis and Coleman, p. 262.

34. Ellner, p. 116.

35. Davis, *Working-Class Mobilization*, p. 32, documents the case of a COPEI-led oil workers' union in which no opposition slate had ever been presented in a union election. Venezuela's large federation of public employees held no national congress for the first twenty-six years of its existence. Confidential interview with a FEDE-UNEP leader, Caracas, June 6, 1985.

36. Davis, ch. 4. However, Davis and Coleman, pp. 247–273, note that the CTV moved in the direction of political unionism after 1980.

37. Davis and Coleman, p. 253.

38. Edward C. Epstein, "Conclusion," in Epstein, ed., *Labor Autonomy and the State in Latin America*, pp. 278–284.

39. Davis, p. 77.

40. Ibid., pp. 98 and 154.

41. Ibid., pp. 120 and 132.

42. This interpretation was suggested by an anonymous reviewer of this article. For the original distinction between state and societal corporatism, see Philippe C. Schmitter, "Still the Century of Corporatism?," in Frederick B. Pike and Thomas Stritch, eds., *The New Corporatism: Social-Political Structures in the Iberian World* (Notre Dame: University of Notre Dame Press, 1974), pp. 85–131.

43. On corporatist arrangements in Venezuela, see McCoy, pp. 35–67; Luis Oropeza, *Tutelary Pluralism: A Critical Approach to Venezuelan Democracy* (Cambridge, Mass.: Harvard University Press, 1983); and Donald Herman, "Democratic and Authoritarian Traditions," in Herman, ed., *Democracy in Latin America: Colombia and Venezuela* (New York: Praeger, 1988), pp. 5–9.

44. Gerhard Lehmbruch, "Liberal Corporatism and Party Government," *Comparative Political Studies*, 10 (April 1977), 91–126.

45. McCoy, p. 53.

46. Ellner, pp. 113 and 101.

47. Eduardo Arroyo Talavera, *Elecciones y negociaciones: Los límites de la democracia en Venezuela* (Caracas: Fondo Editorial CONICIT/POMAIRE, 1988), p. 227.

48. Victor V. Magagna, "Representing Efficiency: Corporatism and Democratic Theory," *Review of Politics*, 50 (Summer 1988), 423.

49. Ross M. Martin, "Pluralism and the New Corporatism," *Political Studies*, 31 (March 1983), 90.

50. Lehmbruch, pp. 99–100.

51. Arroyo Talavera, pp. 215 and 230.

52. Luisa Paré, "Caciquismo y estructura de poder en la sierra Norte de Puebla," in Roger Bartra et al., *Caciquismo y poder político en el México rural*, 5th ed. (Mexico City: Siglo XXI, 1980), pp. 31–61; and Bo Anderson and James D. Cockroft, "Control and Cooptation in Mexican Politics," *International Journal of Comparative Sociology*, 7 (March 1966), 11–28.

53. Confidential interviews with FCV leaders in 1985; see also John Duncan Powell, *Political Mobilization of the Venezuelan Peasant* (Cambridge, Mass.: Harvard University Press, 1971).

54. John G. Corbett, "Linkage as Manipulation: The Partido Revolucionario Institucional in Mexico," in Kay Lawson, ed., *Political Parties and Linkage* (New Haven: Yale University Press, 1980), pp. 327–344.

55. Tonatiuh Guillén López, "The Social Bases of the PRI," in Cornelius, Gentleman, and Smith, eds., *Mexico's Alternative Political Futures*, pp. 243–264.

56. Carlos Martínez Assad and Alvaro Arreola Ayala, "El poder de los gobernadores," in Rafael Segovia and Soledad Loaeza, eds., *La vida política mexicana en la crisis* (Mexico City: El Colegio de Mexico, 1987), pp. 107–130.

57. Rexene Hanes de Acevedo, "El control político en tiempos de crisis: Estudio de caso de una asociación de vecinos en Venezuela," paper presented at the Sixteenth International Congress of the Latin American Studies Association, Washington, D.C., April 4–6, 1991.

58. Before 1989, Venezuelan governors were appointed by the president, not elected. Mexican governors have been elected since the revolution, although they are handpicked for candidacy by the president and all Mexican presidents have forced some of them to resign in order to replace them with new favorites.

59. Author's observations during a campaign swing in October 1985.

60. Consejo Supremo Electoral, *Elecciones municipales 1984* (Caracas: 1985), *passim*. The median is not changed when the large urban districts are excluded from the analysis.

61. José de Jesús Orozco Henríquez, "Legislación electoral en México," in CAPEL, *Legislación electoral comparada: Colombia, México, Panamá, Venezuela, y Centroamérica* (San José, Costa Rica: Ediciones CAPEL, 1986), pp. 255 and 264.

62. Arturo Valenzuela, *Political Brokers in Chile* (Durham: Duke University Press, 1977), found the same consequence of competition at the local level in Chile before Pinochet.

63. Enrique Márquez Jaramillo, "El movimiento Navista y los procesos políticos de San Luis Potosí, 1958–1985," in Segovia and Loaeza, eds., pp. 131–148.

64. Paré.

65. Frans Schryer, "Peasants and the Law: A History of Land Tenure and Conflict in the Huasteca," *Journal of Latin American Studies*, 18 (1986), 283–311. See also Paré.

66. Paré, pp. 31–61.

67. These examples are drawn from Paré's detailed descriptions.

68. Susan Eckstein, "The State and the Urban Poor," in José Luis Reyna and Richard Weinert, eds., *Authoritarianism in Mexico* (Philadelphia: Institute for the Study of Human Issues, 1977), pp. 23–46.

69. Antonio Ugalde, *Power and Conflict in a Mexican Community: A Study of Political Integration* (Albuquerque: University of New Mexico, 1970).

70. Susan Eckstein, *The Poverty of Revolution: The State and the Urban Poor in Mexico*, 2nd ed. (Princeton: Princeton University Press, 1988).

71. Wayne A. Cornelius, *Politics and the Migrant Poor in Mexico City* (Stanford: Stanford University Press, 1975); and Alejandra Moreno Toscano, "La crisis en la ciudad," in Casanova and Florescano, eds., pp. 152–176.

72. M. Pozas García, "Land Settlement by the Poor in Monterey," in Alan Gilbert, ed., *Housing and Land in Urban Mexico* (La Jolla: Center for U.S.-Mexican Studies, University of California, San Diego, 1989).

73. Eckstein, "The State and the Urban Poor," pp. 35–46.

74. Talton F. Ray, *The Politics of the Barrios of Venezuela* (Berkeley: University of California Press, 1969), and Lisa R. Peattie, *View from the Barrio* (Ann Arbor: University of Michigan Press, 1968).

75. Moisés Naím and Ramón Piñango, "El caso Venezuela: Una ilusión de armonía," in Naím and Piñango, eds., pp. 560–563.

76. Author's observations during the election campaigns of 1983.

77. Ray, p. 90.

78. Mina Silberberg, "Change and Continuity in 'Extra-Clientelist' Politics: Alternative Organizations of the Venezuelan Poor," paper presented at the Sixteenth International Congress of the Latin American Studies Association, Washington, D.C., April 4–6, 1991.

79. Acción Democrática, Departamento de Política Municipal, *Reglamento sobre el funcionamiento de las fracciones de concejales de Acción Democrática, 1984: Reglamento del Departamento de Política Municipal*; and interview with the National Director of Municipal Policy, Lewis Pérez Daboín, July 25, 1985.

80. Ray, p. 97.

81. Ibid., p. 89.

82. The PRI was the most favored party in Mexico, even in opinion polls (rather than manipulated votes), even in 1987, even in the states where the opposition was strongest, according to Guillén López, pp. 243–264.

83. Coppedge, "Strong Parties and Lame Ducks," ch. 2.

84. Author's observations of meetings of the AD parliamentary fraction during 1985.

85. Venezuelan police and the National Guard can be quite brutal towards criminals (or suspected criminals), but violent repression was not systematically used against political opponents, unless they went into armed rebellion, as the FALN did in the 1960s.

86. Juan Molina Horcasitas, "The Future of the Electoral System," in Cornelius, Gentleman, and Smith, eds., pp. 274–280.

87. These challenges arose from nonparty organizations before 1988, but they presented the government with what could be considered the functional equivalent of party competition. This experience would support a more basic argument, that *competition* matters, whether it is led by political parties or not.

88. Andrew Reding, "Mexico under Salinas: A Façade of Reform," *World Policy Journal* (Fall 1989), 685–729.

89. Michael Coppedge, "Mexican Democracy: You Can't Get There from Here," in Riordan Roett, ed., *The Politics of Economic Liberalization in Mexico* (Boulder: Lynne Rienner, 1992).
90. Luis Gómez Calcaño and Margarita López Maya, *El Tejido de Penélope: La Reforma del Estado en Venezuela (1984–1988)* (Caracas: CENDES/APUCV/IPP, 1990), pp. 117–160.
91. Margarita López Maya, "Tensiones sociopolíticas en el reciente proceso de descentralización en Venezuela," paper presented at the Forty-seventh International Congress of Americanists, New Orleans, July 1991.

Coming in *Comparative Politics*

"The New Politics of Resentment: Radical Right-Wing Populist Parties in Western Europe" by Hans-Georg Betz

"The Political Economy of Privatization through Divestiture in Lesser Developed Economies" by Luigi Manzetti

"The Meaning of Political Participation in a Nonliberal Democracy: The Israeli Experience" by Uri Ben-Eliezer

"State Leadership in Economic Policy: A Collective Action Framework with a Colombian Case" by David R. Mares

"Party Transformation in France and the United States: The Hierarchical Effects of System Change in Comparative Perspective" by Andrew Appleton and Daniel S. Ward.

"The Wall after the Wall: On the Continuing Division of Germany and the Remaking of Political Culture" by Michael Minkenberg

"Between Theory and History and Beyond Traditional Area Studies: A New Comparative Perspective on Latin America" by Gerardo L. Munck

---

274

Presidents, Ruling Parties, and Party Rules

A Theory on the Politics of Economic Reform in Latin America

Javier Corrales

Between the 1980s and early 1990s numerous statist political parties throughout the world experienced the shock of their lifetimes.[1] In countries as diverse as Australia, Bolivia, Costa Rica, Ecuador, France, Greece, Haiti, India, Jamaica, Mexico, New Zealand, Paraguay, Romania, Spain, and Zambia, statist parties won elections, often running on a traditional platform of state intervention in the economy, only to discover that their very own governments were ready to jettison this platform in favor of market-oriented economic reforms. These turnarounds not only contradicted the parties' historical platforms, but also penalized important constituents of the parties in the short term. Invariably, these parties reacted to these reforms with utter dismay.

This dislocation in executive-ruling party relations is a recurrent and understudied political issue in every process of market-oriented economic reform. In contrast to prevailing theories on the subject, which view reform implementation as contingent on struggles between the executive and antireform interest groups and opposition parties, this article argues that the key conflict to resolve is between the executive and the ruling party. If left unchecked, executive-ruling party dislocation will hamper the capacity of governments to implement reforms.

This article elaborates the reasons why market-oriented economic reforms produce dislocation in executive-ruling party relations. However, it also suggests that this dislocation is resolvable, depending on the strategies adopted by the executive. Three possible responses to these dislocations are discussed. The first is a party-neglecting approach: the executive simply neglects the concerns of the party and attempts to implement the reforms by bypassing the ruling party. The second approach is party-yielding: the executive cedes to the demands of the party, in essence abandoning the reform program. The third approach is party-accommodating: the executive negotiates some compromise with the party, granting political concessions in return for the party's consent to implement reforms.

All of these responses affect the politics of reform implementation. Specifically, they affect two variables: political stability during the reform process and depth of reform implementation. A party-neglecting approach engenders the highest degree of instability and, hence, implementation difficulties. The party-yielding approach might placate tensions in executive-ruling party relations, but at the expense of reform implementation. Whether reform abdication will improve stability in overall

127

state-society relations is, however, less predictable. On the one hand, the ruling party is less likely to be a source of conflict, but, on the other, the abandonment of reforms might lead to such a deterioration of economic variables that state-society relations could turn unstable. Party accommodation, in contrast, generates both greater political stability and deeper reform implementation. By obtaining the consent of the ruling party, the executive wins a crucial political ally, which better equips the executive to wage battles against reform enemies across society. Nevertheless, reform implementation will never be as deep as the executive had hoped. Precisely because the executive is forced to compromise with the ruling party, important illiberal gaps will emerge. In short, reform implementation will be far-reaching and politically smoother, but not entirely neoliberal. These points will be illustrated by discussing Venezuela (1989–1993) and Argentina (1989–1996) in detail and Mexico, Paraguay, and Ecuador in more general terms.

Economic Reforms and Political Parties

Political economists who study processes of economic reform devote little attention to political parties. They prefer instead to see reforms as a political battle between the state and a battery of reform-opposed social groups. Rent-seeking interest groups (either business or labor) are often considered to be the most serious political enemies of the reforms, since they are perceived as the biggest economic losers of these processes, at least in the short term.[2]

Successful economic reform is thus contingent on state officials' ability to neutralize society-based opposition. In some cases, social forces oppose the reforms because they bear heavy economic costs; the suggested remedy is to compensate losers. In other cases, social forces oppose the reforms because they mistrust the executive's commitment to reform; the prescribed solution is for the executive to maximize credibility by adopting the right policy prescription,[3] the right technical experts,[4] or the most radical policy shock ("overshooting").[5] For other scholars, reform implementation is contingent on the executive's ability to concentrate power[6] or simply to persevere until the opposition subsides by attrition.[7] Still others argue that the key is for the state to establish some kind of "link" (for example, *concertación*) with affected groups such as business or popular sectors or both.[8] Others equate reform difficulties to a prisoner's dilemma or a deadlock game between the state and social sectors,[9] which can be resolved to the state's advantage if there is a major economic catastrophe that renders social actors more prone to accept the costs of cooperation.[10]

In most of these works, political parties are either an absent or a secondary variable. To the extent that parties enter into the discussion, it is usually in reference to opposition parties or the manner in which the incumbents interact with them. It has been argued, for instance, that in fragmented, highly polarized, or deinstitutionalized party systems, executives will encounter greater difficulty in governing.[11] Others emphasize that political parties with a tradition of clientelism and statism are unlikely ever to play a constructive role in processes of political or economic renewal.[12]

However, political parties in general—and ruling parties in particular—play crucial roles in the politics of economic reform. Governments that fail to gain the support of their own parties for structural adjustment find it even harder to gain the support of other political forces in society. This failure imperils reform implementation. Strong and unified (as opposed to loose, fragmented, and divided) ruling parties are a precondition of economic governance. However, ruling parties can also act as the most formidable stumbling block in the reform process. To show how, it is important to understand the interaction between executives and ruling parties during economic reforms.

Executive-Ruling Party Relations in Argentina and Venezuela in the Early 1990s

When political parties assume office, they do not cease to exist as separate entities. Not all party leaders join the state, and not all party structures mesh with the state apparatus. At a minimum, ruling parties preserve their hierarchy, which includes a central committee responsible for administering party affairs, setting party policies, influencing voting patterns in the legislature, and conducting relations with outside organs. Not all members of these committees are necessarily state officials (they can be party notables, local officeholders, legislators, financiers, or labor bosses). In addition, ruling parties preserve a set of internal organizations (secretariats, legislative blocs, labor groups, civic associations) that also preserve some autonomy.[13] The political opinions, preferences, and actions of ruling party leaders and organizations need not coincide with those of the executive.

In Venezuela and Argentina the ruling parties reacted in opposite directions to the reform process launched in 1989 by the presidents Carlos Andrés Pérez and Carlos S. Menem. Both presidents came from quintessential statist parties: *Acción Democrática* (AD) and the *Partido Justicialista* (PJ), or Peronist Party, respectively. Halfway into the reform process, executive-ruling party relations became contentious in Venezuela and cooperative in Argentina. Interviews with top party leaders in each country in 1994 support this assessment.[14] When asked if they felt represented in the government, only two AD respondents agreed, whereas all but one PJ respondent agreed. AD's sense of alienation could not be attributed to disagreements about economic ideas: the majority of AD respondents indicated agreement with the administration's economic objectives.

This dichotomy in executive-ruling party relations can not be easily explained by existing arguments. For example, Geddes argues that ruling parties are likely to support

129

efficiency-enhancing reforms when they achieve parity with other parties, which makes parties estimate that the political costs of the reforms will be shared by all political forces more or less equally.[15] However, AD intensified its rebellion against the executive in 1991, when its distance from the opposition was declining (see Table 1).

Table 1 Electoral Results of the Main Parties, Argentina and Venezuela, 1983–1995

Venezuela

	1983	1988	1989	1992a	1992b	1993
Total						
AD	57.7	52.7	39.7	32.3	31.1	23.6
Copei	35.1	40.0	32.8	32.3	38.4	22.7
Convergencia						30.9
Causa R						21.9
Distance between ruling party and first opposition party	22.6	12.7	6.9	0	-7.3	7.3

Notes: 1989 and 1992a are elections for mayors; 1992b represent elections of governors.

Argentina

	1983	1983*	1985*	1987*	1989	1989*	1991*	1993*	1994**	1995	1995*
PJ	39.9	38.4	34.9	41.5	47.5	44.8	40.7	42.3	38.8	49.9	43.0
UCR	51.8	47.8	43.6	37.2	32.5	28.8	29.0	30.0	20.5	17.0	21.8
Frepaso							01.5	02.5	12.7	28.2	21.2
Distance between ruling party and first opposition party	11.9	9.4	8.7	-4.3	15.0	16.0	11.7	12.3	18.5	21.7	21.2

Notes:
* Chamber of Deputies Elections
** Elections to the Constitutional Assembly
Figures for 1989-1995 de Riz (1998)

Source: OCEI; Fraga (1989); Anuario Estadístico de la República Argentina.

Many Venezuelanists actually make the opposite argument. They attribute AD's discontent precisely to its decline in the share of the vote under Pérez. However, the PJ in Argentina also experienced a decline by 1991 (albeit a less significant one), yet it began to cooperate with the executive that same year. Thus, electoral distance between the ruling party and the opposition does not fully determine executive-ruling party relations.

Another set of arguments stresses the imperiousness of the executive. O'Donnell coined the term "delegative democracy" to describe how, in moments of economic crisis, political actors delegate power to the executive at the expense of institutions.[16] Along these lines, Acuña argues that Menem pursued a "Hobbesian strategy," which included colonizing the party's hierarchy and coopting dissenters.[17] Likewise, Venezuelanists tend to see Pérez's administration in similar terms: a forceful executive that attempted to impose its will.[18] The application of the same label to processes that produced different outcomes suggests that it is not useful in accounting for such differences.

Venezuelanists often explain Pérez's conflict with AD as a result of two special circumstances. First, they stress that Pérez became a presidential candidate in defi-

130

ance of AD's leadership, which supported Octavio Lepage. But Menem also won his party's nomination against the wishes of the PJ's leadership, which supported Antonio Cafiero. Second, they stress the role of the Caracazo, the massive riots that enveloped Venezuela's largest cities on February 27–28, 1989, shortly after announcement of the reforms.[19] However, while the Caracazo served to confirm AD's suspicion that the reforms were unpopular, it neither triggered these suspicions (AD had already expressed apprehension when it chided Pérez for not disclosing the letter of intent to the IMF) nor ended completely AD's willingness to cooperate (in late March 1989 AD still endorsed the reforms).

A final set of inadequate explanations is based on economic factors. One version stresses the role of economic catastrophes: Argentina experienced such a devastating economic crisis after 1983, climaxing in the 1989 hyperinflation, that actors finally adopted cooperative strategies in the 1990s. This argument, however, is empirically problematic. The most conflictive period in executive-ruling party relations, both before and during Menem's administration, occurred in the midst of high inflation (1986–1991).[20] Another version stresses economic achievements: once economic conditions turned favorable, the ruling party turned cooperative. This hypothesis is also problematic. In Venezuela AD's rebellion intensified in 1991, the healthiest macroeconomic year of the administration. And in Argentina the PJ began to cooperate also in 1991, when most economic actors and gurus (including the IMF) expected Argentina's new round of stability to collapse, as had happened with every previous stabilization attempt. The PJ thus began to cooperate with the executive in a context of high economic uncertainty—a true act of faith.

How (Statist) Ruling Political Parties React to Market-Oriented Reforms

An explanation of the different evolution of executive-ruling party relations in Argentina and Venezuela must begin with a map of the initial preferences of ruling parties regarding market-oriented reforms. Geddes demonstrated that incumbents have reservations about efficiency-oriented reforms because they bear the political costs of these reforms more intensely than nonincumbents.[21] This situation creates a dilemma for presidents, who realize that reforms threaten their base of support, whereas the absence of reforms threatens their future electorability.

Although Geddes' argument is a sophisticated account of presidents' dilemmas, it says little about the preferences of ruling parties, other than stating that they prefer patronage or cost-avoidance. In reality, ruling parties tend to have a more complex attitude toward reforms, at least initially. Like the executives, ruling parties face their own dilemma: they recognize that reforms can hurt them politically, but they also understand that not cooperating with the executive can be costly. Ruling parties are thus repelled by and attracted to reforms simultaneously.

131

Points of Conflict   Ruling parties are repelled by reforms for a number reasons. First, the calls for spending cutbacks contradict the natural expectation of victorious parties that they should exploit the advantages of officeholding. Second, differences in the timing and location of elections make ruling party officials more risk-averse about reforms than executives. Executives normally face electoral competitions at different times and in different arenas than ruling party leaders, usually four or five years after their election, if at all. In contrast, the ruling party faces more frequent mid term congressional, municipal, and local elections. Because market reforms tend to produce economic hardship in the near term, they appear riskier to politicians facing elections in the near term.[22] In addition, presidents and party officials compete in different electoral arenas. Presidents get elected by nationwide constituencies; party leaders compete in narrower districts. Since market reforms tend to produce concentrated losers (for example, a specific privatization can generate unemployment in a particular locality or hurt a specific interest group), politicians who depend heavily on votes from narrow constituencies (mayors, governors, legislators, labor bosses) will be unenthusiastic about reforms.

If the ruling party happens to be a statist party, the clash between the party and the reforms can be even stronger. Statist parties see themselves as market-correctors rather than market-creators and thus could see the reforms as depriving them of their *raison d'être*, or at least of leaving them with an incongruent ideological posture. Statist parties also fear that the reforms will deprive them of opportunities to carry on as brokers of rents between the state and rent-seeking industrialists and labor groups. Even worse, they fear that the reforms will reduce their involvement in policy decision making. Since many statist parties consider themselves as custodians of the very same institutions that market-oriented *técnicos* seek to dismantle, they will have a strong desire to be consulted over these decisions. *Técnicos*, on the other hand, will have a strong desire to avoid such consultation out of fear that consultation will produce deadlock.

In short, the executive and the ruling party hold opposite primary preferences on two variables: depth of reform implementation and party inclusion in policymaking (see Figure 1). Point A in Figure 1 represents the executive's primary preferences. The executive prefers to pursue deep reform and exclude the ruling party as much as possible from decision making (the executive correctly perceives apprehension about reform within the ruling party). Points B_1 through B_4 represent the possible initial preferences of the ruling party. Compared to the executive, the ruling party certainly prefers less reform implementation and more inclusion in policymaking. However, depending on how many of the previously discussed points these parties share, ruling parties might allow more flexibility. For instance, some parties, such as AD, have a history of granting great autonomy to the executive (point B_1 on Figure 1). Other parties might be less flexible in this regard. Thus, the range of preferences of the ruling party can vary, although it is significantly more averse to reform implementation and exclusion from policymaking than the executive.

132

Figure 1 Reform Implementation and Executive-Ruling Party Relations

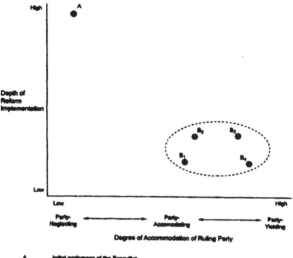

Points of Compatibility The previous analysis suggests that there is no possibility of cooperation between executives and ruling parties. However, ruling parties are not entirely averse to neoliberal reforms. First, there are affinities between neoliberalism and populism, as many scholars have highlighted recently. Both ideologies provide utopian visions of the future, identify clear enemies (privileged interest groups), and seek to mobilize actors that were "hurt" by the preexisting model of economic development.[23] Second, the reforms offer these parties the opportunity to repeat their role as "foundational" parties, that is, to bring modernity to the nation, not unlike what these parties thought they were doing in the mid twentieth century when they introduced statist economic models. Third, many of these parties have nonprogrammatic traditions. Latin American political parties, for instance, operate in extraordinarily presidential systems, in which parties grant executives significant autonomy in policymaking. At most, parties expect the executive to implement policies based on "the philosophical and doctrinal principles of the party," to quote directly from AD's statutes.[24] But these principles are often quite vague (for example, to preserve the sovereignty of the people) and flexible (for example, to promote social justice), and sometimes not at all incompatible with the antirent objectives of market-oriented reforms. Fourth, ties with labor, which are common among statist parties, create a "captive market," which might encourage the parties to take more risks.

133

Finally, there is congruence at the second level of preferences between the executive and the ruling party. While executives and ruling parties disagree on their first order of preferences, their second order of preferences is mutually compatible. For instance, although executives prefer full reform implementation and little accommodation of the ruling party, they nonetheless prefer some implementation and some party inclusion over the third alternative, no reform at all. Likewise, although ruling parties would prefer little reform with total inclusion in the government, they still would prefer some reform with some exclusion over the alternative, the complete failure of their government. Thus, the ranking of preferences of a reformist cabinet is full implementation without modification, implementation with modification, and no implementation. For the ruling party, the ranking of preferences is full incorporation, some reform with some exclusion, and the failure of the government. Thus, at the start of the game the first preferences of the executive and the ruling party are incompatible, but the second level preferences are compatible.[25]

In short, some features of statist parties encourage assimilation of neoliberal reforms or at least more risk-taking. Moreover, the second-level preferences of executives and ruling parties are compatible. Thus, executive-ruling party *rapprochement* is difficult, but not impossible. Argentina and Venezuela illustrate how this *rapprochement* might or might not materialize.

Party-Neglecting Strategies: Argentina and Venezuela, 1989–1991

For the most part, Latin American executives have responded to the initial dislocation in executive-ruling party relations by circumventing the ruling party (party-neglecting policy), attempting to negotiate some policy autonomy in return for some political concession to the party (party-accommodating strategy), or acceding to the party's desire to interrupt the reforms (party-yielding policy). In Argentina and Venezuela the executives began the reform process by adopting the first response. This response exacerbates executive-ruling party relations the most.

Pérez began to neglect the ruling party even before taking office, when he and his advisers essentially ignored the *comisión de enlace* (transition commission) established to coordinate the transfer of power after the 1988 elections. Only ten cabinet posts were filled with AD leaders, a very low number in a country where parties traditionally staffed most governments. Instead of relying on *Adecos*, Pérez mostly appointed political friends (for example, Pedro Tinoco, central bank) and highly trained, nonpartisan, market-oriented social scientists (for example, Miguel Rodríguez, Cordiplan; Moisés Naim, industry; Carlos Blanco, COPRE). Even the ministry of health and social assistance, historically a bastion of the ruling party, was given to a non-*Adeco*. The first major confrontation occurred when AD learned that it was not consulted on the drafting of the letter of intent that Pérez secretly signed

134

with the IMF, which committed Venezuela to the reforms. Pérez and his minister frequently disparaged almost everything related to the "old regime." Pérez attempted to establish alliances with newer parties (*Nueva Generación*) and to appeal directly to new social movements. The executive's policy of party exclusion was high by Venezuelan historical standards, but not as excessive as many *Adecos* argued. Various cabinet positions that are crucial for economic policy were given to AD leaders. In addition, Pérez still gave AD some control over state resources. For example, Pérez granted control of the Corporación Venezolana de Guayana to AD financier Leopoldo Sucre Figarella, thereby insulating this massive state-owned industrial complex and source of state rents from the reform process.

Nevertheless, AD never felt that it carried weight in the government. As a former AD presidential candidate stated, "the CEN of AD feels impotent vis-à-vis Pérez."[26] In response, AD decided to devote itself to raising the transaction cost of the reforms. The few statements in support of the reforms issued by AD typically included salvos such as "the Party would like to be more involved in decision making" and "social issues are being neglected." AD refused to grant Pérez special powers to handle the crisis, attacked almost every cabinet position, and persistently scrutinized and even shelved government bills in congress.[27] In essence, AD granted party members freedom to criticize the government and to restrict the autonomy of the executive in formulating policies.

In Argentina Menem also began his administration by adopting a party-neglecting approach. Rather than turn to the party, Menem sought to build alliances with the private sector (Bunge and Born corporation), neoliberal parties (the *Ucedé*), military sectors (appeasement of the military), and international actors (Argentina's new pro-U.S. foreign policy). Consequently, executive-ruling party relations exploded. Like AD, the PJ plunged into a debate about the extent to which the reforms (and Menem) were truly party-friendly and electorally wise. By January 1990 (in the midst of Argentina's second hyperinflation), approximately twenty leading Peronist legislators (the group of eight) quit the party in protest, and those who stayed intensified their criticisms. By late 1990 executive-ruling party relations were in major disarray, succumbing to "internal cannibalism," to quote Menem.[28]

This disharmony in executive-ruling party relations explains why reform implementation was mixed and instability was relatively high during this first part of the reform in Venezuela and Argentina. There were very few serious structural reforms. Those that were implemented (trade liberalization and a few privatizations) came at the expense of growing political instability and declining public support. In Argentina in 1990 Menem even threatened to use the military to quell opposition to privatizations.

The problem was that the ruling parties, resenting the executive's party-neglecting policy, were becoming the preeminent opposition party in each country. In this situa-

135

tion there was no possibility that other political forces would support the reforms. Often led by ruling party members, congress became unfriendly to the reforms. For the first time ever, for instance, AD sided with opposition parties against the executive. It joined COPEI senator Rafael Caldera to approve a new antireform labor law, the so-called Caldera Law, and Causa-R to delay various privatizations. In Argentina the PJ began to question everything that it had agreed to when it approved the Law of the Reform of the State at the start of Menem's administration. Both AD and the PJ encouraged other social actors to show resistance. Business groups began to see the executive as devoid of political allies and thus as a noncredible actor, and state-business cooperation declined. In mid 1991 Venezuela's leading business federation, *Fedecámaras*, criticized the government; between 1990 and early 1991 Argentine business groups engaged in massive capital flight and speculation, triggering two hyperinflations. In short, party-neglecting strategies destabilized overall state-society relations.

Party-Accommodating Strategies in Argentina, 1991–1996

By early 1991 executive-ruling party relations were on a collision course in both Venezuela and Argentina. This collision occurred in Venezuela. In AD's internal elections of September-October 1991 all the top party positions (presidency, secretary general, organization secretary, all three vice presidents) and a majority of secretariats went to orthodox antireform/government leaders. Henceforth the balance in executive-ruling party relations shifted toward the party, now under the control of recalcitrant reform enemies. In Argentina the collision was avoided. By late 1991 Menem emerged as the unquestionable leader of the PJ.

Two variables account for this difference. The first is a policy-type variable: the switch toward party accommodation in Argentina but not in Venezuela. The second is an institutional variable: AD's relatively higher degree of dependence on state rents and internal cartelization.

Policy Switch: The Rise of Party Accommodation in Argentina In a major about-face in mid 1991 Menem began to address some of the political grievances of the PJ. Essentially, he adopted a party-accommodating strategy. As with every great transformation, this one began at the level of ideology. A new campaign to *aggiornar* the PJ was launched with a massive party congress in March 1991: the Justicialist mobilization for political and doctrinal updating. This congress was an exercise in Peronist adulation and party caretaking. Stating that he came to the congress "feeling more Peronist than ever before," Menem addressed head-on every controversial issue in executive-ruling party relations. He announced a new policy toward the PJ. "Our goal is to assign to Peronism the paternity of an unprecedented process of

136

change in our history....The point is not to destroy the political parties, but to insert them in a model of social democracy...." From a position of neglect, the party was now proclaimed the "main author" of the reforms. Mentioning the word Perón (in reference either to Juan Domingo or Evita) thirty-one times, Menem argued that everything that he was doing was exactly what Perón would have done under today's circumstances. Since 1991 Menem has never shied away from emphasizing that his program was simply an updated version of Peronism.

Menem also renegotiated the rules of executive-ruling party relations. Much has been written about Menem's use of decrees.[29] Less attention is paid to the fact that after 1991 the PJ rarely complained. Moreover, the most important structural reforms (the Convertibility Law, most privatizations, the reform of the pension system) were approved by congress. In 1991 the executive negotiated a tacit pact with the PJ. Ministers and reforms would go to congress more frequently; legislators would be allowed to introduce modifications in the proposed bills and even halt progress on labor market reforms; but the executive reserved the right to veto all or part of congressional output. After 1991 the authorities from the ministry of the economy gave the most frequent depositions in congress in recent Argentine history, consistent with the new tacit pact. These new rules of executive-ruling party relations pleased the PJ. Allowing PJ legislators to present modifications to laws gave the PJ both a say in the reform process and an opportunity to save face vis-à-vis their clients. The "you modify, I might veto" formula proved more functional to the clientelistic interests of the party than the "you watch, I decree" scheme that prevailed during first years of the reforms. The latter formula highlighted the irrelevance of legislators, while the former allowed the party to present itself as an influential player.

The importance of addressing the ideological question and renegotiating rules can not be overstated. As Panebianco argues, ideology acts as the primary source of collective incentives (the benefits or promise of benefits that all organizations must distribute equally among participants) and as a veil to conceal selective incentives (benefits distributed to only a few members of the organization).[30] By Peronizing neoliberalism, Menem gave party leaders the ideological tool to cover up the asymmetry in the distribution of costs and benefits that the reforms imposed among the rank and file. And the newly negotiated rules addressed crucial political concerns of the PJ: brokerage and inclusion in policymaking.

Institutional Variables   In fairness, the Venezuelan executive faced much more constraining circumstances in its dealings with the ruling party. Centrifugal forces in executive-ruling party relations were stronger in Venezuela, due to two institutional factors: AD's greater dependence on state rents and greater internal cartelization.

By 1989 AD had governed Venezuela during most of its democratic history, whereas the PJ had governed Argentina on only two occasions, 1946–1952 and 1973–1976. Even in the opposition, AD still retained important state subsidies and

137

prerogatives. Thus, AD was excessively accustomed to the spoils of office. Moreover, from 1983 to 1989 AD enjoyed a "power feast": it solidly controlled the executive, both houses of congress, and every echelon of the state bureaucracy. President Lusinchi appointed all the provincial secretaries general of AD as governors of their respective provinces. In contrast, the 1980s was an inglorious period for the PJ. For the first time, Peronism lost democratic elections not once, but twice (1983 and 1985), plunging the party into a severe political crisis. As predicted by Anthony Downs, the need to recapture votes caused internal infighting, ideological revision, and leadership turnover.[31] These changes did not turn the party more neoliberal, but they served to dismantle old structures and old leaderships. In addition, the numerous debates about the true meaning of Peronist ideology made Peronist ideology more elastic. Experimenters gained more space, and loyalties became less entrenched.

AD's comfortable control of power and votes in the 1980s exempted it from undergoing a real renovation. AD had always been governed by one of the most entrenched cartels in Latin America, the CEN.[32] Because CEN members were not elected by direct vote but rather by party delegates, it was insulated from the preferences of party members. Because CEN members had direct control over who in the party would occupy positions of power, there was a built-in mechanism for party delegates to vote on behalf of incumbents. Thus, the CEN had more power than the electorate in deciding who would hold public office, including governorships. Lacking internal and external contestation, CEN members did not need to worry too much about competing for votes. In fact, the party could lose presidential elections, but the composition of the CEN would change little. And in contrast to the PRI in Mexico, CEN members were not rotated with a change of administrations. Because the CEN faced no need to find a winning formula, it underwent no internal change.[33] In short, low internal and external contestation entrenched leadership structures, fixed ideologies, and fostered strict admission standards.

Thus, institutional differences—dependence on state resources and internal cartelization—help explain why AD's reaction to the executive and the reforms was much more hostile than the PJ's. However, they were contributing, not sufficient, explanations of executive-ruling party relations. If institutional features were the sole answer, executive-ruling party relations in Argentina would not have been as turbulent as they were between 1989 and 1991 (and under previous Peronist administrations), and AD's relations with Pérez's successors (Ramón Velásquez and Rafael Caldera) would not have been as cooperative as they turned out to be. The executive's policy toward the party was in the end more decisive in shaping ruling party responses.

Consequences for State-Society Relations   When Cafiero and Menem publicly exchanged flatteries in August 1991 for the first time since Menem became presi-

138

dent,[34] they marked a historic realignment in executive-ruling party relations.[35] Essentially, the "dissenting" wing of the PJ granted Menem a negotiated permit to proceed with the reforms. The use of decrees did not end, and not all grievances disappeared, but none of the PJ's debates—until 1996—questioned the spirit of the reform. No previous administration since 1951 had enjoyed such a high level of ruling party support for economic austerity measures.

The animosity in executive-ruling party relations in Venezuela and harmony in Argentina were unprecedented in each country. In the past, factionalism in AD meant only that the party would override the executive's choice of a successor; it never denied the executive autonomy over policymaking, as happened under Pérez.[36] Likewise, the harmony in executive-ruling party relations in Argentina between 1991 and 1996 was new in a country where almost every previous administration, civilian or military, had experienced crippling internal dissent.

The emergence of executive-ruling party cooperation in Argentina had enormous consequences for state-society relations. First, it granted the state an effective shield against attacks from society-based reform opponents. For the first time in Argentina, the PJ became unavailable as an institutional avenue through which social forces could sabotage the state's agenda (a role that the PJ had gladly played since 1955). In fact, after 1991 the PJ became a delegitimizer of social unrest, including labor protests. This party stand discouraged would-be saboteurs from launching attacks. Second, executive-ruling party realignment allowed the state to close the credibility gap. For the first time in decades, an Argentine president could offer guarantees of policy continuity because it had solid political grounding. Reform skepticism—a major reason that stabilization attempts often fail—abated. The result was a reform stampede with relative social acquiescence.

The Costs of Party Accommodation

In countries with strong statist parties, a party-accommodating strategy is therefore necessary for deep reform implementation. However, party-accommodating transitions to the market come with two costs: "illiberal" pockets in the reforms and the strengthening of illiberal tendencies in the ruling party.

The illiberal pockets stem from the compromises that the executive reaches in its negotiations with the ruling party. For instance, Menem had to agree to the PJ's demand not to touch two areas that were dear to the party: labor market reforms and social welfare (*obras sociales*). The executive also offered the party antiliberalization guarantees. Spending on social services, which had always been under the control of the party, increased 64.9 percent between early 1991 and mid 1994. Many Peronist unions were granted opportunities to form their own companies in order to participate in privatizations. Most of the debts of *obras sociales*, controlled by PJ unions,

139

121

were condoned. The federal government granted the province of Buenos Aires, controlled by PJ strongman and former vice-president Eduardo Duhalde, significant funds for discretionary spending.

The second cost stems from conforming to the ruling party's hunger for protagonism. In order to obtain ruling party cooperation, the executive inflated the party's sense of self-importance. The PJ wanted its place in the sun as a condition for reform endorsement, and Menem complied. Once again, a Peronist executive nurtured the party's self-perception as the founder of the nation, the custodian of institutions, and the political force whose say should matter the most. The PJ will emerge from the reform process with an inflated sense of indispensability.

Mexico from 1988 to 1994 is a similar case. Much has been written about how Mexico's market-oriented presidents implemented reforms by courting extrapartisan allies—technocrats and new social groups that were either reform "winners" or simply previously marginalized sectors—to the detriment of traditionalist populist elements in the PRI.[37] This article would propose a different interpretation. Mexico's market reforms were possible, as in Argentina, because the executive succeeded in accommodating, rather than displacing, the traditionalist sectors of the PRI. When President Carlos Salinas de Gortari assumed office in 1988, he encountered a ruling party in disarray. His predecessor, Miguel de la Madrid (1982–1988), had done little to accommodate the "dinosaurs" in the PRI.[38] By 1988 the PRI suffered a massive defection, and those who stayed remained rebellious (in the last months of his administration, de la Madrid faced the most uncooperative congress in decades, and labor leaders were openly calling for a change of economic models).[39]

Salinas de Gortari decided to be far more accommodating. He gave traditionalist PRI members space within his administration (positions in the cabinet, local/gubernatorial offices, and party congresses). He sacrificed certain economic objectives (for example, abandoning the original goal of reducing annual inflation to single digits and allowing it to hover around 19 percent) in order to satisfy the party's demand for economic growth.[40] Rather than insist on de la Madrid's strategy of denying victories to the opposition, Salinas devoted significant resources to enhancing the party's capacity to compete electorally.[41] For instance, Salinas injected massive resources into the PRI's electoral campaigns.[42] The 1993–94 electoral code reforms established very high ceilings for private contributions, allowing the PRI to outspend its rivals.[43] Another electoral booster was PRONASOL (*Programa Nacional de Solidaridad*), a huge state program with a US$3 billion budget nominally intended to fight poverty through public works but in fact a populist machine to enhance the PRI's electoral chances. PRONASOL's budget was targeted at areas where the PRI had experienced electoral defeats (Michoacán, Juchitán, Oaxaca).[44] Although monies went from the president's office directly to local offices, thereby superceding some traditional "corporatist" party chiefs, PRONASOL nonetheless helped the party because it provided "investments" in the geographic areas where the

140

PRI was electorally needy.[45] The result was a negotiated settlement with a rebellious party. In return for political concessions, the PRI allowed the executive to proceed with economic reforms.

In short, party accommodation in Argentina and Mexico enhanced the state's capacity to govern economic change, albeit at a cost: illiberal gaps in the reforms and, more important, the fueling of illiberal tendencies inside the ruling party. Paradoxically, neoliberalism has been introduced in conjunction with—in fact, as a consequence of—illiberal gaps.

The Costs of Party-Neglecting Strategies

However serious the costs of a party-accommodating transition to the market, the costs of a party-neglecting approach can be worse. Given the power resources of ruling parties, especially statist parties, allowing them to become too angry, by neglecting them, can destabilize overall state-society relations. Acrimonious executive-ruling party relations erode the credibility of the executive, which undermines the chances of societal cooperation with the reforms. A political impasse emerges in which the executive tries to push the reforms, while opponents across society, often led or galvanized by the ruling party, resist in full knowledge that the executive is politically isolated. This impasse is an unstable equilibrium. At least two scenarios become plausible.

Scenario 1: The Ruling Party Rebels   Party-neglecting strategies can prompt the ruling party to strike against the executive, as happened in Venezuela in the October 1991 internal elections of AD. The rise of the orthodox sectors and the subsequent executive-ruling party divorce created a political vacuum at the state level. These conditions invited a coup attempt, which materialized in February 1992. After this coup, AD continued to chastise the government, demanding the interruption of all reforms. An embattled and isolated executive had no option but to yield to the party. In the meantime, state-society relations deteriorated further.

Thus, party-neglecting strategies often result, paradoxically, in party-yielding outcomes, which ought not be confused with party accommodation. Party accommodation entails the granting to the party of certain concessions in return for substantial leeway over economic policy. Party yielding, on the other hand, entails the surrender of autonomy to the party, the abandonment of the reform program altogether, and the creation of a political vacuum at the top that provokes instability in state-society relations.

Paraguay (1993–1998) is a comparable case. President Juan Carlos Wasmosy also came from a statist party, the *Partido Colorado*, and unveiled reforms that included structural economic changes as well as the demilitarization of state and party struc-

141

tures.[46] These proposals provoked a double-front opposition from the *Partido Colorado*: the traditionalist civilians, led by Luis María Argaña, rejected economic reforms, and the military sectors of the party, led by General Lino César Oviedo, opposed the efforts to subordinate the military. For a while, Wasmosy also pursued a party-neglecting strategy (hiring Hernan Buchi, the architect of Pinochet's neoliberal reforms in the 1980s, as his main economic advisor). This strategy, too, led to the deterioration of executive-ruling party relations. As in Venezuela, the orthodox gained the upper hand, and Wasmosy began to switch to a party-yielding approach (for example, he yielded to Oviedo's desire to construct a lavish field for military parades, the so-called Linódromo). Rather than placate the orthodox sectors, party yielding only invigorated them. By April 1996 Oviedo staged an unsuccessful coup d'état. He won the party's September 1997 primaries, followed by Argaña and in a distant third place the government's candidate. Not surprisingly, economic reforms have stalled in Paraguay since 1995.

Scenario 2: Opposition Parties Attempt to Exploit the Political Vacuum   The analytical equivalent of a dislocation in executive-ruling party relations is to have no strong ruling party at all. In Brazil (1989–1992), Ecuador (1996–1998), and Peru (1990–1992), for instance, populist leaders won the presidency with weak political parties (Abdalá Bucaram/Fabián Alarcón in Ecuador) or last-minute flash electoral movements (Fernando Collor de Melo in Brazil and Alberto Fujimori in Peru). These executives tried to govern, in effect, without a ruling party. Not surprisingly, the reform programs faltered mostly because opposition parties and interest groups, perceiving the political weakness of the executive, tried to take advantage of the politi- - cal vacuum at the state level by rebelling against the reforms. In Brazil and Ecuador the opposition prevailed.

In Peru Fujimori tried to escape from this situation by carrying out his own coup in 1992. With this coup Fujimori attempted to preempt the possibility of the Brazilian-Ecuadorian scenario. An alternative escape route is to pursue a party-accommodating strategy vis-à-vis the main opposition party. This approach was taken by Venezuelan president Rafael Caldera between 1996 and 1998. Caldera was elected with a very weak ruling party, a last-minute alliance formed in 1993 between an ad hoc coalition of minute parties (*Convergencia*) and a historically small socialist party (*Movimiento al Socialismo*, MAS). This *Convergencia*-MAS alliance came in third in every congressional, gubernatorial, and mayoral election. In 1996 Caldera launched a program of economic reform (*Agenda Venezuela*), which further atomized the ruling coalition. Sectors of *Convergencia* began to defect, and MAS began to break apart. This atomization climaxed in July 1998 when the government's economic czar (and founder of MAS), Teodoro Petkoff, resigned from MAS in protest of MAS's antigovernment decision to endorse Hugo Chávez, the most antireform candidate and author of the February 1992 coup attempt, for the 1998 presidential elections.

142

Caldera's response to the fragility of his ruling party was to build bridges with the main opposition force, AD. He gave AD a few ministries, supported AD's nominations and several laws, and preserved AD's presence in the bureaucracy. In return, AD supported some of Caldera's initiatives, such as a watered-down privatization law. Compared to a party-neglecting strategy, party accommodation toward the opposition offered the advantage of compensating the administration for its fragile ruling coalition with a borrowed supporter. However, compared to party accommodation vis-à-vis the ruling party, party accommodation vis-à-vis the opposition precludes high levels of reform implementation. Opposition parties have little interest in seeing the success of the incumbent. Hence the opposition party sells its support at a much higher price and with greater conditions than the ruling party. Thus, AD supported only the most modest reforms and did not shy away from siding with Caldera's enemy when convenient.

Consequently, reform implementation under Caldera did not go very far. He privatized a few firms and liberalized the oil and banking sectors, but he failed to control·inflation and to enact much needed structural reforms, for example, a stabilization fund to manage windfalls in oil revenues. The Venezuelan economy therefore remained fragile and susceptible to external shocks.

Epilogue: Venezuela's 1998 Elections and the Politics of Economic Reform

In the 1998 presidential elections, in the midst of yet another economic crisis, Venezuelans elected the protagonist of the February 1992 coup attempt, Hugo Chávez Frías. The circumstances of his victory are by now a familiar story in Latin America: a populist, military-linked political novice puts together a last-minute coalition of small, left-leaning parties (the *Polo Patriótico*), runs a populist, antipolitical party campaign, and wins the presidency, but not the congress.

If Chávez decides to implement structural adjustment, political instability is likely. The *Polo Patriótico* will fragment and weaken further, rendering the country susceptible to any of the scenarios discussed previously. Opposition parties in congress, for instance, perceiving the institutional isolation of the executive office, might rebel against the executive (scenario 2). In theory, Chávez could respond by adopting Caldera's approach—accommodating the largest opposition party, AD—but this strategy is unlikely, given Chávez's disdain for traditional political parties. Chávez could also abandon the reform process altogether (scenario 1), but this strategy, too, is unlikely, given the seriousness of Venezuela's economic troubles. Another possibility is some variation of Fujimori's approach—abolishing or superceding congress. Although Chávez has implicitly threatened such action (and many critics contend that his call for a constitutional assembly is a subtle way of accomplishing it), he might be deterred from taking such a bold step because opposition parties in

143

125

Venezuela, however weakened, are not as easy to dismiss as they were in Peru when Fujimori staged his coup. A final option would be to attempt to strengthen his ruling party. Specifically, he could use state resources to strengthen the party within *Polo Patriótico* that is most loyal to him, the *Movimiento Quinta República* (MVR). Anecdotal evidence suggests that Chávez has begun to move in this direction. In preparing the country for a possible election for a constitutional assembly, for instance, Chávez organized "neighborhood committees." In essence, this approach would be a type of party accommodation. If successful, it would no doubt liberate Chávez from the vicissitudes of having to rely on a weak coalition of ad hoc parties and enhance his capacity to overwhelm his opponents. But even under the best of circumstances, party-building will take some time. In the meantime, the politics of economic reform in Venezuela will continue to be tumultuous.

Conclusion

Market-oriented reforms produce a dislocation in executive-ruling party relations. Executives are initially tempted to bypass the ruling party (point Y_1 in Figure 2). At first, party neglect allows the executives to register some progress in reform implementation, but nowhere near the level of implementation desired by the executive (the distance between the dotted line and point Y_1). Because party-neglecting strategies exacerbate conflicts in executive-ruling party relations, which in turn disrupt state-society relations, they are inherently unstable. The tension that they produce is impossible to sustain over time. Eventually, this tension must be resolved in one of . several directions.

One approach is to move toward some kind of settlement with the ruling party (party accommodation, point Y_2, Argentina 1991–1996, Mexico 1988–1994). This approach expands the executive's capacity to deepen the reforms, in part because it discourages social actors from sabotaging or mistrusting the reforms. However, the government will still fail to achieve the levels of reform implementation originally intended (the gap between points A_1 and Y_2). Party accommodation, by nature, entails granting the party certain concessions that translate into gaps in the reform process.

The alternative scenario is a rebellion of the ruling party (point Y_4, Venezuela 1991–1993, Paraguay 1995–1998). Increasingly frustrated with the executive, antireform sectors in the party gain the upper hand, which in turn galvanizes social actors into opposing the reforms. The executive becomes entirely isolated, unable to implement reforms, and likely to abdicate (party yielding). If the ruling party is not strong to begin with, the rebellion will be led by opposition political parties (Brazil 1989–1992, Ecuador 1996–1998), which the executive can preempt by staging some kind of coup against the political system (Peru 1992) or by adopting a party-accom-

144

Javier Corrales

Figure 2 Reform Implementation and Executive-Ruling Party Relations in Argentina and Venezuela, 1989–1996

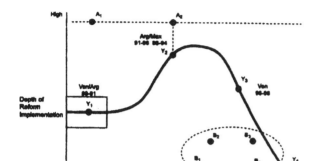

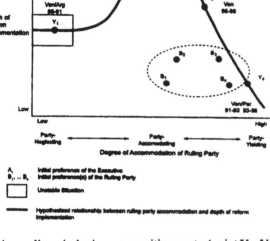

modating policy vis-à-vis an opposition party (point Y_3, Venezuela 1996–1998). The latter might contain some political tensions in state-society relations and allow the government to implement some reforms (more than would be the case at point Y_1), but never to the same extent as would be the case under strong executive-ruling party relations (point Y_2)

This argument has implications for state governance. Essentially, the relationship between state autonomy vis-à-vis the ruling party and state capacity to implement reforms is not linear, but rather curve-shaped. Too much autonomy from the ruling party (party-neglecting policies) and too little autonomy from the ruling party (party yielding) are detrimental to the implementation of reforms. The former is inherently unstable; the latter is a recipe for reform paralysis. Thus, reform outcomes in Latin America have been intrinsically linked to the way in which executives have responded to the dislocation in executive-ruling party relations, sometimes more than to the way in which the executive has interacted with interest groups or opposition parties. Where executives and ruling parties have succeeded in renegotiating the terms of their relationship, rather than superceding each other, the result has been an enlarged process of reform.

145

127

This study also showed that the initially dissimilar preferences of executives and ruling parties, as laid out by Geddes, can be overcome, not so much by the interplay between the ruling party and the opposition, but as a result of policies enacted by the executives, conditioned by the institutional features of these parties. Arguments that stress executive imperiousness in bringing about neoliberal reforms miss this crucial aspect of the politics of reform implementation.

This study, finally, departs somewhat from those studies that argue that neoliberalism has come at the expense of traditional political institutions. On the contrary, where neoliberal reforms have been implemented the furthest (Argentina and Mexico), there has also been a reinforcement of very traditional institutions: statist, ruling political parties. Resolving the dislocation in executive-ruling party required accommodating, rather than obliterating, some of the illiberal demands of ruling parties. Thus, reformist executives in Argentina and Mexico in the 1990s do not leave behind weaker or streamlined political parties. To do away with the old economic model, these executives found it necessary to oxygenate rather than decimate the party as a whole, and especially the traditional sectors. Party-accommodating strategies permitted Menem and Salinas to resolve one of the most serious dilemmas faced by leaders who embrace policies that contradict the historical platforms of their own parties, but they also succeeded in fueling a populist monster. At some point or another this monster will haunt the countries' reform process.

NOTES

I am grateful to the Ford Foundation, the National Research Council, and the David Rockefeller Center for Latin American Studies at Harvard University for funding this project. I am also indebted to the Instituto de Estudios Superiores de Administración (IESA) in Caracas and the Instituto Torcuato di Tella in Buenos Aires for hosting me as a visiting researcher. Jorge I. Domínguez, Robert D. Putnam, Deborah Yashar, Frances Hagopian, Janet Kelly, Michael Coppedge, Miriam Kornblith, Juan Carlos Torres, Aníbal Romero, Jeanne K. Giraldo, M. Victoria Murillo, and Mark Williams provided valuable guidance and comments.

1.   Statist parties are political parties that advocate state intervention in the economy for populist purposes, that is, to mobilize support among urban groups, domestically oriented industrialists, and organized workers. See Robert R. Kaufman and Barbara Stallings, "The Political Economy of Latin American Populism," in Rudiger Dornbusch and Sebastian Edwards, eds., *The Macroeconomics of Populism in Latin America* (Chicago: University of Chicago Press, 1991).

2.   Anne O. Krueger, *Economic Policy Reform in Developing Countries: The Kuznets Memorial Lectures at the Economic Growth Center, Yale University* (Cambridge, Mass.: Blackwell, 1992); Joan Nelson, "The Political Economy of Stabilization: Commitment, Capacity, and Public Response," in Robert H. Bates, ed., *Toward a Political Economy of Development: A Rational Choice Perspective* (Berkeley: University of California Press, 1988).

3.   John Williamson, "In Search of a Manual for Technopols," in John Williamson, ed., *The Political Economy of Policy Reform* (Washington, D.C.: Institute for International Economics, 1994); John Williamson, ed., *Latin American Adjustment: How Much Has Happened?* (Washington, D.C.: Institute for International Economics, 1990).

146

4.   Jorge I. Domínguez , ed., *Technopols: Ideas and Leaders Freeing Politics and Markets in Latin America in the 1990s* (University Park: Penn State Press, 1997); Verónica Montesinos, "El valor simbólico de los economistas en la democratización de la política chilena," *Nueva Sociedad*, 152 (November-December 1997), 108–26.

5.   Anders Åslund, "The Case for Radical Reform," *Journal of Democracy*, 5 (October 1994), 63–74; Dani Rodrik, "Promises, Promises: Credible Policy Reform via Signalling," *The Economic Journal*, 99 (1989), 756–72.

6.   Guillermo O'Donnell, "Delegative Democracy," *Journal of Democracy*, 5 (January 1994), 55–69.

7.   Alberto Alesina and Allan Drazen, "Why Are Stabilizations Delayed?," *American Economic Review*, 81 (1991), 1170–88.

8.   Silvia Maxfield and Ben Ross Schneider, eds., *Business and the State in Developing Countries* (Ithaca: Cornell University Press, 1997); Peter Evans, *Embedded Autonomy: States and Industrial Transformation* (Princeton: Princeton University Press, 1995); Joel S. Migdal, Atul Kohli, and Vivienne Shue, eds., *State Power and Social Forces: Domination and Transformation in the Third World* (Cambridge: Cambridge University Press, 1994).

9.   Leslie Elliott Armijo, "Inflation and Insouciance: The Peculiar Brazilian Game," *Latin American Research Review*, 31 (1997), 7–46.

10.   Aaron Tornell, "Are Economic Crises Necessary for Trade Liberalization and Fiscal Reform? The Mexican Experience," in Rudiger Dornbusch and Sebastian Edwards, eds., *Reform, Recovery and Growth* (Chicago: University of Chicago Press, 1995); Kurt Weyland, "Risk Taking in Latin American Economic Restructuring: Lessons from Prospect Theory," *International Studies Quarterly*, 40 (1996), 185–208; John T. S. Keeler, "Opening the Window for Reform: Mandates, Crises and Extraordinary Policy-making," *Comparative Political Studies*, 25 (1993), 433–86; Allan Drazen and Vittorio Grilli, "The Benefit of Crises for Economic Reforms," *American Economic Review*, 83 (1993), 598–607.

11.   Stephan Haggard and Robert R. Kaufman, *The Political Economy of Democratic Transitions* (Princeton: Princeton University Press, 1995); Scott Mainwaring and Timothy Scully, eds., *Building Democratic Institutions: Party Systems in Latin America* (Stanford: Stanford University Press, 1996).

12.   See Susan Stokes, "Are Parties What's Wrong with Democracy in Latin America?," paper presented at the Twentieth International Congress of the Latin American Studies Association, Guadalajara, Mexico, 1997.

13.   For a cartography of internal structures of AD and the PJ, see Michael Coppedge, *Strong Parties and Lame Ducks: Presidential Partyarchy and Factionalism in Venezuela* (Stanford: Stanford University Press, 1994); James W. McGuire, *Peronism without Perón: Unions, Parties, and Democracy in Argentina* (Stanford: Stanford University Press, 1997); and Steven Levitsky, "Institutionalization and Peronism," *Party Politics*, 4 (1998), 77–92.

14.   I interviewed twelve party leaders in Venezuela and ten in Argentina. All were members of the party's central committee (*Comité Ejecutivo Nacional*, CEN, in AD and the *Mesa Ejecutiva* in the PJ). None was a cabinet member at the time of the interview.

15.   Barbara Geddes, *Politician's Dilemma: Building State Capacity in Latin America* (Berkeley: University of California Press, 1994).

16.   O'Donnell.

17.   Carlos H. Acuña, "Politics and Economics in the Argentina of the Nineties (or Why the Future No Longer Is What It Used to Be)," in William C. Smith et al., eds., *Democracy, Markets, and Structural Reform in Latin America: Argentina, Bolivia, Brazil, Chile, and Mexico* (New Brunswick: North-South Center/Transaction, 1994).

18.   Jennifer McCoy and William C. Smith, "From Deconsolidation to Reequilibration? Prospects for Democratic Renewal in Venezuela," in Jennifer McCoy, Andrés Serbin, William C. Smith, and Andrés Stambouli, eds., *Venezuelan Democracy under Stress* (New Brunswick: Transaction, 1995).

19.   See Miriam Kornblith, "Deuda y democracia en Venezuela: Los sucesos del 27 y 28 de febrero," *Cuadernos del CENDES*, 10 (1989), 17–34.

147

20.   Javier Corrales, "Do Economic Crises Contribute to Economic Reforms? Argentina and Venezuela in the 1990s," *Political Science Quarterly*, 112 (Winter 1997–98), 617–43. Others see crises as contributing (not sufficient) factors in Argentina's turnaround. Juan Carlos Torre, "Critical Junctures and Economic Change: Launching Market Reforms in Argentina," in Joseph S. Tulchin with Allison M. Garland, *Argentina: the Challenges of Modernization* (Wilmington: SR Book, 1998); Vicente Palermo and Marcos Navarro, *Política y poder en el gobierno de Menem* (Buenos Aires: Grupo Editorial Norma, 1996).

21.   Geddes.

22.   See Martha de Melo, Cevdet Denizer, and Alan Gelb, "Patterns of Transition from Plan to Market," *The World Bank Economic Review*, 10 (September 1996), 397–424; Adam Przeworski, *Democracy and the Market: Political and Economic Reforms in Eastern Europe and Latin America* (New York: Cambridge University Press, 1991).

23.   Edward Gibson, "The Populist Road to Market Reform, Policy and Electoral Coalition in Mexico and Argentina," *World Politics*, 49 (April 1997), 339–70; Kurt Weyland, "Neopopulism and Neoliberalism in Latin America," *Studies in Comparative International Development*, 31 (Fall 1996), 3–31; Kenneth M. Roberts, "Neoliberalism and the Transformation of Populism in Latin America: The Peruvian Case," *World Politics*, 48 (October 1995), 82–116.

24.   Acción Democrática, *Acción Democrática: Doctrina y programa* (Caracas: Secretaría Nacional de Organización del Partido Acción Democrática and Instituto Latinoamericano de Investigaciones Sociales, ILDIS, 1993).

25.   Javier Corrales, "El Presidente y su gente," *Nueva Sociedad*, 152 (November-December 1997), 93–107.

26.   Octavio Lepage, *Política, democracia, partidos* (Caracas: Editorial Centauro, 1991), p. 61.

27.   *El Nacional*, Jan. 5, 1991, p. D2.

28.   *Página/12*, Dec. 12, 1990.

29.   Delia Ferreira Rubio and Matteo Goretti, "Gobierno por decreto en Argentina (1989–1993)," *El Derecho* (Universidad Católica Argentina), 32 (1994), 1–8.

30.   Angelo Panebianco, *Political Parties: Organization and Power* (Cambridge: Cambridge University Press, 1988).

31.   Anthony Downs, *An Economic Theory of Democracy* (New York: Harper and Row, 1957).

32.   Miriam Kornblith and Daniel H. Levine, "Venezuela: The Life and Times of the Party System," in Mainwaring and Scully, eds.; Daniel H. Levine, "Venezuela since 1958: The Consolidation of Democratic Politics," in Juan J. Linz and Alfred Stepan, eds., *The Breakdown of Democratic Regimes: Latin America* (Baltimore: The Johns Hopkins University Press, 1978); John D. Martz, "Party Elites and Leadership in Colombia and Venezuela," *Journal of Latin American Studies*, 24 (1992), 87–121.

33.   Corrales, "El Presidente y su gente."

34.   *Clarín*, Aug. 27, 1991, p. 21.

35.   Antonio Cafiero was the president of the PJ and governor of the province of Buenos Aires (the largest bastion of Peronist voters) at the start of the reforms.

36.   See Coppedge.

37.   See Merilee Grindle, *Challenging the State* (Cambridge: Cambridge University Press, 1997); Stephanie Golob, "'Making Possible What Is Necessary': Pedro Aspe, the Salinas Team and the Next Mexican 'Miracle,'" in Domínguez, ed.; Edward L. Gibson, "The Populist Road to Market Reform: Policy and Electoral Coalitions in Mexico and Argentina," *World Politics*, 49 (April 1997), 339–70.

38.   See M. Delal Baer, "Mexico's Second Revolution: Pathways to Liberalization," in Riordan Roett, ed., *Political and Economic Liberalization in Mexico: At a Critical Juncture?* (Boulder: Lynne Rienner, 1993), pp. 53–54.

39.   Miguel Ángel Centeno, *Democracy within Reason: Technocratic Revolution in Mexico* (University Park: Penn State Press, 1994), p. 15; Larissa Adler Lomnitz, Claudio Lomnitz-Adler, and Ilay Adler, "El fondo de la forma: Actos públicos de la campaña presidencial del Partido Revolucionario Institucional"

148

(Notre Dame: Working Paper No. 135, Helen Kellogg Institute for International Studies, March 1990), p. 20.

40.   See Baer, p. 57; and Jorge Buendia, "Economic Reform, Public Opinion and Presidential Approval in Mexico, 1988–1993," *Comparative Political Studies*, 29 (October 1996), 559.

41.   Luis Donaldo Colosio, "Why the PRI Won the 1991 Elections," in Roett, ed.

42.   Ibid., pp. 93–104.

43.   Wayne Cornelius, *Mexican Politics in Transition: The Breakdown of a One-Party Dominant Regime* (San Diego: Center for U.S.-Mexican Studies, University of California, San Diego, 1996), p. 58.

44.   Denise Dresser, "Bringing the Poor Back In: National Solidarity as a Strategy of Regime Legitimation," in Wayne A. Cornelius, Ann L. Craig, and Jonathan Fox, eds., *Transforming State-Society Relations in Mexico: The National Solidarity Strategy* (San Diego: Center for U.S.-Mexican Studies, University of California, San Diego 1991).

45.   Centeno, p. 65; Cornelius, p. 59. Some PRI traditionalists resent PRONASOL because it appears to be a "parallel political party." See Baer, pp. 57–60; Dresser, p. 157.

46.   One legacy of Alfredo Stroessner's dictatorship (1954–1989) was an alliance between Colorado leaders, state bureaucrats (who were required to be affiliated with the party), and military officers (also required to be affiliated with the party). See Domingo Rivarola, "Recomposición Interna del Partido Colorado," in Domingo Rivarola, Marcelo Cavarozzi, and Manuel Antonio Garretón, eds., *Militares y políticos en una transición atípica* (Buenos Aires: CLACSO, 1991).

149

Presidential Power, Legislative Organization, and Party Behavior in Brazil

Argelina Cheibub Figueiredo and Fernando Limongi

Presidential regimes are considered to be prone to produce institutional deadlocks. In the generally shared view, influenced by the work of Juan Linz, presidentialism lacks a built-in mechanism to induce cooperation between the executive and legislative branches of the government.[1] Representatives and the president have different constituencies, and their mandates are independent and fixed. Hence the chances that the legislative and the executive powers will have the same agenda are small. Because the failure of the government does not affect the legislators' political survival, representatives have few incentives to support the government. Minoritarian presidents, in particular, will necessarily face congressional opposition.

Political parties are the only conceivable basis for executive-legislative cooperation. Ideally, the same disciplined party would control the presidency and a majority in the legislature. It follows that "institutional engineering" should focus on electoral formulas that reduce party fragmentation and increase party discipline.

Brazil is viewed as an extreme example of the threats to governability represented by multiparty presidential systems. Constrained by the separation of powers, Brazilian presidents must obtain political support in a congress in which party fragmentation has reached one of the highest levels ever found in the world. In addition, the open list system prevents party leaders from exerting control over candidacies and, consequently, over party members' voting decisions within the congress.[2] With this institutional framework, it is usually inferred that parties will not be disciplined and that presidents will face systematic resistance to their legislative proposals.[3]

This inference is not true. Relying on data on legislative proposals and roll call votes, we show that since the enactment of the 1988 constitution Brazilian presidents have had a considerable degree of success in enacting their legislative agenda. Presidents introduced most of the bills enacted in this period, and the rate of approval of the bills introduced by the executive is high. Presidents have counted on reliable support from the political parties included in the presidential coalition. The average level of discipline of the presidential coalition is 85.6 percent. This support is sufficient to make a presidential defeat in a roll call vote rare. In other words, presidents form governments, and the parties included in the governmental coalition provide political support for the president.

Institutional variables—the legislative powers of the president and the centralized organization of the legislative work—explain these unexpected findings. The extensive legislative powers of the president allow the executive both to control the legislative agenda and to restrict the legislature's "transformative power."[4] The executive controls resources upon which politicians depend for their political survival. The president can affect a legislator's capacity to pursue particularistic policies. In addition, internal rules organize legislative work entirely around political parties, giving rise to highly centralized decision making. Consequently, party discipline is enforced in the legislative arena.

Explanations of parliamentary behavior and of policy outcomes overemphasize the importance of the separation of powers and the characteristics of electoral and party legislation. They overlook the role of other institutional characteristics, especially the president's legislative powers and the internal organization of the legislative work.

Electoral laws and the lack of party control over candidacy may give politicians incentives to cultivate the personal vote and to defy the party line, but individualistic behavior does not thrive in the milieu inside the Brazilian congress. Strategies are not defined exclusively in the electoral arena. What happens within the legislature is also important. The institutional powers held by the executive, on the one hand, and the centralized decision-making system in the legislature, on the other, restrict the agenda and limit the legislators' role in policy outcomes. The executive and party leaders neutralize, through control of the agenda, the representatives' incentive to cultivate "the personal vote."

Brazil is a test case, but the implications of this argument are wide-ranging. The legislative powers of the executive and legislative organization are key variables in the definition of the actual workings of any political system. This observation suggests that the focus of studies of democratic regimes should be shifted to the characteristics of the decision-making system, as defined by the rules regulating the distribution of legislative powers between the executive and legislative branches of government and the rules allocating parliamentary rights within the congress.

Institutional Framework and Legislative Outcomes

The comparison between parliamentary and presidential systems has been the main focus of studies of government performance and regime stability. These studies stress the problems and "perils" of the presidential system, which stem from its constitutional design. Since the origin and survival of each branch of government are independent, presidential systems lack institutional mechanisms to induce cooperation between the executive and the legislature.

According to this view, legislators do not get electoral payoffs from supporting the government. Hence they do not cooperate. They either fail to support legislative proposals or produce incoherent policies. The presidential system is inherently prone

152

to producing conflicts between the executive and the legislature and, consequently, decisional paralysis. The source of conflict is institutional. Specific electoral and party legislation is necessary to rectify this basic flaw.

Shugart and Carey shifted the focus of the comparison between systems by emphasizing the differences among presidential regimes.[5] The distinction among presidential systems, they suggested, should consider two variables, the legislative power of presidents and party support for the executive in the legislature. The former affects the willingness of the executive to negotiate with the legislature. Strong presidents have the means to try to impose their will over the congress, while weak ones have no other option but to negotiate.[6] Thus, Linz's argument that conflicts between the executive and the legislature lead to deadlock applies when presidents hold strong legislative powers. Hence, according to Shugart and Carey, crises under presidential systems are more likely when presidents with strong legislative powers face legislatures in which they lack partisan support.

In a recent book, Shugart and Mainwaring seek to assess the effects of these two variables—partisan support and the president's constitutional powers—on the ability of Latin American presidents to shape legislation.[7] For these authors, two factors are crucial in determining partisan support for the executive: party fragmentation and party discipline. The more fragmented the party system is, the less likely it is that the president's party will control a majority of seats in the legislature. Party discipline, in turn, determines the costs of governing. If parties are not disciplined, presidents may have the nominal support of parties but not the power to translate this support into votes for their policies. Thus, presidents will be forced to rely on ad hoc coalitions based on the distribution of patronage to individual legislators. This strategy will raise the costs of governing and reduce policy coherence.

The relationship between electoral laws and the number of parties is one of the most explored themes in political science. The dominant concerns have been to identify electoral formulas that reduce party fragmentation and to increase party discipline. The goal is to increase the probability that the presidential party will control a majority of seats in the legislature.[8] It is worth noting that this concern indicates that support based upon party coalitions is not considered a politically viable alternative. Either the presidential party controls the majority of the seats, or presidents will have trouble getting their agenda approved.

Party discipline, in turn, is considered to be a consequence of party leaders' capacity to affect the reelection chances of individual candidates.[9] The greater this capacity is, the less likely it is that politicians will look solely to the particular interests of their constituencies. Party leaders' capacity to punish backbenchers in the electoral arena decreases legislators' incentives to follow a strategy based on personal ties with the electorate.

In the absence of the conditions that ensure partisan support, the legislative powers of presidents come into play. In order to get their agenda approved, presidents

153

who lack the support of disciplined and majoritarian parties turn to their constitutional legislative powers.[10] In other words, presidents use their legislative powers to circumvent the legislature. Following these arguments, Mainwaring concludes:

> Between 1985 and 1994, Brazilian presidents had difficulty achieving stabilization and state reform, partly because of the combination of highly fragmented party system, undisciplined parties, and federalism. This combination made it difficult for presidents to secure legislative support for economic stabilization and state reform. Presidents had trouble overcoming congressional opposition and implementing major reforms when their popularity dissipated. This is why president's lack of reliable support in Congress presented problems for effective governance. And it is why Sarney, Collor, and Franco had a hard time getting their agendas accomplished despite possessing sweeping constitutional powers. In the 1985–1994 period, policy coherence often suffered as a result of presidents' efforts to win support in Congress and among governors.[11]

We will show that these conclusions do not hold. The president introduces most of the bills approved by the legislature; parties are disciplined; and presidents can count on political support for their agenda in the congress. Hence we have grounds to dispute conclusions inferred from the model that considers the legislative powers of the president basically as a means to circumvent the lack of partisan support in the legislature. Presidential legislative powers are not the means to confront or bypass the legislative power, but rather the means to entice a centralized legislature to cooperate.

Executive Agenda and Party Behavior in the Legislature

Evidence shows that recent Brazilian presidents have had a high degree of success in enacting their legislative agendas. Post-1988 Brazilian presidents have had most of their legislative initiatives approved by the congress. This conclusion is at odds with the conventional wisdom about the Brazilian political system and presidential systems in general. Even scholars willing to acknowledge this evidence would nevertheless argue that presidents obtained approval for their agenda at a high cost by assembling majorities through bargaining individually with representatives on a case by case basis. This argument is not supported by the evidence. Analysis of roll call votes in the chamber of deputies shows that parties are disciplined and that political support for the presidential agenda comes mainly from the parties participating in the government coalition.

The figures shown in Table 1 do not support the view that Brazilian presidents

154

have met with obstacles in congress. Presidents introduced 86 percent of the bills enacted, and the overall rate of approval of executive bills, 78 percent, is high. Rejection of executive bills is rare: only twenty-four out of the 1,881 bills introduced. In contrast, legislators' proposals have much higher rejection rates, and the number of bills approved by both houses and then vetoed by the president is significant. In addition, congress approves the bills introduced by the executive much faster than it does its own proposals.

Table 1 Results of Bills Presented according to Initiator, 1989–1997

Results		Presented	Enacted	Rejected	Other*	In Progress	Totally Vetoed
Executive	Budgetary	830	825	4	-	1	-
	P. Decree	446	320	14	53	57	2
	Other	605	317	6	146	128	8
	Sub-total	1881	1462	24	199	186	10
Legislature		9454**	236	158**	na***	9006**	114**

* Includes bills or decrees closed, appended to another bill, withdrawn and without efficacy.
** Includes data only until 1994.
*** Not Available

The first two rows of Table 1 represent the bills in which the executive retains the constitutional right of exclusive initiative, budgetary laws and provisional decrees (*medida provisória*). The budgetary laws comprise the annual budget and laws concerning modifications of the previously voted budget through additional, special, and extraordinary transfers of resources from one budget item to another. The annual budget law follows specific proceedings, but the numerous budgetary bills modifying previous appropriations enter the legislative schedule like any other proposal. Only four proposals of budgetary changes were rejected. On average, budgetary changes were approved in about fifty days.

The president can issue provisional decrees with the immediate force of law in urgent and important situations. The constitution requires a vote on the decree by the congress within thirty days. If not voted on, the provisional decree loses its efficacy. However, the reissuing of decrees is allowed. The total number of provisional decrees presented in Table 1 includes only original decrees. All subsequent acts of reissuing the same decree are not counted as new decrees.[12] Even with this method of calculation, the volume of decrees, an average of 4.2 per month, is high. It is no surprise that provisional decrees show the second highest average level of success. The issuing of a provisional decree alters the status quo and thus raises the costs of its repeal.

Only 3 percent of the provisional decrees were rejected, and these rejections occurred during Sarney's and Collor's administrations. The percentage of provisional

155

137

decrees in the remaining categories can not be taken as an indication of difficulties met by the presidents. The category "other," 12 percent of provisional decrees, includes the revoked provisional decrees and those that lost their efficacy, that is, those that expired when the executive did not reissue them. Many of these decrees concerned regulations of programs or policies with a fixed duration, the expiration of which made maintenance of the legislation unnecessary. In other cases, the executive made legal mistakes, as in the unconstitutional decrees contained in Collor's stabilization plan, and subsequently decided to revoke them or let them expire without reissuing them. There were also instances in which two or more decrees were combined into a new one.

The provisional decrees "in progress" are those that were continuously reissued. Most of them were part of the Real Plan, the stabilization plan launched by Cardoso as finance minister right before his election as president. Some of the initial measures have since been reissued. Some of the plan's complementary measures have been reissued for a long time. In fact, most provisional decrees have been reissued with changes that result from executive directives, mostly economic authorities, and were supported by party leaders. Not a single provisional decree has been rejected since the launching of the Real Plan. Hence the proportion of provisional decrees in progress and the time they spent in congress do not indicate that the congress opposes the plan. On the contrary, the majority supporting the president has delegated authority to the executive to legislate on matters related to the plan.[13]

Up to this point we have analyzed proposals whose outcomes derive directly from the executive's institutional position. Rights to exclusivity and the power to issue decrees with the immediate force of law give the executive the capacity to control the legislative agenda in both its timing and content.[14] In the areas of legislation in which the legislature can rival the executive in initiating legislation (third row in Table 1), if compared to the provisional decrees and the budget laws, there is a decrease in the rate of approval of the executive bills.[15] Yet 52 percent of the bills presented are enacted, and the number of bills rejected, only 6 in 605, is insignificant. The proportion of bills not approved may suggest that congress poses resistance or holds up the presidential agenda through inaction. However, the data indicate that this conclusion is not correct.

First, for the bills listed as "other" bureaucratic and procedural reasons, not congressional opposition or inaction, explain most cases in which bills were closed or appended to other bills, and most withdrawn bills (fifty-seven out of seventy-nine) were not introduced by the same president who withdrew them. These bills could hardly be considered controversial and thus capable of arousing congressional opposition. Hence a better explanation of their fate is lack of interest or shifts in policy priorities following a change in the head of the government. Obviously, some bills were in fact controversial and may have been withdrawn due to opposition, especially during Collor's administration, but the number is low.

156

For bills still in progress, 55 percent of them were initiated during the present administration, and the time they have spent in congress is lower than the average time for the approval of executive bills in general. As for those introduced by previous administrations, the same explanation as for the withdrawn bills applies: they did not receive political priority. In fact, the procedural schedule followed by the withdrawn bills and the bills in progress indicates that they have never received high priority. These bills underwent regular scheduling in the congress. The great majority of enacted bills are considered under urgent procedures decided by party leaders. In order to pass its agenda, the executive relies on party leaders' support in scheduling its bills. Hence the bills in progress have not received the political attention needed to be approved.[16]

It is worth stressing the number and the importance of the bills passed in the economic area. Indeed, the main area of executive activity was economic and included three stabilization plans. The content of social and administrative legislation initiated by the executive reveals that it mostly supplemented economic measures; it comprised, for instance, measures that enforced changes in the social security system and administrative reorganization of the state for balancing the budget. Only in the social area did the number of enacted bills initiated by the legislature come close to the number initiated by the executive. However, the number of proposals rejected and vetoed attests to the representatives' inability to pass their social agenda.

These data may not tell the whole story. Legislators can amend the bills submitted by the executive. Representatives present many amendments, and the data do not distinguish the extent to which the original proposal has been changed. But, as we show below, the representatives' amendment capacity is limited by the executive and party leaders' control over the agenda and by the executive's veto. Analysis of specific policy areas reveals that congress plays a minor "transformative role."[17]

A related objection can be raised with regard to the importance of approved bills. In the end, the approved bills may not be the really important ones. One can ask, further, whether there is an association between importance and failure to be passed, that is, whether the noncontroversial measures were passed and the controversial ones failed. Despite the obvious problem in distinguishing controversial from noncontroversial measures, it is indisputable that bills of great importance were approved. The three stabilization plans presented under different administrations—the Summer Plan, the Collor Plan, and the Real Plan—were enacted by provisional decrees, and they were approved by the legislature with minor changes.[18] If the more important measures were rejected, one should observe high rates of rejection of the provisional decrees. However, the opposite is true. The failure of the first two plans was not necessarily due to congressional opposition. Stabilization plans can fail for other reasons than congressional opposition.

One may still object that the proposals sent to the legislature may not have represented the executive's real agenda, since presidents, anticipating the difficulties they

157

would face in congress, might not have submitted it. This type of behavior is indeed possible, and presidents have certainly acted at times in this way, but such behavior is part of the normal working of any democratic system.

We are not arguing that the executive imposes its will on the congress. The congress is not an obstacle simply because it transforms a bill proposed by the president or because the president anticipates its legislative preferences. Under a democratic government one should expect the congress to influence policy. The real question concerns the basis of the bargaining between the president and the congress. The executive's success in winning approval of its legislative proposals in the chamber of deputies was not obtained through bargaining with individual deputies. Roll call data in the Brazilian lower house, the *Câmara dos Deputados*, show that party members tended to vote according to their leaders directives; parties were meaningful collective actors. Brazilian presidents also relied on party coalitions to win approval of their agendas. They obtained political support more or less the same way as prime ministers, by building government coalitions through the distribution of ministries to political parties and thereby securing the votes they needed in congress.

In the Brazilian congress roll call voting is not the norm. Usually, representatives vote by standing up or remaining seated according to the speaker's command. This voting procedure is called symbolic. A roll call vote takes place in two situations. First, it is mandatory for the most important decisions, such as constitutional amendments and legislation that is supplementary to constitutional norms (*leis complementares*). Second, it may be requested by party leaders. Leaders will force a roll call based on political calculations. They may hope to reverse decisions or to increase their adversaries' political costs by recording their votes. Therefore, it is unlikely that party leaders will require a roll call on noncontroversial matters. Their right to call a recorded vote is also limited. The standing orders dictate a period of one hour between the end of a roll call vote and a new request. Thus, the 575 roll call votes included in our data set represent the most important and controversial issues considered by the congress as selected by the political process itself.[19]

According to the standing orders, leaders of parties holding at least 5 percent of the seats may announce their parties' position on an issue before a roll call vote takes place. Party leaders leave members free to vote their conscience only in a few cases. In most cases it is known whether or not members voted according to their parties' publicly announced position. Table 2 reports the average proportion of disciplined votes, that is, those votes cast in accordance with party leaders' announced directives, for the seven biggest parties (PT, PDT, PSDB, PMDB, PTB, PFL, and PPB).[20] For all parties the mean is greater than the median: that is, the distributions are concentrated on the upper tail. The PMDB presents the lowest mean discipline, while the PT is the most disciplined. But three other parties, the PFL, the PDT, and the PSDB, also have a mean discipline above 90 percent. The average floor discipline in the lower house is 90 percent; that is, for any roll call vote nine in ten representatives

158

voted according to party leaders' recommendations. To vote with the party is the norm. In more than 90 percent of the registered cases the proportion of the disciplined vote was superior to 80 percent. In only twelve of 575 cases did the proportion of representatives voting according to party position fall below 70 percent of the floor.[21]

Table 2 Average Proportion of Disciplined Votes by Political Party, 1989–1998

Party	% discipline	N*
PT	98.4	533
PDT	92.1	505
PSDB	90.7	538
PMDB	85.0	538
PTB	87.9	506
PFL	93.1	531
PPB	87.4	509

* Variations are due to roll calls in which the leader does not announce the party position.

These data are at odds with the conventional wisdom about party discipline in Brazil. For instance, they do not support Sartori's following assessment.

Probably no country in the world currently is as antiparty, both in theory and in practice, as Brazil. Politicians relate to their parties as a *partido de aluguel*, as a rental. They freely and frequently change party, vote against party line, and refuse any kind of discipline on the ground that their constituency cannot be interfered with. Thus, parties are powerless and volatile entities, and the Brazilian presidents are left to float over a vacuum, an unruly and eminently atomized parliament.[22]

Roll call data do not support Sartori. His claims about the lack of party discipline in Brazil are inferred from the characteristics of Brazilian electoral laws. Mainwaring and Perez-Liñán's analysis of roll call voting during the Brazilian constitutional congress also found lower levels of discipline than the ones we report here. However, as they recognize, their results do not conflict with ours, since they analyzed roll call votes in a different period and under different institutional rules.[23] Our explanation is based on the constitutional text and on the standing orders approved in 1989; the contrast between the two periods thus reinforces our point.

Assessments of high or low levels of party discipline are inherently comparative. However, we are not comparing levels of discipline among different countries.[24] For this analysis it is sufficient to determine whether the observed levels of discipline are high enough to render the decision-making process predictable. If one assumes perfect discipline, that is, that the members of all parties in the chamber follow the vote

159

141

announced by their leaders, and computes the expected result, one can correctly predict the approval or rejection of 95 percent of the roll call votes. The decision-making process is thus far from random. Parties are meaningful players in the Brazilian congress, and they strongly influence voting outcomes. Parties render the decision-making process predictable.

To analyze the fate of the presidential agenda in the congress, it is necessary to know the presidential position on issues. Roll call votes are taken on the presidential agenda if the bills were introduced by the president or if the government leader stated the government's position on the issue before the voting. In these cases the president had an interest in the result of the votes and made his position on the issues known. Out of the original 575 roll call votes 434 meet at least one of these criteria, and 165 of them were votes on amendments to the constitution that required a three-fifths quorum for approval. The general pattern, high party discipline, is not altered when the sample is restricted to the presidential agenda.

Presidents won the great majority of roll calls votes. The government won 241 of the 269 roll call votes that required a simple majority, and 143 of the 165 that required a three-fifths majority. Victories were achieved through disciplined votes, and defeats due to lack of discipline were rare. For the cases requiring a simple majority, only four defeats can be accredited to a lack of party discipline. For constitutional amendments, the government coalition failed to attain the necessary three-fifths mostly due to absences. If these absences are considered nondisciplined votes, presidents have been defeated on twenty-six of 434 cases due to lack of discipline.[25] Hence discipline is the norm, and presidents relied on parties that were capable of voting in a disciplined way to have their agenda approved.

Presidents may obtain partisan support on a case by case basis or by building stable coalitions. Most students of presidential systems, following Linz's original formulation, rule out the second alternative. Since presidents derive their popular mandate directly from the people, they prefer to impose their will on congress rather than attempt to form party coalitions within congress. In a recent study, Mark P. Jones summarizes this reasoning.

> Presidents have their own independent popular mandate and are likely to be reluctant to cede the degree of power necessary to an opposition party in order to entice it into a legislative coalition. This is due to their independence as nationally elected officials, which often causes presidents to overestimate their power.[26]

Even if the president attempts to form a coalition, nonpresidential parties have no incentive to join it. The dominant strategy of opposition parties is to remain in opposition and wait for the opportunity to win control of the presidency. Their chances of conquering the presidency depend on the incumbent president's failure. The opposition will always behave irresponsibly. Jones also makes this argument.

160

The principal opposition parties (or party) recognize that the executive is, on the whole, the one responsible for the performance of the government. Thus they are often loathe to do anything to help the president succeed. Instead, they often adopt a policy of blind opposition with the end goal of causing the government to fail with the hope that one of their party leaders will be able to win the next presidential election.[27]

Neither of these arguments is convincing. Both implicitly assume that the political game in presidential systems is zero-sum or that political actors suffer from misconceptions. Presidents "overestimate their power"; opposition parties are "loathe to do anything to help the president succeed" and adopt a "blind opposition" strategy. If, as this argument assumes, capture of the presidential office is all parties care about, they will never enter into a coalition government. This assumption is particularly strange when contrasted with studies of parliamentarism, which take for granted that some parties have incentives to join a government as minor parties.[28] Is this claim sustainable? Is there something about presidentialism that impedes formation of coalition governments?

As much as under parliamentarism, political parties under presidentialism face an intertemporal choice between attempting to capture exclusive control of the government in the future and sharing control in the present. No formal analysis is needed to see that the optimal course of action may be different for different parties. Certainly, a party offered some portfolios by the incumbent president will accept them if it does not see much chance of winning the presidency by remaining in the opposition. Hence there are no reasons to assume that government coalitions can not be formed under presidential systems.

Octávio Amorim Neto has shown that during the democratic periods of 1946–1964 and 1985–1997 in Brazil presidents formed cabinets on a partisan basis.[29] He classified about 70 percent of the cabinets in these periods as "party coalition" cabinets as opposed to "cooptation" and "nonpartisan" cabinets. In the period studied here, we identified seven cabinets, six of which can be classified as majoritarian. In only one cabinet, the first one under Collor, the parties participating formally in the government did not hold the majority of the seats in the congress.

We assumed that Brazilian presidents formed party coalition governments through the distribution of portfolios and assessed the support given by the parties in the cabinet on the floor to the presidential agenda. There are four possible situations. First, leaders of all parties holding ministerial portfolios vote in accordance with the government leader. Second, no coalition party opposes the government, but at least one leaves the vote on the issue open. Third, at least one party opposes the government. Finally, all parties within the coalition may oppose the president.

Overall, the parties composing the cabinet voted in accordance with the government leader. All party leaders indicated votes supporting the president in 77 percent

161

of the cases. In addition, at least one party left the vote on the issue open in 11 percent of the cases. Thus, the president could count on the support of cabinet parties in 88 percent of the cases. In 11 percent of the cases the president met with the opposition of at least one party of its congressional political basis. In only four cases did all parties forming the coalition oppose the government. Therefore, cabinet parties in general supported the government. Defections occurred but were rare.

Moreover, party members followed their leaders' positions rather than lend unconditional support to the government. This conclusion can be clearly seen in the figures in Table 3. The proportion of votes given by the party members is strongly related to the type of support given by the leaders of the parties that formed the presidential coalition. The average coalition support for the executive agenda on the floor was very high when all parties that formed the coalition agreed with the indication of the government leader. In these cases, on average, more than 90 percent of the representatives that belonged to these parties voted with the presidents. On the rare occasions when parties left the presidential coalition, support decreased accordingly. The data show that in the event of conflict within the coalition representatives followed their leaders rather than the government. Thus, presidents bargained with parties and not separately with members of the congress.

Parties belonging to the presidential coalition did support the executive. This support was not unconditional or absolute. However, the president rarely faced opposi-

Table 3 Average Proportion of Coalition Votes for Presidential Agenda by Types of Coalition Support, 1989–98

Cabinet	All parties support	At least one party leaves open	At least one party opposes	All parties oppose
Sarney	90.8	65.5	.	19.2
Collor I	92.6	70.4	53.2	10.6
Collor II	93.2	96.8	.	--
Franco I	93.0	74.7	65.8	--
Franco II	96.5	---	73.9	--
Cardoso I	91.4	82.5	51.0	--
Cardoso II	90.8	83.7	67.0	5.0
All	91.4	78.7	60.3	10.1

N= 434

tion from a party that was a member of his coalition. It is worth noting that there was no unconditional opposition either. Even the PT and the PDT supported the government on specific matters. Opposition parties were not confined to an all-or-nothing strategy.

Presidents need party support in order to win approval of their agenda, and they get it. The president and party leaders bargain and strike political deals. The voting pattern revealed by our analysis shows that these deals last over time and that being a

162

member of the cabinet implies political support in the form of votes for the presidential agenda.

Institutional Power, Governability, and Party Support

The data presented here dispute predictions of theories that emphasize the effects of electoral and party legislation on representatives' behavior and legislative outcomes. We have found neither rampant individualistic behavior in the Brazilian congress nor evidence that the legislature acts as an institutional veto player. Why does the Brazilian executive exercise such great dominance on legislative outcomes in a multiparty system with separation of powers? Given electoral incentives and the lack of party control over candidacies, why is the voting pattern in the lower house structured by parties? How does the executive obtain political support in a system with separation of powers?

The 1988 constitution did not change either the form of government or the electoral and party legislation.[30] However, it greatly extended the legislative powers of the president. In fact, it maintained all the constitutional changes introduced by the military regarding the role of the executive in the legislative process. These institutional choices have had profound effects on the Brazilian political system and on the executive-legislative relationship.

Comparison of the role both powers played in enacting laws shows the effects of these institutional choices. Under authoritarian rule the executive introduced 90 percent of laws. The resumption of congress' prerogatives following the adoption of the 1988 constitution did not radically change this situation. The executive remained the main legislator, both de jure and de facto. Its share in initiating laws enacted from 1989 to 1997, 86 percent, is only slightly lower than under authoritarian rule.[31] In contrast, from 1946 to 1964, when the executive lacked most of these powers, it introduced only 43 percent of laws that were enacted.

The current level of executive dominance over legislation resembles that found in parliamentary regimes.[32] Therefore, we are observing, not an executive that simply circumvents the legislature, but rather one that controls the legislative process. Executive dominance is due primarily to the range and extension of legislative powers held by the president, which alter the nature of executive-legislative relations. The legislative powers granted to the executive by the 1988 constitution include the expansion of exclusive initiative, the right to demand urgency procedures in bringing bills up for a vote, and, most important, the power to issue provisional decrees.[33]

The executive has a monopoly on the introduction of proposals in three areas: public administration, taxation, and the budget. The executive is solely responsible for the budget proposal—the annual budget law—which undergoes a special process of appreciation with specific procedures. Legislators may amend the proposed bud-

163

get, but they can not increase expenditures. Once approved, the budget law authorizes but does not mandate expenditures; it leaves considerable discretion over implementation of the approved budget to the executive. Legislators have no guarantee that their amendments will be executed. However, executive control over the budgetary process is enhanced by the lack of constitutional provisions regulating the consequences of failure to approve the annual budget.[34]

According to Article 64 of the constitution, the executive may demand urgency for the consideration of a bill at any moment. The urgency requested by the president sets time limits for the bill's debate. Each house has at most forty-five days to vote on the bill. Thus, no minority can block the presidential agenda. This prerogative is not extensively used since the provisional decree is a much more efficient way of speeding up and approving legislation.

The provisional decree established under Article 62 of the 1988 constitution grants the president the unilateral power to alter the status quo. The provisional decree goes into effect immediately. A vote occurs under the new status quo. Hence, if the congress prefers the prior status quo to the provisional decree but prefers the provisional decree's new status quo to the situation that would obtain with its rejection, the provisional decree is approved. It would have been rejected if it had been introduced as an ordinary bill. According to the constitution, congress has thirty days to deliberate on the decree. After this period, if it is not approved, it loses its legal effects. But the executive can reissue the original decree. This power gives the executive the advantage of keeping its act in force without facing a vote on it. The costs of forming a majority are transferred to the opposition. By avoiding a vote on a provisional decree and allowing its continuous reissuing, the majority may delegate legislative powers to the executive.

Parallel to the executive's extensive legislative power, the legislative organization is highly centralized. The speaker and party leaders exercise tight control over the legislative agenda. They are responsible for the setting of the legislative calendar. Moreover, party leaders have procedural rights that allow them to represent backbenchers (*bancadas*) and thus to control the floor. For instance, the standing orders of the lower house state that a roll call can be held whenever one is requested by a petition signed by 6 percent of the house members. To request a separate vote on an amendment, the petition has to be signed by 10 percent. A request for the consideration of a bill under urgency procedures requires the signatures of one-third of the house members or an absolute majority if the bill is to be voted on in twenty-four hours. In all these cases—requesting a roll call, considering an amendment, and requesting urgency—the party leader's signature automatically represents the will of all members of his party. Hence leaders decide procedures concerning roll calls, amendments, and urgency.

Consideration under urgency limits backbenchers' capacity to participate in the lawmaking process. As noted above, most bills are approved by this route. Under

164

urgency procedures the bill is discharged from the committee, whether the latter has reported on the proposal or not, and then referred directly to the floor. According to house rules and practices, both the request for and the approval of urgency procedures depend on party leaders. Moreover, the right to amend a bill considered under urgency is restricted. To be considered, an amendment needs to fulfill one of the following prerequisites: to be presented by the standing committee; to be subscribed to by 20 percent of house members (about one hundred representatives); or to be subscribed to by party leaders representing this same percentage of the representatives. In practice, only amendments supported by party leaders are considered. Thus, the rules favor party leaders, especially leaders of the larger parties. They restrict the action of the leaders of very small parties.

The extensive legislative powers held by the president and the distribution of legislative rights within the legislature in favor of party leaders explain the patterns observed in the previous section. Constitutional rules and the house's standing orders provide the executive and party leaders with the means to neutralize legislators' individualistic behavior. Members of congress may have electoral incentives to pursue their own particularistic interests, but they do not have the capacity to influence legislation to achieve them. Institutional arrangements conspire against their capacity to realize them.

Why should the leaders of the parties that belong to the presidential coalition cooperate with the executive? Why should they use their agenda powers to help the executive? Participation in the government provides parties with access to resources that individual legislators need for their political survival: policy influence and patronage. Leaders bargain with the executive; they exchange political support (votes) for access to policy influence and patronage. The executive provides party leaders with the means to punish backbenchers. The backbenchers who do not follow the party line may have their share of patronage denied.

Thus, a rather different image of the relationship among the president, party leaders, and individual legislators emerges. The image of a fragile and weak executive, blackmailed by opportunistic legislators who obtain new appointments and positions for each vote, does not hold. The executive, with the resources it controls, is in a very advantageous position. Most cabinets are formed by the formal agreement of parties, and party leaders become the main brokers in the bargaining between the executive and the legislators. Presidents do not need to bargain case by case. They are in a position to demand support for their entire legislative agenda. Once the government is formed and benefits are distributed among the members of the coalition, the president, with the help of party leaders, may threaten representatives and punish those who do not follow the party line.[35]

If representatives' reelection depends, among other things, upon patronage, and if the government controls patronage resources, representatives will try to extract them from the government however and whenever they can. The government will want to

165

reduce these concessions to a minimum. Hence representatives will say that they need to be given something else in order to vote with the government, and the government will say that they have already been given enough and that it can not make new concessions. Each side may threaten the other, and it is reasonable to expect that they will do so. Which side is in a better position to carry out its threat?

Representatives, at least if they act individually, are not in a strong position. They have little say in setting the legislative agenda, that is, in determining which options they will actually vote on. There will be few alternatives. In general, there are only two alternatives, one favored by the government and the other advocated by the opposition. Thus, representatives from the presidential coalition who threaten to vote against the government may end up being forced to vote for an alternative at odds with their true preferences.

Under the restrictions on the submission and consideration of amendments, amendments submitted by representatives have a poor chance of success. In general, amendments are discussed and voted in blocks. Few are reserved for a separate vote. Under the restrictions on requesting a roll call vote, either the main project or one of its amendments is subject to a roll call. Usually, leaders of the presidential coalition favor the symbolic vote and avoid votes on amendments. Given these procedures, the approval of an amendment without party leaders' support is very difficult.

Representatives willing to threaten the government face a coordination problem. Each representative's best strategy depends on the strategy chosen by the others. Representatives need to know what the others will do. If a representative carries out his or her threat but the majority does not, the government will learn that it does not need that specific representative's vote and thus may deny the representative access to the government's benefits in the future.

The structure of the relationship parallels the one depicted by Ferejohn.

> Suppose there is an office whose task is to divide a dollar among a three person constituency governed by a majority rule, and whose occupant is permitted to keep whatever is not given to constituents. Assume that the incumbent seeks to retain office by promising to deliver payments to voters and that a citizen *will* vote for the incumbent if he or she offers a sufficiently high payment. What payment will *a* citizen require of the incumbent in order to vote for his or her reelection? It is easy to see that the required *amount* cannot be greater than zero: if some individuals demand a positive amount, the incumbent will simply deliver payment to the least costly majority, which of course must be of minimum size (containing two voters in this case). The voter with the highest required payment will anticipate receiving nothing in this situation and will therefore be motivated to lower his or her required payment enough to enter the least costly majority.[36]

166

Hence, acting in isolation, representatives will not be able to extract much from the executive. It is clear that representatives have a lot to gain if they coordinate their actions, that is, if they solve their collective action problem. Organizing a party is one of the possible answers to this problem.[37]

Even if all representatives care only about patronage, it may be rational for them to support and strengthen their party. Representatives need to communicate their threats as members of a group that can carry out its promises and threats. They must act collectively. If the executive listens to their claims, they should be able to deliver the promised votes. If they are ignored, they must be able to carry out their threat by denying the government party members' votes. Thus, the executive-legislative bargaining process is structured along party lines. It is rational for each representative to act as a party member and to support the party leaders.

Party discipline may therefore be obtained without the existence of ideological parties with deep roots in the society. A party does not have to fit the Duvergerian model to be capable of acting as a disciplined player in the legislature. Nor do party leaders who do not control key electoral resources such as finances and access to the ballot lack the means to threaten and punish the rank and file. If patronage is a valuable resource for a representative seeking reelection, and if the executive controls access to this resource, then the executive and party leaders retain control over the representatives' political survival.

In sum, despite all the weaknesses Brazilian parties may display in society and in the electoral arena, the standing order of both houses recognizes parties as the main players around which the legislative process revolves. Parties are the actors in the legislative process. Legislative rights are highly concentrated in the hands of the party leaders and are distributed according to their respective membership.

Conclusions

Representatives' behavior can not be inferred exclusively from electoral laws. Incentives to cultivate the personal vote stemming from the electoral arena may be neutralized in the legislature through the internal distribution of legislative rights. The ability of members of the congress to influence policymaking may be small. Besides access to the ballot, there are other means by which leaders can punish recalcitrant rank-and-file members.

Legislative failure is not the inevitable fate of minoritarian presidents. There are no good reasons to rule out the possibility of coalition government under presidentialism. The combination of presidentialism and a multiparty system is not necessarily a threat to governmental performance. The emphasis on electoral formulas that reduce the number of parties is not warranted. Presidents may form governments the way prime ministers do by obtaining support from a coalition of parties.

167

It is widely recognized that executive control over the legislative agenda is a central feature of the parliamentary system. It has been shown that the executive's predominance over legislative output, party discipline, and the working of coalitions depend upon the legislative powers concentrated in the prime minister's hands.[38] However, the legislative powers of the president have been interpreted to have different effects. They have been thought of as a means to circumvent an institution assumed to be antagonistic. In contrast, we have argued that legislative powers may provide presidents with the means to entice a part of the legislature's members into a cooperative strategy. In the end, the legislative powers of the executive may have the same effects on both systems.

This observation allows us to dispute Tsebelis' conclusion about the basic difference between parliamentary and presidential systems. According to him, control over the agenda distinguishes these two systems. "In parliamentary systems the executive (government) controls the agenda, and the legislature (parliament) accepts or rejects proposals, while in presidential systems the legislature makes the proposals and the executive (the president) signs or vetoes them."[39] In Brazil the president controls the legislative agenda. The president proposes, and the legislature accepts or rejects what he has proposed. In fact, the first alternative—acceptance—prevails, because centralized control over the agenda has profound effects on party discipline. The capacity of backbenchers to participate in the policymaking process is curtailed. Centralization denies backbenchers access to the resources they need to influence legislation. The bills and the amendments they introduce do not reach the floor. They can only vote yes or no on an agenda defined by the government. In sum, the characteristics of the decision-making process—the legislative powers of the president and the legislative organization—may be more important determinants of governability than the form of government, the characteristics of party system, or the electoral laws.

NOTES

This paper was made possible by the support of the Conselho Nacional de Desenvolvimento Tecnológico e Científico and the Fundação de Amparo à Pesquisa do Estado de São Paulo. We would like to thank José Antônio Cheibub, Maria Hermínia Tavares de Almeida, Otávio Amorim Neto, Marcus Figueiredo, Scott Mainwaring, John Carey, Adam Przeworski, James R. Vreeland, and the two anonymous referees for their comments.

1. Juan Linz, "Presidential or Parliamentary Democracy: Does It Make a Difference?," in Juan Linz and Arturo Valenzuela, eds., *The Failure of Presidential Democracy: Comparative Perspectives* (Baltimore: The Johns Hopkins University Press, 1994), pp. 3–87; Scott Mainwaring, "Presidentialism, Multipartism, and Democracy: The Difficult Combination." *Comparative Political Studies*, 26 (1993), 198–222.

2. Barry Ames, "Electoral Rules, Constituency Pressures, and Pork Barrel: Bases of Voting in the Brazilian Congress," *Journal of Politics*, 57 (May 1995), 324–43; Barry Ames, "Electoral Strategy under

168

Open-List Proportional Representation," *American Journal of Political Science*, 39 (May 1995), 406–33.

3. Bolivar Lamounier, "Brazil at Impasse," *Journal of Democracy*, 5 (July 1994), 72–87.

4. See Nelson Polsby, "Legislatures," in Fred Greenstein and Nelson Polsby, eds., *Handbook of Political Science*, vol. 7 (Reading: Addison-Wesley, 1975), pp. 257–319.

5. Matthew Shugart and John Carey, *Presidents and Assemblies: Constitutional Design and Electoral Dynamics* (Cambridge: Cambridge University Press, 1992).

6. Ibid., ch. 7.

7. Scott Mainwaring and Matthew Shugart, *Presidentialism and Democracy in Latin America* (Cambridge: Cambridge University Press, 1997).

8. Shugart and Carey, ch. 10.

9. Ibid., pp. 434–35. See also John Carey and Matthew Shugart, "Incentives to Cultivate a Personal Vote," *Electoral Studies*, 15 (December 1995), 417–39.

10. Mainwaring and Shugart, p. 40.

11. Scott Mainwaring, "Multipartism, Robust Federalism, and Presidentialism," in Mainwaring and Shugart, p. 109.

1-2. Including reissued decrees, the executive issued 2,617 from 1988 to 1997.

13. See Argelina Figueiredo and Fernando Limongi, "O Congresso e as Medidas Provisórias: Abdicação ou Delegação?," *Novos Estudos Cebrap*, 47 (February 1997), 127–54. For a comparison with Italy, where reissuing presents a similar pattern, see Argelina Figueiredo and Fernando Limongi, "Institutional Legacies and Accountability: Executive Decrees in Brazil and Italy," paper presented at the Conference on Institutional Legacies, Institute for Latin American and Iberian Studies, Columbia University and Universidade Torcuato di Tella, Buenos Aires, August 27–29, 1998.

14. The laws represented in the first two rows were considered by the national congress as a unicameral deliberative body and referred to special joint committees. However, the votes of deputies and senators were taken and recorded separately. The third and the last rows comprise laws that underwent a bicameral legislative process, that is, separate deliberation in each house of congress.

15. This category also includes some laws regulating public offices and careers that only the executive can initiate. See Argelina Figueiredo and Fernando Limongi, "Mudança Consitucional, Desempenho Legislativo e Consolidação Institucional," *Revista Brasileira de Ciências Sociais*, 29 (October 1995), 24–37.

16. Ibid., p. 31.

17. See Argelina Figueiredo and Fernando Limongi, "Instituições Políticas e Interação Executivo-Legislativo: A Agenda de Estabilização e Reformas" (Working Paper, Cebrap/Ipea, February 1998).

18. Ibid., p. 17.

19. Hence the possibility of a roll call on a noncontroversial issue is small. Yet to avoid biasing the results toward high discipline we excluded cases in which the minority assembled less than 10 percent of the votes. See Fernando Limongi and Argelina Figueiredo, "Partidos Políticos na Câmara dos Deputados: 1989–1994," *Dados*, 38 (December 1995), 497–525. Any sample of roll call votes suffers from self-selection bias. See Peter M. Vanndoren, "Can We Learn the Causes of Congressional Decisions from Roll-Call Data?," *Legislative Studies Quarterly*, 15 (August 1990), 311–40.

20. During this period the PDS changed its name twice, to PPR and to PPB. The behavior of the members of the micro parties is not less predictable. See Limongi and Figueiredo, "Partidos Políticos," p. 520.

21. The distribution is strongly skewed. Hence controlling for presence or the expected margin of victory does not alter the overall picture. Ibid., p. 523.

22. Giovanni Sartori, "Neither Presidentialism nor Parliementarism," in Linz and Valenzuela, eds., p. 113.

23. See Scott Mainwaring and Perez-Liñán, "Party Discipline in Multiparty Systems: A Methodological Note and an Analysis of the Brazilian Constitutional Congress," *Legislative Studies Quarterly*, 22 (November 1997), 471–93. Discipline for the period 1946–1964 was also lower than what

169

we found. See Otávio Amorim Neto and Fabiano Guilherme dos Santos, "The Executive Connection: Explaining the Puzzles of Party Cohesion in Brazil," paper presented to the Twentieth LASA Congress, Guadalajara, Mexico, April 17–19, 1997; Fabiano Santos, "Patronagem e poder de agenda na política brasileira," *Dados*, 40 (December 1997), 465–92.

24.   Few works deal with party discipline in a comparative perspective. Data for selected European countries may be found in Frank L. Wilson and Richard Wiste, "Party Cohesion in the French National Assembly: 1958–1973," *Legislative Studies Quarterly*, 1 (November 1976), 467–90.

25.   Defeat of the government meant failure to change the constitution. There is no case in which the constitution was changed against the government's will. Following Arnold's classification, most of these votes were on politically unfeasible policies, for instance, reform of the social security system. See Douglas Arnold, *The Logic of Congressional Action* (New Haven: Yale University Press), p. 73. For a comparative analysis of social security reforms in different political regimes, see Paul Pierson and Kent Weaver, "Imposing Losses in Pension Policy," in Kent Weaver and Bert Rockman, eds., *Do Institutions Matter?* (Washington, D.C.: The Brookings Institution, 1993), pp 110–47. For an analysis of the current social security reform in Brazil, see Argelina Figueiredo and Fernando Limongi, "Reforma da Previdência e Instituições Políticas," *Novos Estudos Cebrap*, 51 (July 1998), 63–90.

26.   Mark P. Jones, *Electoral Laws and the Survival of Presidential Democracies* (Notre Dame: University of Notre Dame Press, 1995), p. 6.

27.   Ibid., pp. 6–7.

28.   See Michael Laver and Kenneth Shepsle, *Making and Breaking Governments: Cabinets and Legislatures in Parliamentary Democracies* (New York: Cambridge University Press, 1996); Kaare Strom, *Minority Government and Majority Rule* (New York: Cambridge University Press, 1990).

29.   Otávio Amorim Neto, "Cabinet Formation and Party Politics in Brazil," paper presented at the Nineteenth LASA Congress, Atlanta, 1995.

30.   The plebiscite held in 1993 maintained this form of government. No attempt to change electoral legislation has succeeded.

31.   These figures include laws originating from decrees (during the military regime) and provisional measures (after 1988). See Figueiredo and Limongi, "Mudança Constitucional, Desempenho do Legislativo."

32.   See George Tsebelis, "Decision Making in Political System: Veto Players in Presidentialism, Parliamentarism, Multicameralism, Multipartisms," *British Journal of Political Science*, 25 (July 1995), 304.

33.   The 1988 constitution also granted the president the initiative in introducing constitutional amendments, which was absent from the 1946 constitution. It also kept changes to speed up the consideration of legislation subject to the joint deliberation of both houses through the national congress, which has specific internal rules but no permanent organizational structure.

34.   See Antonio Sérgio Rocha, *O Congresso Nacional no Processo Orçamentário Pós-Constituinte (1988–1993): Retomando o "Poder sobre as Finanças?"* (diss., Universidade de São Paulo, 1996).

35.   Legislators have no guarantee that their approved amendments to the budget will be implemented.

36.   See John Ferejohn, "Introduction," in John Ferejohn and James H. Kuklinski, eds., *Information and Democratic Process* (Urbana: University of Illinois Press, 1990), p. 7.

37.   See John Aldrich, *Why Parties? The Origin and Transformation of Political Parties in America* (Chicago: University of Chicago Press, 1995).

38.   Gary Cox, *The Efficient Secret* (New York: Cambridge University Press, 1987); John Huber, *Rationalizating Parliament* (New York: Cambridge University Press, 1996).

39.   Tsebelis, p. 325.

170

Pergamon

Electoral Studies, Vol. 17, No. 3, pp. 351–367, 1998
© 1998 Elsevier Science Ltd. All rights reserved
Printed in Great Britain
0261-3794/98 $19.00+0.00

PII: S0261-3794(98)00034-1

Constituency Influence and Representation[1]

Susan C. Stokes

University of Chicago, Chicago, IL 60637, USA

In their classic study "Constituency Influence in Congress", Miller and Stokes (1966) equated representation with responsiveness to constituent opinion. But when constituents are uncertain about the effects of policies and when they may come to favor a policy which they opposed before its implementation, politicians may represent constitutent's interests even though they are unresponsive to their *ex ante* preferences. Several Latin American governments that switched to unpopular policies early in their terms did so because they thought citizens were ill-informed and their preferences would change. Even though we should consider such policy switches as carried out by governments that are attempting to represent, we should not return to a Burkean ideal whereby legislators do what they deem best regardless of the will of their constituents.

Keywords: Representation, Latin American policies, economic reform, Donald E. Stokes

It is generally recognized that constituency control is opposite to the conception of representation associated with Edmund Burke. Burke wanted the representative to serve the constituency's *interest*, but not its *will*, and the extent to which the representative should be compelled by electoral sanctions to follow the 'mandate' of his constituents has been at the heart of the ensuing controversy as it has continued for a century and a half—Warren E. Miller and Donald E. Stokes, *Constituency Influence in Congress*

In the ensuing 35 years since Warren Miller and Donald Stokes wrote these words, the constituency-control conception, not Burke's, has dominated empirical studies of representation. To the extent that constituencies influence or even 'control' the behavior of their legislators, the legislators *represent* their constituents. Miller and Stokes's elegant study identified two ways that such influence might occur: constituents could elect a representative with convictions like their own, so that "in following his own convictions he does the constituents' will", or the representative could vote according to his perception of constituents' opinion in order to be reelected (Miller and Stokes, 1966, p. 360).

Students of congressional representation in subsequent decades developed new methods to track the people's influence over their legislators. Their results were broadly similar. Constituents, and later 'public opinion', were found to have a powerful influence over the behavior of members of Congress, the President, the Senate, even the Supreme Court (see Stimson *et al.*,

153

1995; Page and Shapiro, 1992; Mishler and Sheehan, 1993; Bartels, 1991; Jackson and King 1989; for a somewhat divergent conceptualization and results see Achen, 1978). And the con ceptual link between citizen influence and representation endured: politicians who enacted th people's will *represented* them. Stimson and his associates, for example, found that change in public opinion induced changes in the behavior of members of Congress in the next perioc and in the same direction. They called this pattern of influence 'dynamic *representation*'.

In the context in which Miller and Stokes wrote, the equation of constituency control wit representation seemed perfectly serviceable. The Congressman whose roll-call behavio reflected constituent opinions about appropriate levels of welfare spending, or civil rights, o even intervention in foreign affairs, was enacting the constituents' will, and there was littl reason to think he wasn't also in some sense advancing their 'interest'. Miller and Stokes an those who followed them in the study of congressional representation saw no reason to drav a distinction between a Representative's *responsiveness* to the people's will and his *represen tation* of their interests.

As the study of constituency, or more broadly citizen, influence over governments move to democracies where the effects of government action are less certain, the people's will les predictable, and the constraints on government action more intrusive, it may be useful to reviv a distinction between responsiveness to citizen opinion and representation of their interests. I what follows I first offer evidence from several Latin American democracies of egregiou failures of governments to respond to citizens' will, as expressed in policy mandates delivere in elections that just took place. Next I explain these break-downs in responsiveness, showin that a plausible case can be made that politicians violated responsiveness because they though doing so was in the best interest of their constituents and hence the surest route to reelection Contrary to the implicit assumption of earlier studies, that politicians are unrepresentative t the extent that their actions respond to the will of actors other than their constituents, in th Latin American cases politicians sometimes thought they had to respond to market actors an not to citizens if they were to be judged successful at the end of their term. In the concludin section I contrast the distinction between the people's will and their interest as conceived b Burke, with the distinction proposed here. I contend that the departure from the representation as-responsiveness conception employed in the positive U.S. literature on representation nee not imply a return to Burke's conception, which rested on his disdain for the people's abilit to make intelligent choices. People's will may at times be at odds with their interests for goo and limited reasons: they may lack important information and the effects of policy may b uncertain. And we expect their will to again become a reasonable reflection of their interes when information is provided and uncertainty resolved.

The Violation of Responsiveness: Three Latin American Cases[2]

In 12 of the 44 presidential election campaigns that took place in Latin America between 1982 and 1995, the winning candidate pronounced himself[3] in favor of some combination of job creation, growth, higher real wages, industrial policy, a gradualist approach to inflation stabiliz ation, and limited repayment of the foreign debt, only to impose austerity and a withdrawal of the state from the economy immediately upon coming to office (see Table 1). All of these immediate, drastic policy switches were in the same direction: from 'welfare-oriented' cam paigns to 'efficiency-oriented' policies (the latter term is borrowed from Elster, 1995).

The most stunning policy switches were those in which the candidate's history, partisan affiliation, campaign-crafted identity, and policy pronouncements all signalled a commitment

Table 1. Presidential elections and policy switches in Latin America's Democracies, 1982–95

Country	Year	Country	Year
Argentina	1983	Ecuador	1984
	1989 s		1988 s
	1995		1992 s
Bolivia	1985	El Salvador	1984
	1989 s		1989
	1993		1994
Brazil	1989	Guatemala	1985 v
	1994		1990 v
Chile	1989		1995
	1993	Honduras	1985
Colombia	1982 s		1989
	1986		1993
	1990	Nicaragua	1984
	1994		1990
Costa Rica	1982v	Peru	1985
	1986		1990 s
	1990 s		1995
	1994 s	Uruguay	1984
Dominican Rep.	1982 s		1989
	1986		1994
	1990 s	Venezuela	1983
	1994 v		1988 s
			1993 s

s Denotes an election followed by a policy switch.
v Denotes an election after a vague campaign, one in which candidates make no policy proposals.

to welfare-oriented policies, and those policies were entirely discarded in favor of a sharp neoliberal turn early in the new government. I first describe three such switches, those of Carlos Menem of Argentina (1989–95) and Alberto Fujimori of Peru (1990–95) in their first terms, and of Carlos Andrés Pérez in Venezuela (1989–93), before turning to an explanation of the general phenomenon of post-election switches.[4]

Argentina

During the early months of 1989, the outgoing Unión Cívica Radical (UCR) government of Raúl Alfonsín struggled against high (though not yet hyper) inflation, recession, and heavy international debt obligations. The ruling party's presidential candidate, Eduardo Angeloz, distanced himself from some specific government policies and called for the resignation of the finance minister after the failure of a late 1988 emergency economic plan. Still Angeloz called for 'deepening' the economic reforms of the Alfonsín government: trade liberalization, good standing with international financial institutions, and privatization of state-owned enterprises.

Alvaro Alsogaray, the candidate of the conservative Unión del Centro Democrático (UCD) called for liberalization of trade, the exchange rate, and wages, for speedy privatizations, and for honoring standing agreements with international creditors.

Carlos Menem was the presidential candidate of the Peronist party (Partido Justicialista, PJ). Menem's was a colorful campaign, which emphasized his fondness for soccer, race cars, and fashion models. His economic message was nationalist and expansionist. He called for stabilizing the economy without imposing hardships on workers or the middle class. A book he and his running mate coauthored during the campaign called for a '*revolución productiva*' or productive revolution (Menem and Duhalde, 1988). With mildly expansionary policies to exploit unused industrial capacity Argentina would overcome depressed real wages, high unemployment, and price instability. At the very moment when the incumbent Alfonsín government was imposing austerity measures, '*paquetazos*', Menem on the campaign trail invented the term '*salariazo*', a big upward shock to wages. Consistent with the Peronist tradition, Menem championed a development model that included state ownership of heavy industry, utilities, and oil, and expressed distrust of Argentina's export bourgeoisie, epitomized by the conglomerate Bunge y Born. Early in the campaign Menem called for a moratorium on payments of Argentina's foreign debt, although he later moderated his position with a call for a five-year cessation of repayment and renegotiation on terms favorable to Argentina. Still, he insisted he would not pay Argentina's debt "by making the people go hungry" (cited in Schuler, 1994). Finally, Menem warned Britain that blood might again flow in the Malvinas or Falkland Islands.

In the election on 14 May, Menem won 47% of the vote, Angeloz 37%, and Alsogaray 6%.

The Alfonsín government was scheduled to stay in office another seven months, until December. Alfonsín announced a new set of economic measures 4 days after the election, but inflation continued to surge, reaching nearly 100% before month's end. Rioting and looting on 23 May left fourteen dead. The crisis produced an agreement between the government and Menem to move the transition forward to July.

When Menem announced his cabinet appointments in July they contained surprises. He named Miguel Roig, a former vice-president of Bunge y Born and "an outstanding symbol of *vendepatria* [sellout] capitalism to all Peronists", as his finance minister (Smith, 1991, p. 52). When Roig died of a heart attack 11 days after taking office, Menem turned the selection of a replacement over to Bunge y Born's president, who chose Nestor Rapanelli, another vice-president of the firm. Menem's labor minister was Jorge Triaca, a conservative labor figure. Triaca's appointment and the government's emerging economic policies precipitated a split in the Peronist labor confederation, the Confederación General de Trabajadores (CGT), and the founding of an antigovernment wing of the CGT under Saúl Ubaldini. Other Menem cabinet appointments were equally surprising, as were his efforts, beginning during his first months in office, to normalize relations with Britain.

Menem's economic policies bore a close resemblance to those advocated by his two opponents in the campaign. By August of 1989, only three months after the election, the language of '*salariazo*' was long forgotten. Menem introduced his austerity program exhorting Argentines to accept "a tough, costly, and severe adjustment" requiring "major surgery, no anesthesia" (cited in Smith, 1991, p. 53). The Bunge y Born plan (as it was known) included a sharp fiscal adjustment and a 170% devaluation of the *austral*. Public service rates rose between 200% and 640%, gasoline 550%. No salary increases were announced to soften the blow, and workers were offered only a bonus, the equivalent of $12.

Privatization was a top priority. Roberto Dromi, the minister of public works, drafted legislation that declared all state-owned companies "subject to privatization". Congress approved the 'Dromi law' in September. Privatized industries included telecommunications, the national airline, television and radio stations, petrochemicals, and steel. In addition to privatization, the government moved to liberalize foreign trade, phasing out export taxes and import tariffs (see Smith, 1991). Having called in the campaign for a moratorium and then five-year cessation of payments on the foreign debt, Menem named Alvaro Alsogaray, the presidential candidate from the right-wing Unión del Centro Democrático as his chief debt negotiator in Washington.

Peru

Peru's 1990 presidential campaign took place against a backdrop of dire economic crisis. In 1989 GNP had contracted by 10.4%, inflation rose to 2775%, and the external debt stood at over US$19 billion (almost $1000 per capita). This was only the worst year in a prolonged period of economic decline. The economic crisis and poor governmental performance discredited the incumbent APRA party's candidate.

Neither Vargas Llosa, the leading candidate at the outset of the campaign, nor Alberto Fujimori, who emerged as Vargas Llosa's main rival, were professional politicians. But Vargas Llosa had a long involvement in national and international politics, and his candidacy was supported by parties of the Right. In contrast, Fujimori had no ties to traditional political parties. Born to Japanese parents, Fujimori was a mathematician and in the 1980s rector of the National Agrarian University. In 1990 he stitched together Cambio'90 (Change'90), more a campaign vehicle than a party, from socially progressive Protestant evangelicals and an association of informal-sector workers. Fujimori rose from obscurity during the last month before the general the election in April. On 8 March, when his name first appeared in public opinion polls (until then he had been an 'Other'), he commanded 4% support. His standing rose to 15% on 25 March, and to 21% on 1 April (Apoyo, Informe de Opinion, March and April, 1990). In the general election on 8 April Fujimori took 25% of the vote, Vargas Llosa 28%.

Economic policy dominated the campaign. Vargas Llosa proposed to resolve the crisis through what would amount to a neoliberal revolution. He viewed Peru's overgrown state as the main barrier to economic growth and 'modernity'. The state's role should be restricted to providing essential health, education, and communications services. He proposed a 'radical attack' on inflation with a drastic reduction of the fiscal deficit. The first weapon of attack was to be a one-time sharp increase of prices of consumer goods and state services, a fiscal adjustment or 'shock'.

Fiscal adjustment would be accompanied by structural reforms including sharp reductions in government personnel, privatization, and an end to 'mercantilist' trade protection. The promise was that these measures, painful in the short term, would increase general welfare in the future. As a Vargas Llosa campaign slogan put it, "It will cost us ... but together we will make the Great Change" ("Nos costará ... pero juntos haremos el Gran Cambio").

Fujimori's campaign rhetoric was of a very different flavor. His strategy was to appeal to the lower- and lower-middle classes by advocating stabilization with a minimum of recession and job loss. Most salient of his economic themes in the campaign was his opposition to a one-time draconian fiscal adjustment, the 'shock'. The view of the 'neo-Keynesian' economic advisors whom Fujimori recruited into his campaign was that an immediate, large increase in the price of government services, removal of subsidies on basic goods, and a devaluation, would be ineffective in controlling inflation and would further concentrate income. The concentration of income would lower private investment and retard growth (see Figueroa, 1993). Fujimori also called for an industrial policy, support for small business, and reinsertion of Peru into international financial institutions (Cambio'90, 1990).

Fears of the fiscal adjustment and neoliberal reforms contributed to Fujimori's 57–35% victory (8% invalid) over Vargas Llosa in the run-off election in June.[5]

Ten days after Fujimori's inauguration, on 7 August, tanks rolled onto the streets of Lima in preparation for the announcement the next day of a package of dramatic price adjustments: the 'shock'. The price of gasoline rose by 3140%; the price of kerosene, used as cooking fuel by poor consumers, by 6964%. Subsidies for many basic foodstuffs were removed and their prices soared: bread by 1567%, cooking oil by 639%, sugar by 552%, and rice by 533%. Medicine prices rose on average by 1385%.

Fujimori's longer-term economic reforms also read remarkably like those Vargas Llosa had proposed: exchange rate unification and liberalization, reduction and simplification of tariffs on imports, elimination of tariffs on exports, capital market liberalization. These measures would later be followed by fiscal reform, reduction of employment in government ministries and state-owned enterprises, privatization of state-owned enterprises and financial institutions, elimination of job security laws, elimination of wage indexation, liberalization of labor relations, and privatization of social security.

Venezuela

To secure the Acción Democrática (AD) presidential candidacy in 1988, Carlos Andrés Pérez had to defeat a rival, Octavio Lepage, who had the support of incumbent President Jaime Lusinchi. Pérez relied on support from AD labor leaders in his struggle against Lepage. Once Pérez had secured the AD candidacy, his campaign went through two distinct phases. In the first phase, from December 1987 to June 1988, Pérez pronounced himself in favor of policies that reflected his debt to labor and recalled his presidency in the mid-1970s, at the height of Venezuela's oil boom. He promised a substantial across-the-board wage increase and a major 'war' against poverty. His opponent, COPEI's Eduardo Fernández, advocated a free-floating exchange rate, a reduced role for the state in the economy, privatization of heavy industry, ports, and services, and inflation stabilization.

Midway through the campaign, with a strong lead in the polls, Pérez appeared to ease toward the center on economic policy, without reversing any previous positions and without moving to the right of his opponent. He called for a multi-tiered exchange rate within a system of continued exchange controls, trade liberalization while maintaining protection for local industry, joint action by Latin American debtors, and 'moderate' and 'selective' privatizations of state activities.

On 4 December, Pérez became the first Venezuelan to win the presidency twice, defeating Fernández 53%–40%.

As president-elect, Pérez announced '*el Gran Virage*' or the Great Turnaround, the liberalization of the Venezuelan economy. It included a fiscal adjustment, aimed at reducing the public-sector deficit from 9.9% to 4% of GDP. Prices of goods and services, frozen by Lusinchi, were raised, and price controls on all but 18 goods were eliminated. The increases were steep: 100% for gasoline, 133% for natural gas, 30% for public transportation. Pérez also quickly reassured the business community, insisting that there would be no substantial across-the-board wage increase. The government adopted a single floating exchange rate, liberalized interest rates, reduced import tariffs to below 40% on average, and announced privatization measures and other structural reforms (see Hausmann, 1995; Naím, 1993).

Consequences of Violations of Responsiveness

Did voters punish politicians who changed course?

In one of the three cases discussed here, the answer is yes. The liberalization of prices, the rst step in Pérez's Great Turnaround, produced an explosion: demonstrations and riots in Caracas that left at least 300 people dead and 1000 injured. The political debacle continued, ed by the excessive costs of the economic program. The first in a series of 'big bang' efforts o correct past policy deficiencies all at once (see Hausmann, 1995; Martinelli and Tomassi, 998), the program unintentionally overshot its targets, causing considerably more hardship han necessary. Non-oil output, which grew by 5.6% in 1988, was predicted to grow by a nore modest 2.0% in 1989 under the austerity program. In fact the non-oil economy contracted y 9.8% in 1989. Even when economic conditions improved after 1990, the public image of he government failed to recover. Pérez was twice challenged in coup attempts in 1992. The hallenges to the constitutional order in Latin America's second oldest democracy were stounding. With abysmal approval ratings, Pérez was impeached on corruption charges in 993. And the share of the vote going to the AD candidate in 1993 was 24%, down from 53% n 1988.

The story of Fujimori's and Menem's first terms contrasts starkly with the Pérez debacle. Both presidents were rewarded for the risk they took in violating their mandate. Fujimori truggled in public opinion during his first year and a half in office. He had highly volatile nd generally declining approval ratings, as Peruvians tried to make sense of this unknown nan who won the election by surprise and then implemented his opponent's program. But two actors made his popularity soar, beginning in 1992. Fujimori led a palace coup in April, in vhich he closed Congress and suppressed the constitution; the public, exhausted by economic risis and insurgency, responded enthusiastically to the apparent return to order. The government's success in reducing inflation also contributed to Fujimori's popularity, even though olls taken at the beginning of the term showed Peruvians to be skeptical of the effectiveness f such programs in reducing inflation (S. Stokes, 1996).[6] This skepticism was especially widepread among the urban lower and lower-middle classes, who provided Fujimori most of his otes in 1990. Growth also resumed after mid-1992. In the last year of Fujimori's predecessor's erm, the economy was contracting at an annual rate of nearly 10%; in the last year of Fujimo- i's first term, output was expanding at nearly 11%. With economic stability restored and olitical authority reestablished, Fujimori engineered a change in presidential term limits after ne coup that allowed him to run again in 1995; he ran and won handily.

The Menem story is similar. Menem also floundered initially. Until 1991 his austerity pro- ram failed to control inflation. But with the success, beginning in early 1991, of finance ninister Domingo Cavallo's 'Convertibilty Plan', which finally rid the Argentine economy of ne bouts of hyperinflation that had characterized the end of the Alfonsín years and the begin- ing of Menem's term. When Menem assumed office output was falling at an annual rate of .4%; by the end of his term it was growing at 6.7%. Price stability and growth placed Menem n a positioned to revise the constitution (this time without a coup), changing term limits so hat he could run again in 1995. He did so, and won handily.[7]

In short, at least two of our unresponsive politicians switched to policies that seemed to nduce a *preference*-switch among voters, who richly rewarded both politicians with reelection.

Analysis of data contained in a cross-national dataset I have assembled suggests that although oliticians who switched policies were at risk of a loss of support in later elections, strong conomic performance could mitigate the damage. I coded all competitive presidential elections hat took place in Latin America between 1982 and 1995 according to whether the winner's conomic policy pronouncements in the campaign predicted well or badly the actual policies ndertaken in the first year of his or her term (the coding was dichotomous: either governments witched or they were consistent). The database also included economic measures (inflation, changes in GDP, international currency reserves, budget deficits; all from *International Finan* *cial Statistics*, IMF), election results, the majority status of governments, term limits, the econ omic policy orientation of the prior government, and other political and institutional measures

Holding economic outcomes equal, end-of-term voteshares were lower for policy switcher than for non-switchers. Consider the regression model of incumbent party voteshare in Tabl 2. The constant, −12.7, is the *y*-intercept for non-switchers. It indicates that under the conditio of no change in GDP, the voteshare of consistent politicians at the end of their term was 12. points lower than their share in the election that brought them to office.[8] The constant for th sub-sample of switchers is the sum of the constant and the coefficient on the SWITCH dummy (−12.7) + (−8.6) = − 21.3. Hence, when the difference between beginning and end-of-tern GDP growth rates is 0, incumbents who switched policies lose almost twice as many votes a non-switchers. The penalty for incumbency is high; for switching it is much higher.

Yet when economic performance was good after a policy switch, voters rewarded policy switchers more richly than non-switchers. Consider again the OLS regression in Table 2, whic includes an interaction term (GDP*SWITCH), the difference in before- and end-of-term GDF growth (DIFGDP) multiplied by the SWITCH dummy. Following Gujarati (1995, 512 ff.), th effect of GDP change in the base category, non-switchers, is given by the coefficient o DIFGDP. We see that the coefficient, 1.04, is significant at the 93% level. The effect of GDF change among switchers is given by the sum of the coefficient on DIFGDP and the interactio term: 1.04 + 2.49 = 3.53. Hence, whereas a 1% increase in GDP over the course of the tern among non-switchers was associated with about a 1% increase in vote share, among switcher: the same change in GDP was associated with a 3.5% increase in vote share. The effect o GDP change on electoral support was magnified three and a half times among politicians whc switched policies early in the term.

Explaining Policy Switches

The three new presidents described here abandoned policies that had just contributed to getting them elected, rejecting them in favor of policies they had sometimes ridiculed in the campaign Their actions were highly visible and politically risky. What explains these dramatic moment: of unresponsiveness?

In all three cases it is clear that, in switching, governments were responding to market actors

Table 2. OLS regression, dependent variable INCUMBENT PARTY VOTESHARE[a], 23 observations

Variable	Coefficient	SE	*t*-ratio	Prob/*l* ≥ *x*	Mean	Std.
Constant	−12.69	2.43	−5.23	0.000		
SWITCH[b]	−8.58	3.73	−2.30	0.033	0.39	0.49
DIFGDP[c]	1.04	0.54	1.94	0.068	3.27	4.37
GDP*SWITCH	2.49	0.69	3.590	0.002	1.49	3.88

$R^2 = 0.786$, Adjusted $R^2 = 0.752$. $F(3,19) = 23.26$, Prob value 0.000.
[a]Percent of the vote election at $t = 2$, at the end of the incumbent's term, minus percent of the vote commanded by that party at $t = 1$, the beginning of the term.
[b]Dummy variable for politicians who switched. Source: LACAP.
[c]Difference between the average GDP growth rate in the two years leading up to term and average growth rate during the last two years of the term. Source: *International Financial Statistics*, IMF.

including international financial institutions, foreign creditors, domestic investors, and currency speculators. In some instances, the pressures came from the uncoordinated, decentralized action of markets. In Peru, Fujimori's election sparked a run on the currency. The *inti* declined 43% in relation to the dollar in the month after the first round of elections, an additional 63% and 67% in June and July. In other instances, the pressure came from powerful individuals who predicted bleak consequences should the politician follow through on the economic program promised in the campaign. When Pérez tried to recruit a young economist to serve as his minister of industrial development, the economist advised the president-elect that Venezuela was about to experience the worst bout of inflation in its history, only to be avoided through a liberalization of prices (interview with Moisés Naím, 1993).[9]

Explicit pressure was also exerted on Fujimori. Weeks after winning the run-off election in June, Fujimori and two advisors traveled to New York (ironically, while the furor still raged over George Bush's then-recent reneging on his 'no new taxes' campaign pledge). Fujimori and one of his advisors, the economist Adolfo Figueroa, attended a meeting at the United Nations with Michel Camdessus, the managing director of the IMF, Barber Conable, the president of the World Bank, and Enrique Iglesias, the president of the Interamerican Development Bank (IDB). At the meeting, as reported to me by Figueroa, the following alternatives were communicated to Fujimori. If the new president tried to avoid an immediate, painful adjustment, his administration would run the course of Alan García's. If he did not adjust, he ought not to turn to the international financial institutions for help. If he did adjust and complemented 'realistic' short-term stabilization measures with structural reforms, the IFIs would be there to help him.

Yet 'market strikes' and overt pressures notwithstanding, what my research makes clear is that most politicians who switched policies already knew during the campaign that the programs they ran on would probably never be implemented. In a 1993 interview with a Buenos Aires journalist, Carlos Menem admitted that he had dissimulated in the campaign, hiding his intentions to privatize industry and pursue other reforms at odds with the Peronist tradition. Campaign strategists whom I interviewed revealed that Menem's decision to pursue liberalization had been taken immediately after the Peronist primary elections—a full year before he took power! Evidence from Venezuela suggests that Pérez planned policies of the Great Turnaround well before his election. Even Fujimori, whose attention was rivetted on the campaign and who thought little about what would happen after the election, was not at all certain that he would remain faithful to his 'anti-shock' slogan. Admonished by an aide to reconsider his no-fiscal-shock promise, "think more like a statesman, less like a politician", Fujimori replied "If I don't act like a politician now, I'll never get to be a statesman" (interview with Fernando Villarán, 1993).

Given the timing of these decisions to pursue efficiency policies, two questions must be answered: first, why did politicians opt for liberalization, and second, why did they hide this decision from voters?

The answer to the second question is that politicians thought they would be rejected by voters if they revealed their efficiency-oriented intentions in the campaign. The answer to the first is that they thought that the risk of economic disaster under the policies they announced in the campaign—disaster induced by the reaction of markets—was great enough to outweigh the risk of switching to policies which a majority of voters had just rejected. And they thought that voters might be coaxed into approving *ex post* policies which they had feared *ex ante*.

Politicians and campaign strategists whom I interviewed in several countries outlined this strategic thinking. One of them Roberto Dromi, the Menem advisor in 1989 who later became minister of public works. What follows is part of my 1994 interview with Dromi:

> S. Stokes: If Menem knew in the campaign that he would pursue austerity and liberalization, why did he talk in the campaign about a moratorium on the debt and about the *'salariazo'*?

> Dromi: If we hadn't talked about a *salariazo* we would have frightened public-sector workers, who are 10% of the working population of Argentina.

> S: But why didn't you announce that you would reduce the deficit, and win the votes of the 90% of Argentine workers who weren't public-sector workers and who wanted inflation to come down?

(At this point in the interview, which took place in Dromi's law office, he pulled from the shelf *Nuevo Estado, Nuevo Derecho* (Dromi, 1994), a book he had written, and opened to the epigraph, a quote from Machiavelli's *The Prince*, which he then read aloud:

> Nothing does so much honor to a new man who emerges as much as his devising of new laws and new institutions. When these things have good foundations and greatness, they make him respected and admired .... [T]here is nothing more difficult to try, nor more doubtful of success, nor more dangerous to deal with, than to take it upon oneself to introduce new institutions, because the introducer makes enemies out of all those who benefit from the old institutions and is feebly defended by all those who might benefit from the new ones. This feebleness arises, in part from the fear of the opposition, who have the laws on their side, in part from the skepticism of men, who do not truly believe in novelties until they see them arising out of firm experience.[10]

> D: We were not sure we would win the election. First we thought Cafiero would win the primaries, then we thought Angeloz would win the general election. We didn't want to risk losing the votes of left Peronists, unions, industrialists in protected industries, and public employees by talking about liberalization and privatization.

> S: Why did you make an alliance with Alsogaray after the election?

> D: We wanted to send a clear signal, so we named Julia Alsogaray as *inventora* of Entel and Frigerio as head of YPF.[11]

> S. A signal to whom?

> D. To God and the devil, to everyone. To Morgan Guaranty, the U.S. government, the World Bank.

To summarize, politicians like Pérez, Fujimori, and Menem adopted welfare-oriented campaign platforms as a strategy to win the up-coming election, but foresaw abandoning these policies, or at least severely modifying them, should they win. They recognized that reneging on campaign pronouncements might be costly. But they believed that their preferred policies would induce salient and tangible results, such as price stability where high inflation had been endemic and that voters would become convinced of the appropriateness of these policies. And perhaps, in volatile political environments, they placed a high value on winning the first election and discounted the future heavily.[12] Some, like Fujimori ("if I don't think like a politician now I'll never get to be a statesman"), knew that losing the present election meant exiting the political arena for good. In close races, therefore, they were willing to risk their post-election future and promise whatever they believed voters wanted to hear.

Caught between the market and voters, voters who may not have appreciated fully the constraints imposed by the market, some presidential candidates in Latin America took the risky move of promising one thing in campaign and immediately doing another in power.

Models by Harrington (1993a,b) suggest the strategic orientation of policy switchers. The models emphasize voter uncertainty regarding the effect of policies on outcomes. Assume two politicians who compete for election and then reelection in a two-period world. They have beliefs about which policies will maximize voters' welfare, beliefs which are private information. Voters also have such beliefs, but are unsure of their correctness. In the second election voters will judge the incumbents' performance according to the net change in their own welfare during the first period. If in the first election the politician promised the policies which a majority of voters initially thought optimal, voters will judge politicians by a retrospective standard which is more lax; if the politician dissimulated his intentions before the first election and switched policies in the first term, voters' retrospective standard will be more demanding. Hence, all things equal, the politician who comes to office announcing the policies he thinks best and then pursues these policies will be reelected more easily than one who comes to office dissimulating his beliefs and then switches. Harrington shows that politicians will dissimulate and switch if they believe their preferred policies will perform sufficiently well to induce unsupportive voters to switch to preferring them.

Harrington's model helps make sense of my findings that voters hold policy switchers to a higher standard than those who enact the policies they ran on, as well as the finding that voters' judgements of incumbents are more sensitive to outcomes when politicians switched course early in their term. We saw that voters did hold policy switchers to a higher standard: with no economic growth, incumbency was worth −12.7% for consistent politicians but −21.3% for governments that had changed course. In turn voters' greater sensitivity to economic outcomes when politicians switched is suggestive of exactly the sort of uncertainty that Harrington emphasizes. These were governments elected by voters for whom the welfare-oriented, pro-growth message was appealing, and whose priors were that austerity and neoliberal reforms would be ineffective or harmful. Such governments had to work harder to persuade voters that neoliberalism in fact had been the right course, where 'working harder' meant producing better economic outcomes. Recall that an increase in GDP produced a three-and-one-half times greater increase in the incumbent party's voteshare when the incumbent switched policies than when his government had been consistent; by the same token, a decline in GDP produced a three-and-one-half times greater decline in the voteshare of incumbent policy switchers than of consistent governments.

Had voters been certain of the effects of policies, they might have attributed unexpectedly good performance under efficiency policies to, say, international conditions rather than to the government's policies. In this case economic performance would have had the same effect on voters' assessment of incumbents, whether their policies had been consistent or inconsistent with their initial mandates. But this was not the case. Voters' greater sensitivity to economic outcomes under inconsistent governments is suggestive of considerable uncertainty, uncertainty which—as we saw—politicians sensed and worked into their stratagems.

To summarize, at least some Latin American politicians were unresponsive to the people's will because they thought voters' beliefs were wrong and that voters would do better (and their own political careers would be enhanced) if the politicians reversed themselves and pursued policies that were *ex ante* unpopular. Or to put it negatively, these politicians thought that if they did what they had promised in the campaign all hell would break loose in the economy, saw all hell beginning to break loose as speculators bet against the currency and international actors threatened financial isolation, and believed there was a good chance their political careers would end after this term—perhaps even sooner—if they did not act to reassure markets. To the extent that politicians anticipated a 'Harrington effect' they were right: voters held governments that switched to a higher retrospective standard than governments that were consistent. Yet our evidence that on average switchers were not punished severely at the polls the next time around suggests that economic performance under *ex ante* unpopular policies was often sufficiently good to change voters' policy preferences.

Citizen Influence, Responsiveness, and Representation

If this is the right way to think about the experiences of Latin American democracies in the midst of pro-market reforms, then the need for a richer conceptualization of representation than mere 'citizen influence' becomes clear. If citizen opinion changes, then which opinions will the politician who aspires to represent them enact? If citizen opinion is better informed after the government has acted than before, will the representative allow her actions to be guided by *ex ante* opinion?

Latin America's recent experience with democracy counsels us to be cautious in equating citizen influence, responsiveness, and representation. These equations, which appeared harmless in the works of Miller and Stokes and their followers in the study of constituency influence, are revealed to be problematic when certain conditions hold:

(1) *Citizens have limited information about the consequences of policy.* Of course in some sense this holds in all kinds of democracies and about all kinds of policies. The work of Donald Stokes and others of the Michigan school taught us that many voters know next to nothing about the policies taken by governments or proposed by candidates, much less the consequences these policies would have. Yet the policies being described here are particularly shrouded in uncertainty: these are major transformations, involving complex chains of causality through the economy, the effects of which will depend on myriad variables the behavior of which is itself difficult to predict (for a particular version of this uncertainty, see Fernández and Rodrik, 1991). It seems safe to say that the consequences of exchange rate unification or trade liberalization are harder for voters to predict than, say, those of civil rights legislation. And it should not surprise us if voters' information and ability to predict the consequences of major economic transformations are limited, given that the ability of experts to predict is hardly perfect. We saw in the Venezuelan experience the drastic errors that highly technical programs can fall into, errors that have been repeated from Mexico to Argentina to Poland.[13]

When people are uncertain about the future effects of policies they may change their mind about them after they have taken effect. The most compelling evidence of people changing their minds is in Peru, where polls revealed skepticism about the effectiveness of shock treatment in bringing down inflation, but when the government's policies proved effective, its approval ratings rose with each reduction of inflation. We would consider people's better-informed, post-policy opinion to better reflect their true interests than their pre-policy, less-informed opinions; and we would therefore regard as representative a politician who was not 'dynamically responsive' to *ex ante* opinion but anticipated the future retrospective judgement of better-informed voters.

Although the authors of 'Constituency Influence in Congress' did not explore the possibility of opinion reversals or 'preference switches,' it is worth noting one of the signal contributions of Donald Stokes in calling attention to the shifting dimensions which form the basis of voters' valuation of politicians from one election to the next. Much of what politicians do, he insisted, was not to respond to public opinion as already formed but anticipate public opinion of future actions of government. Winning reelection, he reminded us, often depends not on following through on past promises, but on shrewdly selecting new themes that would resonate with voters and cast one's party in the best light. In 'Spatial Models of Party Competition' he wrote

> [T]he space in which political parties compete can be of highly variable structure. Just as the parties may be perceived and evaluated on several dimensions, so the dimensions that are salient to the electorate may change widely over time (Stokes, 1966, p. 168).

The evidence Stokes adduced in support of this variability were the 1948 and 1952 presidential elections in the U.S.:

> Whereas the voter evaluations of 1948 were strongly rooted in the economic and social issues of the New Deal-Fair Deal era, the evaluations of 1952 were based substantially on foreign concerns. A dimension that had touched the motives of the electorate not at all in the Truman election was of great importance in turning the Democratic administration out of power four years later .... [T]he skills of political leaders who must maneuver for public support in a democracy consist partly in knowing what issue dimensions are salient to the electorate or can be made salient by suitable propaganda (D. Stokes, 1966, pp. 168-169).

Stokes replaces the picture of politicians as passively responding to constituent influence with the more realistic one in which politicians drum up issues which they anticipate will help them win votes. He replaces the picture of voters delivering to politicians a 'mandate,' one which will provide the criterion for retrospective evaluation at the next election, with one in which voters' criteria of judgement fluctuate with changing circumstances and in response to the strategies of electioneers. His work did not fully explore the implications of these more complex pictures for our notions democratic representation. But his views are highly suggestive of the inappropriateness of reducing representation to responsiveness.

(2) *The welfare effects of a policy on constituents are contingent on the actions of others, whose policy preferences are at odds with those of constituents.* Miller and Stokes recognized that the behavior of members of Congress was shaped by other forces in addition to constituent opinion. They wrote, "*some* constituency influence would not imply that the Representative's behavior is *wholly* determined by constituency pressures .... The constituency can exercise a genuine measure of control without driving all other influences from the Representative's life space" (Miller and Stokes, 1966, p. 361, n.13). It would be natural to consider that this other-than-constituent influence does not interfere with representation as long as the will of non-constituent actors was not preponderant or sharply at odds with the will of constituents. And it would be equally natural to infer that when non-constituent influence sends legislators' behavior in the opposite direction from that desired by constituents, representation is imperiled. Consider a liberal congressional district in which attitudes run strongly in favor of gun control. The Representative from the district is subjected to pressure from the National Rifle Association; and votes to reduce controls on the purchase of firearms. Here there is a zero-sum quality to the influence of constituents and of non-constituents. And to the extent that the Representative is responsive to the latter she is less representative of the former.

This zero-sum quality is mitigated when non-constituents are able to undermine constituer welfare and will do so if the government's policies fail to reflect their own preferences. Voter in Peru and Argentina elected politicians who promised a gradualist approach to inflatio stabilization, higher wages, and jobs. When these candidates won, markets, already unstable reacted by putting loans on hold, shifting out of domestic assets, and betting against the cur rency. This market response threatened price stability, wages, and jobs. Had politicians no acted to reassure markets, the 'market strike' might well have undermined the very goals voter held in electing the welfare-oriented politicians in the first place.

This should not be construed as an argument for absolute 'structural dependence' of th state in capitalist societies, a state that can do nothing that encroaches on the interests o capital; we know such absolute dependence to be false, both empirically and formally (se Przeworski and Wallerstein, 1988; Przeworski, 1985). Nor should it be construed as a justifi cation of the actions of the particular governments discussed here in pulling back from thei mandates when markets appeared to demand it. Whether or not the policies they adopte maximized citizen welfare given the constraints imposed by markets is a question that is diffi cult to answer. What is clear is that politicians acted under substantial pressure from markets and they believed, not implausibly, that the best interests of citizens (and hence their ow political prospects) lay in placating markets.

Back to Burke?

Miller and Stokes opened their pathbreaking study by acknowledging the normative ambiguity of the phenomenon they studied, citizen influence over their representatives. They rightly attri buted to Edmund Burke the position that representation meant not responsiveness to constitu ents' will but to their interest; in fact Burke would not have looked favorably on the represen tation of the interests of a constituency, wedded as he was to the notion of a 'national interest' or other disembodied interests (trading interests, agricultural interests) as the appropriate objec of representation.[14] In arguing for a conceptual distinction between responsiveness and rep resentation, I have also distinguished will—preferences, opinions—from interest. And yet the lesson to be drawn from the Latin American experiences is not that we should return to Burke's idea that the people are an unreliable judge of their own interests. Rather the view emerging here is perfectly consistent with the liberal one that undergirds many of our democratic insti tutions, elections among them. The people should be empowered to select their leaders after judging the effectiveness of the past actions of governments and after listening to alternative proposals for the future, and leaders should be free of institutionalized imperatives to carry out their mandates (Manin, 1997).

Burke believed that to the extent that representative government actually represented, it did so because it was staffed by a natural aristocracy of leaders. Most people in any nation, unculti vated in the matter of rational collective decision-making, were incapable of perceiving the true interests, and would, if given a position of leadership, succumb to passing whims and confuse their own parochial concerns for the greater good. In contrast it is axiomatic in the liberal tradition that individuals are not only capable of reasoned decisions but that they are the best judges of their own interest. As Pitkin explains, this means that when the people are in error regarding their interests there will be clear reasons why this is so, such as that they lack information or misconstrue the significance of an issue (Pitkin, 1967, 164 ff.). Therefore in the liberal democratic framework we do not expect citizens' opinions to be regularly at odds with their interests; and we do not expect their representatives to habitually take actions at odds with their constituents' will. Such an assessment accords well with the Latin American experiences recorded here. To the extent that citizens' *ex ante* economic policy preferences were reversed *ex post*, this was because their later preferences were formulated with the advantage of knowledge of the effects of these policies. And the politicians who were trying to represent them (if for no reason more lofty than to promote their future electoral prospects) by ignoring their mandates fully expected to face the retrospective judgement of voters in the future, and hoped that voters would find the government's unresponsive course of action to have been in their best interest.

If people usually know what's best for them, and if therefore governments usually represent by being responsive to the people's will, how necessary is the distinction that I have been arguing for between responsiveness and representation? In fact it is necessary. The conditions identified here which opened up a gap between the will of the majority and its interests are endemic to democracy, even if they are more commonly found in some democracies than in others. Peru, Argentina, and Venezuela are not the only democracies where politicians sometimes ignore their mandates. Casual observation indicates drastic and early policy switches in West Germany (1976), the United States (1990), France (1995), Australia (1983), and New Zealand (1984) (on the last two, see Nagle, 1996). The dependence of citizens' welfare on the behavior of other actors, actors with preferences at odds with the majority's and whose behavior and preferences are not transparent to the majority, is a feature of a growing number of capitalist democracies in an increasingly interdependent world. And in any democracy, some government actions will have consequences that are not *ex ante* fully predictable. The distinction between representation and responsiveness is an important one to retain as we study government actions in the full range of democracies, even if the distinction will not always shed light on the relation of governors to governed.

Notes

1. Research supported by Nation Science Foundation grant SBR-9617796, and by the SSRC-MacArthur Program in International Peace and Security.
2. Miller and Stokes studied the impact of constituency opinion on the roll-call behavior of Representatives from their districts. The focus of my study is quite different: the relation between voters' opinions and the actions of governments, more narrowly of presidents. This approach reflects the institutions of Latin American democracies. In most, legislatures are elected from large multi-member districts and seats are apportioned by proportional representation. The 'responsible parties' model of legislative representation is more appropriate in this context than one linking the behavior of individual representatives with the opinions of their constituents. Recent studies of party discipline in Latin American legislatures shed light on the responsibility of parties; see, for example, Figueiredo and Limongi (1997). But in many countries national legislatures are deprived of the leading role in law-making characteristic of the U.S. Congress, both by constitutional design and by the *de facto* encroachments of presidents. Hence my focus on executive behavior.
3. Only one woman ran for president, Violeta Chamorro of Nicaragua in 1990. Chamorro, who won and served as president from 1990 to 1996, ran on what I am calling an efficiency-oriented program and implemented that program.
4. The notion that Latin American presidential elections represented any sort of 'mandate' for policies relies on the view that voters responded in part to campaign policy positions in deciding for whom to vote, and not simply to candidates' party, class, or ethnic, identity, or to symbolic and affective impulses. This notion is not an unexamined assumption in the larger project of which this article is a part, although it is not examined in depth here. Survey data from several countries support the view that policy positions were an important factor in voters' decisions, as does the fact that when politicians changed policies, they often elicited an immediate, negative reaction, both in polls and

on the streets. Such a reaction would not be predicted if voters had simply supported candidates as members of a party, or class, or ethnic group.

5. In one post-election poll, 46% of lower-class respondents who had voted against Vargas Llosa said they opposed him because he "represented the interests of the rich", and another 17% "because of his right-wing ideas". These were the responses of the two poorest groups of respondents to Apoyo's June poll of 300 Lima residents (Apoyo, June 1990). 16% opposed Vargas Llosa because they "didn't trust him or didn't like him", and 5% for "other reasons". Fujimori, in turn, attracted support among urban lower classes and middle classes and among the peasantry.

6. Fujimori's other great triumph was quelling the Sendero Luminoso insurgency. The breaking event in that story was the caputure, in September 1992, of Abimael Guzmán, the leader of Sendero. The effect of this event is difficult to detect in public opinion polls, because it happened four months after the coup, when Fujimori's approval ratings were already sky-high, and didn't contribute to any significant increase (S. Stokes, 1996). Nevertheless it stands to reason that victory over Sendero was a salient feature in Fujimori's public image, one that bouyed his popularity into the mid-1990s.

7. The end of the story is yet to be told for these two remarkable politicians. As of this writing, public opinion in their respective countries has turned against them. In both cases, economic stability and macro-level growth came at the cost of high unemployment, stagnant real wages for many workers, and income concentration (see Berry, 1997). Fujimori's trend toward dictatorial behavior also has angered Peruvians.

8. This heavy burden of incumbency is consistent with the findings of Remmer (1993).

9. Naím eventually agreed to join the cabinet and was a major force in the Great Turnaround. For his views of these events see Naím (1993).

10. The translation of Machiavelli is from Sonnino (Machiavelli, 1996). The excerpts are from chapters XXVI and VI. Dromi's rendering in Spanish differs in some details from Sonnino's.

11. Julia Alsogaray, a UcéDé Senator and daughter of the party's presidential candidate, Alvaro Alsogaray, was named by Menem to oversee the privatization of Entel, the state telecommunications company, as well as to other posts. Octavio Frigerio was named chairman of the Yacimientos Petrolíferos Fiscales (YPF), the state oil company. Frigerio's father had attempted to privatize YPF during the Frondizi government in the 1950s.

12. Presidential term-limits might be expected to encourage short time-horizons and policy switches. Analysis of the cross-national dataset reveals no significant impact of term limits on the probability of a switch. See Stokes (1998); see also Carey (1996).

13. If politicians were uncertain about the impact of neoliberal reforms on welfare, is it reasonable to argue, as I have, that many switched to these reforms in an effort to represent citizens' interests? In the area of economic policy, they faced considerable uncertainty no matter what they did. The critical point is that market pressures led them to believe that pro-market reforms were less risky than a program consistent with their own campaign slogans. That is, by the politicians' calculus the expected utility to voters of neoliberalism reforms was higher than the expected utility of welfare policies.

14. The interpretation of Burke offered here relies heavily on Hannah Pitkin's *The Concept of Representation* (Pitkin, 1967), just as Miller and Stokes's comments on Burke relied on Pitkin's dissertation.

References

Achen, C. H. (1978) Measuring representation. *American Journal of Political Science* **22**, 475–510.

Bartels, L. M. (1991) Constituency opinion and Congressional policy making: the Reagan defense build-up. *American Political Science Review* **85**, 457–474.

Berry, A. (1997) The income distribution threat in Latin America. *Latin American Research Review* **32**(2), 3–40.

Cambio'90 (1990) *Lineamientos del Plan de Gobierno 1990.* Cambio'90, Lima.

Carey, J. M. (1996) *Term Limits and Legislative Representation.* Cambridge University Press, New York.

Dromi, R. (1994) *Nuevo estado, nuevo derecho.* Ediciones Ciudad Argentina, Buenos Aires.

Elster, J. (1995) The impact of constitutions on economic performance. *Proceedings from the Annual Bank Conference on Economic Development.* The World Bank, Washington, DC.

Fernández, R. and Rodrik, D. (1991) Resistance to reform: status quo bias in the presence of individual-specific uncertainty. *American Economic Review* **81**(5), 1146–1155.

Figueiredo, A. C. and Limongi, F. (1997). Presidential power and party behavior in the legislature. Paper presented at the Congress of the Latin American Studies Association, April 17–19, Guadalajura, Mexico.

Figueroa, A. (1993) *Crisis distributiva en el Perú*. Pontificia Universidad Católica del Perú, Lima.

Gujarati, D. N. (1995) *Basic Econometrics*, 3rd edition. McGraw–Hill, New York.

Harrington, J. E. (1993a) The impact of reelection pressures on the fulfillment of campaign promises. *Games and Economic Behavior* 5, 71–97.

Harrington, J. E. (1993b) Economic policy, economic performance, and elections. *American Economic Review* 83, 27–42.

Hausmann, R. (1995) Quitting populism cold turkey: the 'big bang' approach to macroeconomic balance. In *Lessons of the Venezuelan Experience*, eds L. W. Goodman *et al*. Johns Hopkins University Press and the Woodrow Wilson Center, Baltimore, MD.

Jackson, J. E. and King, D. C. (1989) Public goods, private interests, and representation. *American Political Science Review* 83, 1143–1164.

Machiavelli, N. (1996) *The Prince*, trans. P. Sonnino. Humanities Press, NJ.

Manin, B. (1997) *The Principles of Representative Government*. Cambridge University Press, New York.

Martinelli, C. and Tomassi, M. (1998) Sequencing of economic reforms in the presence of political constraints. *Economics and Politics* 9, 115–131.

Menem, C. and Duhalde, E. (1988) *La Revolución Productiva*. Buenos Aires.

Miller, W. E. and Stokes, D. E. (1966) Constituency influence in congress. In *Elections and the Political Order*, eds A. Campbell, P. E. Converse, W. E. Miller and D. E. Stokes. Wiley, New York.

Mishler, W. and Sheehan, R. S. (1993) The Supreme Court as a countermajoritarian institution?: the impact of public opinion on Supreme Court decisions. *American Political Science Review* 87, 87–101.

Nagle, J. (1996) Social choice in a pluralitarian democracy: the politics of market liberalisation in New Zealand. Manuscript, University of Pennsylvania.

Naím, M. (1993) *Paper Tigers and Minotaurs: The Politics of Venezuela's Economic Reforms*. Carnegie Endowment, Washington, DC.

Page, B. and Shapiro, R. Y. (1992) *The Rational Public: Fifty Years of Trends in American Policy Preferences*. University of Chicago Press, Chicago.

Pitkin, H. F. (1967) *The Concept of Representation*. University of California Press, Berkeley.

Przeworski, A. (1985) *Capitalism and Social Democracy*. Cambridge University Press, New York.

Przeworski, A. and Wallerstein, M. (1988) Structural dependence of the State on capital. *American Political Science Review* 82, 11–29.

Remmer, K. L. (1993) The political economy of elections in Latin America, 1980–1991. *American Political Science Review* 87, 393–407.

Schuler, M. (1994) An inquiry into the logic behind President Carlos Menem's policy shift. Manuscript. University of Chicago.

Smith, W. C. (1991) State, market and neoliberalism in post-transition Argentina. *Journal of Interamerican Studies and World Affairs* 33, 45–82.

Stimson, J. A., Mackuen, M. B. and Erikson, R. S. (1995) Dynamic representation. *American Political Science Review* 89, 543–565.

Stokes, D. E. (1966) Spatial models of party competition. In *Elections and the Political Order*, eds. C. Angus, P. E. Converse, W. E. Miller and S. C. Stokes. Wiley, New York.

Stokes, S. C. (1998) What do policy switches tell us about democracy? In *Democracy, Accountability, and Representation*, eds. B. Manin, A. Przeworski and S. Stokes. Cambridge Unviersity Press, New York, forthcoming.

Stokes, S. C. (1996) Economic reform and public opinion in Peru, 1990–1995. *Comparative Political Studies* 29, 544–565.

Presidential Election Laws and Multipartism in Latin America

MARK P. JONES, University of Michigan

This article examines the interaction between the rules governing presidential elections and multipartism in Latin America. Data from 16 Latin American systems are examined through the use of a multivariate model to gain an understanding of the independent impact of presidential electoral formula (plurality vs. majority), the timing of presidential and legislative elections (concurrent vs. nonconcurrent) and legislative district magnitude on legislative multipartism, and by extension, on the number of relevant political parties operating in the nation. The findings demonstrate the strong and significant impact which formula and timing have on multipartism. They also point to the importance of examining the interaction between elections for different constituent institutions. Finally, they underscore the applicability of Duverger's law to presidential elections.

This study examines the interaction between the rules governing presidential elections and multipartism in Latin American political systems. All of the Latin American systems examined here possess presidential systems combined with legislatures which are elected utilizing proportional representation (PR).[1] I hypothesize that within this framework (Presidential-PR), the rules by which the president is elected have a strong impact on the degree to which the presidential election is a two-party or multi-party contest, the number of effective parties represented in the lower or single house of the national legislature and, by extension, the number of relevant parties operating in the nation. This study focuses on two prominent features of presidential elections: (1) whether the president is elected with a plurality of the vote or whether (at least in the first round) a majority of the popular vote is required for election, and (2) whether the timing of presidential elections is concurrent or nonconcurrent with the election of the nation's lower or single house.

NOTE: I am indebted to John E. Jackson, E. Terrence Jones, Ruth S. Jones, Warren E. Miller, Matthew S. Shugart and two anonymous reviewers for their helpful comments and suggestions. Errors remaining are solely the responsibility of the author.

[1] The study examines lower/single houses only (hereafter often referred to as the legislature).

41

Previous studies have demonstrated that the level of multipartism in a nation has a significant impact on the level of electoral volatility in that nation (e.g., Remmer 1991). Other studies have discussed the importance of the number of parties for factors such as governmental effectiveness and the representation of interests (e.g., Lijphart 1984; Powell 1982). Most of the scholarly literature which has examined the determinants of multipartism has been based on either parliamentary systems or on presidential systems with legislatures elected utilizing plurality or majority single-member districts. But to study those factors which affect multipartism in Presidential-PR systems such as exist in Latin America, the impact of presidential election laws must be examined.[2]

Shugart and Carey have hypothesized that both the electoral formula used to select the executive and the timing of presidential elections have a noticeable impact on the number of political parties in a nation (Shugart and Carey 1992: 229). They examined the issues of formula and timing using summary statistics from seventeen electoral systems. However, they did not attempt to measure the independent effect of each variable. This study develops a multivariate model (based in part on Shugart and Carey's hypotheses) to examine the independent impact which formula, timing, and legislative district magnitude have on legislative multipartism. This represents both an extension and elaboration of Shugart and Carey's work. The analysis is distinct from their work in three respects. First, and most significantly, in contrast to the serial presentation of statistics employed by Shugart and Carey, a multivariate model is utilized to gain an understanding of the *independent* impact of formula, timing, and magnitude on multipartism, a subject on which Shugart and Carey did not focus.[3] Second, the study restricts its analysis to the impact of these variables in Latin American Presidential-PR systems, which not only constitute an overwhelming majority of the world's presidential systems, but also provide a relatively homogeneous population of nations for analysis. Third, five Latin American systems not incorporated in the analysis of Shugart and Carey are included. In sum, through the utilization of a multivariate model, a concentration on one particular set of presidential systems (one that is composed of the modal type of presidential systems), and

---

[2] The premise that legislatures cannot be studied in isolation, particularly in presidential systems, is an underlying theme of a recent work by Shugart and Carey (1992).

[3] Two variables were excluded from the analysis after preliminary findings yielded null results. One variable measured the presence or absence of a fused ballot where a single vote registers support for both the presidential and legislative candidates. The other variable measured the use of the highest average d'Hondt formula versus the largest remainders Hare formula for the allocation of the legislative seats.

42

the incorporation of additional cases; this article will expand on previous work by seeking to identify the relative salience of formula, timing, and district magnitude for the level of legislative multipartism in an electoral system. Shugart (1988: 3) has offered the generalization that in presidential systems, "The presidential election imposes a single-seat nationwide district over" the legislative elections. This impact would be expected to be particularly strong in systems where the framework for the election of the president (by plurality or majority formula and with a district magnitude of one) tends to contrast with the rules governing the selection of the legislature (PR from multi-member districts). In Latin America this contrast is present, and moreover, the presidency is generally considered to be the dominant elected constitutional institution. While there has not been a great deal of theoretical work that has examined the relationship between electoral mechanisms across institutions, we can infer from what has been written that there is good reason to expect linkages to exist across these institutional boundaries. Thus we would expect the rules governing the selection of the president to have a strong impact on elections for other elected offices (e.g., the legislature) in Latin American systems.

In his work on majority-runoff and plurality formulae Duverger concluded that "the two ballot majority system tends to produce multipartism" and that "the plurality rule tends to produce a two-party system" (1986: 70). He focused primarily on the mechanical and psychological impact of electoral rules for legislative elections on the number of parties receiving votes for and represented in a legislative body. This article takes Duverger's hypotheses one step futher and examines the psychological impact of plurality versus majority-runoff elections for the presidency on the number of parties represented in a nation's lower/single house.

This argument that the psychological effect of Duverger's law goes beyond the actual election it governs to affect elections for other political offices is similar in logic to that of Blais and Carty who argued that "[t]he distribution of votes in an election depends on the interaction between voters and parties, and the latter's strategy is as crucial as the former's. Political elites and party leaders will anticipate the mechanical and therefore the psychological effects of electoral systems as much as voters will" (1991: 80). The impact of this interaction between elections for two different institutions which utilize different electoral formulae (plurality/majority versus PR) and different magnitudes (single-member districts vs. multi-member districts) is intriguing. It suggests that there is a second-order effect associated with Duverger's law, with the impact of the rule (primarily the pyschological effect) apparent not only in the presidential elections, but also in the elections for the nations' legislatures. I hypothesize that the psychological effect of either presidential

43

election formula permeates the legislative electoral contests; has a strong effect on legislative multipartism; and, by inference, affects other elections in the nation as well as the general configuration of the national party system.

DATA, METHODOLOGY, AND MEASURES

The units of analysis for this study are 16 Latin American national electoral systems (see Table 1). The data are the averages for the systems since the goal of the study is to analyze the impact of institutional arrangements on representation and the party system, a task which is best accomplished by examining systems, not individual elections.

▆ Table 1

LATIN AMERICAN SYSTEMS AND THEIR LEGISLATIVE ELECTIONS INCLUDED IN THE STUDY

Electoral Systems	Years of Legislative Elections Included
Bolivia	1985, '89
Brazil IIa	1945, '50
Brazil IIb	1954, '58, '62
Brazil III	1990,
Chile	1949, '53, '57, '61, '65, '69, '73
Colombia	1974, '78, '82, '86, '90
Costa Rica	1953, '58, '62, '66, '70, '74, '78, '82, '86, '90
Dominican Republic	1978, '82, '86, '90
Ecuador	1978-79, '84
El Salvador	1985, '88, '91
Guatemala	1985, '90
Honduras	1985, '89
Nicaragua	1990,
Peru	1980, '85, '90
Uruguay	1942, '46, '50, '66, '71, '84, '89
Venezuela	1958, '63, '68, '73, '78, '83, '88

Note: Brazil IIa and IIb represent the concurrent and nonconcurrent systems respectively of the Brazilian Second Republic while Brazil III is the Brazilian Third Republic (for more information see note 7).

(For information on the sources for the data used, see Tables 2 and 3.) There were two criteria which had to be met for a system to be included in this study. First, the nation had to be a democracy, a nation being considered democratic if its government has been elected via open and competitive elections.[4] A second criterion was that the systems be amenable to analysis using

---

[4] The merits of this institutional approach toward the classification of democratic systems have been discussed by Diamond, Linz, and Lipset (1990: 6-9) as well as by

44

the measures employed in the study.[5] Ordinary least squares (OLS) regression analysis, with a log-log functional form assumed to exist between the independent and dependent (i.e., multipartism) variables, is employed.

Electoral formula is operationalized as a binary variable with the system scored 0 if the executive is elected by a plurality vote (i.e., a relative majority in which the candidate/party receiving the most votes in the first and only round of voting wins the election) and 1 if the executive must receive an absolute majority (over 50 percent of the popular vote) in the first round to be elected. In the majority systems, if no candidate receives a majority in the first round a runoff between the top two challengers is used in five of the seven majority systems to select the president; in two systems however (Bolivia and Chile), the president is then chosen by a majority vote in the legislature (with the upper and lower chambers meeting in joint session).[6]

Remmer (1991). Remmer succinctly summarizes the logic of this institutional approach: "Following the conventions established in the study of Latin American politics over the course of the past two decades, democratic governance is defined here strictly in institutional terms, leaving open to empirical investigation questions regarding the consequences of competitive institutions for popular participation in policy formation, socioeconomic equity, and other political outcomes" (1991: 796).

[5] The Argentine system is excluded from analysis due both to its use of an electoral college, which is distinct from either a plurality or majority system, and to the system's employment of both concurrent and nonconcurrent legislative elections. Colombia is excluded from the multivariate portion of the analysis because legislative elections occur an average of three months prior to the presidential elections and are thus neither concurrent nor purely nonconcurrent. Elections for Uruguay which occurred during that nation's brief post-World War II experience with a collegial executive (1952–66) are excluded from analysis.

[6] Unlike the case in the pure plurality systems, the Costa Rican constitution specifies that to be elected a candidate must receive more than 40 percent of the vote. Costa Rica is however classified as a plurality system due to the low level of this threshold which makes the system much more similar to plurality than majority systems. It should be noted that in the 10 presidential elections which have occurred under the Costa Rican 1949 constitution, at no time has this 40 percent threshold not been surpassed. The Peruvian constitution specifies that to be elected in the first round of voting a presidential candidate must receive over 50 percent of the vote. For the 1980 election a one-time exception lowered this threshold to 36 percent. Nevertheless, Peru is coded as a majority system. Both Bolivia and Chile (only the pre-1973 system is examined) are coded as majority systems. Theoretically Bolivia and Chile are considered to be similar in their functioning to the majority-runoff systems. Like the majority-runoff systems, both require that for a candidate to be elected in the first round he or she has to receive an absolute majority of the popular vote and, also similar to the runoff systems, a choice is made in the second round among the top finishers (two in all of the runoff systems and Chile and three in Bolivia).

45

Timing is operationalized as a binary variable with concurrent presidential and legislative elections being scored as a 0 and nonconcurrent presidential and legislative elections scored 1. Concurrent elections are defined as elections where the first or only round of the presidential election and the election of the legislature are held on the same day. Nonconcurrent elections are defined as elections where the popular selection of the legislature occurs in a separate year from the election of the president.[7] Average district magnitude (i.e., the average number of representatives per electoral district) is calculated by dividing the number of legislative seats by the number of legislative districts.[8]

Legislative multipartism is calculated utilizing a measure based on the percentage of legislative seats won by the various parties in the lower/single house elections (i.e., Laakso and Taagepera's measure of the "effective number of parties" in a party system [1979: 3–27]).[9] Legislative multipartism was used instead of the most prominent alternative, electoral multipartism, for two reasons.[10] First, it better reflects party representation at the governmental

---

[7] For Ecuador, only the 1978–79 and 1984 elections are included in the analysis. During the period 1978–84 the Ecuadoran system had only concurrent presidential and legislative elections. In 1979 the district-level legislative elections were held concurrently with the presidential runoff while in 1984 they were held contemporaneously with the first round of the presidential elections. Beginning in 1986 Ecuador also employed midterm elections for the district-level congressional deputies which renders the post-1984 Ecuadoran system un-amenable to the analysis used in this study. In the Brazilian Second Republic the first two presidential and legislative elections (1945, 1950) were held concurrently, while the latter three elections for the legislature (1954, 1958, 1962) were held separately from the presidential elections. The Brazilian Second Republic was divided into two separate systems: Brazil IIa which represents the elections of 1945 and 1950, and Brazil IIb which represents the elections of 1954, 1958, and 1962.

[8] In four cases complex districting occurs. In Guatemala and Ecuador separate elections are held at the district and national level; in El Salvador a two-tiered district framework is employed (in 1991 only); and in Venezuela compensatory seats are allocated to minor parties. Aided by the work of Taagepera and Shugart (1989: 269), an "effective" magnitude was constructed for each system based on the geometric average of the magnitude of the systems' two levels or tiers. A similar transformation was conducted for those systems which require that a party win a full electoral quotient in order to be eligible to receive any seats in an electoral district (i.e., Bolivia in 1989 only, Brazil IIa, Brazil IIb, Brazil III).

[9] The equation used for the measure of legislative multipartism (N) is: $N = 1/(1-F)$, where N represents the "effective number of parties," F represents the index of fractionalization, and $F = 1-$ the sum of the squared seat shares of each party. Since a log-log functional form is employed (using logarithims to the base 10), the log values of the legislative multipartism and average district magnitude measures are used in the quantitative analysis.

[10] Electoral multipartism measures the effective number of parties in a system based on

---

level, and hence the existence of relevant parties (though at the cost of over-looking the presence of very minor parties). Second, it allows for the inclusion of four systems which could not be analyzed if electoral multipartism were employed.[11] In any event, analysis of the available data revealed electoral and legislative multipartism to be highly correlated (R-.97 for 11 cases), with legislative multipartism consistently lower than electoral multipartism for all systems.

The values for the multipartism variable have a reasonably continuous distribution, with a mean of 3.71 effective parties and a standard deviation of 1.73. Values for this dependent variable range from a low of 2.05 (which is the value for Nicaragua and corresponds to a little more than two effective parties) to a high of 8.62 (which is the value for Brazil III and corresponds to roughly eight and two-thirds effective parties). This distribution is illustrated graphically in Table 2.

▤ Table 2

LEGISLATIVE MULTIPARTISM IN 16 LATIN AMERICAN ELECTORAL SYSTEMS

"Effective Number of Parties" in the Lower/Single House of the National Legislature*

	2.00-2.50	2.51-3.00	3.01-3.50	3.51-4.00	4.01-4.50	4.51-5.00	5.01-
ELECTORAL	Nicaragua	El Salvador	Venezuela	Guatemala	Bolivia	Brazil IIb	Chile
SYSTEMS	Honduras	Uruguay	Brazil IIa			Ecuador	Brazil III
	Colombia	Peru					
	Costa Rica						
	Dom Republic						

* This is Laakso and Taagepera's (1979) "Effective Number of Parties" measure. For more information on its calculation, see note 9.

Sources: Archer 1991; Chang Mota 1986; CINAS 1991; Contreras 1986; Council of Freely Elected Heads of Government 1990; Darlić Mardesić 1987; Delgado Fiallos 1986; Fabregat 1950, 1957, 1964; Hernández Valle 1986; Honorable Corte Nacional Electoral 1990; Inforpress Centroamericana (Guatemala City), 11 January 1991, 4; International Foundation for Electoral Systems 1992; Inter-Parliamentary Union 1981-1990; Jiménez et al. 1988; Jones 1993; Leonard and Natkiel 1986; Listín Diario (Santo Domingo), 12 June 1990, 12; Mainwaring 1994; McDonald and Ruhl 1989; Tribunal Supremo de Elecciones 1990; Urzúa Valenzuela 1986; Wells 1966a, 1966b.

the votes won by each party in an election, as opposed to legislative multipartism which is derived from the number of seats won by each party in an election.

[11] The Brazilian Second (IIa and IIb) and Third Republics and Peru would have to be excluded if electoral multipartism were used. The widespread use of alliances in Brazil where the vote is often recorded for the alliances, not the parties, prevents the use of the Brazilian Second (IIa and IIb) and Third Republics. Lack of adequate vote data for a majority of the Peruvian elections precludes the examination of electoral multipartism for Peru.

47

Finally, the degree to which the presidential elections of a system conform to a two-party framework is measured by summing the percentage of the valid popular vote won by the top two candidates in the elections most closely corresponding to those of the legislative elections examined in this study. This measure is preferable to the "effective number of parties" measure since the question being asked is whether the system conforms to a two-party system, not how many parties compete in the election.

DATA ANALYSIS

Plurality versus Majority Presidential Electoral Systems

The distinction between plurality and majority systems has been a relatively understudied aspect of electoral systems (Riker 1986: 28). Work in this area by Duverger, most rational choice theorists, and to a lesser extent Riker, does however provide support for the hypothesis that whereas plurality elections tend to result in two-party systems, majority-runoff elections tend to lead to multi-party systems (Shugart 1988: 2). Furthermore, Riker's corollaries to Duverger's law do not seem to apply to Latin American presidential elections (Riker 1986: 32). First, the election is a national one and thus Riker's corollary involving parties which are third nationally but one of the top two locally is not relevant. Second, the presence of a Condorcet winner at the presidential level in Latin American systems is doubtful, given the fact that the executive office has been occupied by more than one party in all of the systems included in the study during the period of analysis. This reality is inconsistent with the hypothesis of a Condorcet winner in any of the systems in the study. If any nation approached this level it would have been Chile in the 1960s with the potential of the Christian Democrats becoming a Condorcet party between the left and right; this of course did not occur. In the presidential election of 1970, Chileans elected the Socialist Salvador Allende who "would not have received a majority of the vote in a two-way race" (Valenzuela 1978: 42).

The formula used to elect the president is hypothesized to have a strong impact on the number of parties in a nation's legislature. This strong impact is considered to be the product of an interaction between the rational actions of individuals who do not want to waste their votes in plurality elections (with this factor indirectly influencing their vote choice in legislative elections, in part by limiting the voters' realistic alternatives in the voting booth) and the rational actions of party leaders who in plurality presidential electoral systems tend to coalesce into larger parties than is the case in majority presidential systems, since the principal electoral prize, the presidency, goes to the plurality winner. Thus, given the regular occurrence of presidential elections (in the absence of a Condorcet winner) there is less incentive in plurality (as

48

opposed to majority) systems for most politicians to form alternative parties whose probability of capturing the presidency is quite low. This dynamic has been identified by Shugart and Carey as being linked to strategic decisions of political elites in response to the electoral formula used to select the executive. In plurality systems there exists a tendency among party elites to "form a broad coalition behind the front-runner" as well as when in opposition "to coalesce behind one principal challenger" (Shugart and Carey 1992: 209). This contrasts with the majority-runoff systems which "actually discourage the coalescence of opposing forces," with political elites making the decision to run their own presidential candidates with the goal of either finishing in the top two in the first round, or else demonstrating an electoral following that can be delivered in the runoff election to one of the top two finishers in exchange for selective benefits in the future (ibid.: 210). Strategic bargaining occurs among relevant political actors in all of the Latin American presidential elections. When this bargaining occurs however depends to a great extent on the electoral formula employed. In plurality systems it takes place prior to the election whereas in majority systems it occurs after the first round of elections (ibid.: 216). Consolidation prior to the election as occurs in the former systems should result in a lower level of presidential, and indirectly legislative, multipartism than should the post-first round bargaining which occurs under the majority framework.

The sixteen Latin American systems examined are almost evenly split between those which utilize a plurality selection process to select their executive (nine) and those that employ a majority system to select their executive (seven). Due to the assumed differential psychological impact of plurality versus majority systems on both rational voters and rational party leaders, we would expect plurality presidential elections to be dominated by two parties, with the first round of the majority system elections involving strong competition among multiple parties. This premise is confirmed by an initial analysis of data for presidential elections corresponding to the legislative elections included in the study.[12] Presidential elections in the plurality systems tend to be dominated by two parties, with the top two in the plurality systems averaging 86.86 percent of the vote as opposed to the majority systems where the top two parties average only 62.60 percent of the vote in the first round. This relationship is illustrated graphically in Table 3 with the plurality systems concentrated in the upper ranges and the majority systems falling (though with less regularity) at the lower end of the scale.[13]

---

[12] For Ecuador results from the 1988 and 1992 presidential elections (in addition to those from 1978 and 1984) were used in this portion of the analysis.

[13] An anonymous reviewer suggested that the anomalous status of El Salvador and Chile

49

▤ Table 3

PERCENTAGE OF THE VALID POPULAR VOTE RECEIVED BY THE TWO LEADING PARTIES IN FIRST ROUND PRESIDENTIAL ELECTIONS FOR 15 PLURALITY AND MAJORITY LATIN AMERICAN SYSTEMS

Presidential Election Formula	Percentage of the Vote Received by the Two Leading Parties in the First Round of Elections					
	100–90	89.5–80	79.5–70	69.5–60	59.5–50	49.5–40
Plurality	Nicaragua	Colombia	Venezuela			
	Honduras	Dom Republic	Brazil II			
	Costa Rica	Uruguay				
Majority		El Salvador	Chile		Bolivia	Brazil III
			Peru		Guatemala	
					Ecuador	

Sources: Europa Publications Limited 1978–1991; Jornal do Brasil, 22 November 1989; Keesing's 1974–1992; McDonald 1971; Ruddle and Gillette 1972. For additional sources see Table 2.

The basic multivariate analysis combines the hypothesis of Duverger (that plurality elections lead to two-party systems while majority systems favor multi-party systems) with Shugart's assertion that presidential elections can have a strong impact on legislative elections in presidential systems. The result is a prediction that, holding other factors constant, systems which utilize the plurality presidential electoral formula will have lower levels of legislative multipartism than will systems that employ the majority formula.[14] By extension, and using legislative multipartism as a proxy for the national party system, this choice of presidential election formula is hypothesized to influence the number of effective parties in the nation as well.

As is seen in the OLS regression results presented in Table 4, the presidential election formula (plurality or majority) does have a very strong impact on the number of effective parties in the legislature, with a t-ratio (2.371, 11-df) which is significant at less than .05 for a one-tailed test.[15]

---

could be due to their use of nonconcurrent elections. These legislative elections might be used by parties to test their electoral strength, with weaker parties then joining with other (perhaps stronger) parties to support a common candidate in the next presidential contest. Subsequent analysis suggested that such a process did not occur in El Salvador and was only partially present in Chile (where the timing of municipal elections was also important in this regard).

[14] A slightly different version of this hypothesis is offered by Shugart and Carey (1992: 224–25).

[15] The possibility of the existence of multicollinearity, especially between the formula and

---

50

▤ Table 4

ORDINARY LEAST SQUARES ESTIMATES OF INSTITUTIONAL DETERMINANTS OF LEGISLATIVE MULTIPARTISM

Independent Variables	Estimated Coefficient	Exponential of Estimated Coefficient #	T-Ratio (11 DF)
Presidential Formula	0.176	1.500	2.371*
Election Timing	0.155	1.429	1.924*
District Magnitude	0.148		1.408
Constant	0.256		2.008*

R-Square = .563
*p < .05 one-tailed test
Note: a Log-Log functional form is employed.

Note that the exponential of the estimated coefficient indicates the ratio of the expected value of Y (i.e., the dependent variable multipartism) when the binary variable (either presidential formula or election timing) equals one to the expected value of Y when the binary variable equals zero. The district magnitude variable coefficient (as is the case with all continuous variables) is interpreted via its elasticity. In a log-log model however, one cannot interpret the binary variable coefficients using their elasticities, and thus for purposes of interpretation, the exponentials of the estimated coefficients of the binary variables are employed. For more information on the interpretation of these coefficients, see notes 16 and 17.
Sources: See sources listed in Table 2.

Here, the presence of a majority system results in a level of multipartism which is 1.500 times the level of multipartism of a plurality system (holding other factors constant).[16] For example, based on this model, in the Dominican Republic (multipartism: 2.46, with a plurality formula and concurrent timing) a 50 percent increase in multipartism from 2.46 to 3.69 would make the Dominican Republic's level of multipartism comparable to that of Guatemala (multipartism: 3.80, majority formula and concurrent timing). This change would amount to an increase of roughly one and one-fourth effective parties in the legislature and to a three-column shift to the right in Table 2.

---

timing variables, was examined. These tests revealed low R-Squares when each independent variable was regressed on all of the other independent variables, with the highest R-Square being .182 (Lewis-Beck 1980: 58–62).

[16] 1.500 is merely the exponential of the estimated coefficient (i.e., Exponential .176 = 1.500). The value 1.500 indicates that the expected value of the multipartism variable, when the presidential formula variable equals one (i.e., a majority system), is 1.500 times the expected value of the multipartism variable when the presidential formula variable equals zero (i.e., a plurality system). Since logarithims to the base 10 are employed, this exponential is given by 10 raised to the power of the estimated coefficient (0.176) for the formula variable. I am indebted to John E. Jackson for his advice regarding the general use and interpretation of dummy variables in a log-log model.

51

In sum, these data in Table 3 and 4 provide strong support for the hypothesis that the presidential electoral formula has a noticeable impact on both the number of parties effectively competing in presidential elections as well as on the number of effective parties represented in the legislature and by extension in the nation. This implies that rules for elections for one constitutional office have an impact on the nature of elections and representation in other elective bodies.

Concurrent versus Nonconcurrent Presidential and Legislative Elections

There is strong theoretical support for the hypothesis that in Presidential-PR systems the timing of presidential and legislative elections has a significant impact on the level of multipartism in the latter elections (Shugart and Carey 1992: 226–53). Concurrent systems should be expected to have lower levels of multipartism than is the case when the two elections are held at different times when the restraining impact of the executive selection process is much weaker.

Multivariate analysis provides solid support for the hypothesis that election timing has a strong impact on legislative multipartism, with a t-ratio (1.924, 11-df) which is significant at less than .05 for a one-tailed test. Table 4 indicates that the use of nonconcurrent elections results in a level of multipartism that is 1.429 times the level of multipartism that occurs when concurrent elections are used (holding other factors constant).[17] Here the model indicates that a 42.9 percent increase in multipartism in a system such as Venezuela (multipartism: 3.18, plurality formula and concurrent timing) would lead to an increase in multipartism from 3.18 to 4.54. This change would result in a transformation of Venezuela's party system (with slightly more than three effective parties) to a situation very similar to that of Brazil IIb (multipartism: 4.54, plurality formula and nonconcurrent timing), with the difference being the presence of roughly one and one-third more effective parties in the legislature. On Table 2 this change would shift Venezuela three columns to the right.

Analysis of Argentina's system which experiences both concurrent and nonconcurrent presidential and legislative elections provides further support for the salience of timing for multipartism. In the concurrent elections Argentina

---

[17] Similar to the case of the presidential formula variable, the value 1.429 indicates that the expected value of the multipartism variable, when the election timing variable equals one (i.e., a nonconcurrent system), is 1.429 times the expected value of the multipartism variable when the election timing variable equals zero (i.e., a concurrent system). This ratio is given by 10 raised to the power of the estimated coefficient (0.155) for the timing variable.

52

had levels of legislative multipartism which were much lower than the multipartism of the nonconcurrent elections (2.39 vs. 2.62).[18] These results provide support for Shugart's previous findings and demonstrate the salience of election timing for multipartism in a nation.

District Magnitude

In an examination of 31 Anglo-European systems Arend Lijphart (1990: 488) detected a small positive relationship between district magnitude and electoral multipartism. A replication of Lijphart's study using data from twenty-two Latin American and Caribbean nations revealed the same positive relationship, albeit in an even more limited status (Jones 1993: 66).

Table 4 reveals the impact of district magnitude on legislative multipartism to be in the hypothesized direction, but not significantly strong. The estimated coefficient (0.148, t-ratio: 1.408, 11-df) does however reveal that district magnitude influences legislative multipartism to a certain extent. This finding should not be taken to imply that district magnitude is not a very important structural factor in other contexts. For example, Lijphart (1985, 1990), Taagepera and Shugart (1989), and others have repeatedly demonstrated the strong salience of magnitude for the degree of proportionality of an electoral system.

DISCUSSION

Four important conclusions can be drawn from this study. First, Duverger's law does apply to presidential systems. The data clearly demonstrate that Latin American systems which employ a plurality system to elect their president have presidential elections which correspond much more closely to those of a two-party system than do those systems which utilize a majority framework and thus tend to have a larger number of parties effectively competing in presidential elections. Second, the choice between a plurality and majority presidential election formula has a strong impact on the level of legislative multipartism and, by inference, on the number of relevant parties in the nation's party system. Plurality systems clearly possess lower levels of legislative multipartism than do majority systems. Third, Shugart's hypothesis regarding the salience of presidential and legislative election timing was supported by these data. Systems in which these elections were held concurrently have lower levels of multipartism than do those systems where these two elections were held at separate times. Finally, district magnitude was found to

---

[18] Argentina had concurrent presidential and legislative elections in 1983 and 1989, and nonconcurrent legislative elections in 1985, 1987, and 1991. The source for these data is the files of the Argentine Ministerio del Interior, Dirección Electoral Nacional, Departamento de Estadísticas.

53

have only a modest impact on multipartism, with the finding in the hypothesized direction (positive), but not significant.[19]

The focus of this article has been on the impact of presidential electoral rules on elections for the legislature. However, the potential impact of legislative electoral arrangements on presidential multipartism should be kept in mind (Shugart and Carey 1992: 240). When examining the impact of legislative election rules on presidential multipartism, one crucial variable is the electoral formula, in particular the differential impact of PR formulae versus the plurality formula. This variable, held constant in the Latin American cases, probably goes a great distance in explaining the lower level of presidential multipartism in Presidential-Plurality systems (e.g., Philippines 1946–69, United States) than in the Presidential-PR systems.

The findings of this study point to the importance of examining the interaction between elections for different constituent institutions. In at least two instances (formula and timing) the electoral rules governing the selection of the chief executive in presidential systems have a strong impact on the degree of multipartism in a nation's legislature and, more generally, on the number of relevant parties operating in a nation's party system. These effects are both proximal and distal in nature, affecting both the results of the actual elections and (potentially) the long-term nature of a nation's party system.[20] The increasing popularity of the Presidential-PR and Premier-Presidential-PR frameworks in Eastern Europe, Africa, and Asia (e.g., Namibia, Poland, Romania, Senegal, Sri Lanka), as well as the Presidential-PR system's continued presence in Latin America, begs for a more complete understanding of the interaction between the rules governing the selection process for the systems' two most important constituent units (the presidency and the lower/single house).[21]

---

[19] While most of the results reported were quite strong, given the strength of the theoretical argument, why were they not stronger? A partial explanation would be based around four points: (1) many of the systems have only experienced a few elections under the current rules, and it may take time for both voters and party elites to conform to the electoral rules through a learning process; (2) there are many electoral rules (e.g., rules on party formation) which were not examined here but may influence the level of multipartism in specific systems; (3) the small size of the population examined increases the probability of partial outliers exerting a strong influence on the results; and (4) many other factors (e.g., socioeconomic, religious, cultural, regional, ethnic) can also affect the level of multipartism in a nation.

[20] The political consequences of the number of legislative parties in an electoral system is an important topic of inquiry. It is, however, beyond the scope of this article. For a discussion of some important consequences, see Lijphart (1984), Powell (1982), Remmer (1991), and Shugart and Carey (1992).

[21] A majority of the more recent presidential systems are of the Premier-Presidential type. While the same basic systemic effects which occur in the Presidential-PR systems are

---

54

This research has demonstrated the relevance of presidential electoral frameworks for the partisan configuration of a nation's legislature. It has provided support both for previous work that examined the system-wide importance of certain presidential electoral arrangements for lower level elections as well as for work which identified the salience of Duverger's psychological effect for the conduct of elections. Furthermore, it is apparent that the choice of rules governing presidential elections is important not only for the outcome of the election of the chief executive, but also for the elections of other representative bodies, particularly the national legislature. These points should therefore be incorporated into any discussion of presidential systems as well as into any consideration of constitutional revisions or constructions, such as are occurring in the 1990s throughout the world.

REFERENCES

Archer, Ronald P. 1991. Unpublished manuscript. Durham, NC: Duke University.
Blais, André, and R. K. Carty. 1991. "The Psychological Impact of Electoral Laws: Measuring Duverger's Elusive Factor." *British Journal of Political Science* 21: 79–93.
Centro de Investigación y Acción Social (CINAS). 1991. *El Salvador Boletín de Análisis e Información*, #7.
Chang Mota, Roberto. 1985. *El Sistema Electoral Venezolano: Su Diseño, Implantación y Resultados*. Caracas: Consejo Supremo Electoral.
Contreras, Dario. 1986. *Comportamiento Electoral Dominicano: Elecciones Dominicanas 1962-1982*. Santo Domingo: Editora Corripio.
Council of Freely Elected Heads of Government. 1990. *Observing Nicaragua's Elections 1989-90. Special Report #1*, Atlanta, GA: The Carter Center of Emory University.
Darlić Mardesić, Vjekoslav. 1987. *Estadísticas Electorales de Ecuador 1978-1987*. Quito: ILDIS.
Delgado Fiallos, Anibal. 1986. *Honduras Elecciones (Más allá de la fiesta cívica) 85*. Tegucigalpa: Editorial Guaymuras.
Diamond, Larry, Juan J. Linz, and Seymour Martin Lipset, eds. 1990. *Politics in Developing Nations: Comparing Experiences with Democracy*. Boulder, CO: Lynne Reiner.
Duverger, Maurice. 1986. "Duverger's Law: Forty Years Later." In Bernard Grofman and Arend Lijphart, eds., *Electoral Laws and Their Political Consequences*. New York: Agathon Press.
Europa Publications Limited. 1978-1988. *The Europa Year Book*. London: Europa Publications Limited.

---

also hypothesized to hold true in these sytsems, the fact that the two represent two distinct systems should not be obscured. I thank Matthew Shugart for clarifying this point for me.

55

———. 1989-1991. *The Europa World Year Book*. London: Europa Publications Limited.

Fabregat, Julio T. 1950. *Elecciones Uruguayas: Febrero de 1925 a Noviembre de 1946*. Montevideo: Republica Oriental de Uruguay, Poder Legislativo.

———. 1957. *Elecciones Uruguayas de Noviembre de 1950 a Noviembre de 1954*. Montevideo: Republica Oriental de Uruguay, Camara de Representantes.

———. 1964. *Elecciones Uruguayas de 25 de Noviembre 1962*. Montevideo: Republica Oriental de Uruguay, Camara de Senadores.

Hernández Valle, Ruben. 1986. *Costa Rica: Elecciones de 1986, Análisis de los Resultados*. San Jose, Costa Rica: IIDH-CAPEL.

Honorable Corte Nacional Electoral. 1990. *Elecciones Generales 1985-1989*. La Paz: Honorable Corte Nacional Electoral.

Inforpress Centroamericana (Guatemala City). 1991. *Central America Report* 11 January.

International Foundation for Electoral Systems. 1992. Unpublished foundation country data files.

Inter-Parliamentary Union. 1981-1990. *Chronicle of Parliamentary Elections and Developments*. Geneva: International Centre for Parliamentary Documentation.

Jiménez, Edgar C., et al. 1988. *El Salvador: Guerra, Política y Paz (1979-1988)*. San Salvador: CINAS.

Jones, Mark P. 1993. "The Political Consequences of Electoral Laws in Latin America and the Caribbean." *Electoral Studies* 12: 59-75.

Jornal do Brasil, 1989, 22 November.

Keesing's. 1974-1992. *Keesing's Contemporary Archives*. Bristol: Keesing's.

Laakso, Markku, and Rein Taagepera. 1979. "Effective Number of Parties: A Measure With Application to West Europe." *Comparative Political Studies* 12: 3-27.

Leonard, Dick, and Richard Natkiel. 1986. *World Atlas of Elections: Voting Patterns in 39 Democracies*. London: The Economist Publications Limited.

Lewis-Beck, Michael S. 1980. *Applied Regression: An Introduction*. Newbury Park, CA: Sage.

Lijphart, Arend. 1984. *Democracies: Patterns of Majority and Consensus Rule in Twenty-One Countries*. New Haven, CT: Yale University Press.

———. 1985. "The Field of Electoral Systems Research: A Critical Survey." *Electoral Studies* 4: 3-14.

———. 1990. "The Political Consequences of Electoral Laws, 1945-85." *American Political Science Review* 80: 481-96.

Listin Diario (Santo Domingo), 1990, 12 June, p. 12.

Mainwaring, Scott. 1994. "Brazil: Weak Parties, Feckless Democracy." In Scott Mainwaring the Timothy Scully, eds., *Building Democratic Institutions: Parties and Party Systems in Latin America*. Stanford, CA: Stanford University Press.

McDonald, Ronald H. 1971. *Party Systems and Elections in Latin America*. Chicago: Markham.

McDonald, Ronald H., and J. Mark Ruhl. 1989. *Party Politics and Elections in Latin America*. Boulder, CO: Westview Press.

Powell Jr., G. Bingham. 1982. *Contemporary Democracies: Participation, Stability, and Violence*. Cambridge, MA: Harvard University Press.

Remmer, Karen L. 1991. "The Political Impact of Economic Crisis in Latin America." *American Political Science Review* 85: 777–800.

Republica Argentina. Ministerio del Interior. Dirección Electoral Nacional. Departamento de Estadísticas. Department data files.

Riker, William H. 1986. "Duverger's Law Revisited." In Bernard Grofman and Arend Lijphart, eds., *Electoral Laws and Their Political Consequences*. New York: Agathon Press.

Ruddle, Kenneth, and Philip Gillette, eds. 1972. *Latin American Political Statistics*. Los Angeles: Latin American Center, University of California, Los Angeles.

Shugart, Matthew S. 1988. "Duverger's Rule, District Magnitude, and Presidentialism." Ph.D. dissertation, University of California, Irvine.

Shugart, Matthew Soberg, and John M. Carey. 1992. *Presidents and Assemblies: Constitutional Design and Electoral Dynamics*. Cambridge: Cambridge University Press.

Taagepera, Rein, and Matthew Soberg Shugart. 1989. *Seats and Votes: The Effects and Determinants of Electoral Systems*. New Haven, CT: Yale University Press.

Tribunal Supremo de Elecciones. 1990 *Cómputo de Votos y Declatorias de Elección-1990*. San Jose, Costa Rica: Imprenta Nacional.

Urzúa Valenzuela, Germán. 1986. *Historia Política Electoral de Chile 1931–1973*. Santiago de Chile: Tarmacos.

Valenzuela, Arturo. 1978. "The Breakdown of Democratic Regimes: Chile." In Juan J. Linz and Alfred Stepan, eds., *The Breakdown of Democratic Regimes*. Baltimore, MD: Johns Hopkins University Press.

Wells, Henry, ed. 1966a. *Costa Rica Election Factbook: February 6, 1966*. Washington, DC: Institute for the Comparative Study of Political Systems.

———. 1966b. *Uruguay Election Factbook: November 27, 1966*. Washington, DC: Institute for the Comparative Study of Political Systems.

Received: September 23, 1992
Accepted for Publication: March 10, 1993

57

Political Parties and Candidate Selection in Venezuela and Colombia

JOHN D. MARTZ

Stasiology, the study of political parties, has experienced a check-ered career at the hands of social scientists specializing in Latin America. This is not the space in which to engage in a review of the literature.[1] For present purposes, suffice it to say that the powerful democratizing hemispheric move-ment occurring since the close of the 1970s has inevitably sparked a revival of interest in the parties as well. Yet the veritable inundation of literature dealing with regime change—both the transition to and the consolidation of democ-racy—has not probed deeply the subject of parties. A review essay considering a dozen recent publications about democratization and development has con-firmed the fact that notwithstanding a general recognition of parties as important agents affecting the fate of democratization, this has not been accompanied by concomitant research.[2] In short, theorizing about transitions to democracy and subsequent success or failure has been sharply constrained by the relative lacunae surrounding the study of parties. Furthermore, there are those who contend that it is precisely as contemporary democratization occurs that the parties are declin-ing in importance. Thus Philippe C. Schmitter, while conceding that parties re-main indispensable for the formal organization of electoral competition, con-tends that "they have lost a great deal in terms of militants, followers, internal participation, programmatic coherence, and credibility with the general public."[3]

[1] A brief bibliographic overview is included in John D. Martz, "Party Elites and Leadership in Co-lombia and Venezuela," *Journal of Latin American Studies* 24 (February 1992): 87–89.
[2] John D. Martz, "Economic Challenges and the Study of Democratization," *Studies in Comparative International Development* 31 (Spring 1996).
[3] Philippe C. Schmitter, "Transitology: The Science or the Art of Democratization?" in Joseph S. Tulchin with Bernice Romero, eds., *The Consolidation of Democracy in Latin America* (Boulder, CO: Westview, 1995), 23.

The late JOHN D. MARTZ was professor of political science at Pennsylvania State University. He wrote numerous works on democratic transition and United States–Latin American relations, and was editor of the journal *Studies in Comparative International Development*.

189

Whether one accepts this view with or without qualification, there can be little doubt that contemporary parties are confronting serious problems in adapting to political reality, even in the merely formalistic democracies. Questions of internal democracy are among the most critical. If broadly systemic democratization has been unfolding in the hemisphere, one must ask whether a similar current is flowing inside the parties themselves. Traditionally, the better organized parties and those enjoying the greatest electoral success have been characterized by centralized authority. There has been a general resistance to organizational democratization and a reluctance to move toward increased participation. As a point of departure, it is assumed here that party elites seek to preserve their organizational domination. This requires control of participation and of activity at the grassroots. It is nowhere more crucial than in matters of candidate selection, most particularly that of a presidential nominee. This suggests that a basic research question must inquire into the nature and strength of party elites. It is especially fruitful to pursue the issue over the years, rather than merely examining a single snapshot frozen in time. Have changes evolved and, if so, what direction have they taken?

In seeking some understanding of the Latin American experience, it is useful to explore the phenomenon of selection by studying two of the longer-established democracies, Venezuela and Colombia. This choice is justified by the fact that within the hemispheric context they have been among the more mature democracies, with their respective party systems playing a fundamental role. In each nation, today's contemporary systems date from their creation in 1958 and were effectively consolidated long before the host of severe dislocations occurring in recent years. Furthermore, a drive toward a liberalizing and democratizing *apertura* has included proposals to further the internal democratization of the parties.[4] For traditional party elites, more comfortable with hierarchical processes and centralist control, the choice of president has predictably constituted a critical matter ever since the emergence of the two contemporary democracies four decades ago.

This article is oriented around the role and influence of party leadership in the selection of presidential candidates. We must first determine whether party elites are united in their preference of candidate and if so whether their control is sufficient to avoid meaningful internal competition among would-be aspirants. In cases where the answers are negative, the nature of the competition

---

[4] This is not the place for a detailed restatement that has already received considerable attention in the literature. In general, in Venezuela then-President Jaime Lusinchi in December 1984 established a special blue-ribbon committee for the reform of the state (COPRE—Comisión Presidencial para la Reforma del Estado). Its continuing efforts have encouraged a variety of provisions aimed at the revitalization of democracy; those directly related to internal party structure and organization have not been extensively implemented. For Colombia, the far-reaching reforms embedded in the new 1991 constitution, along with growing demands for new legislation regulating internal party affairs, have also received far greater rhetorical than practical attention. Among several convenient sources for more extended discussion, see Martz, "Party Elites and Leadership," 114–20.

TABLE 1

Candidate Selection — Venezuela

Year	Party	Leadership	Candidacy	Participatory	Candidate	Leadership Choice
1958	AD	united	noncompetitive	no	Betancourt(W)	yes
	COPEI	united	noncompetitive	no	Caldera	yes
1963	AD	united	noncompetitive	no	Leoni(W)	yes
	COPEI	united	noncompetitive	no	Caldera	yes
1968	AD	divided	competitive	yes*	Barrios	yes
	COPEI	united	noncompetitive	no	Caldera(W)	yes
1973	AD	united	noncompetitive	no	Pérez(W)	yes
	COPEI	divided	competitive	yes†	L. Fernández	yes
1978	AD	divided	competitive	yes*	Piñerua	yes
	COPEI	united	noncompetitive	no	Herrera(W)	yes
1983	AD	divided	competitive	yes#	Lusinchi(W)	yes
	COPEI	united	noncompetitive	no	Caldera	yes
1988	AD	divided	competitive	yes#	Pérez(W)	no
	COPEI	divided	competitive	yes†	E. Fernández	yes
1993	AD	divided	competitive	yes#	Fermin	no
	COPEI	divided	competitive	yes*	Paz	yes

* Party primary
† Party convention
# Party electoral college
W Winner

and rank-and-file participation must be examined. A variety of mechanisms may be employed in candidate selection, including party conventions, primaries, and electoral colleges. The first of these may range from a mere rubber-stamping of decisions already adopted by the central leadership to an open fight with the outcome in doubt. With primaries, the significance may run the gamut from decisive to symbolic, depending upon structure, timing, and the rules for representation. An electoral college provides another option, one which is also greatly influenced by the selection of delegates who will cast votes. Whatever the mechanism, there is then the question asking whether the party leadership can accept the outcome if contrary to its wishes or alternatively ends up by dividing the party. Beyond this, finally, is the electoral fate of the candidate tapped by the party. All of this incorporates a wide variety of factors, as suggested in the following analyses. It also raises questions about potential trends over time. In the interests of clarifying dynamic processes that are often complex, discussion of both Venezuelan and Colombian candidate selection is summarized in Tables 1 and 2.

The study of individual cases predictably encompasses a broad array of elements. Beyond the preferences of party elites, there are questions about the doctrinal orientation of aspiring precandidates. Whether or not these become germane for a particular contest, there are also personal factors reflecting the vote-getting abilities of potential candidates. Given a situation of competition that the leadership cannot avoid, the character of grassroots participation ac-

TABLE 2

Candidate Selection—Colombia

Year	Party	Leadership	Candidacy	Participatory	Candidate	Leadership Choice
.... [Frente Nacional] ....
1958	Libs	united	noncompetitive	no	Lleras C.(W)	yes
	Cons	united	noncompetitive	no	Lleras C.(W)	yes
1962	Libs	united	noncompetitive	no	Valencia(W)	yes
	Cons	united	noncompetitive	no	Valencia(W)	yes
1966	Libs	united	noncompetitive	no	Lleras R.(W)	yes
	Cons	united	noncompetitive	no	Lleras R.(W)	yes
1970	Libs	united	noncompetitive	no	Pastrana(W)	yes
	Cons	united	noncompetitive	no	Pastrana(W)	yes
1974	Libs	united	noncompetitive	no	López(W)	yes
	Cons	united	noncompetitive	no	Gómez	yes
1978	Libs	divided	competitive	yes##	Turbay (W)	yes
	Cons	united	noncompetitive	no	Betancur	yes
1982	Libs	divided	competitive	yes##	López	yes
	Cons	united	noncompetitive	no	Betancur(W)	yes
1986	Libs	united	noncompetitive	no	Barco(W)	yes
	Cons	united	noncompetitive	no	Gómez	yes
1990	Libs	divided	competitive	yes**	Gaviria(W)	yes
	Cons	divided	competitive	no	Lloreda	yes
1994	Libs	divided	competitive	yes**	Samper(W)	yes
	Cons	united	noncompetitive	no	Pastrana	yes

Congressional elections
** Consulta popular
W Winner

quires immediate relevance. This also focuses attention on organizational centralism and the capacity of the leadership to maximize control. The mechanisms whereby authority may be maintained and participatory forces minimized are various. In the final analysis, party elites seek to win the presidency. Beyond that obvious if fundamental reality lie those matters related to organizational strength and to enduring authority within the party. Where participation may be permitted but essentially held in check, party elites will happily accommodate liberalizing pressures that do not challenge their control. To unravel this configuration of interrelated variables requires the examination that follows.

VENEZUELA

During the initial years of Venezuela's democratic era, party politics were marked by factionalism, fragmentation, and a proliferation of presidential candidates. There were three candidates and four parties in 1958; five years later there were seven competitors; by 1968 there were six presidential competitors appearing on the ballots of sixteen different parties, while another seventeen parties competed in congressional and municipal races. The zenith was reached in 1973 with no fewer than a dozen presidential candidates and more than twice as many national or regional parties competing for legislative and municipal positions.[5] That was the year of Venezuela's critical election, which recast the party system into one reflecting the biparty hegemony of Acción Democrática (AD) and the Social Christian COPEI. The two parties alternated in the presidency every five years until 1988, while winning at least three-fourths of the vote in congressional races. To study candidate selection in Venezuela, therefore, centers upon the respective experience of the social democrats (AD) and the Christian democrats (COPEI). Of the two, Acción Democrática has been confronted more frequently with serious competition and thus has experimented with a variety of means to guide the party without jeopardizing either electoral outcomes or internal unity. Its failures have nearly equaled its successes.

In 1958, there was no question about the candidacy of the dominant member of the AD's founding generation, already one of the recognized leaders of Latin American democracy. Thus Rómulo Betancourt was chosen and subsequently won office. Five years later, the competition was framed within a systemic rather than personal context. Given the fragility of Venezuelan democracy, buffeted by attempted military *golpes* (coups) as well as by serious *fidelista* (Castro supporter) violence, the departing Betancourt explicitly supported a procedural formula to choose his successor—perhaps an independent—acceptable to both COPEI and AD. In this he was firmly opposed by both the party hierarchy and the rank-and-file. Thus at the national convention there was a clear expression of party sentiment in the selection of Raúl Leoni, who subsequently won office. In the runup to the 1968 national elections, however, internal competition was fierce over what was presumed to be a certain party victory, thereby retaining the presidency for yet another five years. The nomination was seen as the preserve of one of the two remaining leaders of the party's founding *vieja guardia* (old guard). The contenders were Party President Luis Beltrán Prieto Figueroa and Secretary-General Gonzalo Barrios. From mid-1967, the competition escalated dramatically. There was the element of personalism, for each of the two contenders felt that the loser would be too old to win nomination five years hence. In addition, there were clear policy differences. Prieto and his supporters believed that after ten years during which the party had emphasized the survival and strengthening of democracy, it was time for a return to traditional party commitments toward social welfare and an uplifting of the masses. Barrios and his backers argued that continuity with the Betancourt and Leoni administrations was the highest priority, and that the nascent democracy still required more time to mature before directing primary attention to potentially disruptive social reforms.

[5] John D. Martz and Enrique A. Baloyra, *Electoral Mobilization and Public Opinion: The Venezuelan Campaign of 1973* (Chapel Hill: University of North Carolina Press, 1976), 9–10. In a contemporary study of that nation's parties, no fewer than 159 legally organized parties or electoral groups were identified for the 1958–1973 years. See Manuel Vicente Magallanes, *Los partidos políticos en la evolución histórica venezolana* (Caracas: Editorial Mediterraneo, 1973).

Given this deeply felt personalistic and doctrinal rationale for competition, the party sought to resolve matters through the untried mechanism of a party primary. Conducted in September 1967, with all card-carrying *adecos* (members of AD) eligible to participate, it was disrupted by violence in several regions of the country. A climactic dispute over the vote in Cumaná culminated in the simultaneous withdrawal of *prietistas* (supporters of Prieto) from party executive bodies and their expulsion by the so-called loyalists backing Barrios. By all indications—including partial vote totals—Prieto had won a majority in some fifteen of the party's twenty-five regional organizations. However, the party machinery was controlled by Barrios, and the extended dispute led to a party division and the Barrios candidacy for the AD and that of Prieto for his newly minted Movimiento Electoral del Pueblo (MEP). Thus the primary had not merely exacerbated party disunity but had divided the previously undefeated AD. The December 1968 electoral contest brought victory to COPEI's Rafael Caldera by one percentage point over Barrios. The combined total for Barrios and Prieto was 49 percent as contrasted with the Caldera total of 29 percent. Speculation about the emergence of the AD as a Venezuelan counterpart of the PRI in Mexico was dissipated as a result. The division clearly cost the AD the election and a continuation of its monopoly of presidential power. The consequences of the selection process, therefore, had mirrored party problems, which led to results of historic proportions. For Acción Democrática itself, party unity was not swiftly or easily reconstructed and even then was achieved with a high price in the loss of major leaders of the party organization.

Five years later the *adeco* elites decided matters without recourse to a primary or even to concerted pre-convention competition. Former President Betancourt, constitutionally eligible for a second term that appeared his for the asking, froze the internal party situation by withholding his eventual announcement of noncandidacy until the last moment. This left as serious contenders only Gonzalo Barrios and Bentancourt's one-time protégé and leader of the party's second generation, Carlos Andrés Pérez. Betancourt quietly discouraged Barrios from a second candidacy, and the convention then rubberstamped the selection of Pérez, who went on to a smashing electoral victory in December 1973. By 1978, the party faced an internal difference in preferences between Secretary-General Luis Piñerua Ordaz, who enjoyed organizational strength plus the approval of Rómulo Betancourt, and David Morales Bello, a confidante of President Pérez. Morales's candidacy was anathema to Betancourt, who urged and sparked the movement to another internal primary. Ultimately, Piñerua was opposed instead by the AD's congressional leader, Jaime Lusinchi, who had the implicit backing of President Pérez. The two aspirants agreed upon the convening of a direct primary, one in which all 1.3 million party members were eligible to participate. The pre-primary competition was intense, and there were several outbursts of violence between partisans of the contenders. However, the struggle was less ferocious than that of 1967. In August of 1977, Piñerua won an estimated 62 percent of the vote, capturing all but one state and one federal territory from Lusinchi. In general elections, however, Piñerua lost by some 3 percent of the vote, and there were many recriminations charging that the internal fight had weakened the party and contributed to an admittedly poorly organized campaign on Piñerua's part.

By 1982, the leadership had recognized that discord and disharmony were merely strengthening COPEI's hand, and there was a diminution of preconvention hostility. In August of 1981, Jaime Lusinchi assured his eventual selection in competition with Morales Bello by negotiating a deal that assured the support of the party's Labor Bureau. He backed Labor Secretary Manuel Peñalver for party secretary-general. Peñalver became the first labor leader in party history to achieve this powerful and influential position. At the same time the party's *cogollo* (internal circle), preoccupied with any threat of serious dissent and the potential challenge to its own authority, devised a kind of electoral college to choose the candidate. A variety of controls were engineered to limit eligibility for participation and assure that loyalists would hold key positions. The result was a ready confirmation of Lusinchi over Morales Bello, paving the way for Lusinchi's defeat of Rafael Caldera in the 1983 general elections. Even so, some animosities within the party again arose.[6] This assured even greater caution over the choice of the 1988 candidate. On this occasion the candidate of the party leadership, as well as President Lusinchi, was the veteran Octavio Lepage. His opponent was Carlos Andrés Pérez, seeking to be the first president under the 1961 constitution to win a second term in office.[7]

Much as had been the case in 1967, there was a sharp contrast between the organizational preference and popular sentiment, causing a renewal of tensions between elitist controls and democratic participation. Lengthy negotiations centered on the question of the number of party members (as identified by elected or party positions) eligible to participate. The smaller the number, the greater the organizational control; the larger the number, the better for the popular Pérez. Once the terms were set, the process went forward smoothly and resulted in a Pérez victory by nearly 2-1. By the time of the electoral college, it was widely believed—as polls were showing consistently—that the former president was a virtual certainty to win the election against COPEI's Eduardo Fernández, while a Lepage candidacy was far from a guarantee of victory. The outcome of the college competition was not in doubt, and in the end the Pérez forces joined in some manipulation of results in order to avoid an unduly one-sided outcome.

The second Pérez presidency proved to be highly contentious, eventually building toward a nearly universal popular rejection of his leadership and policies, which culminated in his impeachment. This left Acción Democrática in a mood of dispirited defeatism, while the entire party system was generally

---

[6] Commentaries that closely examine party matters are republished in Manuel Felipe Sierra, *Los hilos del poder* (Caracas: Ediciones Galera, 1986).
[7] See Carlos Andrés Pérez, *El quehacer y la historia* (Caracas: Afadil Ediciones, 1988).

viewed by the public as corrupt and self-serving. In April 1993, the party once again turned to the electoral college as a mechanism, this time loosening somewhat the organizational controls. The competition pitted Carmelo Lauría (a Lusinchi confidante and the preferred choice of the *cogollo*) against a prominent leader of the AD's younger generation, Claudin Fermín, until recently the mayor of Caracas. With the party largely resigned to defeat as a consequence of Pérez's unpopularity, the contest was relatively desultory. While figures were carefully withheld, the Fermín victory margin exceeded 3–1; for the first time, there was also a problem of abstention.[8]

In turning to the case of COPEI, we find a contrasting history in the degree to which the process of candidate selection was dominated for many years by the party's founder and unchallenged leader, Rafael Caldera. The brief symbolic candidacies of 1947 and 1952 are not significant, but the experience of the democratic era reveals an organization controlled by the personal rule of one man. Caldera was the party's nominee in 1958, 1963, and 1968, reaching the presidency on the third of these efforts. Yet he was not without his critics inside the party, especially rising figures in the Juventud Revolucionario Copeyano (JRC), the party's youth wing. Although Caldera had run second in 1963 with 20 percent of the vote—an improvement over a distant third place finish five years earlier—there were elements on the party's left that were unenthusiastic about his candidacy in 1968. Had he been defeated in national elections, the internal conflict might have been severe. As it was, he retained his power and moved to name his putative successor in 1973 when, for the first time, he could not be the *copeyano* standard bearer. Thus the competition in truth focused on control of the party, as reflected by precandidates Lorenzo Fernández for the *calderistas* and Luis Herrera Campins for party reformers. The contest had in effect begun before 1973 in such matters as selecting the party secretary-general. However, it was the subsequent party gathering that confirmed Caldera's authority. At the Second Extraordinary Convention in March of 1972, the first ballot eliminated all the secondary precandidates, and Fernández, with Caldera's evident backing plus the weight of the government, prevailed over Herrera in the second round by a vote of 506 to 444.[9]

Following the AD defeat of Lorenzo Fernández, Luis Herrera Campins emerged as the obvious frontrunner for the 1978 nomination. Rafael Caldera was decidedly unenthusiastic, while Herrera had swallowed his pride in accepting defeat without bolting the party—something uncharacteristic of Vene-

---

[8] There is discussion of these conflicts in Michael Coppedge, *Strong Parties and Lame Ducks: Presidential Partyarchy and Factionalism in Venezuela* (Stanford: Stanford University Press, 1994), 97–109, although his focus is more on the rivalry between "Ins" and "Outs."

[9] For detailed discussion of internal *copeyano* conflict through the 1960s and 1970s, see Donald L. Herman, *Christian Democracy in Venezuela* (Chapel Hill: University of North Carolina Press, 1980). See his treatment of Herrera's campaign in "The Christian Democratic Party" in Howard R. Penniman, ed., *Venezuela at the Polls: The National Elections of 1978* (Washington, DC: American Enterprise Institute, 1980), 133–54.

zuelan parties of the 1960s and 1970s. For Caldera, desirous of cementing his enduring domination of the party while anticipating another candidacy in 1983, his choice for party secretary-general was defeated, and the Herrera forces gradually gained the upper hand in most state organizations. At this juncture, Caldera sought to restore his hegemonic position through a revision of methods that might resolve internal conflict. He proposed a so-called Gran Congreso Nacional, designed to include independents and sympathizers as well as card-carrying party members. The victor would presumably be a national rather than partisan nominee and at the same time might more likely be susceptible to Caldera's preeminent personal role. However, the mechanism proved inoperable until later, for Herrera's candidacy became a foregone conclusion well before his official nomination at the Fifteenth National Convention in August of 1977. He won national office, *herrerista* forces joined him in the administration, and Rafael Caldera—eligible for a 1983 candidacy after two full terms out of office—prepared for his next presidential bid.[10]

When the time came, there was no serious opposition to his candidacy, with the Herrera forces having been decimated by the manifest failures of his government and the resounding rejection by the public. Indeed, the latter assured Caldera's defeat by Jaime Lusinchi, and it has only been after 1983 that the historic *calderista* dominion fell into question. In the wake of the 1983 elections, it was generally believed that Eduardo Fernández, party secretary-general and longtime protégé of Caldera, would carry the party banner in 1988. As time passed, however, it became evident that Caldera intended yet one more try for a second term. The rationale for this competition was preeminently personalistic while also implicitly generational as well; certainly ideological factors were not in question. After a lengthy and divisive struggle, much of it hidden from public eyes, Fernández's control of the party machinery prevailed against the prestige and reputation of the former president. At a Gran Congreso Nacional, which Caldera had again seen as a mechanism for assuring his own success in gaining the nomination, he was instead rejected. Stunned that his party could deny him the nomination and embittered at what was to him a personal betrayal by Fernández, he sat out the campaign and was distinctly unperturbed by COPEI's loss to Acción Democrática. The selection of Fernández and denial of Caldera resulted in a fundamental rift that has plagued COPEI ever since. After the 1988 elections, Fernández retained control of the apparatus while Caldera remained a vocal figure on the national scene. His was an eloquent voice in defense of the democracy when it was threatened in 1992 by two attempted military uprisings, at the same time decrying the shortcomings of the government and harshly attacking prevailing political elites. By mid-1993 his independent candidacy had become official, and in December the 78-year-old won his cherished second term.[11]

---

[10] An examination of party meetings and conventions is found in Paciano Padrón, *Siembra de democracia (COPEI a través de sus convenciones nacionales)* (Caracas: Ediciones Centauro, 1982).

[11] The events of the early and mid-1990s are neatly analyzed and recapitulated by Richard S. Hillman, *Democracy for the Privileged: Crisis and Transition in Venezuela* (Boulder, CO: Rienner Publish-

For COPEI, Eduardo Fernández had retained control of the apparatus. However, his sporadic attempt to buttress the embattled Pérez administration—designed in no small part to protect the democracy in which COPEI might regain power in 1993—merely tarnished his position inside the party. Furthermore, lingering doubts about Caldera's party status contributed indirectly to the rapid ascent of Zulia Governor Oswaldo Alvarez Paz. Even before Caldera's official announcement of his independent candidacy, Alvarez Paz had parlayed disenchantment with Fernández to introduce his own candidacy. In a competition, the rationale for which was purely personal and opportunistic, the challenger unexpectedly struck through the mechanism of a primary, the first in COPEI's history. With the party machinery rusty and ill prepared by Fernández, Alvarez Paz capped a few weeks of intense campaigning to defeat his opponent by a decisive margin of more than 2 to 1. The organization of the primary itself had been haphazard, and an estimated 2 million ultimately participated—a number well above COPEI's official claims for party membership. The consequences included a national campaign in which Fernández supporters gave no more than token support to Alvarez Paz, who ran a poorly planned and weakly organized campaign. While it is highly unlikely that this candidacy might have carried the *maracucho* (person from Maracaibo) to power, the loss stimulated a new round of organizational infighting. Above all other considerations, however, the departure of Caldera—his election, his choice of advisers, and his adamant unwillingness to deal with *copeyanos* as other than traitors to his cause—destined COPEI to a position that in the short run is scarcely encouraging. In the final analysis, while Rafael Caldera had periodically been challenged and was for a time outmaneuvered by Luis Herrera Campins and his supporters, his extraordinary personification of Venezuelan Christian democracy has been so profound that whatever the methods employed, the consequences would revolve about the fate of the party's organizational founder and ideological mentor.[12]

---

ers, 1994). Analyses by Venezuelan social scientists are now burgeoning, although some is little more than episodic narrative. Among recent works which seriously examine the crisis of the system, a few of the more notable include Aníbal Romero, *Aproximación a la política* (Caracas: Editorial PANAPO, 1994); also his *Decadencia y crisis de la democracia* (Caracas: Editorial PANAPO, 1994); Heinz R. Sonntag and Thais Maingon, *Venezuela: 4-F 1992: Un análisis sociopolítico* (Caracas: Editorial Nueva Sociedad, 1992); and Andrés Serbin, Andrés Stambouli, Jennifer McCoy, and William Smith, eds., *Venezuela: la democracia bajo presión* (Caracas: Editorial Nueva Sociedad, 1993). For a somewhat idiosyncratic but highly suggestive study that appeared shortly after the presidential inauguration of Rafael Caldera, see Joaquín Matte Sosa, *Patios cerrados/puertas abiertas: cambios, democracia y partidos en Venezuela 1988/1993* (Caracas: Monte Avila Editores Latinoamericana, 1994). In addition, there are useful if often outdated remarks appearing in a conference report prepared by both Venezuelan and North American academics. See Louis W. Goodman et al., eds., *Lessons of the Venezuelan Experience* (Washington, DC: Woodrow Wilson Center Press, 1995). For a highly useful set of electoral analyses by experienced Venezuelan scholars accompanied by relevant data, see CENDES. *El proceso electoral de 1993: análisis de sus resultados* (Caracas: Centro de Estudios del Desarrollo, Universidad Central de Venezuela, 1995).

[12] A contentious journalistic treatment, which nonetheless portrays tellingly important facts of Rafael Caldera as political leader, was published as he returned to office in an exceptionally difficult and

Taking the Venezuelan experience as a whole, generalization cannot be pushed too far. This reflects, among other factors, the extraordinary position of Rafael Caldera in COPEI over nearly a half-century. Yet it is nonetheless evident that COPEI as well as Acción Democrática has periodically been confronted with competition over candidate selection. For the AD, there were meaningful doctrinal and generational disputes through 1967–1968, after which the competitive motivation has been essentially driven by personalistic ambitions. The party *cogollo* has consistently sought to exercise authority on behalf of the officialist candidate, relying on primaries or more recently on its self-styled electoral colleges. Yet the popular choice has generally won out, owing in part both to polling evidence and intuitive sentiment over the probable outcome of general elections. Thus a high degree of political pragmatism has marked the *adeco* leadership; over the years its utilization of primaries and other means of allegedly democratizing mechanisms has not tilted the party away from its most viable vote-getters, such as Pérez in 1988 and Fermín in 1993. In short, the consequences of varied forms of candidate selection have not cost the party an election since the increasingly distant exception of 1967–1968. Rather, the organizational channeling of party sentiment has tended to validate the choice of the strongest and most popular candidate.

In this sense, it can be said that although the party rank-and-file has been consulted via several mechanisms, the leadership has survived without any lasting diminution of its power. With COPEI, procedures for candidate selection have customarily been of less critical importance than for Acción Democrática. Caldera has so spread-eagled the process, granted his necessary if unhappy acceptance of the Herrera candidacy in 1978, that his departure has left the Christian Democrats bemused and confused. Their ultimate fate may yet await the eventual retirement from the political scene of Rafael Caldera, the party's intellectual guide, organizational founder, and today the last surviving founder of modern Venezuelan democracy.[13] In a broad sense, somewhat contradictorily, a pattern emerges in which a party's most popular precandidate is selected, and yet at the same time the organizational and political elite of the party succeeds in maintaining its position. This predominance, of course, is exercised between elections and over matters having little or nothing to do with candidate selection. In any event, the Venezuelan experience does mirror a change from

---

intimidating situation. See Departamento de Investigación de la Actualidad Política, *Caldera en el ojo de la tormenta* (Caracas: Fondo Editorial Venezolano, Colección Cultura Política, 1994).

[13] In company with the late Eduardo Frei Montalvo of Chile, Caldera is the leading intellectual and ideological exponent of Latin American Christian Democracy. His writings are too extensive to be listed here. One of many representative samples would be Caldera, *Especifidad de la democracia cristiana* (Caracas: Editorial Nova Terra, 1972). For a broad overview of his writings, see Miguel Jorrin and John D. Martz, *Latin-American Political Thought and Ideology* (Chapel Hill: University of North Carolina Press, 1970), esp. 411–21. Two important and readily accessible, if general, works are Edward A. Lynch, *Christian Democratic Parties: A Political Economy* (Westport, CT: Praeger Publishers, 1993); and the seminal work by Edward J. Williams, *Latin American Christian Democratic Parties* (Knoxville: University of Tennessee Press, 1967).

past domination of party leaders. They have learned to live with political reality when it does not assure their own choice of candidate. Acción Democrática has thus far adjusted effectively to this passing of unchallenged central authority; the situation for COPEI is more uncertain as the Social Christians seek to redefine themselves for the next century in the absence of Rafael Caldera.

COLOMBIA

The Colombian party system can be traced back all the way to its founding in the mid-nineteenth century. The historic division between Conservatives and Liberals has endured to the present, with minor parties rarely enjoying significant political influence. The deterioration and breakdown of the party system in 1953 led to an atypical military interregnum, after which a democratic regime was reestablished in 1958. The latter, however, adopted a series of broad systemic limitations, which among other things assured a biparty monopoly. It also deeply affected the process of presidential candidate selection in Colombia for the next sixteen years.[14] A pair of agreements between the two parties led to the creation of the Frente Nacional in the wake of military rule. This rested on the principles of *paridad* and *alternación*: the first divided public positions equally between Conservatives and Liberals; the latter called for alternation of the presidency between the two parties, first for twelve, then ultimately renegotiated for sixteen years and for the next four governments. These measures enhanced the traditional domination of Colombia's small political elite while resisting meaningful civic participation. While the parties were not as tightly organized as the Venezuelan, they were nonetheless controlled by national leaders, most particularly during the artificiality of limited democratic choice during the 1958–1974 years. It was tacitly agreed that the party responsible for naming the Frente Nacional president would make its own selection and convey this to the other party, which would presumably validate the decision at its national convention. All of this was expected in actual practice to confirm the selection of party elites; interparty disagreement or an absence of public approval were not possibilities to be seriously entertained. The tradition of biparty hegemony, formulated by elitist arrangements, would presumably be strengthened and reified by the Frente Nacional.

With the initiation of the Frente, it was ultimately decided that the first president would be a Liberal—Alberto Lleras Camargo, that party's representative in the lengthy pre-Frente negotiations with the Conservatives. Four years later, the mantle fell upon the Conservative Guillermo León Valencia, to be followed in 1966 by the Liberal Carlos Lleras Restrepo. Only in 1970 was there serious question about the choice of the Frente. The longstanding Conservative

[14] An early comparison of parties that remained valid throughout the Frente Nacional years is John D. Martz, "Political Parties in Colombia and Venezuela: Contrasts in Substance and Style," *Western Political Quarterly* 18 (June 1965).

rivalry between the followers of ex-presidents Laureano Gómez (*laureanistas*) and Mariano Ospina Pérez (*ospinistas*) complicated matters. The Conservative leadership was divided, and the customary national convention was unable to render a decision while Liberal leaders impatiently awaited the outcome. Only after extended and opportunistic negotiations between Conservative and Liberal elders—strongly influenced by outgoing President Lleras Restrepo—was it finally possible to select a candidate.[15] Yet this process, while assuring a standard bearer to retain the Frente's administrative control for its final four years, produced instead a dull and unimpressive nominee who was confronted by the revived electoral movement of former dictator Gustavo Rojas Pinilla. Misael Pastrana Borrero eventually was declared victor by a small margin, following a succession of questionable manipulations and political calculations by the Frente elites.[16]

Only since 1974 has there been meaningful electoral competition, thereby opening the process of candidate selection to potential competition.[17] For the Conservatives, the conflict for years revolved about the basic division between *laureanistas* and *ospinistas*, a legacy that survived into the 1990s. It was based on personal rivalries, which had long since come to supersede the doctrinal differences of the 1940s and 1950s between Laureano Gómez and Mariano Ospina Pérez. With leadership of the two factions passing to Laureano's son Alvaro Gómez Hurtado and to Ospina's loyal follower, Misael Pastrana Borrero, candidate selection became relevant in 1974,when Pastrana was leaving the presidency and thus ineligible for a second consecutive term. Alvaro Gómez was consequently named by the Conservatives' national convention, after which he was soundly defeated in general elections. This left the internal competition unresolved while also opening the way to a longtime aspirant, Belisario Betancur. Although in earlier years a *laureanista*, he had become something of a maverick, and sought the support of both Conservative groups. In 1978, with neither Gómez nor Pastrana personally seeking the nomination, he succeeded in gaining the nomination and ran an effective if ultimately unsuccessful race against the Liberals, in the process building national support for the party and for his own future candidacy.[18] His strong showing, which reflected his capacity to reach non-Conservative independents, assured his selection once again in

[15] For a detailed accounting of the mechanistic process that ultimately led to the relatively unpopular selection of Lleras Restrepo's colorless minister of government, the *ospinista* Conservative Misael Pastrana Borrero, see John D. Martz, *The Politics of Clientelism in Colombia: Democracy and the State* (New Brunswick, NJ: Transaction Publishers, 1996).

[16] Useful sources include Marlo Latorre Rueda, *Elecciones y partidos políticos en Colombia* (Bogotá: Uniandes, 1974); Robert H. Dix, "The Varieties of Populism: The Case of Colombia," *Western Political Quarterly* 31 (September 1978): 334–51.

[17] Detailed analysis is found in Rodrigo Losada Lora, *Realidades de la concentración/dispersión del poder político en Colombia 1966–1978* (Bogotá: Pontificia Universidad Javeriana, 1983). Also see Losada, *Clientelismo & elecciones* (Bogotá: Pontificia Universidad Javeriana, 1984).

[18] See the discussion in Marlo Latorre Rueda, *Hechos y crítica política* (Bogotá: Universidad Nacional de Colombia, 1986), 147–93.

1982. When the Liberals divided that year, he seized upon the moment and led his party to victory in a competitive race for the first time since 1946, when the Liberals had also divided behind two rival nominees.

During his presidency and thereafter, Betancur held himself aloof from internal conservative factionalism. Thus the fortunes of the two party groups continued to wax and wane, with the presidential candidacy customarily negotiated by the elites and thereby avoiding unseemly public conflict. For 1986 it was evident that Alvaro Gómez was due another bid for office, a choice which the Pastrana forces accepted without great public complaint well in advance of the nominating convention. The decisive Liberal victory in general elections effectively marginalized the *laureanistas* from their normally powerful position, seemingly assuring an easy candidacy for the Pastrana-controlled *ospinistas* in 1990. However, political reality was to dictate otherwise, leading to a virtual division of the Conservatives at a time when the party's electoral appeal was at its lowest ebb in years. Facing the 1990 general elections, the party validated Misael Pastrana's chosen candidate, Rodrigo Lloreda Caicedo. However, the *laureanistas*, by this time more commonly identified as *alvaristas*, had already effectively broken away to proclaim the dissident Movimiento de Salvación Nacional (MSN) and put forward Gómez as candidate. In May of 1990, the MSN candidate finished second in the presidential race with 24 percent of the vote; Pastrana and his chosen candidate were humiliated by a distant fourth-place finish with 12.4 percent. The MSN subsequently maintained its independence in elections for the Constituent Assembly and Congress which were to follow.[19]

As 1994 elections neared, the panorama for the Conservatives remained cloudy, although once again candidate selection was conducted by political elites behind closed doors. While Alvaro Gómez and Misael Pastrana remained distanced from one another, many Conservative regulars were attracted to the latter's son, Andrés Pastrana Arango, a former media star and Bogotá mayor who had already created his own personal apparatus, the Nueva Fuerza Democrática (NFD). By late 1993, the younger Pastrana was running strong in the polls while carefully appearing to keep his father at arms' length. Announcing his formal NFD candidacy in February 1994, he gradually won the support and then the formal endorsement of other Conservative factions, importantly including Alvaro Gómez and the MSN. As he began campaigning for May 1994 presidential elections, he did so with broad Conservative acceptance, which he secured without a convention fight, primary contest, or other form of even minimal civic participation in the process. While the contest for 1998, following the prolonged agony of the embattled Samper administration, appears to be more open than ever before, it is probable that the historic Conservative division may

[19] Excellent analyses are found in Patricia Pinzón de Lewin, "Las elecciones de 1990" and Pinzón de Lewin with Dora Rothlisberger, "La participación electoral en 1990: un nuevo tipo de votante?" both in Rubén Sánchez David, comp., *Los nuevos retos electorales: Colombia 1990; antesala del cambio* (Bogotá: CEREC, 1991), 116–67.

be drawing to a close. Alvaro Gómez was murdered in November 1995, while Misael Pastrana died in 1997. The pattern throughout the post-1958 democratic era, however, has been one in which the two historically hostile forces generally reached an accommodation over the presidential nomination. For all practical purposes, Conservative party elites generally reflected the best Colombian political tradition in quietly resolving conflict by informal and noninstitutional means, consciously hidden from the view of the electorate. For the Liberals, the competition has produced somewhat greater procedural complications.

When the Frente Nacional drew to a close, there were three prominent figures vying for power and influence, and their ongoing struggle constituted the essence of the Liberal candidate selection process up to the 1990s. Each served his own term in the presidency of the nation: Carlos Lleras Restrepo, Alfonso López Michelsen, and Julio César Turbay Ayala. The first of these, who remained significant in party affairs until the day of his death in 1994, consistently advocated a reformist commitment to the restructuring of important sectors of the Colombian economy and body politic. The second, himself the son of a Liberal president, was a critic of the Frente in its early years, leading his own dissident forces in the 1960s but then returning to the traditional Liberal mainstream with the encouragement of Lleras Restrepo during the latter's presidency. Turbay was the machine politician incarnate, one who pulled strings inside the party for years and successfully maneuvered himself into the presidency. When the Liberals faced the first post-Frente race in 1974, the candidacy of López Michelsen was a natural. Lleras Restrepo's prestige and Turbay's control of local and regional leaders carried López to an easy nomination at the Liberal convention, after which he won the general elections. The party selection for 1978, however, was very much at issue. With Turbay having assiduously courted and won the backing of most Liberal congressmen, Lleras Restrepo sought a method other than the usual party convention. To this end he advocated some form of primary or similar pre-convention test in which his own personal appeal might compensate for Turbay's control of the machinery.

In a characteristically Colombian elitist accord, the two aspirants and their advisers settled upon a legislative reform separating 1978 congressional and presidential elections. This Consenso de San Carlos accepted the congressional contest as the surrogate for a Liberal party primary. The pre-candidate whose identifiable followers won out with Liberal voters would thereby be designated and anointed at the subsequent convention, with the loser withdrawing from the contest. This mechanism, which Lleras Restrepo believed would be decided on the basis of his own personal appeal and reputation, instead proved responsive to Turbay's reliance on pure patronage and clientelistic incentives. President López Michelsen also quietly but unmistakably tilted toward Turbay, thus repaying the latter for his 1984 labors on behalf of the outgoing chief executive. The *turbayista* party victory led to his electoral defeat of Belisario Betancur, but did little to heal the wounds from the long conflict among the three men for political power, influence, and ascendancy to the presidency. When the Liberals turned to candidate selection once again in 1982, they were initially without a clear and obvious choice, although Virgilio Barco Vargas seemed to be standing at the head of the traditional Liberal *fila india*, or row of Indian chieftains lined up for their turn at the presidency. For Barco, whose past career as a technocrat did not greatly enhance his political standing, 1982 seemed the right time for his candidacy. Lleras Restrepo was viewed by some as having grown too elderly, while Turbay could not succeed himself. Talk of another run by López Michelsen began to spread, and a divided Liberal party leadership fell back on a common organizational tactic: turning over matters to a special electoral directorate that included three former presidents—Alberto Lleras Camargo, Lleras Restrepo, and Alfonso López Michelsen. In due course it produced another López candidacy, while Barco quietly withdrew from the field and Lleras Restrepo angrily denounced the decision and washed his hands of the contest.

Although traditionalists of the party establishment had thus imposed their choice via the familiar path of behind-the-scenes maneuvering, their victory was contested by a young pro-Lleras figure who picked up the reformist banner. Thus Luis Carlos Galán Sarmiento entered the picture. A critic of prevailing Liberal elitism whose demands for political reform were accompanied by proposals for relatively modest economic changes, Galán attracted a coterie of younger Liberals and independent professionals and created his own organizational vehicle, Nuevo Liberalismo (NL). Unwilling to accept a López renomination, he fought it out in the March congressional elections. When roundly defeated, he chose not to withdraw. Consequently, in the June 1982 general elections, Galán's 10.9 percent of the vote left López with 41.0, and the Conservative Betancur prevailed with 46.8 percent of the vote. It remained for the Liberals, out of power for the first time in years, to contemplate the 1986 nomination within the context of Galán and the NL's continuing challenge.[20] Once again the Liberal selection was to be decided by the outcome of March congressional elections, which had in turn been preceded by the virtually unanimous choice of Virgilio Barco by party regulars. As López put it when discussing the figure who had loyally stepped aside in 1982, "if not Barco, then who?" The Liberals proceeded to thrash the Conservatives (54.2 to 37.2 percent) while NL candidates won a mere 6.6 percent. Galán soon withdrew from the presidential race and endorsed Barco, who won the general elections in May decisively against Alvaro Gómez (58.3 to 35.8 percent).

The slow but perceptible impact of *systemic apertura* and a generalized movement toward a democratization of Colombia's rigidly controlled system registered on the institutional arrangements for 1990. Luis Carlos Galán, much like the onetime maverick Jorge Eliecer Gaitan in the 1940s, succeeded in parlaying his years as a Liberal outsider, critical of both the party's functioning and

[20] The literature on Galán is extensive. For a massive retrospective volume, admittedly partisan, which records his career in detail, see Luis Carlos Galán, *Ni um paso atrás, siempre adelante!* (Bogotá Fundación Luis Carlos Galán, 1991).

of its traditionalist policy orientation, into the position of clear frontrunner for the nomination. Although others were contesting the choice, Galán drew on his personal appeal to emerge as the leader in the polls. The Liberal leadership agreed to a more structured pre-convention mechanism by adopting what was termed a *consulta popular*. A virtual party primary, it was held in conjunction with March 1990 congressional elections and in practice moved toward a removal of the choice of candidate from the hands of elitist-controlled conventions or party directorates controlled by a small handful of leaders and former presidents. Thus the characteristics of a genuine party primary were introduced in Colombia, although only for the Liberals at the time. For Galán, the *consulta popular* was seen as a method to assure that his popularity would not be rebuffed or ignored by party elites; moreover, he expected an impressive victory that would confirm the strength of his mandate. In turn, the party leadership, unprepared for an independent Galán candidacy such as had cost them the 1982 race, hoped that if he could not be stopped, his independence might at least be curbed in the process. All of this changed when Galán was cut down by an assassin's bullets in August of 1989.

This thrust the Liberals into a competitive situation far more unpredictable and unstructured than they had undergone in many years. The son of the slain leader promptly announced his family's choice of César Gaviria Trujillo, a rising young Liberal who had recently become Galán's campaign manager. However, it was initially uncertain how successful Gaviria might be in assuming the *galanista* mantle in the eyes of the public. He was also confronted by two serious rivals. Hernando Durán Dussan was a veteran party leader representing traditionalist leaders and backed by regional party *caciques* (bosses), while Ernesto Samper Pizano was a younger figure, at least as much a reformist in orientation as Galán, whose national experience was more extensive than that of Gaviria. The bases of the competition were a mixture of doctrinal and generational factors, along with the potential for a shifting of party power internally. The use of the *consulta popular* had already been put in place, and thus the outcome was framed by the respective pre-candidates' campaigns. César Gaviria labored to retain the balk of Galán's supporters while skillfully maneuvering to capture the political center, forcing Durán to the right and Samper to the left. The result was a decisive victory for Gaviria with 60 percent of the vote, followed by Samper's 18.5 and Durán with 14.4 percent. The remainder was shared by three minor candidates. This paved the way for Gaviria's clear-cut victory in the general elections of May 1990. It also left Ernesto Samper as the leading contender for the nomination in 1994.[21]

After serving for a time in Gaviria's cabinet, Samper went to Madrid as ambassador and held himself aloof from domestic politics while other aspirants

---

[21] A detailed treatment of electoral party politics during this period is Rubén Sánchez David and ʾatricia Pinzón de Lewin, "Elecciones y democracia en Colombia" in Rodolfo Cerdas-Cruz, Juan Rial, nd Daniel Zovatto, eds., *Uno tarea inconclusa: elecciones y democracia en América Latina 1988–1991* San José, Costa Rica: IIDH-CAPEL, 1992), 287–311.

engaged in continual efforts to assail his position.[22] No fewer than seven Liberals officially declared their intentions, eventually including Gaviria's minister of government, Humberto de la Calle Lombana. The Liberal Dirección Nacional, badly fragmented and fearing a breakdown in party unity, called back Julio César Turbay Ayala to oversee the contest, reduce the threat of factionalism, and assure a regularized and legitimized process. The former president eventually secured the agreement of all but one contender to participate in another election and accept the verdict: this test produced a decisive victory for Ernesto Samper Pizano on 13 March 1994. While his doctrinal trajectory had been to the left of the Liberal center, Samper sought the middle of the spectrum by persuading the runner-up, de la Calle, to join the ticket as vice-presidential candidate. This move in all probability was decisive in Samper's narrow victory in both the first and second round elections, while also seeming to enhance de la Calle's own future prospects. Party unity was also strengthened as Samper was inaugurated in August 1994.[23] However, the prolonged systemic crisis into which Colombia was plunged in the controversy over the financing of the 1994 campaign by the drug cartels, reaching all the way to the Casa del Nariño and Samper himself, so unsettled political conditions that party behavior for the immediate future was uncertain.

Taking the post-1958 democratic era as a whole, Colombia has been marked by largely successful efforts to decide the selection process on the part of both Conservative and Liberal leaders. As Harvey F. Kline aptly remarked, Colombian parties "have always been elitist instruments of control . . . . For the past thirty years, the real conflicts in elite politics have been between the various factions of the two parties."[24] With the Conservatives, it has been the split between Laureano Gómez and Mariano Ospina Pérez, which dates back a half-century. While originally reflecting doctrinal division between more rightist and more centrist forces respectively, this difference has been largely dissipated. Thus contests for presidential candidate selection have rested on the political ambitions of the two factions. Circumstantial conditions have largely shaped the official party choice, with the traditional convention nominally employed to legitimize the previous decision of the elites. The complications surrounding the naming of Misael Pastrana in 1970 as the anointed Frente Nacional candidate were based as much on Liberal as on Conservative factionalism. In later years, there was either no clear competitor to block a Gómez candidacy

---

[22] A long-honored Colombian tradition is the dispatching abroad of leading presidential contenders, thus removing them from the pressures and pitfalls of daily politicking. This stands in sharp contrast to Venezuela, for example, where few serious presidential precandidates have held an ambassadorial post.

[23] A detailed account appears in Martz, *The Politics of Clientelism*. For a thorough presentation and review of the general elections' presidential candidates and their programs, see Juan A. Castellanos and Jorge Tellez, *Presidenciales '94* (Bogotá: Planeta Colombiana Editorial S.A., 1994).

[24] Harvey F. Kline, *Colombia: Democracy Under Assault*, 2d ed. (Boulder, CO: Westview Press, 1995), 78.

(1974 and 1986); both factions found acceptable the inevitable nomination of Belisario Betancur (1978 and 1982); total disunity led to separate Conservative organizations and candidates (1990); or there was an elitist agreement based on the absence of a clear *alvarista* option. With Gómez having been murdered and a rather disliked Misael Pastrana having died in 1997, the younger Pastrana was but one of several would-be Conservative candidates as the party faced a new century. Whether the tradition of closed party elitism will be altered remains in question.

The record for the Liberals has been more varied. This has perhaps responded in no small part to the value of the party nomination, for the only Liberal defeats at the national level have come when factionalism produced two candidates who canceled out one another's chances. Internal divisions have also been less structured and more complicated than those of the Conservatives. The years of competition for power, influence, and control among Lleras Restrepo, López Michelsen, and Turbay led to a host of complex, sometimes Machiavellian shifts in loyalties and alliances. Added to this was the role played by Galán and Nuevo Liberalismo, to be followed by the rise of a distinctly young generation headed by Gaviria and Samper, themselves rivals despite occasional collaboration. Moreover, supporters of Gaviria have more recently meddled behind the scenes in domestic issues, while Samper has been forced to confront problems and pressures that at times have threatened to destroy his administration. Such internal conflict has virtually forced upon the party the adoption of methods other than straight conventions based on elitist understandings. The primary-like approach, which led in time to the *consulta popular*, has worked reasonably well since its adoption and may well continue to thrive, especially as the influence of former presidents gradually recedes. While the tradition of former presidents' direct involvement in party affairs is alive and well, it is presently in decline. Lleras Camargo, Lleras Restrepo, Pastrana, and Barco have died. Betancur has largely rejected political activism, although López Michelsen and Turbay continue to voice their opinions about party and governmental affairs. Cesar Gaviria is ineligible for another term under provisions of the 1991 constitution as well as currently serving as OAS Secretary-General, although critics note that he and his colleagues remain very much interested in the course of both national and party affairs at home. What may follow the conclusion of the Samper presidency is open to speculation, but the possibilities of internal party upheaval suggest that candidate selection may be intensely contested, thereby necessitating ever closer attention to the mechanics of the process.

CONCLUSION

In considering the broad question of internal party democratization as documented through the process of presidential candidate selection, the examination of Venezuela and Colombia provides both contrasts and similarities. Venezuela has shown a relatively greater willingness for aspirants to test their appeal directly with party loyalists. There has been more reluctance to do so in Colombia, notwithstanding situations in which there were grave political divisions and rivalries demanding some form of compromise and resolution. However, the evidence in both nations supports the belief that party leaders are determined to maintain their traditional control, and that this is their overriding objective when candidate selection is the issue at hand. Whatever the pressures for greater and more meaningful participation, central party authorities seek measures and mechanisms that in the final analysis do not diminish unduly their hegemonic organizational control. The presence of a competitive situation constitutes a testing of the capacity of party elites to protect their power.

The reasons for competition are varied. However, for Venezuela and Colombia, these are most typically personalistic, with rival aspirants and their supporters vying for primacy. Where the dispute is largely ideological or doctrinal, party elites find themselves especially tested in attempting to contain the dispute, usually with damaging consequences. In Venezuela this was most noteworthy in the 1967 struggle within the AD. Introduction of a party primary merely hastened an eventual division of the party, which led to its first electoral defeat and a concomitant loss of national power. In similar fashion, the closest approach to a true doctrinal conflict in Colombia came with the rise of Nuevo Liberalismo and Luis Carlos Galán, resulting in the candidacy of two Liberals and the accompanying loss to the Conservatives in 1982. Otherwise, the competition has proved more susceptible to manipulation by organizational leaders' capacity to devise and introduce new procedures. Such measures as primaries, electoral colleges, and so-called *consultas populares* all succeeded in broadening participation by the party rank and file. Yet the basic intention of the elites was clearly to meet demands for democratization while covertly keeping a tight rein on the situation. A prime example is the repeated tinkering by Acción Democrática with the bases for participation in its electoral college voting, always with an eye to protecting the interests of the *cogollo*. Furthermore, in both countries the party leaders have usually (although not always) recognized the popular strength of the respective precandidates and have responded accordingly. In Venezuela, for instance, the AD accepted the primacy of Carlos Andrés Pérez in 1988; ten years earlier Rafael Caldera had ceded the *copeyano* nomination to Luis Herrera Campins. In Colombia, the Liberals, albeit reluctantly, had acceded to a Galán candidacy when he was murdered. The Conservatives until recently were more deeply divided because of the *laureanista-ospinista* heritage. But at least they accepted the seemingly strongest of its aspirants, including the two Betancur candidacies.

All of the evidence confirms that party leaders, predictably committed to their own political interests, remain determined to preserve their power and authority. At the same time, they recognize that as a practical matter, the sentiment for internal democratization cannot be ignored. It must somehow be accommodated. Through varied permutations of internal mechanisms and procedures, the elites have become more sophisticated and sensitive to the reformist challenge. In a few instances, the major parties have been unable to avoid divisions over the candidacy. The notable exceptions have been for Venezuela the AD split in 1967–1968 and the unresolvable conflict in COPEI surrounding yet another Caldera candidacy in 1993. In Colombia, the Liberals divided in 1982 and the Conservatives were unable to unite in 1990. Customarily, however, candidate selection has been negotiated without lasting damage to internal unity, and the ultimate party standard-bearer has generally proved the strongest of the aspiring contenders. Within the context of internal party organization, the dynamics revolving about presidential candidate selection mirrors the continuing determination of party elites to finesse popular demands for democratization. In both Venezuela and Colombia, the trend seems to be in the direction of greater internal competition among presidential precandidates; the inclination of the party leadership to provide at least cosmetic participation by the rank-and-file; and in a few instances a grudging willingness to accept candidates who were not the preference of the leadership. Centralized control today has become less inflexible than in the past. Nevertheless, it still lies at the very core of the parties' apparatus, even in such systemic democracies as Venezuela and Colombia.

NEOLIBERALISM AND THE TRANSFORMATION OF POPULISM IN LATIN AMERICA
The Peruvian Case

By KENNETH M. ROBERTS*

CONTEMPORARY Latin American scholarship has been confronted by a novel paradox—the rise of personalist leaders with
broad-based support who follow neoliberal prescriptions for economic
austerity and market-oriented structural adjustments. Leaders like Fujimori and Menem have been difficult to characterize and interpret, as
their personalistic style of leadership evokes images of populist leaders
of the past, but their economic policies diverge sharply from the statist
and distributive (or redistributive) emphases of traditional populism.

This paradox may be more apparent than real, however, since it rests
upon a widespread presumption that neoliberalism and populism are
antinomies that represent fundamentally divergent economic projects.
It also reflects the belief (or hope?) that populism corresponded to an
earlier phase of socioeconomic development—one usually associated
with import substitution industrialization—that has been eclipsed by
the debt crisis and the neoliberal revolution. However, several recent
works have noted a coincidence between neoliberal economics and
populist politics,[1] raising basic questions about the meaning of populism and its relationship to different economic models. Is populism re-

* The author would like to thank Kurt Weyland, Karen Remmer, Gilbert Merkx, Robert Kaufman,
Philip Oxhorn, and Steve Levitsky for helpful comments on earlier drafts of this article.
    [1] See, for example, Luiz Carlos Bresser Pereira, José María Maravall, and Adam Przeworski, *Eco-
nomic Reforms in New Democracies: A Social Democratic Approach* (Cambridge: Cambridge University
Press, 1993), 10; Denise Dresser, *Neopopulist Solutions to Neoliberal Problems: Mexico's National Solidarity Program* (San Diego: Center for U.S.-Mexican Studies, 1991); Carmen Rosa Balbi, "Del Golpe de
5 de Abril al CCD: Los Problemas de la Transición a la Democracia," *Pretextos* 3–4 (December 1992),
53–55; Julian Castro Rea, Graciela Ducatenzeiler, and Philippe Faucher, "Back to Populism: Latin
America's Alternative to Democracy," in Archibald R. M. Ritter, Maxwell A. Cameron, and David H.
Pollock, eds., *Latin America to the Year 2000: Reactivating Growth, Improving Equity, Sustaining Democracy* (New York: Praeger, 1992), 145; and Kurt Weyland, "Neo-Populism and Neo-Liberalism in Latin
America: Unexpected Affinities" (Paper presented at the annual meeting of the American Political Science Association, New York, September 1–4, 1994).

silient enough to adapt to the socioeconomic and political conditions of a new era in Latin America, or is it inextricably associated with an earlier phase or model of socioeconomic development? And if populism has not been extinguished, is it possible to reconcile its essential features with those of its putative antithesis, neoliberalism?

Although previous works have argued persuasively that populism is a recurring phenomenon, rather than a period-specific historical anomaly,[2] there is still a tendency to associate it with statist and redistributive policies that are antithetical to neoliberalism. As such, the specter of populism in contemporary Latin America is usually equated with a lower-class backlash against the austerity, inequalities, and market insecurities attendant on neoliberalism.[3] Likewise, presidents and finance ministers who implement IMF-approved stabilization plans routinely pledge to resist the "populist temptation"—that is, the politically expedient but fiscally "irresponsible" increase of government spending to ameliorate the social costs of market reforms. The possibility that populist tendencies could arise *within*—rather than *against*—a neoliberal project has yet to be fully explored.

Drawing from an analysis of the Fujimori regime in Peru, this study suggests the emergence of new forms of populism that are compatible with and complementary to neoliberal reforms in certain contexts. This new, more liberal variant of populism is associated with the breakdown of institutionalized forms of political representation that often occurs during periods of social and economic upheaval. Its emergence demonstrates that populism can adapt to the neoliberal era and that it is not defined by fiscal profligacy; indeed, even when constrained by fiscal austerity and market reforms, personalist leaders have discovered diverse political and economic instruments to mobilize popular sector support when intermediary institutions are in crisis.

To understand this transformation of populism in the neoliberal era, a framework is needed for the comparative analysis of different expressions or subtypes of populism. This framework should help identify change and continuity in populist phenomena, while facilitating analysis of the conditions that spawned the unconventional partnership be-

---

[2] Ernesto Laclau, *Politics and Ideology in Marxist Theory* (London: NLB, 1977), 153; Robert H. Dix, "Populism: Authoritarian and Democratic," *Latin American Research Review* 20, no. 2 (1985); Gamaliel Perruci, Jr., and Steven E. Sanderson, "Presidential Succession, Economic Crisis, and Populist Resurgence in Brazil," *Studies in Comparative International Development* 24 (Fall 1989); and Cynthia Sanborn, "The Democratic Left and the Persistence of Populism in Peru, 1975–1990" (Ph.D. diss., Harvard University, 1991).

[3] See Sergio Zermeño, "El Regreso del Líder: Crisis, Neoliberalismo, y Desorden," *Revista Mexicana de Sociología* 51 (October–December 1989); or Jorge Castañeda, *Utopia Unarmed: The Latin American Left after the Cold War* (New York: Vintage Books, 1993), 49–50.

tween neoliberalism and populism in Peru. The following section develops a comparative framework that can be applied to both the Peruvian case and other examples of populism, whether of liberal or statist orientation. This framework suggests that intertemporal and cross-regional generalizability could be enhanced by decoupling the populist concept from any specific phase or model of development.

COMPETING PERSPECTIVES ON POPULISM

The analysis of potential linkages between populism and neoliberalism is highly contingent upon the conceptualization of populism. Unfortunately, few social science concepts can match populism when it comes to nebulous and inconsistent usage; like the proverbial blind man trying to describe an elephant by feeling its individual parts, conceptions of populism are shaped by selective attention to its multiple components, as well as by national or regional particularities. These multiple dimensions have allowed the populist concept to be applied to a wide range of loosely connected empirical phenomena, ranging from economic policies and development phases to political ideologies, movements, parties, governments, and social coalitions.[4]

Within this mélange, four principal perspectives on populism can be identified in the Latin American literature: (1) the historical/sociological perspective, which emphasizes the multiclass sociopolitical coalitions that typically arise during the early stages of industrialization in Latin America;[5] (2) the economic perspective, which reduces populism to fiscal indiscipline and a set of expansionist or redistributive policies adopted in response to pressures of mass consumption;[6] (3) the ideological perspective, which associates populism with an ideological discourse that articulates a contradiction between "the people" and a "power bloc";[7] and (4) the political perspective, which equates populism

---

[4] Different conceptions of populism are discussed in Margaret Canovan, *Populism* (New York: Harcourt Brace Jovanovich, 1981).

[5] Prominent examples include Gino Germani, *Política y Sociedad en una Epoca de Transición: De la Sociedad Tradicional a la Sociedad de Masas* (Buenos Aires: Editorial Paidos, 1968); and Gino Germani, Torcuato S. di Tella, and Octavio Ianni, *Populismo y Contradicciones de Clase en Latinoamerica* (Mexico City: Ediciones Era, S.A., 1973).

[6] The best representatives include Jeffrey Y. Sachs, *Social Conflict and Populist Politics in Latin America* (San Francisco: ICS Press, 1990); and Rudiger Dornbusch and Sebastian Edwards, "The Macroeconomics of Populism," in Dornbusch and Edwards, eds., *The Macroeconomics of Populism in Latin America* (Chicago: University of Chicago Press, 1991). Limitations of the economistic interpretation are discussed in Eliana Cardoso and Ann Helwege, "Populism, Profligacy, and Redistribution," in Dornbusch and Edwards.

[7] The best representative of the ideological perspective Ernesto Laclau (fn. 2), chap. 4. See also Canovan (fn. 4), 294.

with a pattern of top-down mobilization by personalist leaders that bypasses or subordinates institutional forms of political mediation.[8] Taken in isolation, each perspective is limited either by a static tendency to bind the populist concept to a particular stage in history, thus denying its dynamic and adaptive properties, or by a reductionist tendency to transform a complex, multidimensional phenomenon into a unidimensional one. The historical/sociological perspective, for example, captures much of the richness and complexity of populism, but weds it to a particular stage in the socioeconomic and political development of Latin American societies. For writers like Germani and Ianni, populism corresponded to a transitional stage on the path between traditional and modern societies, when the breakdown of the oligarchic order in the 1930s allowed newly mobilized urban working and middle classes to be incorporated into the political process. Even scholars from the Marxist and dependency traditions who did not adopt this functionalist orientation shared a basic conception of populism as a multiclass political movement corresponding to the stage of import substitution industrialization (ISI).[9] According to this interpretation, the statist and nationalist policies of ISI allowed populist leaders to build cross-class alliances between urban labor, the middle sectors, and domestic industrialists. However, the "exhaustion" of ISI strategies after the 1950s eroded the material foundations for multiclass coalitions, accentuating class conflicts and spawning new forms of exclusive authoritarianism to demobilize popular sectors.[10] More recently, it has been argued that the viability of populism has diminished as a result of the debt crisis and neoliberal adjustments, which have undermined the fiscal base of distributive programs and emasculated labor unions and other collective actors whose economic interests defined traditional populist agendas.[11]

[8] See, for example, the definition offered by Julio Cotler, in Carlos Franco, Julio Cotler, and Guillermo Rochabrún, "Populismo y Modernidad," *Pretextos* 2 (February 1991), 105. See also Castro Rea, Ducatenzeiler, and Faucher (fn. 1), 126; and Nicos Mouzelis, "On the Concept of Populism: Populist and Clientelist Modes of Incorporation in Semi-Peripheral Polities," *Politics and Society* 14, no. 3 (1985).

[9] The "structural approach" of Carlos M. Vilas is unusually explicit in this regard, as it interprets populism as a strategy for accumulation corresponding to "the first stage of the growth of national industry and the consolidation of the domestic market"; see Vilas, "Latin American Populism: A Structural Approach," *Science and Society* 56 (Winter 1992–93), 411.

[10] Several of the most influential works on twentieth-century Latin American politics adopt variants of this interpretation; see Guillermo O'Donnell, *Modernization and Bureaucratic-Authoritarianism* (Berkeley: Institute of International Studies, 1973), chap. 2; and Fernando Henrique Cardoso and Enzo Faletto, *Dependency and Development in Latin America* (Berkeley: University of California Press, 1979), chaps. 5, 6. See also Michael L. Conniff, "Introduction: Toward a Comparative Definition of Populism," in Conniff, *Latin American Populism in Comparative Perspective* (Albuquerque: University of New Mexico Press, 1982).

[11] See, for example, Robert R. Kaufman and Barbara Stallings, "The Political Economy of Latin American Populism," in Dornbusch and Edwards (fn. 6), 31–32; and the "Comment" by Paul Drake in the same volume, 40.

However helpful for understanding the rise and fall of classical populism in Latin America, evolutionary theories of developmental stages conceptualize populism in a way that is static and spaciotemporally bounded—as a fixed stage in a sequential pattern of development that has already moved on to more advanced levels in Latin America and may not have clear parallels in other regional experiences. As such, they provide little insight into kindred phenomena in other development contexts,[12] and they fail to identify the social conditions or coalitions that could generate new forms of populism in the post-ISI era. Likewise, they do not anticipate adaptations in populist expressions that would allow significant forms of continuity under changing social and economic conditions.

Alternatively, the economic and ideological perspectives skirt the problem of multidimensionality by prioritizing a single component of populism. The economic approach, for example, equates populism with expansionist or redistributive economic policies that are untempered by fiscal considerations. Accordingly, this perspective purges the populist concept of its political and sociological content beyond the desire of populist leaders to build political support by enhancing mass consumption. It is also less bound to any particular phase of development, because it treats fiscal laxity as a permanent temptation facing governments of diverse ideological orientations within the context of Latin America's social inequalities and distributive conflicts.[13] The narrowness of this reductionist and economistic approach makes it at once too elastic and too restrictive. Its elasticity allows the populist epithet to be hurled at virtually any government, from that of Allende to that of Sarney, which fails to extract resources commensurate with its spending commitments, whether or not it possesses a populist social coalition or leadership style.[14] Conversely, its restrictiveness excludes contemporary political phenomena that have striking parallels with classical populism, but coexist with a different type of economic project, whether out of ideological conviction or due to fiscal constraints. In particular, it defines away forms of clientelism and other economic instruments for mobilizing lower-class political support that do not rely upon inflationary wage increases or deficit spending.

[12] This holds true not only for liberal variants of populism in contemporary Latin America but also for rural manifestations of populism in Russia and the United States in the late nineteenth century.

[13] The hypothesis linking populism to social inequality and distributive conflict is most fully elaborated by Sachs (fn. 6). A good discussion of class and sectoral distributive conflicts can also be found in Kaufman and Stallings (fn. 11), 19–22.

[14] Warnings of excessive elasticity have also been made by Drake (fn. 11), 38; and Cardoso and Helwege (fn. 6).

Finally, the political perspective focuses attention on the deinstitutionalization of political authority and representation under populism—that is, on the direct, paternalistic relationship between personalist leaders and their heterogeneous mass of followers, which numerous scholars see as a central feature of classical populism.[15] This perspective is essential for understanding new forms of populism in contemporary Latin America that both exploit and accelerate the erosion of institutionalized forms of political representation in countries like Peru. However, it does not explain how some of Latin America's classical populist figures, such as Cardenas and Haya de la Torre, combined personalist leadership with significant forms of institution building. A unidimensional political perspective may also find it difficult to explain the successful generation and reproduction of popular support, even by a charismatic leader. Populist leaders may be able to mobilize support by articulating political issues or symbols such as the fight against corruption, the extension of citizenship rights,[16] or the need for "the people" to challenge entrenched bureaucrats and political elites. As such, populist economic measures are *not* a necessary condition for populist authority relations.[17] Nevertheless, in a region of profound inequalities and widespread economic insecurity, most populist expressions will try to establish a material foundation to cultivate lower-class support. This is a challenge for any conception of populism that is extended to a neoliberal project, and it is the principal reason why populism is presumed to be incompatible with neoliberalism.

These competing perspectives can produce radically different interpretations of the same phenomenon. For example, writing essentially from an economic perspective, Kaufman and Stallings argue that the electoral platform of Brazil's leftist leader Lula in 1989 was populist, whereas the conservative Fernando Collor represented an "antipopulist" project.[18] However, a political perspective could easily lead to the conclusion that Collor was the populist; whereas Lula's candidacy was grounded in the institutional support of party, labor, and civic associations, Collor was an archetypal personalist leader of the atomized and unorganized poor.[19]

[15] See, for example, Carlos de la Torre, "The Ambiguous Meanings of Latin American Populisms," *Social Research* 59 (Summer 1992), 396–99; and Conniff (fn. 10), 21–22. Paul W. Drake acknowledges the importance of this element but warns that populism cannot be reduced to it; see Drake, "Conclusion: Requiem for Populism?" in Conniff (fn. 10), 220–23.
[16] Germani (fn.5), 325–27, for example, argues that Peron's working-class support was based less on tangible material rewards than on perceived gains in personal power and citizenship rights.
[17] The author is indebted to Philip Oxhorn for clarifying this point.
[18] Kaufman and Stallings (fn. 11), 33.
[19] See Weyland (fn. 1), 13.

Given the inconsistent meanings generated by these alternative perspectives, it is hardly surprising that scholars have questioned the utility of the populist concept for social science inquiry.[20] However, as Collier and Mahon warn, important empirical content can be lost when concepts are discarded prematurely as a result of ambiguity or an incomplete "fit" across cases.[21] The populist concept should be retained, but conceptualized synthetically, as there are no clear theoretical or empirical grounds for adopting an essentialist perspective that prioritizes any single property of this multidimensional phenomenon. An integral, prototypical populist experience such as that of Argentina under Peron would thus aggregate the core features from the four perspectives outlined above. By disaggregating, it is then possible to identify populist subtypes that share a "family resemblance" and manifest some but not all of the core attributes. For example, the reductionist notion of economic populism could signify a subtype that incorporates core economic properties, but not all of the pertinent social and political attributes.

To facilitate comparative analysis of different populist expressions, a synthetic construction of populism can be founded on the following five core properties that are derived from these competing perspectives.

1. a personalistic and paternalistic, though not necessarily charismatic, pattern of political leadership
2. a heterogeneous, multiclass political coalition concentrated in subaltern sectors of society
3. a top-down process of political mobilization that either bypasses institutionalized forms of mediation or subordinates them to more direct linkages between the leader and the masses
4. an amorphous or eclectic ideology, characterized by a discourse that exalts subaltern sectors or is antielitist and/or antiestablishment
5. an economic project that utilizes widespread redistributive or clientelistic methods to create a material foundation for popular sector support

[20] See Ian Roxborough, "Unity and Diversity in Latin American History," *Journal of Latin American Studies* 16 (May 1984), 14.
[21] David Collier and James E. Mahon, Jr., "Conceptual 'Stretching' Revisited: Adapting Categories in Comparative Analysis," *American Political Science Review* 87 (December 1993), 846. Their suggestion to treat problematic concepts as "radial categories" provides a potential escape from the conceptual morass that plagues the study of populism, and it guides the reformulation that follows. A radial category is anchored in a prototypical case that incorporates a bundle of core elements or properties. Secondary categories (or subtypes) are variants of the prototypical case that share some (but not all) of its defining attributes and have no necessary connection to one another. Radial categories have three principal methodological advantages in this context: (1) they allow aggregation of the distinct properties of multidimensional concepts; (2) they provide precise specification, while still allowing a concept to be extended across cases that approximate the prototype in varying degrees, and (3) they facilitate the identification of distinct subtypes within a particular category.

These core properties are consistent with the classic cases of populism from the import substitution phase of development, and they closely follow the multidimensional conceptualizations of authors like Conniff, Drake, and De la Torre. However, a number of subtle modifications enable these properties to transcend spaciotemporal boundaries and travel more easily to the social and economic terrain of contemporary Latin America, as well as to non-Latin American contexts. The inclusive notion of "subaltern sectors" is more appropriate than the conventional focus on the working class, given the increasing informality and heterogeneity of the workforce and the diminished political centrality of organized labor in Latin America. Likewise, an antielitist and/or antiestablishment discourse allows for mobilizing ideologies that are directed against an entrenched political class (or the institutions that they embody),[22] as well as traditional oligarchs or economic elites. Finally, the emphasis on direct relationships between leaders and followers highlights the weakness of institutionalized channels of political representation in contexts where populism is likely to emerge.

Although these core properties focus primarily on the political and sociological dimensions of populism, they maintain its economic content without binding the concept to any specific phase or model of development. This conceptualization presumes that populist leaders tend to design economic policies to build or sustain political support by providing material benefits to subaltern groups. The specifics of macroeconomic policy are variable, however; they may be market or state oriented, open or closed to international competition, fiscally lax or disciplined, and progressive or regressive in their overall distributive effect. This flexibility enables the populist concept to travel across different development strategies, recognizing that there exist multiple and diverse economic instruments for the cultivation of lower-class support.

But does this reconceptualization allow populism to coexist with neoliberalism, which for both economic and political reasons is presumed to be antithetical to populism? Economically, its free-market orientation contrasts with the statist and interventionist policies of classical populism, which relied heavily upon a proprietary state, protected industries, and price controls or subsidies. Likewise, the fiscal austerity and international economic integration advocated by neoliberalism clash with the mass consumption and economic nationalism of classical populism. Finally, neoliberalism has generally redistributed in-

---

[22] This aspect of populism is discussed in Canovan (fn. 4), chap. 7.

come upward rather than downward, at least in its initial stages. Indeed, in the drive to create more "flexible" labor markets, it has often harmed the working-class constituency of classical populism by lowering wages, reducing formal sector employment, and emasculating workers' legal protections. The primary beneficiaries of neoliberalism—and presumably its core sociopolitical constituency—are thus conventionally seen as more elitist and exclusive than those of populism.

Moreover, neoliberalism is thought to have a very different political logic than populism—one that rejects any sort of rent-seeking behavior by the "redistributive combines" in civil society that specialize in extracting resources or economic privileges from the state.[23] Populism is widely alleged to reflect the inability of the state to resist the competing claims of organized class or sectoral groups; indeed, it is often equated with the efforts of personalist leaders to inflate societal demands for their own political gain. In contrast, neoliberalism often relies upon technocratic decision making, which helps to insulate the state from societal demands and to subject individual economic agents to the competitive logic and discipline of the marketplace. As the state retreats from welfare, redistributive, and integrative functions, it is left largely to the market to process conflicting individual and collective demands.

However, these perspectives rest upon stage theories or narrow economic interpretations of populism, and they have two principal limitations. First, they emphasize economic demands in the genesis of populism to the neglect of authority relations. As such, they fail to recognize that by weakening or circumventing organized interests and institutional forms of representation—the alleged purveyors of populism—the stage is cleared for the direct, unmediated mobilization of atomized masses by personalist leaders. As the Peruvian case shows, both neoliberal adjustments and the economic crises that precede them have weakened organized labor and political parties, the classic forms of institutional representation for subaltern sectors. They have thus created a political context where populist leadership is likely to thrive, that is, one in which autocratic authority is suspended above organized interests and institutionalized forms of accountability.[24]

Second, arguments that see neoliberalism and populism as inherently incompatible ignore not only the variability of populist (and neoliberal) economic formulas but also the ingenuity of leaders who need to main-

[23] The classic critique of redistributive combines is Hernando de Soto, *The Other Path: The Invisible Revolution in the Third World* (New York: Harper and Row, 1989), chap. 6.
[24] See Guillermo O'Donnell, "Delegative Democracy," *Journal of Democracy* 5 (January 1994); and Bresser Pereira, Maravall, and Przeworski (fn. 1), 10.

tain political support while implementing structural adjustments. Classical populism used a mixture of selective and universal measures as economic levers to cultivate popular support. In a context of fiscal austerity, neoliberal adjustments may preclude some generalized material benefits such as higher wages or subsidized consumer goods, both instruments commonly used by classical populists. However, political dividends may be derived from the alleviation of hardships inflicted by hyperinflation upon the most vulnerable sectors of society. Moreover, neoliberal adjustments may facilitate the provision of more selective, targeted material benefits to specific groups, which can be used as building blocks for local clientelist exchanges. Targeted programs have a more modest fiscal impact than universal measures, but their political logic can be functionally equivalent, as both attempt to exchange material rewards for political support.

Besides their lower cost, targeted programs have the advantage of being direct and highly visible, allowing government leaders to claim political credit for material gains. By allowing leaders to personally inaugurate local projects or "deliver" targeted benefits, selective programs are highly compatible with the personalistic leader-mass relationships of populism. Much like Olson's argument that selective incentives provide more powerful inducements to collective action than do public goods,[25] selective benefits may create stronger clientelist bonds than universal benefits, especially politically obscure ones like permanent price subsidies or exchange controls. Selective rewards bestowed upon a particular community or group provide powerful inducements for an exchange of political support, creating localized reciprocal relationships where paternalism and clientelism thrive. In short, leaders may seek to establish a material foundation for populism at the microlevel even where macrolevel policies are apparently exclusive or antipopular.

The Peruvian case suggests that a strict neoliberal project at the macrolevel may be compatible not only with populist-style political leadership but also with populist economic measures at the microlevel. This amalgam is not exempt from contradictions, and it is far from certain that it will prove effective over the long term in reproducing a popular political constituency to undergird a neoliberal project. However, the existence of such an unexpected amalgam and its indisputable short-term political success warrant closer examination.[26]

[25] Mancur Olson, *The Logic of Collective Action* (Cambridge: Harvard University Press, 1971).
[26] As of this writing (April 1995), President Alberto Fujimori has translated public approval ratings of over 60 percent into a landslide first-round reelection in his presidential contest with former United Nations Secretary General Javier Perez de Cuellar and twelve other candidates.

THE TRANSFORMATION OF POPULISM IN PERU:
AN ANALYSIS OF *FUJIMORISMO*

At first glance, Peru appears to offer a classic case of what Drake calls "bait and switch" populism[27]—that is, personalist leaders who campaign on a populist platform, only to switch abruptly to neoliberal policies following election. However, the about-face in economic policies does not necessarily signify a complete abandonment of populism, nor the sacrifice of political support from popular sectors. Although Peru's economic crisis and the neoliberal revolution imposed novel constraints upon populism, they did not extinguish it, as new forms of populist expression emerged in the political vacuum bequeathed by the collapse of the party system.

Indeed, the political career of Alberto Fujimori is a testament to the malleability of populism. Since Fujimori's meteoric rise to political prominence in 1990, three populist features have been constant: a personalistic style of leadership, a heterogeneous social constituency with widespread lower-class support, and the absence of institutionalized forms of political mediation between the leader and his followers. However, the ideological and economic formulas used to generate (or sustain) this popular support have changed over time, with three distinct phases identifiable. The first phase was associated with Fujimori's electoral campaign, when his populist formula cultivated a "man of the people" image and proposed a gradualist economic program to avoid the social consequences of a neoliberal "shock." During the second phase, which covered roughly Fujimori's first two years in office, economic populism essentially disappeared, but a populist constituency was sustained through attacks on the political establishment. The third phase, which began in the period following Fujimori's April 1992 "presidential coup" (the *autogolpe*) and continued through his 1995 reelection campaign, was characterized by a resurgence of economic populism at the microlevel. These three phases highlight the diversity of populist instruments, as well as their transformation in the neoliberal age.

PHASE 1: FROM OUTSIDER TO THE PRESIDENCY

A virtual unknown a mere month before the first round of the April 1990 presidential election, Fujimori surged to victory by capitalizing on the crisis of established parties and running against the neoliberal

---

[27] Drake (fn. 11), 36.

"shock" program promised by the conservative novelist and over-whelming favorite Mario Vargas Llosa, who had the backing of Peru's traditional elite.[28] Indeed, Fujimori built his political base on the rubble left by the collapse of more traditional populist experiments, namely, those of incumbent president Alan García and leftist leader Alfonso Barrantes. García inherited the leadership of APRA, Latin America's oldest populist party, following the death of the party's founder and longtime leader Victor Raul Haya de la Torre.[29] The young, charismatic García cultivated an enormous personal following and in 1985 led APRA to the presidency for the first time in its history. His support grew as he pledged to limit debt service payments, then implemented a het-erodox program of wage hikes, price controls, and tax breaks in order to stimulate aggregate demand and lift Peru out of recession, thus gen-erating a short-lived economic boom. However, García and APRA were devastated politically as foreign exchange constraints and government deficits led to hyperinflation, the collapse of real wages, and a 25 per-cent contraction of the Peruvian economy between 1988 and 1990.[30]

The demise of *Aprismo* seemed to open new political space for the United Left (IU) coalition, the strongest electoral force on the South American left for most of the 1980s, and APRA's principal competitor for lower-class support.[31] However, long-standing conflict between moderates and radicals culminated in a division of the IU in 1989 and the collapse of the left as a serious electoral force. IU moderates wanted to support Barrantes, an independent leftist and former mayor of Lima, as a presidential candidate, believing his personal appeal would expand the coalition's electoral constituency among centrist and independent voters. In contrast, more radical parties in the IU viewed Barrante's pop-ulist tendencies as an impediment to the development of a more in-stitutionalized left-wing alternative, and they rejected his conciliatory call for a multilateral "national accord" to buttress Peru's tentative

---

[28] For an analysis of Fujimori's victory, see Carlos Ivan Degregori and Romeo Grompone, *Elecciones 1990: Demenios y Redentores en el Nuevo Perú* (Lima: Instituto de Estudios Peruanos, 1991). Fujimori's meteoric rise to prominence was not the first symptom of the crisis in Peru's system of partisan repre-sentation; it was preceded in 1989 by the populist-style election of the independent television person-ality Ricardo Belmont as mayor of Lima.

[29] The populism of APRA and Haya de la Torre is discussed in Steve Stein, *Populism in Peru: The Emergence of the Masses and the Politics of Social Control* (Madison: University of Wisconsin Press, 1980).

[30] The collapse of García's heterodox program is analyzed in Mañuel Pastor, Jr., and Carol Wise, "Peruvian Economic Policy in the 1980's: From Orthodoxy to Heterodoxy and Back," *Latin American Research Review* 27, no. 2 (1992).

[31] Both APRA and the IU garnered substantial support from workers and the urban poor in the 1980s; see Maxwell A. Cameron, *Democracy and Authoritarianism in Peru: Political Coalitions and Social Change* (New York: St. Martin's Press, 1994), chaps. 2, 3.

democracy against the economic crisis and the Shining Path guerrilla insurgency. Hoping to marginalize the radical left, Barrantes and his supporters broke with the IU in 1989, gambling that an independent candidate who promised economic relief and political "concertation," or accommodation, could capture the floating mass of centrist and center-left voters who were seeking a viable alternative to the discredited APRA and the neoliberal "shock" of Vargas Llosa.

Barrantes figured right, except that the independent candidate favored by these voters was a political novice and outsider, Alberto Fujimori, rather than the familiar populist of the Peruvian left.[32] In effect, Fujimori won the election using Barrantes's game plan: a personalist campaign that avoided partisan obligations, an appeal to lower-class and unattached voters, and an emphasis on political concertation rather than a neoliberal shock as the solution to the national crisis. After finishing a close second to Vargas Llosa in the first round of the election, Fujimori crushed his conservative rival in the second round by picking up the support of leftist and *Aprista* voters.

In order to avoid alienating voters, Fujimori eschewed ideological definition and cultivated the image of the untainted leader who was above the fray of partisan politics. He thus claimed to represent the interests of common people against the sectarianism and self-interested machinations of traditional politicians. While campaigning against the shock treatment promised by Vargas Llosa, he said little about his own program beyond espousing a vague commitment to a concertationist strategy to address social and economic problems. His campaign slogan of "honesty, technology, and work" contrasted with the demagoguery of traditional politicians and evoked images of probity, efficiency, and technocratic modernization, rather than ideological motivation. This lack of ideological definition was ideal for attracting unattached, lower-class voters with predominantly centrist or uncertain political orientations.[33]

Given the delegitimation of Peru's creole political elite, Fujimori's Japanese heritage was an asset rather than an obstacle in this process of image building. Besides spawning hopes for an infusion of Japanese capital, it allowed him to benefit from popular stereotypes of the Japanese immigrant community as a hardworking and successful minority

---

[32] Barrantes, who had led polls of voter preferences in 1988 before the division of the IU, finished fifth in the first round of the election with a disastrous 4.8% of the vote. IU candidate Henry Pease received 8.2%, compared with 22.6% for APRA candidate Luis Alva Castro, 29.1% for Fujimori, and 32.7% for Vargas Llosa.

[33] For a discussion of these orientations, see the spatial analysis of the Peruvian electorate in Cameron (fn. 31), chap. 6.

group, and to portray himself as a political outsider of humble origins who had risen through personal talent and initiative. Efforts by some of Vargas Llosa's supporters to stir up nationalist sentiments against Fujimori backfired, as Fujimori took advantage of the profound cultural cleavage between Peruvians of European descent and those of indigenous descent. Indeed, Fujimori's facial features, migratory experience, and modest origins were more reminiscent of Peru's *mestizo* and indigenous majority than those of the Europeanized Vargas Llosa.[34] Fujimori, then, cultivated a double image: as a political outsider who was untainted by an association with established institutions[35] and as a leader who had emerged from the common people to offer a fresh alternative. Consequently, while the urbane Vargas Llosa obtained the backing of conservative parties and the coastal creole elite, Fujimori swept the Andean highlands and the sprawling urban lower-class districts populated by the *mestizo* and indigenous majority. In so doing, he earned votes that had previously gone to APRA or the IU, and he took most of the floating, independent votes in the political center that were generally decisive in Peruvian elections.[36]

In short, along with his vague promise to avoid a harsh economic stabilization program, Fujimori's personal qualities were central to the heterogeneous political support that he garnered. Fujimori's relationship to his supporters during the campaign was direct and highly personalistic; to highlight his background as an agronomist, he traversed the Andean higlands and urban shantytowns on a tractor, and he ate in public marketplaces among the masses. Institutional mediation was exceptionally weak; Fujimori's "party," Cambio 90, was cobbled together shortly before the election from personal acquaintances in business and academic circles, after Fujimori had failed to obtain a position on the senatorial list of the pro-Barrantes Izquierda Socialista.[37] Fujimori's running mates were drawn from a federation of small businesses and a Protestant organization, but relations with these groups frayed quickly after his election to the presidency.

[34] See Aldo Panfichi, "The Authoritarian Alternative: 'Anti-Politics' among the Popular Sectors of Lima," in Carlos Vilas, Katherine Roberts-Hite, and Monique Segarra, eds., *Rethinking Participation in Latin America* (forthcoming).
[35] The advantages of being an outsider in a time of institutional crisis are perhaps best captured in an anecdote told by Alma Guillermoprieto in *The Heart That Bleeds: Latin America Now* (New York: Alfred A. Knopf, 1994), 81. A market vendor was approached by a prominent leftist leader who asked why she was displaying a poster of Fujimori during the presidential campaign. She responded that she supported him "because he hasn't done anything yet."
[36] The social bases of Fujimori's victory are dissected in Cameron (fn. 31), chap. 5.
[37] Alberto Adrianzén, "Dispersión Política, Partidos y Rito Electoral," *Quehacer* 91 (September–October 1994), 5.

Given Fujimori's campaign themes and political constituency, Peruvians were stunned when, within two weeks of his inauguration, the new president reversed course by adopting a stabilization program that was even tougher than that proposed by Vargas Llosa.[38] As shown below, this new economic model did not force Fujimori to abandon populism; it did, however, require significant modifications in the content of his populist message, with a deemphasis of the material components and the intensification of antiestablishment political themes.

PHASE 2: DEINSTITUTIONALIZATION AND THE POLITICS
OF ANTIPOLITICS

When Fujimori assumed the presidency, he inherited an economy in its third year of four-digit hyperinflation, along with a prolonged recession that had plunged Peruvians' per capita income back to the levels of the late 1950s. In response, he imposed a draconian package of neoliberal reforms with three principal components. The first step was a stabilization program adopted in August 1990 to control inflation and capture revenues needed to renew payments of the debt service. Price subsidies, social spending, and public sector employment were slashed, interest rates and taxes on government services were increased, and exchange rates were unified, producing a de facto devaluation of the currency. A second set of institutional reforms, begun in February 1991, was designed to move beyond stabilization toward a market-based restructuring of the Peruvian economy. These reforms included the deregulation of financial and labor markets, a reduction and unification of tariffs, the privatization of public enterprises, and efforts to broaden the tax base and reduce tax evasion. Finally, these market reforms, improving fiscal health, and the resumption of debt-service payments allowed Peru's reintegration into international financial circuits, perhaps the foremost objective of Fujimori's economic plan.[39]

This structural adjustment was harsh medicine for an economy that had already suffered through a prolonged crisis, with devastating effects upon popular living standards. After losing 800,000 jobs in the 1988–89 economic crisis, employment declined by another 13.9 percent in

---

[38] The change in policy was encouraged by a trip that president-elect Fujimori made to the U.S. to meet with representatives of the IMF, the World Bank, and the Inter-American Development Bank. Following the resignation of the economists who advised Fujimori during his campaign, a new team—heavily influenced by neoliberal apostle Hernando de Soto—implemented the shock progam in early August 1990, shortly after Fujimori assumed the presidency.

[39] Overviews of Fujimori's economic reforms can be found in Efraín Gonzales de Olarte, "Peru's Economic Program under Fujimori," *Journal of Interamerican Studies and World Affairs* 35 (Summer 1993); and Carol Wise, "The Politics of Peruvian Economic Reform: Overcoming the Legacies of State-Led Development," *Journal of Interamerican Studies and World Affairs* 36 (Spring 1994).

industry, 13.7 percent in services, and 21.8 percent in commerce in the first eighteen months under Fujimori.[40] Inflation, which had been running at about 40 percent per month, shot up to 398 percent in August 1990, before declining sharply to 3–5 percent per month in late 1992 and 1–2 percent per month in 1994. The number of Peruvians living in poverty rose to 54 percent of the population in the aftermath of the "Fujishock"; the percentage of the workforce considered underemployed or unemployed rose from 81.4 in 1990 to 87.3 in 1993; the informal sector grew from 45.7 percent of the workforce in 1990 to 57 percent in 1992; and real wages fell by 40 percent between 1990 and 1992, to 33 percent of the 1980 level in the private sector and 9 percent in the public sector. A decade-long trend toward increasing inequality also continued: the share of the national income represented by wages declined from 46.7 percent in 1980 to 19.9 percent in 1990 and 13 percent in 1992, whereas the share represented by profits rose from 25.9 percent in 1980 to 49.3 percent in 1990 and 54.5 percent in 1992.[41]

The severity of this stabilization plan, with its regressive distributive impact and firm commitment to austerity, makes it difficult to think of Fujimori as a populist figure. Indeed, supporters often praised his willingness to break with Peru's entrenched populist tradition.[42] However, upon closer examination it can be seen that Fujimori sustained his populist project through an astute manipulation of political and symbolic themes, even during a period when populist economic measures were notable for their absence.

Like classical populists, Fujimori's discourse was antielitist and antiestablishment. However, rather than targeting the traditional oligarchy for its economic dominance, Fujimori began a systematic attack on Peru's political elites and the establishment institutions they controlled—namely, the political parties, Congress, and the judiciary. This antiestablishment orientation was always present in Fujimori's status as a political outsider. It intensified, however, after he took office, lacking an organized political base of his own and having to confront alternative, independent institutions; and it peaked when the Congress posed more assertive challenges to his economic and security policies in late 1991 and early 1992. Consequently, Fujimori sought to mobilize pub-

---

[40] *Peru Country Profile, 1992–93* (London: Economist Intelligence Unit, 1992), 11.
[41] Data are taken from Denis Sulmont Samain, "Ajuste sin Reestructuración," *Cuadernos Laborales* 100 (May 1994), 8–12; and Eliana Chávez O'Brien, "El Mercado de Trabajo y las Nuevas Tendencias en la Estructura del Empleo en el Perú," *Socialismo y Participación* 60 (December 1992), 20.
[42] See Rafael Romero, *El Pragmatismo de Fujimori: Del Exceso Ideológico al Realismo Político* (Lima: Sediot S.A., 1992).

lic opinion against what he called the *partidocracia*,[43] charging that the corruption, inefficiency, and sectarianism of entrenched party elites had brought Peru to the brink of economic collapse and civil war. He thus portrayed Peru's political establishment as a privileged, self-reproducing dominant class that threatened to block the implementation of economic reforms while placing partisan interests above the public good.

This "politics of antipolitics"[44] is a classic populist technique, by which a leader poses as the embodiment of national unity and the public interest against the dispiriting divisiveness of partisan or particular interests.[45] In Peru it resonated deeply with popular sentiments, as it capitalized on the delegitimation of institutions that had failed to contain the Shining Path insurgency or redress a deepening economic crisis. In 1989 only 43.5 percent of the individuals surveyed in lower-class sections of Lima said Peru had a democratic system, compared with 42 percent who said it was undemocratic.[46] By 1992 over 87 percent of respondents from lower-class sectors claimed that Congress and the judiciary had failed to fulfill their constitutional role.[47] In March 1992 only 12 percent of Peruvians expressed confidence in political parties, the lowest confidence level accorded any national institution.[48] This delegitimation of established institutions was so thorough that Fujimori received popular acclaim when he suspended the constitution, dissolved Congress and regional governments, and purged most of the judiciary in a military-backed *autogolpe* in April 1992.[49]

Popular struggle, therefore, was redefined by Fujimori: no longer "the people" versus "the oligarchy," it became instead "the people"—represented by their elected president—versus the "political class." For Fujimori, this political class comprised not only professional politicians and

[43] Fujimori's attacks on the party system and the generalized crisis of political representation in Peru are analyzed in Alberto Adrianzén Merino, "Democracia y Partidos en el Perú," *Pretextos* 3–4 (December 1992), 7–19.

[44] For an analysis of the "politics of antipolitics," see Panfichi (fn. 34).

[45] See Canovan (fn. 4), chap. 7.

[46] Walter Alarcón Glasinovich, "Clases Populares, Cultura Política y Democracia," *Socialismo y Participación* 54 (June 1991), 4.

[47] Sandro Macassi Lavander, "Cultura Política de la Eficacia: Qué Hay Tras la Discusión Dictadura-Orden Constitucional?" *Socialismo y Participación* 58 (June 1992), 70–71.

[48] Apoyo S.A., *Informe de Opinión* (September 1992), 32. One study of the urban poor found that only 1.5% belonged to a political party, while 94% claimed that "the people have always been deceived by politicians"; see Jorge Parodi and Walter Twanama, "Los Pobladores, la Ciudad y la Política: Un Estudio de Actitudes," in Parodi, ed., *Los Pobres, La Ciudad y la Política* (Lima: Centro de Estudios de Democracia y Sociedad, 1993), 68–70.

[49] Fujimori's public approval rating jumped from 59% of the population to 82% during the week of his *autogolpe*; see Apoyo S.A. (fn. 48), 8. For an analysis of this support, see Balbi (fn. 1). An excellent account of the changes in the Peruvian state associated with the *autogolpe* is provided in Philip Mauceri, "State Reform, Coalitions, and the Neoliberal Autogolpe in Peru," *Latin American Research Review* 30, no. 1 (1995).

political parties, but virtually any organized interest group in the public domain, including those spawned by previous waves of populist mobilization. Therefore, in contrast to most classical populist experiences, the organized labor movement was not a central component of Fujimori's multiclass, catch-all coalition. Although Fujimori obtained backing from the major labor federations in the second-round election against Vargas Llosa, their organizational autonomy and political ties to the United Left made them uncertain allies. Indeed, organized labor turned quickly into a bitter opponent of Fujimori after his sudden embrace of neoliberal economics. Three failed national strikes, however, demonstrated organized labor's impotence in resisting the structural changes proposed by Fujimori. A bulwark of the protest movement that undermined military rule in the late 1970s, organized labor was then decimated by a decade of economic crisis that produced widespread factory layoffs, rising underemployment, and an informalization of the workforce. By 1991 the level of unionization had fallen by one-third to 12 percent of the workforce,[50] while over half of the economically active population in Lima worked in the informal sector and 49 percent of salaried workers in the private sector had temporary contracts.[51]

In short, structural changes in the Peruvian economy had fragmented and atomized the workforce, obstructing organizational efforts that relied upon class-based collective interests and identities. These changes made organized labor less broadly representative of diverse working-class interests, and it ceased to be the axis of popular political movements.[52] Fujimori's economic model was therefore able to challenge the interests of a politically prostrate labor movement at relatively little cost—through wage cuts, decreased public and private sector formal employment, and changes in the labor law that emasculated collective rights.[53] Indeed, Fujimori had more to gain politically by aiming his message at the burgeoning microenterprise and informal sectors; they incorporated nearly five times as many people as the labor unions, and their ambiguous class identities, malleable political loyalties, and lack of autonomous organizational power facilitated personalist mobilization. As Franco has argued, Peru's urban masses have favored a long succession of highly differentiated populist figures in the absence of au-

---

[50] *Foreign Labor Trends: Peru* (Washington, D.C.: U.S. Department of Labor, 1991), 7.

[51] Sulmont Samain (fn. 41), 11.

[52] In particular, unions staunchly defended legal rights to employment security in response to widespread layoffs and government efforts to make the labor market more "flexible." Such concerns were of limited interest to the more numerous informal and temporary contract workers.

[53] The impact of neoliberal reforms on the labor movement is analyzed in Carmen Rosa Balbi, "Miseria del Sindicalismo," *Debate* 15 (November 1992–January 1993), 38.

tonomous and institutionalized forms of political representation.[54] Given the collapse of the state's capacity to deliver public services in the late 1980s, the urban masses were increasingly inclined to pursue individual rather than collective channels for advancement, and they were drawn to Fujimori's message of hard work, self-reliance, and efficiency. Fujimori thus selected running mates who were symbols of the self-made individual, and he cultivated the support of informals by promising to legalize street vendors and establish a bank to make loans to the informal sector.[55] He was rewarded with overwhelming political support.[56]

The most notable features, then, of *Fujimorismo* were its personalism, atomization, and lack of institutionalization. The crises of APRA and the United Left had undermined partisan identities and created an institutional vacuum that predisposed the popular sectors to follow personalist leaders. Likewise, the weakening of organized labor and the informalization of the workforce created a fragmented, heterogeneous mass electorate that lacked autonomous organizational power. Fujimori's government was thus largely suspended above organized interests in civil society; given the preference for direct, unmediated linkages between the personalist leader and an atomized mass electorate, no significant efforts were made to construct institutionalized partisan or corporatist channels of representation. Indeed, the armed forces—or, at least, sectors within them—became Fujimori's principal base of institutional support, as the president quickly demobilized Cambio 90 and broke with the leadership of the Protestant and small business groups that had initially supported him. Following the 1992 *autogolpe* Fujimori helped create a new movement among supportive technocrats; Nueva Mayoría was to sponsor a slate of candidates in elections for a constitutional assembly and was subsequently used by Fujimori to subordinate Cambio 90 even further.

In short, Fujimori owed his political ascendance to the crisis of Peru's representative institutions, and he actively encouraged political dispersion and atomization to enhance his personal authority. This is best seen, perhaps, in his decision to greatly ease requirements to field candidates in the 1993 municipal elections. Since mayoral candidates did not need to mobilize the support or resources of party organizations to

[54] Carlos Franco, *Imagenes de la Sociedad Peruana: La Otra Modernidad* (Lima: Centro de Estudios para el Desarrollo y la Participación, 1991). See also Parodi and Twanama (fn. 48).
[55] See Cameron (fn. 31), chap. 6.
[56] The support of informal sectors for Fujimori is analyzed in Carmen Rosa Balbi, "Modernidad y Progreso en el Mundo Informal," *Pretextos* 2 (February 1991).

run for office, the result was a proliferation of independent candidacies and ephemeral political fronts. Predictably, there was a diffusion of smaller-scale populist experiences across the political spectrum; an extraordinary fifteen thousand independent lists ran in municipal races across the country,[57] capturing 73 percent of the vote nationwide.[58] By 1994 the institutional vacuum was so profound that 86 percent of the population claimed to be politically independent, with Cambio 90 receiving the highest level of public identification at 5 percent. Only 9 percent said they would vote for a candidate from a political party, with 77 percent claiming to prefer an independent.[59] The 1995 national elections confirmed that the Peruvian party system had essentially collapsed, as Fujimori and other independent candidates garnered 90 percent of the vote in the presidential race. Indeed, the traditional parties that had dominated Peruvian politics before 1900—the conservative Popular Action Party, the centrist APRA, and the United Left coalition—all lost their legal status after failing to obtain 5 percent of the vote.

Fujimori thus governed in a highly autocratic style, deliberately weakening or eliminating institutional checks on his authority, and allying himself with military officials to neutralize the only force that could threaten his regime. According to O'Donnell, such autocratic forms of authority—what he calls "delegative democracy"[60]—are found in societies where economic crises and institutional weaknesses allow personalist leaders to pose as the embodiment or savior of the nation. These leaders may then govern arbitrarily, unchecked by institutional constraints, campaign promises, or organized interests. In the absence of institutionalized accountability, they can reverse direction suddenly, with relatively little concern for political ramifications.

Bresser Pereira, Maravall, and Przeworski see neoliberalism as having a natural inclination toward such autocratic and technocratic forms of rule, given the need to evade or override the political opposition of organized interests that would be hurt by structural adjustments. Furthermore, they argue, autocratic neoliberalism encourages rather than suppresses populist behavior—understood as the immediate pursuit of particularistic interests—by weakening the social and political institutions that can mediate and contain particularistic demands.[61]

[57] Julio Cotler, *Descomposición Política y Autoritarismo en el Peru* (Lima: Instituto de Estudios Peruanos, 1993), 27.
[58] Maxwell A. Cameron, "Political Parties and the Informal Sector in Peru" (Paper presented at the Eighteenth Congress of the Latin American Studies Association, Atlanta, March 10–12, 1994), 23.
[59] *Semana Económica*, March 20, and April 24, 1994, p. 6.
[60] O'Donnell (fn. 24).
[61] Bresser Pereira, Maravall, and Przeworski (fn. 1), 10.

This analysis of Peru goes further by suggesting that autocratic neoliberalism in and of itself may embody the core political and sociological elements of populism outlined above. By crafting an image as a man of the common people, articulating the life experiences and aspirations of an informalized workforce, and confronting a corrupt and elitist political establishment, Fujimori was able to sustain a populist coalition even during a period of severe economic hardship. The question remains, however, whether autocratic neoliberalism can craft populist economic measures to help reproduce lower-class political support. The third phase of *Fujimorismo* began after the 1992 *autogolpe* opened the possibility of a constitutional change to allow presidential reelection. It was marked by a systematic effort to reconstruct a material foundation for populism at the microlevel. Once reelection became a distinct possibility, Fujimori was no longer content to rely primarily upon political mechanisms in his populist formula; indeed, he discovered that structural adjustments could provide unexpected economic instruments and political space for populist leadership, despite the macrolevel constraints of economic austerity.

PHASE 3: THE RESURRECTION OF ECONOMIC POPULISM
UNDER NEOLIBERALISM

During Fujimori's first years in office, few economic instruments were available to ameliorate the social costs of the stabilization plan and sustain his initial base of popular support. The shock program of August 1990 had a severe impact on popular living standards; it was administered largely without anesthesia, that is, with only a paltry compensation plan to cushion the impact of price increases, job losses, and wage cuts. The problem was twofold: a lack of resources, given the fiscal crisis of the Peruvian state and the austerity requirements of stabilization, and a lack of administrative capabilities, due to the erosion of the state's institutional presence in society.[62] Consequently, although Fujimori promised to spend over $400 million in the months after the shock program to protect the poorest sectors, only $90 million was actually spent on programs to alleviate poverty, and other forms of social spend-

---

[62] For example, budget cuts forced the central government to reduce its administrative staff and workforce from 633,000 in 1990 to only 338,000 in 1993—an extraordinary 47% cut in only three years. See "VIII Foro Económico: Pobreza, Política Económica y Política Social," *Actualidad Económica* 16 (June 1994), 31. As Carol Graham points out, Fujimori inherited a state whose tax receipts had fallen from 15% to 3% of the GDP under García; see Graham, *Safety Nets, Politics, and the Poor: Transitions to Market Economies* (Washington, D.C.: Brookings Institution, 1994), 93. Nevertheless, Graham argues that given the availability of external resources, Fujimori's minimal effort to construct a social safety net to cushion the impact of market reforms was attributable more to a lack of political will than to fiscal constraints.

ing were being cut.[63] A new program, the Fondo Nacional de Compensación y Desarrollo (FONCODES), was established in 1991 to direct local infrastructure and poverty relief programs, but it lacked the administrative capability to spend all the funds it was allocated. In early 1992 FONCODES was spending less than 20 percent of its allocated budget; that figure barely topped 50 percent in early 1994.[64]

As such, the only significant economic gain for popular sectors in the early years of structural adjustment was the sharp decline in the inflation rate, which fell from 7,650 percent in 1990 to under 20 percent in 1994. This gain was significant, as popular sectors were especially vulnerable to hyperinflation, given the inefficacy of wage indexation and the inability of the poor to protect income levels by holding foreign currency or sending capital abroad. But if stabilization reduced economic uncertainty, it was achieved at the cost of significant economic contraction and reduced consumption. Fujimori thus relied heavily upon nonmaterial factors to sustain his popular support—in particular, his campaign against the political establishment and the growing success of police intelligence units in the war against the Shining Path, which culminated in the capture of messianic rebel leader Abimael Guzman in September 1992. Additionally, at least some features of the economic model had a popular cast, even if they did not provide direct economic benefits to subaltern sectors. For example, Fujimori cracked down on large-scale tax evaders and withdrew a number of subsidies and tax exemptions that had traditionally favored large enterprises with political connections over smaller competitors.

By 1993, however, Fujimori's strategies began to change slowly, as a resumption of economic growth and tax reform, as well as a restoration of ties to international lending institutions, alleviated fiscal constraints. Government spending on social emergency programs, which totaled a paltry $100 million in both 1991 and 1992, doubled in 1993. By the end of 1993 FONCODES had initiated ten thousand small-scale projects in agriculture, health care, education, sanitation, nutrition, transportation, and microenterprise promotion in an effort both to provide public services and to generate new employment.[65] A new residential infrastructure program (PRONAVI) was also expanded to begin housing construction, and Fujimori sharply increased the pace of his visits to

[63] José María Salcedo, "Sí Hay Alternativas," *Quehacer* 85 (September–October 1993), 18.
[64] In 1994 the budget of FONCODES called for an expenditure of $170 million, but it only spent $45 million over the first half of the year; see *Caretas*, July 27, 1994, p. 22.
[65] See the interview with Arturo Woodman, former executive director of FONCODES, in *El Comercio*, November 14, 1993, p. A4.

poor communities to inaugurate public works projects. Between the April 1992 *autogolpe* and the November 1993 constitutional referendum, Fujimori personally dedicated seventy-one schools, mostly in lower-class urban districts.[66]

A more dramatic change occurred in early 1994, however, when the Fujimori regime received an unexpected economic windfall—a privatization settlement worth over $2 billion from the sale of Peru's state-owned telephone and telecommunications industries to a Spanish-led consortium of investors. The sale price, higher than what the government had anticipated, suddenly added to the state coffers a quantity of money that was equivalent to more than half of Peru's annual export earnings and more than 240 percent of the currency in circulation. While business interests clamored to have the money used for tax relief and the IMF insisted that it go for debt payments so as not to reignite inflation, Fujimori insisted that a sizable portion of the money be directed to social programs as part of a new "war on poverty." After getting IMF approval to double social emergency spending to $450 million, Fujimori held out for additional increases before signing a new letter of intent, and he eventually received authorization to spend $876 million on social and investment programs.[67] Meanwhile, Fujimori's minister of the presidency—whose office is responsible for FONCODES, PRONAVI, and the food assistance program PRONAA—promised to create a million new jobs before the 1995 elections through housing and public construction projects.[68] Fujimori announced a new $400 million campaign to build thirty-one thousand homes, and promised to build one school per day in 1994 and two to three per day in 1995.[69] He also decreed special bonuses for public sector workers, a doubling of the minimum wage in the public health and education sectors, and an 83 percent increase in the private sector minimum wage, the first in two years.[70]

Given Peru's accumulated social deficit, the urgent need for commitments of new resources can hardly be denied; if they fully materialize, it will be only a first step toward making up some of the ground lost from

[66] *Caretas*, November 25, 1993, p. 22. Regular visits to urban shantytowns began in earnest after the 1992 *autogolpe*; following the poor showing for Fujimori's constitution in the 1993 referendum, when it failed to get 50% of the vote outside of Lima, presidential visits to the provinces to inaugurate public works and deliver supplies increased as well, to an average of more than one per week. See "El No Candidato," *Quehacer* 88 (March–April 1994).

[67] *Latin America Weekly Report*, June 2, 1994, p. 237.

[68] See "El Camino a la Reelección Pasa por el Millón de Empleos," *Actualidad Económica* 152 (March 1994), 6–7.

[69] *La República*, June 29, 1994, p. 6.

[70] "La Buena Estrella del Presidente Fujimori," *Argumentos* 2 (April 1994), 7.

the collapse of public services over the past decade,[71] and it will represent only a fraction of the resources required to meet the basic needs of the fifteen million Peruvians estimated to be living below the poverty line.[72] However, the timing and manner in which these new social programs were implemented involved transparent political manipulation, and they have generated widespread charges of electoral populism in Peru.[73] With only a year to go before standing for reelection—an opportunity made possible by rewriting the constitution—Fujimori suddenly embarked upon a dramatic expansion of state social spending, deriving political advantages from sympathetic media coverage of his daily visits to inaugurate public works in poor communities. Indeed, Peruvian airwaves and newspapers were replete with images of Fujimori, often wearing an Indian poncho and woolen cap, visiting remote Andean communities or urban shantytowns to inaugurate public works, distribute computers or other materials to schools and health clinics, and pass out calendars with his photo to indigenous peasants. The political manipulation of social spending was so blatant that the council which oversees national elections—a body not known for its independence from the executive branch—proposed legislation in late 1994 that would prohibit an incumbent president from inaugurating public works, distributing goods, or even speaking of public works during a presidential campaign.[74] Earlier in the year the director of FONCODES, a respected leader of the business community, resigned his position following conflicts with the minister of the presidency over the political manipulation of social projects to build support for Fujimori and neutralize the influence of municipal authorities.[75]

Although this expansion of social spending was not based upon inflationary deficit financing—the bête noire of critics of economic populism—it relied heavily upon temporary funds made available by international financing and the short-term sale of state assets. FONCODES, for example, has received 70 percent of its funds from in-

[71] According to one estimate, government social spending declined from 4.7% of GDP in 1980 to 0.9% in 1993; see *Latin America Weekly Report*, June 9, 1994, p. 244.
[72] Félix Jiménez estimates that the budget of FONCODES is approximately one-tenth what would be required to attend to the basic needs of Peruvians living below the poverty line; see Jiménez, "Estrategias de Desarrollo y Política Social," *Socialismo y Participación* 67 (September 1994), 22.
[73] See, for example, *Resúmen Semanal*, March 29–April 5, 1994, p. 2. Graham (fn. 62), chap. 4, has argued that even the minimalist social programs of Fujimori's first two years were riddled with political manipulation; the electoral motivations and economic resources at stake more recently make such manipulation even more tempting.
[74] A watered-down version of this legislation was passed by the pro-Fujimori majority in Congress as the 1995 presidential race formally began. The final bill allowed Fujimori to inaugurate public works in "noncampaign" settings, where he did not advocate his reelection or criticize electoral opponents.
[75] *Caretas*, February 3, 1994, p. 25.

ternational sources,[76] and FONAVI and PRONAA have also received international support. Although Fujimori's neoliberal reforms made these new financial resources available through privatization and renewed access to international credits, their sustainability is questionable. Reliance upon international financing to sustain social consumption is a risky endeavor, and although Peru will likely earn several billion dollars more before completing its privatization project, this is by definition a short-term fiscal palliative. It is not surprising, then, that FONCODES is designed to be an emergency social compensation project rather than a long-term development program.

Furthermore, the expansion of social spending has entailed an extraordinary concentration of power and resources in the hands of the president and a further weakening of intermediary social and political institutions. The major poverty alleviation programs are managed directly by the Ministry of the Presidency, which has acquired a virtual monopoly over public works in Peru. Social spending in other government ministries has been cut, regional governments were eliminated in the 1992 *autogolpe*, and municipal governments have been emasculated by a 1993 decree that eroded their financial autonomy.[77] Municipal governments are generally bypassed in the targeted social projects of FONCODES, which works directly with base-level community groups, or *nucleos*, in project design and implementation. These *nucleos* typically have an ephemeral existence, as they are project specific rather than permanent grassroots community organizations; their role is not one of political representation or demand making. Indeed, Fujimori has been widely criticized for marginalizing more autonomous and institutionalized popular organizations, particularly the community soup kitchens that are legally entitled to government subsidies.[78] The wariness toward independent groups in civil society can also be noted in his reliance upon military troops for projects like highway construction.

In short, Peruvian social policies have relied upon direct, highly paternalistic relationships that are conducive to the microlevel exchange of material benefits for political support, even in a context of relative macroeconomic austerity. The material foundation for populism thus

[76] Interview by the author with Mariano Castro, FONCODES manager of programs and projects, Lima, June 30, 1994.
[77] The municipal reform is analyzed in Angel Delgado Silva, "Autocracia y Régimen Local," *Socialismo y Participación* 65 (March 1994). This decree not only weakened municipal governments as a counterweight to executive authority, but also undermined the political position of Mayor Ricardo Belmont of Lima, one of Fujimori's major competitors for the presidency in 1995. By the end of 1994 the Lima municipality was essentially bankrupt, public services and employee salaries had been interrupted, and Belmont was floundering politically.
[78] *Resúmen Semanal*, December 21–27, 1993, pp. 2–3.

shifted from costly, impersonal programs such as universal consumer subsidies to less expensive, community-based projects that could be directly attributed to presidential initiative as a result of the concentration of resources in the executive branch and the systematic erosion of intermediary institutions in both civil and political society. As fiscal constraints gradually diminished and electoral considerations rose to the forefront, Fujimori expanded community projects and even resorted to more generalized populist mechanisms—such as wage increases—without jeopardizing the macroeconomic equilibria of the neoliberal model.

Fujimori has thus demonstrated how populist economic measures—at times, remarkably traditional ones—can be incorporated into an overarching neoliberal project, and how the privatization programs that are central features of neoliberalism can easily spawn new types of populist agendas. Indeed, privatization can help circumvent the fiscal constraints of neoliberal austerity by providing resources for the type of pork-barrel distributive politics that incumbents everywhere find so hard to resist. Such distributive measures may not add up to populism in and of themselves, especially where they follow channels of partisan representation or enduring forms of social organization. However, in the Peruvian context of social atomization and political deinstitutionalization, they have become a central component of a broader populist project that ties a heterogeneous subaltern constituency to the unmediated authority of an autocratic ruler.

In effect, Fujimori has crafted a mixed political strategy that combines technocratic neoliberalism with microlevel populism. In a recent study, Geddes found that Fujimori, as the consummate outsider and independent political entrepreneur, had the highest score out of forty-four Latin American presidencies for his reliance upon meritocratic criteria rather than partisan patronage when making political appointments.[79] But while opting for technocratic competence in the state bureaucracy, he has not had to forgo patronage opportunities made possible by public works in local communities; indeed, his personal visits to lower-class communities to deliver goods are highly reminiscent of Peru's military populist of the 1950s, General Mañuel Odría.[80]

---

[79] Barbara Geddes, *Politicians's Dilemma: Building State Capacity in Latin America* (Berkeley: University of California Press, 1994), chap. 6.

[80] See David Collier's analysis of Odría's paternalistic relationship to shantytown settlements; Collier, *Squatters and Oligarchs: Authoritarian Rule and Policy Change in Peru* (Baltimore: Johns Hopkins University Press, 1976), chap. 4. Fujimori also resembles Odría in his efforts to transform the unorganized poor into a bastion of personalist support, as Odría had to bypass the organized social and political constituencies of APRA.

Whereas Geddes speaks of efforts to create "islands of competence" within states that are otherwise riddled with political patronage, Fujimori has nurtured "islands of populism" within an otherwise highly technocratic and exclusive model of economic development. The question remains, however, whether these populist measures have been efficacious in reproducing Fujimori's base of popular support. The flirtation with more generalized populist mechanisms followed the narrow victory of Fujimori's new constitution in an October 1993 plebiscite, when it obtained broad support in wealthy districts but failed to get a majority in many of the provinces and urban popular communities that had supported him overwhelmingly in 1990.[81] Clearly, there would be little reason to identify Fujimori as any type of populist if his social constituency were to shift definitively toward more elite sectors. However, as of June 1994, Fujimori's approval rating among Lima's poorest sectors (67.3 percent) remained higher than that among the middle and upper classes (56.9 percent),[82] and the memory of the economic debacle of the García years seemed to outweigh the social costs of Fujimori's structural adjustment. Indeed, in January 1994, 68.9 percent of the poorest sectors in Lima said the economy was in better shape than it had been under García (compared with 10.4 percent who said it was worse); more revealing is the fact that 42.7 percent of the poor said their own standard of living had improved under Fujimori, compared with 25 percent who said it had declined.[83] It seems plausible, then, that after a traumatic period of hyperinflation, the material— or, perhaps, the psychological—benefits of economic stabilization and selective populist measures may cushion the impact of austerity and thus provide breathing space for government efforts to address social problems.

COMPARATIVE PERSPECTIVES

Although *Fujimorismo* provides an unusually transparent example of the affinities between populism and neoliberalism, it is hardly a unique

[81] In the second round of the 1990 election, Fujimori won over 62% of the vote in the poorest districts of Lima, compared with only 24.6% in the wealthiest districts. In the 1993 referendum, over 64% in the wealthiest districts voted for the new constitution, compared with 56% in the poorest districts; see *Caretas*, November 18, 1994, p. 24B. Fujimori's constitution fared even worse outside of Lima, losing in fifteen of Peru's twenty-two departments. The two elections are not directly comparable, however, since the 1990 figures were affected by the presence of an alternative candidate who was attractive to elite sectors. Nevertheless, the 1993 results are revealing, and the narrowness of Fujimori's referendum victory gave added political impetus for increased social spending in 1994.

[82] *Imasen Confidencial*, June 1994, p. 12.

[83] Ibid., January 1994, p. 18.

case. In Mexico debate has emerged over the characterization of the Programa Nacional de Solidaridad (Pronasol), the targeted social compensation plan that President Carlos Salinas de Gortari designed to cushion the impact of neoliberal reforms. Some observers have denied that the program is populist, either because it has maintained fiscal discipline[84] or because it has been incorporated into a broader neoliberal conception of the state.[85] As conceptualized above, however, neither fiscal indiscipline nor statist economic models are intrinsic to populism; of greater relevance are the nature of authority relations and the manipulation of government economic resources in an exchange for political support.

On paper, Pronasol is not a populist project, as it is designed to be a nonpartisan, demand-based program in which autonomous local committees play a major role in the proposal, design, and implementation of government-financed community projects. The practice, however, often diverges from this model, although it is difficult to generalize, given the variation in the program's political implementation according to the strength and autonomy of preexisting grassroots organizations and the proclivities of local government officials.[86] In some localities grassroots initiative and autonomy have been maintained; in others local committees have been created out of or incorporated within the clientelist networks of the governing party, the PRI.

In practice, there are several characteristics of Pronasol that endow it with populist features,[87] namely, a personalistic, centralized authority structure and the widespread manipulation of resources to marginalize opposition parties and build local bases of political support for the government. As Cornelius, Craig, and Fox assert, Pronasol developed as "a presidentialist program par excellence."[88] President Salinas and his advisers held tight control over highly discretionary funds; in some cases, funds were disbursed through municipal governments or the PRI's traditional corporate institutions, but in other cases institutional intermediation was bypassed in favor of direct disbursement to the grass roots,

---

[84] José Córdoba, "Mexico," in John Williamson, ed., *The Political Economy of Policy Reform* (Washington, D.C.: Institute for International Economics, 1994), 266.

[85] Carol Graham, "Mexico's Solidarity Program in Comparative Context: Demand-Based Poverty Alleviation Programs in Latin America, Africa, and Eastern Europe," in Wayne A. Cornelius, Ann L. Craig, and Jonathan Fox, eds., *Transforming State-Society Relations in Mexico* (San Diego: Center for U.S.-Mexico Studies, 1994), 323.

[86] See Jonathan Fox, "The Difficult Transition from Clientelism to Citizenship: Lessons from Mexico," *World Politics* 46 (January 1994).

[87] For an elaboration, see Dresser (fn. 1).

[88] Wayne A. Cornelius, Ann L. Craig, and Jonathan Fox, "Mexico's National Solidarity Program: An Overview," in Cornelius, Craig, and Fox (fn. 85), 14.

especially where municipal governments were under the control of opposition parties or traditional PRI bosses opposed to Salinas's reforms.
With considerable fanfare, Salinas made weekly visits to poor communities to inaugurate projects and receive petitions for new ones. Alloca-
tive decisions were heavily influenced by political considerations, and
not merely technical criteria or poverty levels; resources were distributed to reward areas of PRI support and either punish or "buy back" opposition voters, depending upon partisan loyalties and the proximity of
regional elections.[89] Funds were targeted to "buy back" voters in areas
that were strongholds of support for Cuahtemoc Cardenas and his leftist opposition party, the PRD.[90] Not surprisingly, empirical studies have
demonstrated that access to Pronasol benefits had a significant impact
on lower-class support for the PRI in the 1991 legislative elections.[91]

   This is not to argue that the targeted social compensation programs
advocated by neoliberal reformers are intrinsically populist; where the
political will exists, as Graham's analysis of the Bolivian Emergency
Social Fund demonstrates, such programs can be designed to follow
relatively technical and nonpartisan criteria and to strengthen local organizational and administrative capabilities.[92] But as the Peruvian and
Mexican cases show, these programs can easily be manipulated by personalist leaders seeking microlevel exchanges of material benefits for
political support. The broader context of neoliberal austerity does not
negate the essentially populist character of such authority relations. Indeed, as in Peru, the privatizations that accompanied structural adjustment provided resources that could be used (temporarily) to help
finance clientelist exchanges; Salinas used earnings from privatizations
not only to help fund Pronasol but also to finance electrification projects in lower-class communities.

   In Argentina, Carlos Menem also proved adept at maintaining a
populist coalition despite his reversal of traditional Peronist economic
policies. Like Fujimori, Menem has tried to incorporate selective populist economic measures into an overarching neoliberal project, especially since constitutional change made reelection a possibility. This can
be seen in his 1994 adoption of a $7 billion public works campaign fol-
lowing political unrest in the northern provinces, along with his advo-

<hr />

[89] See Juan Molinar Horcasitas and Jeffrey A. Weldon, "Electoral Determinants and Consequences
of National Solidarity," in Cornelius, Craig, and Fox (fn. 85).
[90] See Kathleen Bruhn, "Taking on Goliath: The Emergence of a New Cardenista Party and the
Struggle for Democracy in Mexico" (Ph.D. diss., Stanford University, 1993), chaps. 6, 7.
[91] Charles L. Davis and Kenneth M. Coleman, "Neoliberal Economic Policies and the Potential for
Electoral Change in Mexico," *Mexican Studies/Estudios Mexicanos* 10 (Summer 1994).
[92] Graham (fn. 62) chap. 3

cacy—over the objections of Finance Minister Domingo Cavallo—of a scheme to sell off shares of the state-owned oil company to help finance a low-cost housing project.[93] More important, perhaps, has been Menem's astute employment of selective material and political incentives to garner support from strategically located labor unions. Although neoliberal reforms undercut the collective rights and power of organized labor in general, Menem used his Peronist links to divide and rule the labor movement by targeting cooperative unions for selective wage increases, control over social welfare funds, political appointments, and legal privileges.[94] These measures at the microlevel blocked the emergence of a unified labor opposition and helped Menem maintain a popular constituency despite a macroeconomic model that sharpened inequalities and drove up unemployment to record levels. Such forms of selective incorporation fragment subaltern sectors, impede horizontal linkages between popular organizations, and encourage vertical forms of political clientelism; as such, they follow in the long tradition of Latin American populism, which typically bestowed its rewards upon "privileged" sectors of the lower classes (especially organized labor) while neglecting others (the urban underclass and rural poor). The social actors may have changed, but the logic remains one of promoting social fragmentation to facilitate vertical political domination and dependency.

Social fragmentation has gone hand in hand with autocratic rule and political deinstitutionalization in Argentina, although the process has been less extreme than in Peru. Not only did Menem produce a schism in the labor movement, the historic institutional pillar of Peronism, but he has also subordinated the legislature by governing extensively by decree, packed the Supreme Court with loyalists, personalized the leadership of the Peronist party, built personal bases of support outside the party, and concentrated power in the hands of a charismatic executive.[95] Recent Argentine elections have also witnessed an erosion of the traditional party system and the emergence of new political fronts, provincial parties, and personalist leaders. In both Argentina and Peru, political deinstitutionalization has been a conscious strategy of personalist leaders, enabling them to establish unmediated relationships with

[93] *Latin American Weekly Report,* June 16, 1994, p. 262, and December 8, 1994, p. 557.
    [94] Sarah Kelsey and Steve Levitsky, "Captivating Alliances: Unions, Labor-backed Parties, and the Politics of Economic Liberalization in Argentina and Mexico" (Paper presented at the Eighteenth International Congress of the Latin American Studies Association, Atlanta, March 10–12, 1994).
    [95] Aldo C. Vacs, "Attending Marvels: The Unanticipated Merger of Liberal Democracy, Neo-Liberalism, and Neo-Populism in Argentina" (Paper presented at the annual meeting of the American Political Science Association, New York, September 1–4, 1994).

atomized mass followings while overcoming institutional checks on the imposition of neoliberal reforms. By helping to remove such institutional constraints, populism has proven to be highly functional to the neoliberal project.

CONCLUSION: THE POLITICAL IMPLICATIONS OF POPULIST LIBERALISM

Since neoliberalism first arrived in Latin America under the iron fist of Chile's military dictator Augusto Pinochet, its political implications have been widely—and hotly—debated. Early critics saw authoritarian coercion as a functional requisite to suppressing political opposition to strict market reforms.[96] More recently, the "Washington consensus" presumes a natural harmony between political and economic liberalism, and thus an affinity between free markets and democratic politics.[97] Over time neoliberalism has demonstrated its political versatility; nevertheless, as political dealignment spawns personalist regimes across much of Latin America, it is time to consider whether the most natural political correlate to the neoliberal era may actually be populism, the option most widely seen as its antithesis.[98]

This study suggests that neoliberalism and populism contain unexpected symmetries and affinities. The Peruvian case demonstrates that populism can complement and reinforce neoliberalism in certain contexts, even if its form differs from the classical populism associated with the likes of Peron, Vargas, Cardenas, Haya de la Torre, and Gaitán. Rather than representing the eclipse of populism, neoliberalism may actually be integral to its transformation, as populism adapts to changing structures of opportunities and constraints.

Given this resiliency and malleability, populism should be decoupled from any specific phase or model of socioeconomic development. Indeed, its multiple expressions enable it to survive—and even thrive— under diverse political and economic conditions. Simply put, populism is a recurring feature of Latin American politics. Its recurrence is attributable not so much to a personalist strain in the region's political

[96] Mañuel Antonio Garretón, *El Proceso Político Chileno* (Santiago: FLACSO, 1983).
[97] See, for example, Anthony Lake, "The Reach of Democracy," *New York Times*, September 23, 1994, p. A17.
[98] There is no assumption here that this correlation is perfect; Chile has experienced neoliberalism under both authoritarian and democratic rulers without significant manifestations of populism, while Venezuela under Rafael Caldera demonstrates to date that personalist leadership and political deinstitutionalization do not inevitably strengthen neoliberalism. Nevertheless, the theoretical and empirical linkages between populism and neoliberalism are compelling and suggest a form of association that goes well beyond political coincidence.

culture, or even to the distributive conflicts engendered by entrenched socioeconomic inequalities, as to the fragility of autonomous political organizing among popular sectors and the weakness of intermediary institutions that aggregate and channel social demands within the political arena. That is, it is the failure of representative institutions like political parties, labor unions, and autonomous social organizations to mediate between citizens and the state that paves the way for the direct, personalist mobilization of heterogeneous masses which is synonymous with populism.[99]

Populism is a perpetual tendency where political institutions are chronically weak. However, it surges most strongly in contexts of crisis or profound social transformation, when preexisting patterns of authority or institutional referents lose their capacity to structure the political behavior and identities of popular sectors. It is in such contexts that popular sectors are most likely to deposit their confidence in powerful men of action, in national "saviors" who promise to sweep away the detritus of the past and usher in a new social order. Classical populism, for example, emerged in the 1930s in Latin America as industrialization and urbanization eroded the social controls of the oligarchic order and created a new urban mass sector disposed to political mobilization. Given the nascent state of institutional channels for popular representation, emerging working and middle classes were often incorporated into the political arena through direct mobilization by personalist leaders. In contemporary Latin America the prolonged economic crisis of the 1980s culminated in the collapse of the developmentalist state, clearing the deck for neoliberal structural adjustments. This process, however, undermined the institutional forms of representation that characterized the developmentalist state—in many cases, the political parties and labor unions spawned by earlier populist movements. The outcome has been a fragmentation of civil society, a destructuring of institutional linkages, and an erosion of collective identities that enables personalist leaders to establish vertical, unmediated relationships with atomized masses.[100] The theoretical nexus between populism and neoliberalism, then, is grounded in their reciprocal tendency to exploit—and exacerbate—the deinstitutionalization of political representation. Ultimately, the two phenomena are mutually reinforcing.

Therefore, in periods of economic crisis, social fragmentation, and

---

[99] These factors are also stressed by Castro Rea, Ducatenzeiler, and Faucher (fn. 1).

[100] An excellent synthesis of the relationship between social fragmentation and personalist authority can be found in Eugenio Tironi, "Para Una Sociología de la Decadencia: El Concepto de Disolución Social," *Proposiciones* 6 (October–December 1986), 12–16.

political deinstitutionalization, the personalist mobilization of lower-class support is not necessarily contingent upon statist or redistributive macroeconomic policies. Indeed, personalist leaders from Boris Yeltsin to Ross Perot have found ways to combine populist, antiestablishment messages with programs of economic austerity during periods of institutional failure. Likewise, the Peruvian case demonstrates that it may be possible to craft populist formulas that complement neoliberalism by exploiting popular disillusionment with established institutions and selectively allocating limited public resources to create local bases of clientelist support.

If this is the case, the collapse of import substitution industrialization and the onset of the neoliberal era do not require a "requiem for populism," as some anticipated.[101] Instead, the new era may be associated with the transformation and revival of populism under a new guise, one that is shaped by the breakdown of more institutionalized forms of political representation and the fiscal constraints that inhere in a context of public indebtedness and a diminished state apparatus. The Peruvian case suggests that this new, more "liberal" variant of populism not only represents a different economic project than traditional, "statist" populism,[102] but also rests upon new social bases (that is, informal sectors rather than organized labor) and a new articulation of the contradiction between "the people" and the "power bloc."

Like classical populism, this new form of liberal populism is likely to manifest contradictions and limitations. Once the initial political dividends of inflation control have worn off, the long-term capacity of targeted social programs to provide political cover for an economic model that generates growth without employment is subject to doubt, especially when social programs rely on one-shot infusions of financial resources. When one out of every five workers in the nation's capital is a street vendor, as is the case in Lima, it is hardly surprising that jobs are a more salient concern for most individuals than public works projects.[103] Likewise, there is an inherent volatility in political systems that are devoid of representative institutions, and thus rely on fluctuating personalist appeal for legitimation and aggregation. Such expressions of

---

[101] Drake (fn.15).

[102] Methodologists may note that these liberal and statist forms of populism correspond to what Collier and Mahon (fn. 21) call "classical" categories, rather than subtypes of a radial category. That is, since both of these forms are capable of manifesting all the core properties of populism outlined above, the attachment of a descriptive adjective signifies the addition, not subtraction, of defining attributes—in this case, alternative expressions of populist economic policies.

[103] See Francisco Verdera V., "La Preocupación por el Empleo," *Debate* 16 (July–August 1994), 43–44.

populism do little to bridge the chasm that separates the state from society in Latin America, and they can leave personalist leaders dangerously isolated, as evidenced by the failure of Fujimori to transfer his own popularity to candidates of his choosing in Peru's 1993 municipal elections. The more enduring classical populists built party or labor organizations to complement their personal appeal and integrate followers into the political system, something the new generation of liberal populists has shown little inclination to do. Although the inclusiveness of classical populism was always selective, it was far deeper than that of liberal populism, which spawns little organization, no political role for citizens beyond that of voting, and a more limited and exclusive set of economic rewards.

Finally, the "politics of antipolitics" is a weak substitute for the cross-class nationalist appeal of classical populism, and it is likely to be self-limiting as a populist formula for legitimizing an incumbent government. However potent it may be for political outsiders and protest movements, it becomes self-negating once the outsiders displace the traditional political class, turn into incumbents, and construct a new political establishment. It is therefore a formula that is not equally effective during all phases of a populist phenomenon, much less one that provides a permanent governing rationale, which helps explain Fujimori's turn toward economic populism after he swept away competing institutions in the 1992 *autogolpe* and became the embodiment of the political establishment. The "politics of antipolitics" becomes especially dissonant at a time when Fujimori's governing style and relationship with the masses are increasingly reminiscent of more traditional politicians and populist leaders.

These limitations may be sources of long-term instabilities, but they hardly diminish the importance of *Fujimorismo*; populism, after all, has never been noted for producing sustainable economic improvements or durable governing formulas. The importance of the Peruvian case rests in its demonstration of the potency and viability of liberal populism during periods of institutional crisis and social transformation. As such, it has profound implications for opponents as well as supporters of neoliberalism. For opponents, it warns against the comforting assumption that neoliberalism is incapable of generating a broad base of political support, and thus will inevitably produce a popular backlash in favor of progressive alternatives. Indeed, it provides compelling evidence that neoliberalism is both a consequence and a cause of the weakening and fragmentation of the popular collective actors who are essential to any progressive alternative.

For those who share in the "Washington consensus" favoring neoliberal reforms, the Peruvian case is a sobering reminder that economic restructuring may come with unexpected political ramifications. Proponents of neoliberalism may find it unsettling to contemplate whether they are presiding over the transformation and revival of populism, rather than its burial. More important, the emergence of liberal populism casts a large shadow over facile assumptions that free markets and representative democracy are kindred phenomena. The historical development of representative democracy in the West was heavily influenced by the efforts of subaltern groups to organize collectively to exert political control over market insecurities;[104] in order to eliminate such controls, modern neoliberal technocrats have routinely suppressed or circumvented the mechanisms of accountability that inhere in democratic organization. The correlation between neoliberalism, deinstitutionalization, and autocratic rule is hardly unique to Peru, or even Latin America, as there are clear parallels to recent events in the former Soviet bloc. Although personality may be an effective force for political aggregation and legitimation in tumultuous times, the shifting sands of public infatuation and the whims of autocratic rulers are hardly desirable long-term foundations for the neoliberal edifice, as the Russian case amply demonstrates. As such, the predilection for autocracy—for the political power to implement economic reforms unencumbered by institutionalized mechanisms of representation and accountability—is likely to clash with both the political need to establish institutional roots in civil society and the popular tendency to rely on democratic organization as a counterweight to individual market insecurities. These tensions can be expected to shape the evolutionary dynamics of liberal populism in the years to come; more fundamentally, they will be decisive in determining whether the denouement of the neoliberal era will be democratic or authoritarian.

[104] See Dietrich Rueschemeyer, Evelyne Huber Stephens, and John D. Stephens, *Capitalist Development and Democracy* (Chicago: University of Chicago Press, 1991); or Karl Polanyi, *The Great Transformation* (New York: Farrar and Rinehart, 1944).

THE POPULIST ROAD TO MARKET REFORM
Policy and Electoral Coalitions in Mexico and Argentina

By EDWARD L. GIBSON*

INTRODUCTION

DURING his tenure of office between 1988 and 1994, Mexican President Carlos Salinas de Gortari proclaimed a new guiding ideology for his presidency and his country's ruling party, the Partido Revolucionario Institucional (PRI). Liberalismo Social (Social Liberalism) would replace the statist and corporatist Nacionalismo Revolucionario (Revolutionary Nationalism) as the vision advanced by the party in a new age of free-market development. During much the same period, five thousand miles away, Argentina's President Carlos Saúl Menem committed his government to the pursuit of a new development model, the Economía Popular de Mercado (Popular Market Economy), a policy shift that reversed the Peronist party's historic commitment to state-led economic development. These leaders headed the two most important populist movements in Latin America, movements that had strong ties to labor and embodied their countries' pursuit of state-led economic development. The policy shifts thus had tremendous coalitional and institutional consequences. They implied a restructuring of the social coalitions that had historically supported the Peronist party and the PRI, and the alteration of many of the representational arrangements that linked key social actors to the state. Although these reforms reversed historic policy commitments and

* I would like to thank Robert Ayres, Valerie Bunce, Ernesto Calvo, Tulia Falleti, José María Ghio, Judith Gibson, Bela Greskovits, Michael Hanchard, Blanca Heredia, Mark Jones, Kevin Middlebrook, María Victoria Murillo, Mick Moore, Hector Schamis, Ben Ross Schneider, Jeffrey Winters, and Meredith Woo-Cumings for comments on earlier versions of this article. The Centro de Investigación y Docencia Económicas (CIDE) in Mexico and the Universidad Torcuato Di Tella in Argentina provided much appreciated forums for presentation of the article. I am grateful as well to the Center for International and Comparative Studies and the Department of Political Science at Northwestern University for the financial support that made the research for this article possible.

adversely affected the parties' key social constituencies, both parties handily won their respective presidential elections held in 1994 in Mexico and in 1995 in Argentina.

How did leaders of the PRI and the Peronist party carry out such shifts and remain electorally viable? What coalitional characteristics, which shaped the dynamics of these transitional periods, did these movements share? This essay offers a rethinking of the internal coalitional dynamics of these broad-based national parties. The literature on populist coalition building has tended to stress the importance of these parties' strategic links to labor and developmental cross-class alliances. This essay, however, conceives of these parties as unions of two distinctive regional subcoalitions and suggests a historical division of labor between the subcoalitions in the realms of policy-making and electoral politics. Peronism and the PRI are thus understood as encompassing a "metropolitan" coalition and a "peripheral" coalition. The metropolitan coalition functioned primarily as a policy coalition that gave support to the parties' development strategies. The peripheral coalition functioned largely as an electoral coalition, which carries the burden of generating electoral majorities. This perspective, which stresses the interaction between the electoral and policy-making dimensions of coalition building, sheds light on important complexities in the historical evolution of these parties and on the current process of coalitional realignment and economic reform.

METROPOLITAN AND PERIPHERAL COALITIONS IN THE EVOLUTION OF POPULISM

The literature on the origins and dynamics of populist parties in Latin America is vast, and the PRI and Peronism have taken up the lion's share of attention. Debates on the historical meaning, coalitional dynamics, and ideologies of these parties have dominated Latin American scholarship, but consensus exists on a number of points: populist parties incorporated labor and popular sectors into political life, just as mass politics transformed national politics in the early and mid-twentieth century. Building on this incorporation, they linked labor to nascent cross-class support coalitions for state-guided capitalist development.[1] Regardless of the many differences that separated individual cases, the

---

[1] In Latin American studies the "populism" concept has been subject to continuous stretching over the years to include types of movements, policy-making patterns, ideologies, coalitions, styles, or 'ways of doing politics.' Some conceptualizations have included all these features. The concept of "populism" in this essay is more restrictive, denoting parties that incorporated labor during the historical and developmental period mentioned above. These characteristics link Peronism and the PRI conceptually to

strategic link to labor and the developmentalist policy orientation were two features indissolubly linked to populist parties generally and to Peronism and the PRI in particular.[2] Peronism and the PRI have thus been largely analyzed as labor-based movements whose political and electoral clout resided in the most urbanized and modern regions of the country.[3] These were, after all, the movements that put an end to oligarchic rule and organized new social forces for the reorganization of their countries' political economies. But the picture is not complete until we look more carefully at other aspects of the populist coalitions, aspects which have not received much attention relative to the much analyzed relationship of these parties to labor. Labor and the developmental coalition to which it was linked were important, but often electorally insufficient components of the PRI and Peronist coalitions. If we look at these movements as national parties, as mobilizers of electoral victories throughout the national territory, we see that there was more to populism. The other less illuminated, perhaps even seedier, side of populism is its rural, nonmetropolitan side. In the metropolis, populism was a revolutionary force, incorporating labor into its fold and promoting a new class of domestically oriented entrepreneurs as carriers of new state-led strategies of economic development. It was the metropolis that gave populism its modern face—that gave it the social and economic clout to build a new economic order. It was the periphery, however, that linked populism to the traditional order, gave it coherence as a national electoral force, and extended its reach throughout the national territory.

such movements as, Alianza Popular Revolucionaria Americana (APRA) in Peru, Acción Democrática in Venezuela, and Varguismo in Brazil. For a less restrictive definition of populism, see Kenneth M. Roberts, "Neoliberalism and the Transformation of Populism in Latin America: The Peruvian Case," *World Politics* 48 (October 1995).

[2] See, for example, such works as Ruth Berins Collier and David Collier, *Shaping the Political Arena: Critical Junctures, the Labor Movement, and Regime Dynamics in Latin America* (Princeton: Princeton University Press, 1991); Michael L. Conniff, ed., *Latin American Populism in Comparative Perspective* (Albuquerque: University of New Mexico Press, 1982); Ruth Berins Collier, *The Contradictory Alliance: State-Labor Relations and Regime Change in Mexico* (Berkeley: Institute of International and Area Studies, University of California, 1992); Kevin Middlebrook, *The Paradox of Revolution: Labor, the State, and Authoritarianism in Mexico* (Baltimore: Johns Hopkins University Press, 1995); Miguel Murmis and Juan Carlos Portantiero, *Estudios sobre los orígenes del peronismo* (Buenos Aires: Siglo XXI Editores, 1971); Joel Horowitz, *Argentine Unions, the State, and the Rise of Perón, 1930–1945* (Berkeley: Institute of International and Area Studies, University of California, 1990); Juan Carlos Torre, ed., *La formación del sindicalismo peronista* (Buenos Aires: Editorial Legasa, 1988); and Guillermo A. O'Donnell, *Modernization and Bureaucratic Authoritarianism: Studies in South American Politics* (Berkeley: Institute for International and Area Studies, University of California, 1971).

[3] The role of the PRI in mobilizing peasants, as a pillar of its corporatist structure, has been widely addressed, but analysis has rarely gone beyond its controlled and subservient status within the coalition. The functions of the regional subcoalition, which organized peasant and rural sectors, in the maintenance and internal power struggles of the PRI have been understudied aspects of the party's politics.

As electoral movements, the PRI and Peronism were national coalitions that harbored two very disparate and regionally based subcoalitions. These were dualistic movements, encompassing at once the most modern sectors of society and the most traditional, the most urbanized and the most rural, the most dynamic and the most stagnant, the most radical and the most conservative. The secret of their success was due largely to their ability to make effective the dualistic nature of their societies in the coalitional realm by bringing together the most antagonistic sectors of society and giving them distinct tasks in the creation and reproduction of populist power.

The metropolitan coalition was located largely in urban areas and economically important regions of the country.[4] Its most important constituencies were labor and business groups, geared toward the domestic economy and dependent on state subsidies and protection. These social groups were vital for the implementation of developmentalist economic policies. They generated support for state policies and ensured, through corporatist bargaining, mobilization, and legitimation, the viability of the development model and the governability tasks of the political system.

The peripheral coalition was located primarily in rural areas and relatively underdeveloped regions. Its primary constituencies were peasants, rural labor, and town dwellers, but it also included local elites who controlled local populations and could deliver their votes and support to the national party. These constituencies remained, by and large, marginalized from the design and implementation of the development strategies pursued from the center, but in the organization and maintenance of populist power, they were not merely a residual coalition. As the Peronists and the PRI became consolidated as national parties, they came to play a vital role in maintaining their parties' electoral strength. Populist parties came to rely increasingly on the peripheral coalitions to deliver national electoral majorities. Tradition and modernity coexisted in Peronism and the PRI because of the indispensability of the peripheral coalition for the maintenance of populist power.

THE ORIGINS OF THE POPULIST COALITIONS

THE FORMATION OF THE PERONIST PARTY

The mobilization of labor in Argentina's metropolitan regions was decisive in the rapid rise to power of army colonel Juan Perón after the

[4] The term "metropolitan" is thus employed here to mean more than "urban," although the relationships described in the following pages tend to accentuate levels of urbanization. The term here denotes the most dynamic and economically dominant areas of the country.

1943 military coup that overthrew a conservative civilian regime. Appointed secretary of labor shortly after the coup, Perón galvanized the moribund agency and made it an aggressive champion of workers' rights. He also used his position in office to tie labor organizations more closely to the state, to purge them of communist and opposition influences, and to build networks of supporters in the labor movement. Perón thus used the power of the state to tap a constituency that, in spite of its organizational clout and importance in the country's urban occupational structure, had been largely unclaimed by the national political establishment.

In 1946 Perón ran for president as the candidate of the Partido Laborista, an independent labor party founded by union leaders in 1945. The party was modeled on European social democratic parties and was seen by its founders as an autonomous vehicle for labor representation in the electoral arena.[5] The Partido Laborista's links to organized labor gave Perón a powerful organizational base for running his presidential campaign and for mobilizing the urban vote.

In regions with a negligible proletarian population, however, Perón's 1946 electoral victory was driven by other factors. The Partido Laborista's labor networks gave his campaign some organization in the capitals of less backward provinces in the interior, but provided it with little access to voters in towns and rural areas or to urban voters not controlled by the fledgling regional labor organizations. These areas tended to be firmly controlled by existing caudillo-dominated electoral machines. A national presidential victory required more than powerful organization in metropolitan regions. It also required the formation of an electoral coalition in the peripheral regions of the country.

To this end, Perón reached out to the enforcers of the periphery's status quo. Throughout the interior provinces, he recruited local conservative leaders into his alliance, from the top leaders of provincial governments to local party hacks who controlled electoral machines in rural areas and small towns.[6] The defection of conservative caudillos facilitated the massive transfer of votes from conservative electoral networks throughout the country to the 1946 Peronist ticket.[7]

---

[5] Murmis and Portantiero (fn. 2).

[6] The Junta Renovadora, a conservative faction of the Radical Party dominated by leaders from the "interior" provinces, supported Perón's candidacy. So did the Partido Independiente, a small group of provincial conservative-party leaders. These two electoral groupings and additional coalition building with local caudillos helped, build support in areas beyond the Partido Laborista's geographical reach. See Darío Cantón, *Elecciones y partidos políticos en la Argentina* (Buenos Aires: Siglo XXI Editores, 1973); and Sandra J. Aidar, "Electoral Reform in Argentina and the Revival of the Peronist Party" (Master's thesis, MIT, February 1994).

[7] Systematic case studies of the Peronist party's formation in the interior provinces are unfortunately almost nonexistent. However, a glimpse of processes taking place throughout the country is provided

In this way, Perón forged the key pillars of his national electoral coalition. In metropolitan regions he mobilized the unincorporated working class as the primary constituency of his new political movement. Outside those areas he co-opted existing provincial electoral machines, which delivered large numbers of votes from among the rural poor and town dwellers to the Partido Laborista's electoral campaign. After the 1946 election President Perón transformed this circumstantial electoral alliance into a new national political party, the Partido Justicialista.

The creation of the Partido Justicialista established Peronism's electoral presence throughout the country. It also created a new internal balance of power between the movement's national coalition members. The social and political forces that had brought Perón to power underwent major reorganization in the period following his election. The union movement experienced a dramatic expansion of its membership, and its organizations were strengthened and linked closely to the state. In the metropolitan regions, labor organizations, with their expanding mass mobilizational capabilities, became the primary organizers of the Peronist electoral machine. After the 1946 elections the union movement's dominance over party leaders was almost complete in the metropolitan areas' electoral organization.[8]

Political caudillos remained important, however, for mobilizing votes outside the working class, and they were most important in less developed regions with few industrial workers and union members. In the 1940s the industrial working class was largely located in the greater Buenos Aires urban area, and to a lesser extent in such budding industrial cities as Rosario and Córdoba. Throughout the rest of the country, however, traditional social structures dominated, and the paternalistic political control of caudillos held sway. The conservative political machines that had controlled political life for decades, and which had

---

by two studies of the 1946 election in the provinces of Córdoba and Buenos Aires, both of which experienced endorsements of Perón by prominent conservative leaders. Luís González Esteves and Ignacio Llorente report a significant transfer of conservative organizational resources and votes to the Peronist ticket. The exceptions were large urban areas, where the working-class constituencies of Peronism were congregated. See Luis Gonzáles Esteves, "Las elecciones de 1946 en la provincia de Córdoba," and Ignacio Llorente, "Alianzas políticas en el surgimiento del peronismo: El caso de la provincia de Buenos Aires," in Manuel Mora y Araujo and Ignacio Llorente, eds., El voto peronista: Ensayos de sociología electoral argentino (Buenos Aires: Editorial Sudámericana, 1980). A more recent work, both historical and partisan, provides details of local-elite networks that supported the rise of Peronism in the nortwestern province of La Rioja, President Menem's home province. See Hugo Orlando Quevedo, El Partido Peronista en La Rioja, 3 vols. (Córdoba: Marcos Lerner Editora, 1991).

   [8] Manuel Mora y Araujo, "Introducción: La sociología electoral y la comprensión del peronismo," in Mora y Araujo and Llorente (fn. 7), 49.

helped put Perón in power in 1946, were dominant facts of local political life. Incorporating them into the national party was vital to making Peronism a truly national electoral force.

Thus, the period following Perón's assumption of the presidency was marked by the reorganization of the peripheral electoral coalition that had helped him win. Temporary deals with autonomous conservative machines were followed by the outright absorption of these leaders and organizations into the national Peronist party. Former conservative caudillos became Peronist caudillos, or their organizations and followers were absorbed by the national party and given new leaders from among their ranks. Control of the state also gave Perón the ability to engage in the autonomous mobilization of rural and nonmetropolitan constituencies. This mobilization, however, was far less threatening to local power relations than the mobilization then taking place in the country's metropolitan regions. Measures passed during Perón's first term, such as the Estatuto del Peón, extended benefits and legal rights to rural laborers, but did not threaten existing land-tenure patterns or disrupt local-elite control over economic life.[9] They were, however, effective in mobilizing support among the lower social strata for a national Peronist party whose local political and social structures closely resembled those that had dominated life in the pre-Peronist political order.

With the founding of the Partido Justicialista, the autonomous electoral creation of the Argentine labor movement, the Partido Laborista, was dissolved. In its place, Perón created a national party supported by two distinctive and regionally specific pillars. The urban labor organizations, which had declared in the founding documents of the Partido Laborista that no "members of the oligarchy" would be permitted in its ranks,[10] were incorporated alongside the conservative-dominated party machines of the interior regions of the country. By doing this, Perón institutionalized not only the Peronist party's presence throughout the nation, but also a new internal balance of power in the party. As a national party, Peronism would not be exclusively dependent on its powerful and highly mobilized constituencies in the labor movement. Their clout in the area of mobilization would be countered by the electoral weight of the caudillo-dominated and socially heterogeneous constituencies in the peripheral coalition. Perón was thus able to fuse disparate coalitions under one national party structure, and each coalition provided a counterweight to the other. The two pillars were rooted

[9] Robert J. Alexander, *The Perón Era* (New York: Columbia University Press, 1951), 141–53.

[10] Cited in Murmis and Portantiero (fn. 2), 96.

in very different social contexts and organized by different types of machines: corporatist and mobilizational in the metropolis, clientelistic and conservative in the periphery. The Peronist party's seeming invulnerability at the polls in subsequent decades as well as the continuous (and often polarizing) tensions between the party's metropolitan labor organizations and its provincial party organizations were both results of Peronism's successful fusion of these two national subcoalitions.

Electoral studies of the Peronist vote, written during the 1970s, provide a sense of the continuities involved in the relations between metropolitan and peripheral coalitions after Perón's rise to power. The most consistent finding is the negative relationship between the Peronist vote and indicators of economic development and modernization as the Peronist coalition became established.[11] In the 1946 election the Peronist vote was positively associated with such variables as industrialization, urbanization, and size of the working-class population, and ambiguously associated with indicators of economic backwardness. These results reflected Perón's reliance in 1946 on labor mobilization and the weakness in the organization of the independent Peronist electorate in the interior. However, by 1954 these relationships had changed. Peronism was most positively associated with indicators of social and economic backwardness, and most negatively associated with indicators of economic development and modernization.[12] Studies of the 1973 presidential elections suggest that these tendencies persisted after decades of repression and electoral proscription of the Peronist movement by authoritarian governments. In the 1973 presidential elections, Peronism's performance in rural and underdeveloped regions far outstripped its performance in urban regions, a performance which gave the Peronist party its slim national electoral majority in March 1973.[13]

<hr />

[11] As Mora y Araujo and Smith note, summarizing the literature on the subject, "the conclusion has been categorical: the higher the level of development, the lower the Peronist vote." Manuel Mora y Araujo and Peter Smith, "Peronism and Economic Development: The 1973 Elections," in Frederick C. Turner, ed., *Juan Perón and the Reshaping of Argentina* (Pittsburgh: University of Pittsburgh Press, 1983), 177. Electoral studies of Peronism that have noted this trend include Ignacio Llorente, "La composición social del movimiento peronista hacia 1954," in Mora y Araujo and Llorente (fn. 7); Peter Smith, "The Social Bases of Peronism," *Hispanic American Historical Review* 52 (1972); Lars Shoultz, *The Populist Challenge: Argentine Electoral Behavior in the Postwar Era* (Chapel Hill: University of North Carolina Press, 1983); Manuel Mora y Araujo, "La estructura social del peronismo: Un análisis interprovincial," *Desarrollo Económico* 14 (1975); Darío Cantón and Jorge R. Jorrat, "Occupation and Vote in Urban Argentina: The March 1973 Presidential Election," *Latin American Research Review* 13, no. 1 (1978); and Douglas Masden and Peter G. Snow, *The Charismatic Bond: Political Behavior in Time of Crisis* (Cambridge: Harvard University Press, 1991).

[12] This pattern is detailed in Llorente (fn. 11).

[13] In the March 1973 election, the Peronist party consistently received over 60 percent of the vote in rural districts, while failing to get a majority in most urban districts. As Mora y Araujo noted, "It is very clear that if only those districts with urban populations higher than 40 percent had been counted,

TABLE 1
CORRELATIONS BETWEEN SELECTED SOCIOECONOMIC VARIABLES
AND THE PERONIST VOTE[a]

	1946	1954	March 1973	Sept. 1973
Per capita product	.07	-.39	-.75	-.80
Illiteracy	-.08	.63	—	—
Literacy	—	—	-.59	-.59
Urbanization	.20	-.48	-.64	-.55
EAP in primary sector[b]	-.24	.28	.28	.12
EAP in secondary sector[b]	.32	-.18	.03	-.04
EAP in tertiary sector[b]	.09	-.34	-.11	-.36
Urban working class	.30	-.14	-.39	-.40

SOURCES: Calculations for 1946 and 1954 from Ignacio Llorente, "La composición social del movimiento peronista hacia 1954"; calculations for 1973 from Manuel Mora y Araujo, "Las bases estructurales del Peronismo"; in Mora y Araujo and Llorente, eds., *El voto peronista: Ensayos de sociología electoral argentina* (Buenos Aires: Editorial Sudamericana, 1980).
[a] N=479 electoral counties. Significance levels of coefficients not listed.
[b] EAP=Economically active population.

The coefficients listed in Table 1[14] measure correlations between the Peronist vote and selected socioeconomic indicators from the Argentine census, giving an indication of the nonmetropolitan bias to the Peronist vote which emerged after 1946.[15]

---

the Peronist party would not have attained the 50 percent vote total which gave it its victory in the March elections." Manuel Mora y Araujo, "Las bases estructurales del Peronismo," in Mora y Araujo and Llorente (fn. 7), 423.

[14] Working from a similar database, Manuel Mora y Araujo and Peter Smith provide further support for this argument in a multiple regression analysis of the 1973 elections, in which indicators of social deprivation and underdevelopment have the strongest positive impact on the Peronist vote, while indicators of urbanization register a strong negative impact. See Mora y Araujo and Smith (fn. 11), 177–81.

[15] The correlations presented in Table 1 and elsewhere in this essay are ecological correlations; that is, they measure the association between aggregate economic indicators and aggregate electoral results for given geographic units (in this case, Argentine electoral counties, which today number 520). The unit of analysis is not the individual voter, but the geographic unit. The negative associations between such variables as "urban working class" and Peronist party vote should not, therefore, be interpreted as indications of the preferences of working-class individuals, but of Peronist electoral performance in geographic areas where workers live. These tend to be areas of high urbanization and economic development, which also include other social sectors whose electoral preferences may differ dramatically from those of working-class voters. In fact, studies based on survey data or urban-area data sets consistently find strong working-class support for the Peronist party. See, for example, Jeane Kirkpatrick, *Leader and Vanguard in Mass Society: A Study of Peronist Argentina* (Cambridge: MIT Press, 1971); Masden and Snow (fn. 11); Schoultz (fn. 11); Peter Ranis, *Argentine Workers: Peronism and Contemporary Class Consciousness* (Pittsburgh: University of Pittsburgh Press, 1992); Smith (fn. 11); and Gino Germani, "El surgimiento del peronismo: El rol de los obreros y de los migrantes internos," *Desarrollo Económico* 13 (October–December, 1973).

253

The Origins of the PRI in Mexico

The formation of what is today named the Partido Revolucionario Institucional went through several stages. The first stage was the creation by Plutarco Elías Calles of the Partido Nacional Revolucionario (PNR) in 1929. The creation of the PNR was first and foremost an effort to impose central authority on a fractious nation in the aftermath of the armed conflicts and intraelite struggles that had rocked the nation since the outbreak of the 1910 revolution. The PNR's founders sought to bring together under one institutional umbrella the disparate regional power holders that had emerged from these conflicts. They also sought to establish procedures of negotiation and political succession that would institutionalize intraelite conflicts and provide electoral hegemony to elites in control of national and regional governments.[16] The PNR was thus an effort to organize the existing Mexican political strata, whose composition was as regionally varied as the reach of the Mexican revolution itself. They included progressive and conservative governors, local revolutionary caciques, landlords, and military caudillos.[17] In an effort to establish institutional control throughout the territory, the PNR incorporated the array of old and new, revolutionary and prerevolutionary power holders who were left standing after decades of armed conflict.[18]

---

[16] A detailed treatment of the formation of the PNR is provided by Luis Javier Garrido, *El partido de la Revolución institucionalizada: La formación del nuevo Estado en México, 1928–1945* (Mexico City: Siglo XXI Editores, 1986). For this period see also, Jean Meyer, *Estado y sociedad con Calles*, vol. 11 of *Historia de la Revolución Mexicana* (Mexico City: El Colegio de México, 1977); and Lorenzo Meyer, Rafael Segovia, and Alejandra Lajous, *Los inicios de la institucionalización*, vol. 12 of *Historia de la Revolución Mexicana* (Mexico City: El Colegio de México, 1978); and Samuel León, "Del partido de partidos al partido de sectores," in Carmen Corona, ed., *El partido en el poder: Seis ensayos* (Mexico City: Partido Revolucionario Institucional-Instituto de Estudios Políticos, Económicos y Sociales [IEPES], 1990).

[17] The terms "caudillos" and "caciques" seem to have slightly different meanings in Argentina and Mexico. In Argentina, "caudillo" denotes a political boss. The Argentine caudillo can be a local boss or a national leader. In Mexico, "cacique" explicitly denotes a local political boss, while "caudillo" generally denotes a civilian or military political leader whose authority is national in scope. In both Mexico and Argentina, caciques and caudillos can draw their political authority from socioeconomic power relations, political institutions, or both. I am indebted to Blanca Heredia, of the Centro de Investigaciones y Docencia Económicas (CIDE), and Fernando Escalante, of the Colegio de México, for these distinctions. For typological and analytical discussions of this issue, see Fernando Díaz Díaz, *Caudillos y Caciques: Santa Anna y Juan Alvarez* (Mexico City: El Colegio de México, 1971), and Gilbert Joseph, "Caciquismo and the Revolution: Carrillo Puerto in Yucatán," in D. A. Brading, ed., *Caudillo and Peasant in the Mexican Revolution* (Cambridge: Cambridge University Press, 1980).

[18] As Alan Knight notes, "Through the 1920's and 1930's Mexican elites remained variegated and fractious, especially if the vital provincial, as against national, perspective is adopted. In parts of the south the plantocracy still ruled, albeit under pressure; the northern bourgeoisie prospered (at least until the later 1920's); and the new revolutionary elite—generals, above all, acquired property to match their power. But there were also elites, some of popular extraction, who depended on continued popular support for their advancement." Knight, "Mexico's Elite Settlement: Conjuncture and Consequences," in John Higley and Richard Gunther, eds., *Elites and Democratic Consolidation in Latin America and Southern Europe* (New York: Cambridge University Press, 1992), 128.

Responding to worker and peasant masses mobilized by the revolution was also a concern of PNR founders, but it was subordinated to the imperative of territorial consolidation. The PNR's creation was thus a deal between the center and the regions, involving the incorporation of regional elites into the national party in exchange for local autonomy. The party was organized territorially, with little or no efforts made toward the sectoral incorporation of the masses.[19]

The presidency of Lázaro Cárdenas from 1934 to 1940 temporarily shifted the party's internal balance of power in favor of sectoral incorporation of workers and peasants. In an effort to consolidate new power bases against the continuing influence of Callistas and their networks of regional power bosses, Cárdenas carried out the most sweeping labor and land-reform initiatives ever seen in the country's history.[20] During this period the first manifestations of what would become the metropolitan and peripheral coalitions emerged in the party's national coalitional structure. The national labor movement was mobilized as an official constituency of the party, an act that made it a pivotal part of the party's emerging metropolitan coalition. In the countryside, massive land-reform initiatives were accompanied by the sectoral organization of peasants and rural workers and their formal incorporation into the party structure. Cárdenas then spearheaded the reform of the party itself, renaming it the Partido de la Revolución Mexicana (PRM) and converting its territorial organization to the functional organization of national peasant, labor, and middle sector groups.[21] With the functional reorganization of the party, Cárdenas thus empowered new social groups whose loyalty and political clout strengthened the national party leadership. By adding a new line of cleavage to the previously dominant regional cleavage within the party, he also diluted or neutralized those elite groups whose power had resided in the party's territorial structures. The tension between territorially based elites and functionally

[19] In fact, the territorial deal underlying the PNR was a mechanism for dealing with the threat of class conflict. In exchange for their support, the PNR offered regional elites protection against continued revolutionary change. See Garrido (fn. 16), 127–28.

[20] On the internal struggles that drove the Cárdenas reforms, see Wayne Cornelius, "Nation-building, Participation, and Distribution: The Politics of Social Reform under Cárdenas," in G. A. Almond, S. C. Flanagan, and R. J. Mundt, eds., *Crisis, Choice, and Change: Historical Studies in Political Development* (Boston: Little, Brown, 1973). See also Nora Hamilton, *The Limits of State Autonomy: Post-Revolutionary Mexico* (Princeton: Princeton University Press, 1982).

[21] The military was organized into a "sector" as well, but this sector was dissolved shortly thereafter. The reorganization of the PRM and party-constituency relations is analyzed in Middlebrook (fn. 2), and in Ruth Berins Collier (fn. 2). Detail on the dynamics of the Cárdenas presidency is provided by Luis González in *Los artífices del cardenismo*, vol. 14 of *Historia de la Revolución Mexicana* (Mexico City: El Colegio de México, 1979), and *Los días del presidente Cárdenas*, vol. 15 of *Historia de la Revolución Mexicana* (Mexico City: El Colegio de México, 1981).

organized sectors of the party would persist within the party to the present day.

The Cárdenas-led land reforms and peasant mobilizations had another effect on what would become the party's peripheral coalition. In regions affected by land reform, they placed party-controlled electoral machinery throughout the countryside. A result was the controlled mobilization of rural masses in support of national leaders and a large captive rural electorate that would become instrumental to the party's electoral success. Once the reformist euphoria of the Cardenista period subsided in the cóuntryside, a new system of rural electorate control remained in place. Caciques loyal to the PRM (later renamed PRI) came to replace those of pre-Cardenista days. Thereafter the PRI's peripheral coalition throughout the country would consist of a blend of revolutionary and prerevolutionary systems of rural electoral mobilization and control. In areas swept by the winds of the revolutionary periods, PRI caciques, dispensing land titles and party patronage, ensured the overwhelming support of rural voters for the ruling party. In areas that escaped the effects of the revolution, more traditional forms of cacique-led political and social control prevailed. The guardians of the old order were given free rein to perpetuate local power arrangements in exchange for reliably delivering massive PRI victories at election time.[22]

A glance at the PRI's electoral performance over the last several decades reveals the party's reliance oh the peripheral coalition. (See Table 2.) Prior to the 1970s the PRI enjoyed hegemonic status, and while its electoral margins were consistently larger in rural and less developed areas, it won overwhelmingly throughout the country.[23] The peripheral coalition was thus less important as a mobilizer of electoral majorities than as a guarantor of order and political support for the PRI-dominated regime throughout the country. Its importance as an electoral coalition, however, grew dramatically from the 1970s onward, as

---

[22] In both cases, of course, the mobilization and control of rural electorates were complemented, when needed, with electoral fraud. For an analysis of rural power dynamics in the postrevolutionary period, see Werner Tobler, "Peasants and the Shaping of the Revolutionary State, 1910–1940," in Friedrich Katz, ed., *Riot, Rebellion; and Revolution: Rural Social Conflict in Mexico* (Princeton: Princeton University Press, 1988). Illustrative local case studies include Guillemo de la Peña "Populism, Regional Power, and Political Mediation: Southern Jalisco, 1900–1980," in Eric Van Young, ed., *Mexico's Regions: Comparative History and Development* (San Diego: Center for U.S.-Mexican Studies, University of California, 1992); Romana Falcón, "Charisma, Tradition, and Caciquismo: Revolution in San Luis Potosí," in Katz (fn. 17); as well as essays in Brading (fn. 17).

[23] According to one study, between 1964 and 1976 the PRI averaged over 70 percent of the vote in highly urbanized areas, while its averages in rural areas exceeded 90 percent of the vote. Leopoldo Gomez, "Elections, Legitimacy, and Political Change in Mexico, 1977–1988" (Ph.D. diss., Georgetown University, 1991), 242.

TABLE 2
ELECTORAL SUPPORT FOR THE PRI BY LEVEL OF URBANIZATION

Level of Urbanization	1979	1982	1985	1988	1991
>95 % urban	54%	50%	44%	30%	48%
50–74% urban	71%	68%	61%	50%	61%
<25 % urban	84%	82%	78%	64%	71%

SOURCE: Joseph L. Klesner, "Realignment or Dealignment? Consequences of Economic Crisis and Restructuring for the Mexican Party System," in Maria Lorena Cook, Kevin J. Middlebrook, and Juan Molinar Horcasitas, eds., *The Politics of Economic Restructuring: State-Society Relations and Regime Change in Mexico* (San Diego: Center for U.S.-Mexican Studies, University of California, 1994), 165.

national elections became more competitive and the party faced growing electoral challenges in metropolitan areas.

The PRI's electoral support has been strongly correlated with indicators of ruralness, primary production, and illiteracy, and negatively correlated with indicators of urbanization, education, and occupations characteristic of the metropolitan economy. (See Table 3.) In spite of the party's historic role as an incorporator of working classes and a transformer of the metropolitan political economy, rural Mexico, in the words of one observer, "has been the PRI's bastion for six decades."[24] Furthermore, these trends increased as decades of stabilizing development changed the country's demographic and social structures. Ironically, the PRI's metropolitan constituencies, which were vital supporters and beneficiaries of the party's economic development policies, played an ever decreasing role in the generation of electoral majorities for the PRI.[25]

Populist leaders in Argentina and Mexico thus solved the problems of governance by bringing two distinctive subcoalitions together under one movement. In their founding periods, they succeeded in exploiting the two dominant lines of cleavage in national politics, class and region, and made both lines of cleavage the organizing principles of their national coalitional structures. Pact making between classes permitted Peronism and the PRI to seize the initiative in the transformation of the national political economy. Pact making between regions permitted

[24] Joseph L. Klesner, "Realignment or Dealignment? Consequences of Economic Crisis and Restructuring for the Mexican Party System," in Maria Lorena Cook, Kevin J. Middlebrook, and Juan Molinar Horcasitas, eds., *The Politics of Economic Restructuring: State-Society Relations and Regime Change in Mexico* (San Diego: Center for U.S.-Mexican Studies, University of California, 1994), 164.

[25] A multiple regression analysis carried out by Joseph Klesner from the same database in the above-cited study confirms the tendencies shown in Tables 2 and 3, particularly with regard to the impact of industrialization, urbanization, and education on the PRI vote. See Klessner (fn. 24), 170.

TABLE 3
CORRELATIONS BETWEEN ELECTORAL SUPPORT FOR THE PRI AND
SELECTED SOCIOECONOMIC VARIABLES[a]

	1967	1970	1982	1988	1991
% in localities >2,500	-.68	-.73	-.76	-.71	-.65
% with no schooling	.62	.61	.62	.49	.48
% with post-primary ed.	-.68	-.76	-.74	-.58	-.62
% EAP in primary sector[b]	.74	.80	.74	.60	.62
% EAP in secondary sector[b]	-.63	-.73	-.79	-.64	-.69
% EAP in tertiary sector[b]	-.72	-.75	-.44	-.32	-.35
Urban working class	NA	NA	-.80	-.66	-.66
Rural popular classes	NA	NA	.82	.67	.71

SOURCE: Joseph L. Klesner, "Realignment or Dealignment?" Consequences of Economic Crisis and Restructuring for the Mexican Party System," in Maria Lorena Cook, Kevin J. Middlebrook, and Juan Molinar Horcasitas, eds., *The Politics of Economic Restructuring: State-Society Relations and Regime Change in Mexico* (San Diego: Center for U.S.-Mexican Studies, University of California, 1994), 163.
[a]Range of N=159-290 federal districts. All correlations significant at the .001 level.
[b]EAP=Economically active population.

them to constitute themselves as national governing parties.[26] The contrasting social and political contexts in both subcoalitions also created very different local electoral situations. The populist parties' links to traditional and clientelistic power structures in the periphery made them electoral bastions, and the populist coalitions drew support from all social strata. In the more diverse metropolitan regions, the populist coalitions mobilized relatively fewer votes, had more organizational links to working and popular classes, and would become more vulnerable electorally to the effects of social change and organized political opposition.

INTERNATIONAL AND DOMESTIC CAUSES OF THE CURRENT
TRANSFORMATIONS OF PERONISM AND THE PRI

Pressures from global and domestic socioeconomic change converged and prompted major policy and coalitional shifts by the PRI and the Peronist party in the 1980s. Just as the crisis of the global economy in the 1930s led to the adoption of developmentalist economic policies and to the ascendance of populist coalitions, the global reorganization

[26] Although exploring the issue further is beyond the scope of this essay, it might be suggested that this successful institutional fusion of metropolitan and peripheral coalitions is one factor that distinguishes Peronism and the PRI from Varguismo in Brazil and might account for the greater endurance and cohesion of the former two cases.

of production and capital and the debt crisis of the 1980s signaled the beginning of the end for developmentalism and its support coalitions in Mexico and Argentina. The free-market policy reorientation was led in both countries by their historic populist parties. It also fell to these parties to restructure the populist coalitions that had undergirded decades of developmentalist policies.

But while international economic change drove the turn toward free-market development, the coalitional changes pushed by the PRI and Peronism also had a domestic electoral logic of their own. Even before the global economy put pressure on domestic policymakers, the populist electoral coalitions had been running out of steam. Much of this was due to secular changes in their countries' demographic and occupational structures. Rural to urban migration since the 1950s and 1960s had eroded the peripheral coalitions' electoral weight. The shrinking of the rural electorate was accompanied by changes in the demographic and occupational structures of the countries' metropolitan regions, notably the expansion of social sectors not linked to populist parties or state-controlled corporatist structures that had mobilized votes for the populist metropolitan coalitions.[27] In cities the expansion of populations employed in service activities, informal sectors, and white-collar occupations meant the expansion of a middle stratum of voters that had been most resistant to electoral mobilization by the populist parties' urban "pillars" in the labor movement and corporatist organizations. In effect, decades of social change and economic crisis had produced, in both countries, decline or stagnation in the electoral bastions of Peronism and the PRI, and significant growth in the social categories most negatively associated with populist party vote.[28]

---

[27] For studies on Mexico's changing social and occupational structure, see Emma Liliana Navarrete and Marta G. Vera Bolaños, eds., *Población y Sociedad* (Toluca, Mexico: El Colegio Mexiquense, 1994); Brigida Garcia, *Desarrollo económico y absorción de fuerza de trabajo en México, 1950–1980* (Mexico City: El Colegio de México, 1988); and Gloria Vázquez Rangel and Jesús Ramírez López, *Marginación y pobreza en México* (Mexico City: Editorial Ariel, 1995). For Argentina, see Susana Torrado, *Estructura social de la Argentina, 1945–1983* (Buenos Aires: Ediciones de la Flor, 1992); José Nun, "Cambios en la estructura social de la Argentina," in José Nun and Juan Carlos Portantiero, eds., *Ensayos sobre la transición democrática en la Argentina* (Buenos Aires: Puntosur, 1987); Hector Palomino, *Cambios ocupacionales y sociales en la Argentina, 1947–1985* (Buenos Aires: CISEA, 1987); and Alberto Minujín, et al., eds. *Cuesta abajo: Los nuevos pobres: Efectos de la crisis en la sociedad argentina* (Buenos Aires: Editorial Losada, 1992).

[28] Studies on Mexico analyzing the effect of social and demographic change on party vote include Juan Molinar Horcasitas, *El tiempo de la legitimidad* (Mexico City: Cal y Arena, 1992); Joseph Klesner, "Modernization, Economic Crisis, and Electoral Alignment in Mexico," *Mexican Studies/Estudios Mexicanos* 9 (Summer 1993); and Gómez (fn. 23). I deal with the impact of social and demographic change on Argentine electoral politics during the 1980s and 1990s in Edward L. Gibson, *Class and Conservative Parties: Argentina in Comparative Perspective* (Baltimore: Johns Hopkins University Press, 1996).

These secular trends made themselves felt in the populist parties'
electoral performance, producing a declining trend in electoral support
for the PRI and an electoral stagnation for the Peronist party. In Mexico
the PRI lost its electoral majorities in urban areas in the 1980s, and
while it maintained its majorities in rural areas, these too were on the
decline (see Table 2). Meanwhile, party opposition grew by leaps and
bounds, supported largely by middle and upper strata in the metropolitan regions.[29] The 1988 presidential elections put the PRI's electoral crisis into bold relief. It was able to claim the slimmest of victory margins
only after major electoral irregularities and denunciations of fraud by
the opposition. It was quite clear by this time that the PRI was on the
verge of losing not only its hegemonic status but also its ability to generate bare electoral majorities.

In Argentina the presidential elections of 1983 resulted in Peronism's
first electoral defeat. This event signaled the end of the iron law of Argentine elections, which assumed Peronist victories in freely held elections. A variety of circumstantial factors contributed to this defeat, but
the secular trends discussed above played an important part. The peripheral coalition's contribution to the total national vote of the party
declined noticeably from the 1973 election and has remained at this
new level ever since.[30] This was compounded by the party's poor performance in the metropolitan regions, which demonstrated a clear
aversion by affluent voters to the electoral campaign mobilized by the
party's labor supporters.[31] The 1989 Peronist electoral victory, which
took place amid a profound hyperinflationary crisis, appeared to signal
a revival of the classic Peronist coalition. This, however, was to be the
last flexing of its populist muscle. Thereafter it would be dramatically
restructured.

[29] See Klesner (fn. 24); Molinar Horcasitas (fn. 28); and Yemile Mizrahi, "A New Conservative Opposition in Mexico: The Politics of Entrepreneurs in Chihuahua (1983–1992)" (Ph.D. diss., University
of California, Berkeley, 1994).

[30] One measure of this tendency is the proportion of votes received by Peronism from the country's
less developed provinces, calculated here as all provinces and districts excluding Buenos Aires province,
the Federal District, Córdoba, Santa Fe, and Mendoza. After 1973 this proportion declined. Since
1946 the poorest provinces provided the following proportion of Peronism's total votes: 1946, 23 percent; 1951, 30 percent; 1973, 37 percent; 1983, 27 percent; 1989, 28 percent; 1995, 27 percent. Percentages for 1946–73 were taken from Mora y Araujo (fn. 13). Percentages for 1983–95 were
calculated from official election results.

[31] In one key urban district, the city of Buenos Aires, the 1983 election results constituted a sharp
acceleration of a declining trend of support for the Peronist party. The following election totals for the
party detail this trend: 1946 presidential elections, 53 percent; 1954 congressional elections, 54 percent; 1973 presidential elections, 37 percent; 1983 presidential elections, 27 percent. Luis Gonzáles
Esteves and Ignacio Llorente, "Elecciones y preferencial políticas en Capital Federal y Gran Buenos
Aires: El 30 de Octubre de 1983," in Natalio Botana et al., eds., La Argentina Electoral (Buenos Aires:
Editorial Sudamericana, 1985).

The combined effects of international economic pressure and domestic social change placed strains on the policy-making and electoral capabilities of Peronism and the PRI. It is thus useful to understand the current restructuring of the populist coalitions in light of both these dimensions. Global economic pressures produced a clear policy-making logic to the recrafting of populist coalitions: to identify the beneficiaries of neoliberal reform and mobilize them in support of a new economic model. But this recrafting also had an electoral logic: to adapt the populist coalitions to long-term social changes and render them electorally viable in new contexts of social heterogeneity and urbanization of politics. The need to establish new social bases of support for free-market development converged with the need to build new electoral coalitions for populist parties in decline.

The main target of transformation became the metropolitan coalition. The historic pillars of the metropolitan coalition were obviously no longer suited to supporting the development model being adopted by the governing party leaders. Neither were they delivering the goods electorally. Thus, new constituencies and organizations had to be developed in metropolitan regions that would perform both these tasks. The division of labor between policy-making and generating electoral majorities could not continue to be regionally determined. In essence, the metropolitan coalition had to be made both relevant in the policy realm and viable in the electoral realm.

RECASTING THE METROPOLITAN COALITION

BUSINESS AND LABOR IN THE REMAKING OF POPULIST POLICY COALITIONS

Populist leaders had used the power of the state to forge new social coalitions at the start of the developmentalist age in the 1930s and 1940s. They would do so again at the start of the neoliberal age in the 1980s and 1990s. The recasting of the populist policy coalition in metropolitan regions involved the use of state power to reward winners and neutralize losers, to forge alliances with new constituencies, and to rearrange relations with old constituencies. It also involved the opening of new channels of access to policymakers for the coalition's new social protagonists and the dismantling of the institutional structures that had linked old constituencies to the decision-making process. At a general level, it can be asserted that these changes shifted the balance of power within the policy coalition away from labor and toward business.

However, if this were the only dimension, then it would merely be a continuation of the decades-long pattern whereby business interests in the pursuit of developmentalist policies have prevailed over those of labor. The objectives pursued in the 1980s and 1990s were more nuanced and institutionally discontinuous. They were more nuanced because they involved the selection of winners within both business and labor—the more concentrated and internationally competitive sectors of business and those parts of the labor movement that were linked to those sectors and were able to gain economic and political benefits from the decentralization of the labor movement and the flexibilization of industry-labor relations.[32] They were institutionally discontinuous because they involved the dismantling of legal, regulatory, and financial frameworks that for decades had undergirded the labor movement's institutional power.

In both Mexico and Argentina the plan toward business involved the building of a new strategic relationship with the most diversified, concentrated, and internationally competitive sectors of business. Ties to domestically oriented industrialists and nondiversified, single-sector firms—the traditional business supporters of populist coalitions—were weakened. Corporatist organizations that had traditionally linked them to state decision makers were marginalized in favor of new institutional channels or direct state-firm links for the beneficiaries of economic reform.

From the beginning of their administrations, Presidents Salinas and Menem actively courted leaders of major business firms for the new economic models being pursued.[33] The presidents affirmed publicly the importance of large-scale modern entrepreneurs, with their links to foreign capital and technology. Political cooperation in the formulation and implementation of economic policy between populist-controlled governments and big business reached new heights. In Mexico, access to state policymakers by leaders of large business and financial concerns

[32] On the "modernization" of sectors of the Mexican labor movement and its role in President Salinas's coalition-building strategies, see Ilán Bizberg, "Restructuracion productiva y transformacion del modelo de relaciones industriales: 1988–1994," *Foro Internacional*, no. 143–144 (January–June, 1996). The different strategies of adaptation by sectors of the Argentine labor movement to President Menem's reform policies are analyzed by Maria Victoria Murillo in "Organizational Autonomy and the Marketization of Corporatism," in Douglas Chalmers et al., eds., *The New Politics of Inequality in Latin America: Rethinking Participation and Representation* (New York: Oxford University Press, 1997).

[33] During his presidential campaign, Peronist candidate Carlos Menem was somewhat discrete about his overtures toward business. His discretion, however, was not shared by candidate Salinas during his own presidential campaign. Salinas openly courted big business during the campaign, reportedly meeting with the largest entrepreneurs in every state he visited. See Carlos Elizondo, "Privatizing the PRI? Shifts in the Business–PRI Relationship" (Manuscript, CIDE, Mexico City, March 1994).

was greatly enhanced during the Salinas period. Collaboration between business and state elites in the design of economic policy "became unprecedentedly tight, fluid, and public."[34] During his first year in office Argentine President Carlos Menem went so far as to give control of the Ministry of Economy to executives of the Bunge y Born corporation. This move went beyond the Peronist corporatist tradition, whereby key ministries and secretariats were occasionally assigned to representatives of the sectors they oversaw. Bunge y Born was the country's only multinational corporation and Peronism's most truculent adversary in the business community. The appointment of Bunge y Born executives to the high command of the Ministry of the Economy, along with the appointment of conservative leaders to other policy-making positions, signaled an important coalitional shift by the Peronist government toward historically non-Peronist business constituencies. It also marked a shift in the institutional forms of linkage between the state and business, displacing traditional links in favor of direct interaction between state policymakers and large business firms.[35]

Beyond these political links to the business community, populist governments also provided powerful material incentives for their newfound constituencies. The liberalization of financial systems and the opening of the domestic market created major economic opportunities for competitive firms and financial groups. The widescale privatization of state-owned enterprises favored domestic entrepreneurs with access to large amounts of capital and accelerated the process of economic concentration.[36] Privileged economic actors tapped for political support by populist governments thus saw their economic leverage expand during this period.[37]

[34] Blanca Heredia, "State-Business Relations in Contemporary Mexico," in Monica Serrano and Victor Bulmer-Thomas, eds., *Rebuilding the State: Mexico after Salinas* (London: The Institute of Latin American Studies, University of London, 1996).

[35] As Carlos Acuña notes, "Immediately upon taking office, the new minister of economy reached agreements with 350 leading firms to stabilize prices in exchange for maintaining stable public-sector prices and tariffs, as well as interest and exchange rates. These agreements bypassed entrepreneurial representatives." Acuña, "Politics and Economics in the Argentina of the Nineties (Or, Why the Future No Longer Is What It Used to Be)," in William C. Smith, Carlos H. Acuña, and Eduardo Gamarra, eds., *Democracy, Markets, and Structural Reform in Latin America* (Miami: University of Miami, North-South Center, 1994), 39.

[36] In Mexico it is estimated that the privatization of parastatal enterprises fostered the creation of at least fifty big economic *grupos*. See Yemile Mizrahi, "Recasting Business-Government Relations in Mexico: The Emergence of Panista Entrepreneurs," Working Paper, no. 29 (CIDE, División de Estudios Políticos, 1995). For a journalistic analysis of the consolidation of economic conglomerates in Argentina during the Menem period, see Luis Majul, *Los dueños de la Argentina* (Buenos Aires: Editorial Sudamericana, 1992).

[37] For a discussion of the uses of market reform for constituency formation and political coalition building, see Hector Schamis, "Re-forming the State: The Politics of Privatization in Chile and Great Britain" (Ph.D. diss., Columbia University, 1994).

The co-optation and strengthening of big business was accompanied by the division of labor and the weakening of its institutional and economic power. In the economic realm, the governments' reforms sought to reduce labor costs and neutralize labor obstacles to marketization. The measures signaled an end to decades-long populist commitments to maintain employment and wage levels and to use state power to bolster labor's bargaining position in the labor market and political arena.[38] In both countries, decrees and legislation were passed restricting the right to strike, decentralizing collective bargaining, limiting wage hikes, and flexibilizing hiring and firing practices in the private sector. The selling-off of state-owned enterprises, which eliminated tens of thousands of jobs in each country, also marked an end to populist commitment to full employment and job security. The reforms also sought to curtail the labor movement's organizational and financial power in measures ranging from the imprisonment of prominent union leaders in Mexico to the restriction of labor control over vast pension plans and social security programs in Argentina.[39]

Not all sectors of labor were clear losers in this reform process. While the labor movement as a whole suffered from the weakening of its political organization and from its membership's declining economic clout, some sectors benefited from the reforms and were able to adapt to a new context of flexibilized labor markets and decentralized state-labor relations. The restructuring of the populist metropolitan policy coalition involved the selection of winners and losers within both the business community and the labor movement, not the wholesale strengthening or weakening of either group. In part, the success of the reform process involved the division of the labor movement and the co-optation of certain sectors to prevent unified labor opposition to economic reform. Populist governments made concerted efforts to co-opt key union leaders and sectors and make them partners in the economic

---

[38] Weak as this commitment might have seemed in Mexico, especially after the conservative turn of government policy after the Cárdenas period, government policies did nevertheless ensure that real wages for labor rose steadily for labor from the 1950s to the late 1970s. See Esthela Gutierrez Garza, "De la relacion salarial monopolista a la flexibilidad del trabajo, Mexico 1960–1986," in Esthela Gutierrez Garza, ed., La crisis del estado del bienestar, vol. 2 of Testimonios de la crisis (Mexico City: Siglo XXI Editores, 1988), 146–54. In the 1980s, however, this objective changed. Average wages in manufactuing plummeted 38 percent between 1982 and 1985 and continued their downward trend after that. The urban minimum wage fell nearly 46 percent during President De la Madrid's sexenio. Ruth Berins Collier (fn. 2), 105.

[39] For a discussion of the institutional changes in state labor relations made by the Salinas administration in Mexico, see Enrique de la Garza Toledo, "The Restructuring of State-Labor Relations in Mexico," in Cook, Middlebrook, and Molinar Horcasitas (fn. 25). James McGuire analyzes Menem's labor reforms in Argentina in Peronism without Perón: Unions, Parties, and Democracy in Argentina (Stanford: Stanford University Press; forthcoming, 1997), chap. 8.

reform process. These unions tended to be in the more competitive industrial and export-oriented sectors of the economy. In these sectors a
new unionism emerged, which emphasized firm-level industry-labor
collaboration, worker ownership of stock in privatized firms, and the
decentralization of employer-worker negotiations. Their leaders were
often rewarded with government positions or were visible interlocutors
with state officials in the reform process.[40] The economic and institutional arrangements in the new policy coalition gave clear preference to
the larger and internationally competitive sectors of business. However,
those labor sectors that could take advantage of economic opportunities offered by policy reforms as well as political opportunities provided
by cooperation with the executive, were integrated into the new populist policy coalition.

TECHNOCRATS AND PERIPHERAL COALITION POLITICIANS IN THE RECASTING OF THE METROPOLITAN COALITION

With the restructuring of the business and labor components of their
metropolitan policy coalitions, Peronism and the PRI established new
bases of support for market reform. But in the process they reversed the
social pact with key metropolitan constituencies, which had been a
bedrock of populist governance. In the interim, this reversal could be
accomplished by relying on sectors outside the metropolitan coalition.
In both Mexico and Argentina, peripheral coalition politicians and
nonparty technocrats played key roles during the reform period. A
much publicized displacement of traditional PRI politicians by technocrats within the Mexican state in the 1980s was crucial for reformers
to change economic policy and recast the metropolitan policy coalition.
To an extent, this pattern was repeated by Menem in Argentina.
Throughout his administration, the key economic policy-making institutions were assigned to non-Peronists. The Ministry of the Economy
was first assigned to Bunge y Born executives, then briefly to Erman
Gonzalez, a close collaborator of Menem during his years as governor
of the remote La Rioja province, and finally to Domingo Cavallo, a
non-Peronist technocrat with well established neoliberal credentials.
The Central Bank was also assigned to non-Peronist conservative
technocrats.

Menem's background as governor of a poor province in the interior
of the country also permitted him to rely on leaders, supporters, and

[40] In Mexico this also led to the formation of a new union grouping of the "modern" sectors of the
labor movement, the *Federación de Sindicatos de Empresas de Bienes y Servicios* (Fesebes) that took a
prominent role supporting government-led reforms. See Bizberg (fn. 32).

party structures from the peripheral coalition as he brought the day of reckoning to the party's traditional supporters in the metropolis. Menem's presidential victory signaled a shift in Peronism's internal balance of power between metropolitan and peripheral coalitions. Key ministries in the areas of labor relations, management of public enterprise, and institutional reform were assigned to leaders from the peripheral coalition—leaders with few ties and few debts to the party's urban labor constituencies.

The peripheral coalition in Mexico was also vital to Presidents de la Madrid and Salinas as they went about restructuring the metropolitan coalition. Their most important contribution was electoral. As the PRI continued to take a beating in metropolitan regions, the peripheral coalition continued to deliver consistent, albeit decreasing electoral majorities throughout the country. These majorities were enough to counter the losses suffered by the party in urban areas and to deliver the presidency to the ruling party. The peripheral coalition also ensured continued PRI dominance over local politics in many parts of the country. Tensions between technocratic elites in the executive branch and the PRI's traditional políticos running the peripheral coalition were very real in Mexico, as they were in Argentina. However, a marriage of convenience was sustained by the interest of both groups in holding on to their quota of state power. It provided an unlikely alliance between internationalized technocrats and parochial politicians that saw the reform process through.

MAKING THE METROPOLITAN COALITION ELECTORALLY VIABLE

The neoliberal reformers in Mexico and Argentina were state elites seeking governability for their economic reform programs, but they were also party leaders concerned with the long-term viability of their parties in the postreform period. The clock was ticking on the peripheral coalition's ability to deliver national majorities. New constituencies in the countries' most developed regions had to be built if Peronism and the PRI were to remain competitive in the postdevelopmentalist era. An updating of the metropolitan coalitions was thus pursued by leaders of these parties in the late 1980s and early 1990s. In essence, this meant replacing the mobilizational power of labor with the financial power of business as the foundation of the metropolitan coalition's electoral organization. The populist parties also needed to organize a new mass base among contested urban constituencies. These included middle and upper-middle sectors that lay outside the corporatist system and the increasingly fragmented lower classes that lay beyond the reach of traditional populist party organization.

Party leaders sought to make effective in the electoral realm the coalitional changes wrought in previous years in the policy realm. Business, now a vital member of the policy coalition, was thus organized as a core constituency in the metropolitan electoral coalition. Both PRI and Peronist leaders aggressively courted business support for the parties' electoral campaigns. In Mexico this process advanced the furthest, for it involved not only the mobilization of financial support but also the opening of formal links between the party and business. Business had historically been excluded from representation in the party's corporatist organization and, at least formally, from the party's campaign activities. In spite of business's privileged access to state institutions, one major legacy of the revolutionary period was the norm of the illegitimacy of business participation in ruling-party politics. This changed quickly during the Salinas period. Party finance committees, which included prominent entrepreneurs as members, were established. As part of his dealings with business beneficiaries of his government's economic policies, President Salinas actively sought their financial support for the ruling party's campaign operations.[41] At the regional level, business also began to play a more prominent role in the financing of local PRI campaigns, as increasingly competitive local contests compelled local leaders to become more autonomous in the financing and organizing of electoral campaigns.[42]

PRI campaign leaders also tapped the business's power to mobilize. Seeking to renovate the party's image in key urban regions, the PRI often imposed new candidates on local party officials. Many of these candidates were well-known local business leaders. According to one report, 17 percent of PRI candidates in the 1991 midterm elections came from the business community.[43] In the 1994 presidential campaign, committees of local entrepreneurs organized by the PRI, known as Células Empresariales, were established throughout the country. The Células mobilized support for the PRI presidential candidate in the

---

[41] The most notorious incident was the president's "request" at a gala dinner for business leaders for $25 million in campaign contributions from the participants for the PRI. See Lorenzo Meyer, "El PRI se abre a la inversión privada: Auténtica elite de poder," *Excelsior*, March 4, 1993. See also Tim Golden, "Mexican Leader Asks Executives to Give Party $25 Million Each," *New York Times*, March 9, 1993, p. 1.

[42] Salvador Mikel, national PRI deputy for the state of Veracruz, interview by author, Mexico City, February 4, 1995.

[43] Fernando Ortega Pizarro, "Los empresarios, poderoza fuerza en el PRI, aunque no sean sector," *Proceso* 800, March 2, 1992, p. 21.

business community, identified entrepreneurs for recruitment into the PRI, and generated funds for local campaigns.[44] The Células tapped local business of all sizes, but made special appeals to small- and medium-sized sectors that had been actively courted by the PRI's party rivals, the conservative Partido Acción Nacional (PAN) and the center-left Partido de la Revolución Democrática (PRD). As such, they gave the party an organizational device for luring these constituencies away from the opposition, as well as a wedge into the urban middle classes where the party's organized presence was weak.

The now open relationship with business was accompanied by the restructuring of the party's relationship to its mass base. The operative term for party reformers during this period was "desectoralization," which meant a move away from reliance on the party's sectoral organizations, particularly its labor sector, in the mobilization of the urban vote. It also meant a stress on the party's territorial organization, neighborhood-level organizations, and media campaigns.[45] Under President Salinas, the circumvention of sectoral organizations and traditional party leaders was given further impetus by the creation of a new national antipoverty program with strong electoral dimensions, the Programa Nacional de Solidaridad (PRONASOL). There has been much debate about PRONASOL's political and electoral impact, but it formed a key part of the PRI's strategy for recapturing the urban vote in key electoral districts.[46] PRONASOL provided a combination of pork barrel, lead-

---

[44] The Células Empresariales were established by collaborators in Luis Donaldo Colosio's campaign. After his assassination, they formed part of Ernesto Zedillo's campaign. Details on the strategy behind the organization of the Células Empresariales are provided by Antonio Arguelles, one of the chief PRI organizers of the Células, in "Las células empresariales en la campaña de Ernesto Zedillo," in Antonio Arguelles and Manuel Villa, eds., *México: El voto por la democracia* (Mexico City: Grupo Editorial Miguel Angel Porrua, 1994). The political organizers of the Células maintain that these were organized strictly for mobilizing political support and establishing communication between local entrepreneurs and the party's presidential candidate, not to mobilize financial support; Luis Antonio Arguelles and Marco Antonio Bernal, interviews with the author, Mexico City, February 4 and 5, 1995. However, Roberto Campa, a top party leader in Mexico City, affirmed that these were also important devices for raising funds from the local business community; Roberto Campa, interview with author, Mexico City, June 8, 1995. Journalist Andrés Oppenheimer also describes the importance of the células for PRI fundraising in *Bordering on Chaos: Guerrillas, Stockbrokers, Politicians, and Mexico's Road to Prosperity* (Boston: Little, Brown, 1996).
[45] This new emphasis away from sectoral organization was asserted officially by party leaders at the landmark XIVth National Assembly of the PRI in September 1990. For an analysis of the results of the XIVth assembly, see John Bailey, Denise Dresser, and Leopoldo Gómez, "XIV Asamblea del PRI: Balance Preliminar," *La Jornada*, September 26, 1990.
[46] Campa (fn. 44). An edited volume devoted entirely to this subject is *Transforming State-Society Relations in Mexico: The National Solidarity Strategy*, ed. W. Cornelius, A. Craig, and J. Fox (San Diego: Center for U.S.-Mexican Studies, University of California; 1992). In their article in this volume, "Electoral Determinants and Consequences of National Solidarity," Juan Molinar Horcasitas and Jeffrey Weldon show a strong electoral bias to PRONASOL expenditures and a marked impact on electoral outcomes in key electoral districts. For a recent study questioning the electoral impact of

ership recruitment, and vote-getting resources in contested urban districts that, in some cases, stemmed the party's slide and, in others, permitted it to recapture majorities back from opposition parties.[47]
After 1988 the PRI managed to recover many of the losses suffered that year. Its metropolitan coalition in particular seemed to have been reinvigorated in subsequent elections. While the peripheral coalition continued to deliver solid majorities in 1991, the PRI's average vote total in urban areas increased significantly over 1988 (see Table 2). In the 1994 presidential elections, the party retained its hold on the metropolitan vote. In the urbanized central region of the country, the PRI's presidential campaign mobilized close to 50 percent of the vote—up from around 37 percent in 1988.[48] Similar results were registered in the advanced northern regions, where the PAN was strongest.[49] The 1994 election results also indicated that the PRI's appeals to privileged voters seemed to be bearing fruit. Exit polls showed the PRI running evenly with the PAN among well-educated and affluent voters, while at the same time winning overwhelmingly at the bottom of the social ladder.[50] While retaining a mass base that overwhelmed its opponents, the PRI in 1994 also mobilized substantial electoral support from affluent sectors of Mexican society.

In Argentina the building of business support for the Peronist party was reflected in close collaborative relationships between key entrepreneurs and top party officials and by the organization of party campaign-finance committees sponsored by prominent members of the business community. The main strategy for building new support among urban upper and upper-middle sectors was evidenced in the party's alliance with local conservative parties. By the late 1980s these parties commanded over 20 percent of the vote in the pivotal city of

---

PRONASOL, see Kathleen Bruhn, "Social Spending and Political Support: The 'Lessons' of the National Solidarity Program in Mexico," *Comparative Politics* 28 (January 1996).

[47] As Paul Haber notes, PRONASOL was instrumental in eroding organizational and electoral gains by the PRI in Durango and other electoral districts. Haber, "Political Change in Durango: The Role of National Solidarity," in Cornelius, Craig, and Fox (fn. 46).

[48] Federico Estevez, Instituto Tecnológico Autónomo de Mexico. Electoral data from research in progress.

[49] Joseph Klesner, "The 1994 Mexican Elections: Manifestation of a Divided Society?" *Mexican Studies/Estudios Mexicanos* 11 (Winter 1995). In this study Klesner also shows that, even with the PRI's urban advances, the peripheral and rural electoral bias displayed statistically in Tables 2 and 3 was maintained in 1994.

[50] Exit polls conducted by Mitofsky International, Inc. indicated that the PRI received 45 percent of the "wealthy" vote and 49 percent of the "high income" vote, compared to 44 percent and 33 percent respectively for the conservative PAN. However, at the bottom of the social ladder the PRI obtained 54 percent of the "below poverty level" vote as opposed to 25 percent for the PAN. Similarly, the exit polls indicated that the PRI captured 41 percent of voters with university education, compared to 36 percent for the PAN. For poll results, see *New York Times*, August 24, 1994, p. A4.

Buenos Aires and held the balance in several districts throughout the country. The parties ran joint candidates with the Peronist party in local elections or declared their support for Peronist candidates in national elections. In several cases conservative party leaders were absorbed outright into Peronist party ranks.[51]

During this period, the power of party leaders within the Peronist movement increased over leaders in corporatist organizations, marking a shift within the Peronist movement's historic internal division of power.[52] In metropolitan areas, new leaders from urban party organizations began to play a major role in organizing Peronist urban campaigns and running the Peronist party apparatus.[53] In a sense, this shift mirrored the PRI's shift from sectoral to territorial organization in the running of urban campaigns. It gave rise to new party leaders and organized channels for mobilizing electoral support, and displaced labor and functional organizations in the party's metropolitan electoral organization. After President Menem seized control of the Peronist party by becoming its chair in 1991, loyal políticos within the urban party organization provided him with an important base of support in his struggles with opponents in the Peronist movement.

The 1995 presidential elections gave the Peronist party a major electoral victory. President Menem won the election with nearly 50 percent of the vote. The Peronist party in 1995 won big throughout the country, but its highest vote totals were in the least developed provinces, and its most contested showings were in the major metropolitan areas.[54] Nevertheless, during the six-year presidency of Carlos Menem, the Peronist metropolitan coalition experienced considerable change, particularly the addition of upper and upper-middle class voters to its electoral ranks. Part of this shift is captured in the results of multiple regression analyses presented in Tables 4 and 5 for Buenos Aires, a

---

[51] See Gibson (fn. 28).

[52] Peronist party leaders usually played second fiddle to labor leaders and corporatist organization figures in the Peronist movement. See Ricardo Sidicaro, "¿Es posible la democracia en Argentina?" in Alain Rouquié, ed., *Argentina Hoy* (Buenos Aires: Siglo XXI Editores, 1985); and McGuire (fn. 39).

[53] One of these leaders, was Eduardo Duhalde, governor of the province of Buenos Aires. Formerly the mayor of the greater Buenos Aires municipality of Lomas de Zamora, he became Menem's vice-presidential running mate in 1989 and later won election as governor of Buenos Aires. In the 1995 presidential election, the Duhalde party machine in Buenos Aires was credited with orchestrating President Menem's electoral victories in the greater Buenos Aires region, bucking a general trend of urban electoral losses.

[54] The Peronist party's presidential percentage vote total in the twenty poorest provinces was 54 percent in 1995. In the four most economically advanced provinces it was 47 percent. In the country's four largest cities, the city of Buenos Aires, Córdoba, Rosario, and Mendoza, the party's average vote percentage was 38 percent.

TABLE 4
PERONIST ELECTORAL PERFORMANCE AND SELECTED SOCIOECONOMIC
VARIABLES: PROVINCE OF BUENOS AIRES, PRESIDENTIAL ELECTION, 1995
(MULTIPLE REGRESSION ANALYSIS)[a]

	Regression Coefficient	Beta Coefficient	t-value
Intercept	29.73		
Managers	.36	.17	1.2
Higher education	-.05	-.06	-0.8
Unemployed	-.66	-.27	-2.2[b]
Retirees on pension	-.74	-.44	-4.2[c]
Poverty	.31	.35	2.3[b]
Self-employed	.39	.27	2.1[b]
Employee/worker	.30	.35	1.8

[a] N=122 electoral countries. R-squared coeffieicnt is .440. Dependent variable: Peronist party vote per-centage, 1995. Independent variables from the 1990 census measured in percentages: managers = pop-ulation employed as managers or owners of firms; higher education = population with postsecondary education; unemployed = population unemployed; retirees on pension = population collecting retire-ment pensions; poverty = population with unsatisfied basic material needs; self-employed = business operator or professional with no employees; employee/worker = salaried white- or blue-collar worker.
    [b] Significant at the .05 level.
    [c] Significant at the .001 level.

major metropolitan province. Table 4 measures the impact of selected sociodemographic variables on the Peronist party's electoral perfor-mance in 1995, while Table 5 measures the impact of the same variables on the party's growth between 1989 and 1995.

The results suggest two things about the Peronist party's shifting metropolitan coalition. Keeping with tradition, historically Peronist pop-ulations in the lower and lower-middle social strata had the strongest positive impact on the party's electoral performance in 1995, as evi-denced particularly by the "poverty" and "self-employed" variables in Table 4. However, the party's growth between 1989 and 1995 (Table 5) was most positively affected by the high-social-status variables of "uni-versity education" and "managers."[55] The party's changing metropolitan social profile appeared to be moving in an increasingly discontinuous direction between 1989 and 1995. Its support was strongest at the bot-

[55] The negative coefficients registered for "retirees on pension" and "unemployment" in both tables reflect predictable costs to the governing party of fiscal adjustment in the metropolis. Unemployment, in particular, was a major issue during the electoral campaign, edging toward historically high levels of 20 percent in the first half of 1995.

TABLE 5
PERONIST PARTY GROWTH BETWEEN 1989 AND 1995 AND SELECTED
SOCIOECONOMIC VARIABLES: PROVINCE OF BUENOS AIRES,
PRESIDENTIAL ELECTIONS
(MULTIPLE REGRESSION ANALYSIS)[a]

	Regression Coefficient	Beta Coefficient	t-value
Intercept	-5.23		
Managers	.79	.31	2.0[b]
Higher education	.22	.24	2.3[b]
Unemployed	-1.45	-.49	-3.5[c]
Retirees on pension	-1.12	-.53	-4.5[c]
Poverty	.03	.03	0.2
Self-employed	.30	.17	1.2
Employee/worker	.20	.18	0.8

[a]N=122 electoral counties. R-squared coefficient is .282. Dependent variable: Peronist party vote percentage change between 1989 and 1995.
[b]Significant at the .05 level.
[c]Significant at the .001 level.

tom and the top of the social ladder, and weakest in between, suggesting a possible displacement of the old working-class-based electoral
coalition by one with distinctively popular-conservative markings.

CONCLUSION

This article has attempted to cast a new perspective on the coalitional
dynamics of Peronism in Argentina and the PRI in Mexico. The analysis starts off with the suggestion that coalition building is strongly
shaped by the interplay between policy-making and electoral politics,
and that constituencies within a governing party's coalition can be
distinguished according to their importance in the pursuit of either
of those tasks. For analytical purposes, it is thus useful to conceive of
governing parties as relying upon a policy coalition and an electoral
coalition.

The division of policy and electoral tasks between the social constituencies of Peronism and the PRI was strongly shaped by regional factors. This insight leads to one of the main arguments of this essay: the
emphasis on class dynamics of populist coalition building that has
dominated scholarship on these two movements should be complemented by attention to the regional dynamics of the Peronist and PRI
coalitions. Peronism and the PRI were more than class coalitions with
strong ties to labor. They were also regional alliances encompassing two

subcoalitions with markedly different social characteristics and different tasks in the reproduction of populist power. A metropolitan coalition incorporated new social actors into the political process. It gave impetus to the reorganization of the national political economy and to state-led models of development. A peripheral coalition extended the parties' territorial reach throughout the more economically backward regions and became vital to generating national electoral majorities. Modernity and tradition thus coexisted as part of the regional bargain that gave populism its national reach, created an internal balance of power, and led to a political division of labor vital to the political viability of populist movements.

The regional division of policy and electoral tasks was determined by the markedly different social characteristics of the metropolitan and peripheral regions, as well as by the social and demographic importance of the latter regions. This pattern appears to have been reproduced in other experiences of reformist or populist-party coalition building in contexts of underdevelopment. It also sheds light on the factors limiting the reformist potential of populist and center-left parties in developing countries or contexts of marked regional economic imbalances. Such parties must reconcile their drive for social change with their need for political order and support throughout the national territory. Disparities in socioeconomic development between regions render it almost inevitable for national parties, regardless of their transformative policy orientations, to enter into a pact with the forces of tradition that can guarantee order and political support in the territories they control. If these territories lie outside the reach of the original transformative agenda of the reformist parties, so much the better. If not, the pact itself will set clear geographic limits to that agenda. The Democratic Party coalition in the United States in the 1930s, which linked labor and progressive northern constituencies to a southern segregationist plantocracy, gave the Democratic Party a national electoral reach while placing the American South off-limits to the progressive agenda of New Deal policies.[56] Similarly, the Congress Party of India, and the center-left SLFP-led coalition in Sri Lanka, were unions of policy and electoral coalitions that were regionally differentiated and unevenly affected by the reformist economic policies pursued by the central government.

⁵⁶ For an analysis of the regional bargain involved in the New Deal, as well as of other effects of regionalism on U.S. national politics, see Robert F. Bensel, *Sectionalism in American Political Development: 1880-1980* (Madison: University of Wisconsin Press, 1984).

The more recent experiences of free-market reform, however, suggest that the relationship between coalitions does not render the party's social and policy orientations immutable. Quite the contrary, the coexistence of two functionally distinctive coalitions under one institutional umbrella can provide leaders with the resources and coalitional flexibility required for enacting major policy shifts. The dual dependence on policy and electoral coalitions by Peronism and the PRI placed limits on their original transformative potential, but it also created an internal balance of power that aided political leaders greatly during the reform periods of the late 1980s and early 1990s. In Mexico and Argentina the electoral leverage provided by the peripheral coalitions gave leaders a critical degree of autonomy from their old policy coalitions when they decided to pursue free-market reforms. The disruption caused by the recasting of the metropolitan policy coalition was countered by the stabilizing effect of the peripheral coalition's electoral weight. This situation in essence made the transitional costs of policy change sustainable in electoral terms. Similarly, in the case of Sri Lanka today, the once leftist governing coalition has relied on its peripheral coalition's electoral support while pursuing major free-market reforms against the resistance of its metropolitan constituencies.[57] Disaggregating the functional and territorial components of coalition building is thus important not only for an accurate historical understanding of the origins and evolution of populist parties, but also for a more nuanced understanding of the coalitional dynamics at play when such parties undertake market-oriented economic reforms.

Regarding the specific evolution of Peronism and the PRI, certain trends in their historic subcoalitions might be highlighted. In the metropolitan coalition one visible development has been a new political incorporation of business. Business politics has become a new coalitional "fulcrum" in this period of political and economic realignment, and this development has reshaped both the policy and electoral dimensions of its political action.[58]

At the policy level, business, which for decades had been a favored interlocutor in the state's relations with social groups, now finds itself in a prominent and more autonomous role. It is less fettered, in its deal-

[57] For an analysis of the Sri Lankan case, which adopts the analytical framework presented in this essay, see Mick Moore, "Leading the Left to the Right: Populist Coalitions and Economic Reform," *World Development* 25 (July 1997).

[58] In its institutional and political consequences, this might·be seen as a historical sequel to Collier and Collier's portrayal of labor politics as a coalitional "fulcrum" in twentieth-century Latin American politics. Collier and Collier (fn. 2), 40.

ings with populist-controlled governments, by a corporatist balance of power that once forced it to negotiate with a centralized and politically integrated labor movement. At the electoral level, business now finds itself openly drawn into party politics, an arena that until recently it had avoided. In both Mexico and Argentina the relationship between business and political parties has become open, and populist parties are vigorous contenders for the electoral support of the propertied and socially privileged. This may portend, as a political sequel to the economic reform process, a "popular conservative" future for Peronism and the PRI as they organize for political competition in the neoliberal era. If so, it would still be a struggle to be won. Opposition parties, such as Mexico's PAN, may well thwart the PRI's overtures to the business community,[59] and resistance within Peronism and the PRI to the social conservatization of their metropolitan constituencies threaten its development at every turn.

Another issue relates to the changing relationship between the metropolitan and peripheral coalitions. Tensions between the parties along regional lines are likely to increase as the reform process shifts resources and power between regional leaders and constituencies. The declining electoral weight of the peripheral coalitions and the modernization and urbanization of Mexican and Argentine societies suggest that the division of functional tasks between regional constituencies will decline in the future.[60] The restructuring of the metropolitan coalition and the shifting of electoral tasks to the parties' metropolitan constituencies and political organization will undoubtedly spark important internal power struggles as peripheral coalition members strive to hold on to their declining shares of power.

In addition, tensions between the peripheral coalition and the populist parties' free-market policy orientations are likely to wrack both parties in the years to come. Although this essay has focused on conflicts between the parties and their metropolitan constituencies, it should be stressed that tensions between party leaders and the peripheral coalition over market reform also exist. In Argentina the interior provinces have historically been the most dependent on central government subsidies

[59] The economic crisis unleashed by the December 1994 devaluation in Mexico certainly increases the possibilities that the PAN will erode privileged strata support for the PRI.

[60] In Argentina this trend can be expected to accelerate as a result of the 1994 reform of the national constitution. Under the old constitution the provinces of the interior of the country were overrepresented in national elections because of the regional apportionment of votes in the national electoral college. With the abolition of the electoral college, the peripheral coalition's electoral weight in presidential elections will more closely reflect its actual population size.

and were spared the more ravaging effects of fiscal adjustment during President Menem's first term.[61] During his second term they will face a harsh period of adjustment imposed by the central government.[62] In Mexico the peripheral coalition forms a powerful bastion of opposition to further economic reform and political democratization. PRI "dinosaurs" are strongly entrenched in the peripheral coalition, and conflicts between them and PRI elites in the presidency have been a powerful source of disharmony in the party. The temporary alliance between technocrats and peripheral-coalition políticos, which access to state power helped to maintain, cannot be expected to last indefinitely. In both Mexico and Argentina, continued conflicts between them will shape the evolution of populism well into the postdevelopmentalist era.

[61] Edward L. Gibson and Ernesto Calvo, "Electoral Coalitions and Market Reforms: Evidence from Argentina" (Manuscript, Northwestern University, December 1996).
[62] The Menem economic team's "Second Reform of the State," announced in late 1995, envisages a major fiscal reform for the country's provincial governments.

Acknowledgments

Ames, Barry. "Electoral Strategy under Open-List Proportional Representation." *American Journal of Political Science* 39, no. 2 (1995): 406-433. Reprinted with the permission of the University of Wisconsin Press.

Domínguez, Jorge and James McCann. "Shaping Mexico's Electoral Arena: The Construction of Partisan Cleavages in the 1988 and 1991 National Elections." *American Political Science Review* 89, no. 1 (1995): 34-48. Reprinted with the permission of the American Political Science Association.

Shugart, Matthew Soberg. "The Electoral Cycle and Institutional Sources of Divided Presidential Government." *American Political Science Review* 89, no. 2 (1995): 327-343. Reprinted with the permission of the American Political Science Association.

Siavelis, Peter. "Continuity and Change in the Chilean Party System: On the Transformational Effects of Electoral Reform." *Comparative Political Studies* 30, no. 6 (1997): 651-674. Reprinted with the permission of Sage Publications.

Coppedge, Michael. "Parties and Society in Mexico and Venezuela." *Comparative Politics* (1993): 253-274. Reprinted with the permission of the editors of *Comparative Politics*.

Corrales, Javier. "Presidents, Ruling Parties, and Party Rules: A Theory on the Politics of Economic Reform in Latin America." *Comparative Politics* 32, no. 2 (2000): 127-149. Reprinted with the permission of the editors of *Comparative Politics*.

Figueiredo, Argelina Cheibub, and Fernando Limongi. "Presidential Power, Legislative Organization, and Party Behavior in Brazil." *Comparative Politics* 32, no. 3 (2000): 151-170. Reprinted with the permission of the editors of *Comparative Politics*.

Stokes, Susan. "Constituency Influence and Representation." *Electoral Studies* 17, no. 3 (1998): 351-367. This article was first published in *Electoral Studies* and is reproduced here with the permission of Butterworth-Heineman, Oxford, UK.

Jones, Mark. "Presidential Election Laws and Multipartism in Latin America." *Political Research Quarterly* 47, no. 1 (1994): 41-57. Reprinted with the permission of *Political Research Quarterly*.

Martz, John D. "Political Parties and Candidate Selection in Venezuela and Colombia." *Political Science Quarterly* 114, no. 4 (2000): 639-659. Reprinted with the permission of the author and The Academy of Political Science.

Roberts, Kenneth. "Neoliberalism and the Transformation of Populism in Latin America: The Peruvian Case." *World Politics* 48 (1995): 82-116. Reprinted with the permission of Johns Hopkins University Press.

Gibson, Edward. "The Populist Road to Market Reform: Policy and Electoral Coalitions in Mexico and Argentina." *World Politics* 49, no. 3 (1997): 339-370. Reprinted with the permission of Johns Hopkins University Press.

For Product Safety Concerns and Information please contact our EU
representative GPSR@taylorandfrancis.com
Taylor & Francis Verlag GmbH, Kaufingerstraße 24, 80331 München, Germany